A Traveler's Guide to

THE CIVIL
RIGHTS
MOVEMENT

JIM CARRIER

FOREWORD BY JOHN LEWIS

A Harvest Original

Harcourt, Inc.

ORLANDO   AUSTIN   NEW YORK   SAN DIEGO   TORONTO   LONDON

A Traveler's Guide to
THE CIVIL RIGHTS MOVEMENT

...UNTIL JUSTICE ROLLS DOWN LIKE WATERS
AND RIGHTEOUSNESS LIKE A MIGHTY STREAM

MARTIN LUTHER KING JR

www.HarcourtBooks.com

Maps copyright © 2004 by Rodney Diaz

Frontispieces: p. ii The Lorraine Motel in Memphis, now the National Civil Rights Museum;
photo by Jim Carrier. p. iii from top left: Alex Haley's boyhood home and gravesite in
Henning, Tennessee; *photo by Jim Carrier.* Rosewood, site of an infamous 1923 massacre;
photo by Jim Carrier. Detail on the African-American Civil War monument; *courtesy
Washington, D.C. Convention and Tourism Corporation.* Sit-in at the Woolworth's counter
on February 2, 1960; © *Jack Moebes/CORBIS.* Civil rights memorial designed by
Maya Lin; *courtesy Thomas England/Southern Poverty Law Center.*

Library of Congress Cataloging-in-Publication Data
Carrier, Jim, 1944–
A traveler's guide to the civil rights movement/Jim Carrier.—1st ed.
p. cm.
Includes index.
ISBN 0-15-602697-X
1. African Americans—Civil rights—History—20th century.
2. Civil rights movements—United States—History—20th century.
3. African Americans—History.   4. Historic sites—Southern States—
Guidebooks.   5. Historic sites—Middle Atlantic States—
Guidebooks.   6. Southern States—Tours.
7. Middle Atlantic States—Tours.   I. Title.
E185.61.C267 2004
323.1196'073'009—dc22   2003015557

Text set in Fairfield Light
Designed by Lydia D'moch

Printed in the United States of America
First edition
A C E G I K J H F D B

Contents

Foreword by John Lewis • vii

Introduction • xiii

WASHINGTON, D.C. • 1
A Matter of Law • 19
The Pioneering Military • 28

VIRGINIA • 35
Pocahontas • 56
The Role of the Media • 69

NORTH CAROLINA • 73
Nonviolent? Not Always • 88
The Thirst for Education • 95

SOUTH CAROLINA • 107
Jim Crow in a Nutshell • 116
Terrorism—Now and Then • 130
About the Gullahs • 135

GEORGIA • 137
Black Institutions Led the Way • 161
The Women of the Movement • 165

FLORIDA • 169
Sports Heroes and Civil Rights • 182

ALABAMA • 211
Freedom Riders • 240
The Right to Vote • 249

MISSISSIPPI • 257
Ordinary Icons • 264
The Vote • 288

LOUISIANA, ARKANSAS, TENNESSEE • 291
The Music of Civil Rights • 324

OTHER STATES, OTHER SITES • 335
Brown v. Board of Education • 336

Bibliography • 355

Acknowledgments • 361

Index • 363

Photo Credits • 383

Foreword

The modern-day civil rights movement of the 1950s and 1960s is one of the most stirring chapters in American history. It was a period of tremendous hope and optimism, but it was also a time of great crisis and confrontation. It compelled the whole of America to face its history of racial injustice.

Page by page, *A Traveler's Guide to the Civil Rights Movement* takes readers on a journey to the memorials, museums, battlegrounds, and sacred places that tell the amazing story of America's continuous struggle for freedom and justice, a struggle that reached its zenith during the nonviolent revolution for civil rights.

It was one of my greatest privileges to be a part of that movement. As a product of the segregated South, I was swept up by its vision for an all-inclusive American community—a truly interracial democracy rooted in peace, justice, and brotherhood. It was a vision so bright that no form of evil could dim its glow.

With the use of the creative tactic of nonviolent direct action, people of great moral courage, black and white, set out to destroy the barren and corrupt system of racial segregation and discrimination. We wanted to do what Dr. Martin Luther King Jr. called "redeem the soul of America."

Yes, we were engaged in a war, but not war in the traditional sense. We did not embrace violence. We did not use ammunition, bombs, and guns against our attackers. Our message was love, our method was nonviolent action, and our weapon was truth.

We put our bodies and our very lives on the front lines in the sit-ins and demonstrations across the Jim Crow South. We prayed, protested, marched, and shed blood together in Nashville, Birmingham, Selma, and Montgomery. In essence, we were *living witnesses* of the evil tools and tactics of racial segregation.

Our mission came with a price. Throughout the South, civil rights workers and indigenous people protesting to desegregate public accommodations and for the right to vote were thrown in jail and brutally beaten; some were shot and killed. Innocent people, including old women and young children, were attacked with fire hoses, tear gas, and police dogs.

Yet we did not allow anger or bitterness to defeat our cause. We had the capacity and the desire to forgive, understand, and sing, "Ain't going to let nobody turn me around." Our belief in the fundamental principles of democracy was stronger than the system of racial segregation that had oppressed black people for hundreds of years.

Because of the sacrifice of ordinary men and women who petitioned their government by sitting down and standing in unmovable lines, today Americans of every race and ethnicity benefit from the protections of the 1964 Civil Rights Act and the 1965 Voting Rights Act—the most sweeping civil rights legislation since the Civil War.

As I look back on this period of incredible change, I know that the civil rights movement was not an isolated phenomenon, but part of our nation's unending pursuit for freedom and justice.

This human yearning for freedom is driven by what I like to call the *Spirit of History*—that moment when inspiration and commitment combine to produce a turning point in the evolution of humankind.

It was the Spirit of History that gave birth to the five most powerful words in America's founding creed: "All men are created equal."

It was the Spirit of History that stirred the conscience of Abraham Lincoln and compelled him to formally end more than two centuries of human bondage on American soil.

This Spirit empowered the descendants of slaves and slave owners with the moral fortitude to create an interracial coalition called the civil rights movement.

The Declaration of Independence, the Emancipation Proclamation, *Brown v. Board of Education,* the Montgomery Bus Boycott, the Freedom Rides, the March on Washington, the March from Selma to Montgomery (Bloody Sunday)—each occurrence represents another milestone in America's journey toward freedom.

We have a mission, a mandate, and a moral obligation from the Spirit of History to follow in the footsteps of those brave and courageous men and women who fought to make our nation and our world a place of justice and brotherhood.

Generations yet unborn will study a *Traveler's Guide to the Civil Rights Movement,* they will pause with each chapter and say, "At this site is where the Freedom Riders were beaten. . . . Here is the place where children faced police dogs. . . . On this bridge we shed a little blood to replenish the fountains of our democracy. . . . This moment gave birth to the nonviolent movement for civil rights."

We must know our history as a nation and a people. We must study it and visit its birthplaces—in essence we must *live* history in order to understand and appreciate it. For better or for worse, our past is what brought us here, and it will help lead us to where we need to go. Our forefathers and foremothers came to this land in different ships, but we are all in the same boat now.

The civil right movement has literally reshaped our world. Its legacy serves as an enduring foundation upon which we must continue to build.

—*U.S. Congressman John Lewis*

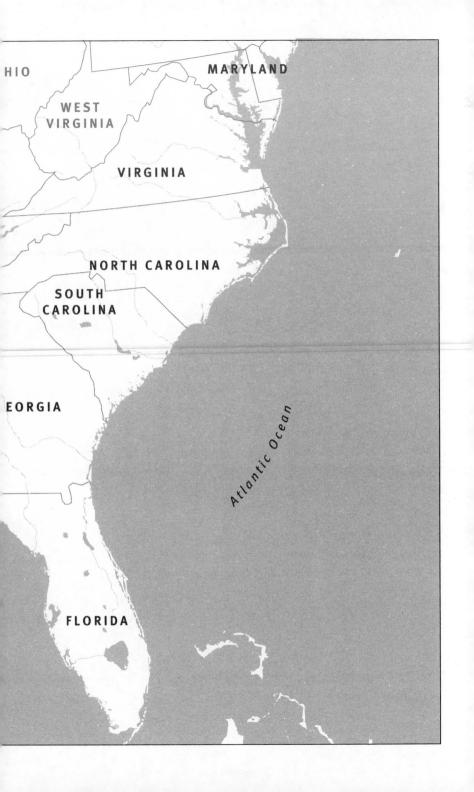

Introduction

FIFTY YEARS AGO, a revolution known as the civil rights movement began to sweep the United States. A decade of tumult and soul-searching later, America agreed to honor its founding creed that we are created equal.

The movement wiped away legalized segregation and discrimination. It resolved racial questions left hanging by colonists. It capped a civil rights century that transformed the world's largest slaveholding nation into a beacon for human rights. It created a country to be proud of, with standards to reach for.

Led by African Americans in former slave states, the civil rights revolution was the South's great gift to the world. This book guides you to the scenes of that struggle.

Montgomery. Little Rock. Greensboro. Birmingham. Selma. Memphis.

The names alone evoke battlefields. Beginning with a bus boycott and ending with the assassination of Dr. Martin Luther King Jr., events in those cities defined the period. In each place, museums and sites tell the story, and people from all over the world visit. For many, it is a pilgrimage.

But this guide takes the view, shared by many historians, that the civil rights movement did not blossom suddenly in 1955 when Rosa Parks refused to give up her seat on a bus. Modern-day events were based on generations of sacrifice and effort that came to a climactic confluence of morals and law.

The 1954–1955 Supreme Court case that integrated schools, for example, involved years of legal work in four states by the National Association for the Advancement of Colored People (NAACP), which had been created forty-five years earlier to fight lynchings and other injustices.

All civil rights sites, in fact, sit atop layers of events that are connected. Where resistance was strongest, history ran deepest. Voting rights marchers in 1965, for example, thronged a Montgomery street where, 104 years before, crowds cheered the president of the new Confederacy as he signaled the start of the Civil War. The context is important because the Civil War could be called the bloodiest of all civil rights events.

In a curious way, the past itself was transformed by the movement. With the rise of black pride and black studies, stories of slavery, terrorism, and heroism were rediscovered. Suddenly we could ask, wasn't Nat Turner, who led a rebellion in 1830, a civil rights leader? Or Harriet Tubman, who helped in the Underground Railroad? And what about black freedom fighters in all American wars? This resurrection of stories long absent from textbooks has prompted a major history rewrite at dusty parks and national heritage sites from Fort Sumter to Thomas Jefferson's Monticello.

Many historians date U.S. civil rights to January 1, 1863, when Abraham Lincoln issued the Emancipation Proclamation, freeing slaves in rebel states. Or, his Gettysburg Address, ten months later. That speech, carved in stone at the Lincoln Memorial, is a must stop in a civil rights tour, if only to contemplate the century that lay ahead before Lincoln's dream was realized. While in Washington, this guide recommends a side trip to Antietam, the Civil War battlefield where a slim victory gave Lincoln the fortitude to free the slaves. And a stop at the Supreme Court, both to celebrate school desegregation and to contemplate an earlier string of decisions that supported segregation.

What is—and isn't—a civil rights story is subjective. This book is a primer, and not encyclopedic on the history of African Americans. Not every church that played a part in civil rights is in this book. Not every hero is named.

On the other hand, events not normally linked to the civil rights movement are included. Equality grew in many fields. Thus, a visitor to Daytona Beach is directed to a small minor league stadium where Jackie Robinson integrated baseball. And who would miss the Muscle Shoals, Alabama, studio where Aretha Franklin sang "R-E-S-P-E-C-T"?

No matter where you stop in the South you can find a civil rights story. This guide includes a few key stops in select cities, chosen because of their unique history, things to see, or a sense of place. In some cases, a story is told in the hopes that something will be done to memorialize it. This book was written, in large part, to preserve the history of civil rights for new generations that may take them for granted.

Read as a whole the guide takes visitors deep into America's most important social movement, indeed, one of the most painful and triumphant chapters in human history. Although begun by African Americans, the civil rights movement in time ennobled women, Native Americans, people with disabilities, Latinos, gays and lesbians, and freedom fighters the world over.

Truthfully, the struggle is not over. But this guide reminds us how a people demanded to be part of the American dream, and by doing so, brought freedom and honor to us all.

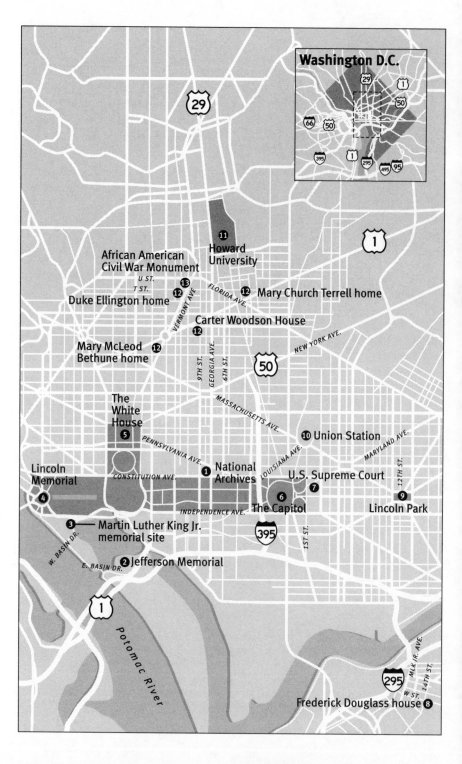

Washington, D.C.

THE NATION'S CAPITAL encapsulates the story of human rights in America—from its beginning as mere words to their embodiment in law and granite. Nowhere in this country are there more powerful symbols of the quest for an ideal.

Befitting a city of politics, many famous moments—events, speeches, and decisions whose images and impact reverberate across time—have since become symbols of the movement. The Gettysburg Address, *Brown v. Board of Education,* and the "I Have a Dream" speech are examples. The best of America came to fruition here.

Reflecting the nation, the worst also passed through. All three branches of government at times were infected by official racism and discrimination. Below the Capitol's crowning Statue of Freedom, successive congresses discriminated against Native Americans, African Americans, Asian Americans, and others before passing the Civil Rights Act of 1964. Behind the royal curtains of the Supreme Court, segregation was upheld as legal for more than half a century before it was declared unconstitutional. This history stands as a reminder that what government decrees it also can amend.

All this took place in the District of Columbia, a southern city—some called it a colony—where black residents faced the gamut of civil rights roadblocks and successes, from slave trading and segregation to full access and elected office. The city produced brilliant black minds, entrepreneurs, artists, and a strong middle class whose work helped fuel the national movement.

For all this, distinct memorials to civil rights are scattered throughout the D.C. area and sometimes hard to find. There are several statues and museums. But two monuments planned for the National Mall at this writing remain only place stands. And a national museum to African American history is years away.

Many of the recommended sites, such as the White House, will be familiar to a Washington visitor. Others, like Civil War battlefields, are rarely included in civil rights histories. Viewed through the lens of the nation's oldest, most divisive issue, these venues take on a different cast. Behind the facade of nearly every icon, a civil rights story awaits discovery.

Washington, D.C., and Civil Rights

Since its founding in 1790, the hundred-square-mile city surrounding the U.S. capitol has been a bittersweet beacon for black Americans. A lightning rod for sectional differences, Washington collected racial tension and absorbed the racial policies of each administration. In the years leading up to the Civil War, the national fracture appeared along Pennsylvania Avenue in an 1835 riot at a black-owned restaurant called Snow's Eating House. Roving white gangs destroyed black neighborhoods, and the city thereafter prohibited black-owned businesses. Slave trading along the Potomac finally stopped in 1850 as a result of complicated congressional horse trading over free and slave states in the West.

When the Civil War started, Washington emptied of southern congressmen while thousands of refuge slaves set up camps north of downtown around a Union hospital. In 1862 Congress officially freed them. In the vicinity of the camps, black entrepreneurs built a village for themselves with banks, businesses, newspapers, churches, and, especially, schools. Education became the bedrock of black Washington, and black schools—M Street High, Dunbar High, Armstrong Technical, and Howard University— created pools of talent, many of whom found federal jobs, beginning with the post office. Yet D.C. remained a ward of the federal bureaucracy that had again become dominated by southerners. Jim Crow roamed the halls of government and, often, the streets. During the Red Summer of 1919, blacks were pulled from streetcars and beaten in what James Weldon Johnson called a "pogrom." In the Shaw neighborhood, black GIs and merchants lined the street and fought back.

The first rumblings of black activism in the twentieth century were concentrated here as African Americans migrated to the district with the goal of changing the nation. Mary Church Terrell founded the National Association of Colored Women. Carter Woodson started the Association for the Study of Negro Life and History. In 1935 Howard University hosted the first National Negro Congress. "Washington was where the flutter of national conscience alighted gingerly upon the racial customs of the South," Richard Kluger wrote in *Simple Justice*. By 1950, Kluger reported, one of every three black D.C. jobs was with Uncle Sam. The district's police and fire departments had four hundred blacks, though they, like the city, were segregated.

"Nowhere was the change in the status of African Americans more dramatic than in the nation's capital," wrote John Hope Franklin, at the time a young scholar combing the National Archives for material later used in his pioneering black history books. But Franklin couldn't eat lunch at segregated government lunchrooms and had to grab a bite at Union Station.

Hotels began integrating in 1947. President Truman integrated swimming pools. In 1950 Mrs. Terrell, then in her eighties, led an elegant group into Thompson's Restaurant on Fourteenth Street and asked to be seated for lunch. After her group was turned away, her lawsuit went to the Supreme Court, where in 1953, it integrated D.C.'s restaurants.

In 1964 D.C. voters were granted the right to vote for president, and three years later, Walter Washington was appointed the first black mayor. Under home rule granted by President Nixon, Washington was selected in the city's first mayoral election in 1974. Marion Barry, the former Student Nonviolent Coordinating Committee activist, was elected mayor in 1978 for four tumultuous terms that included an infamous conviction for possession of cocaine. He was reelected in 1994.

Washington, D.C., Civil Rights Tours

Civil rights in the United States evolved from a few powerful words in the Declaration of Independence and any tour should include a stop to see the original document, on display at the National Archives. The Constitution, the Bill of Rights, and the Emancipation Proclamation are also housed here.

The arc of this history can be walked from the Jefferson Memorial to the Lincoln Memorial, past the site chosen for the Martin Luther King Jr. Memorial. The National Mall's other popular stops, like the White House, the Smithsonian, the Supreme Court, and the Capitol, have civil rights tales to tell, too.

The District of Columbia is a story unto itself, as black residents fought against a blind or recalcitrant Uncle Sam with sit-ins, lawsuits, and hard work. Frederick Douglass, Mary Bethune, and nearly two hundred thousand blacks who fought in the Civil War are remembered with museums, but much of the local history is unmarked.

This guide also recommends a side trip outside Washington to three Civil War sites that proved critical in the human rights struggle: Harpers Ferry, Antietam, and Gettysburg.

D.C. sites are easily accessed by public transportation, including the Metro. "The Nation's Capitol," a free brochure from the National Park Service, is a must. **Cultural Tourism D.C.** also has created walking tours with brochures and numbered sidewalk kiosks of both national and district civil rights sites (*www.culturaltourismdc.org*).

Maps also are available from the **Washington Convention and Visitor's Bureau** (*1300 Pennsylvania Avenue; 866-324-7386; www.washington. org*). For a comprehensive guidebook, see *Black Washington* by Sandra Fitzpatrick and Maria Goodwin.

1 | *National Archives*
(*National Mall at Pennsylvania Avenue; 866-272-6272; www.archives.gov*)

DECLARATION OF INDEPENDENCE

We hold these truths to be self-evident, that all men are created equal . . .
The five most powerful words in human rights history were scratched with a quill on paper on or shortly after June 11, 1776, in a second-floor room of a house in Philadelphia, Pennsylvania. Writing on deadline to start a revolution, thirty-three-year-old Thomas Jefferson borrowed words from a number of authors to justify independence from England. His first rough draft looked like a messy grade-school assignment with scratch-outs and words

squeezed between lines. (That version resides at the Library of Congress.) But the lyrical call to arms he presented to the Continental Congress, later transcribed onto parchment by a professional "engrosser" and signed by members of congress, lies in the rotunda of the National Archives. On display in a thick, gas-protected case and guarded around-the-clock, this most cherished of U.S. documents is fragile and faded and yet, arguably, the world's most powerful document. Through well over two centuries, Jefferson's words have remained a beacon of hope for oppressed people.

Jefferson, who died on the fiftieth anniversary of the July 4 signing, would never know the full impact of his bold, clear line. In fact, the words meant something very different in a fledgling nation with five hundred thousand slaves, women who couldn't vote, Indians regarded as "savages," and a ruling class of white male property owners. Struck from his first draft, at the insistence of slave owners from South Carolina and Georgia, was a denunciation of the slave trade. But Jefferson the slave owner would most likely applaud the broader meaning of his words today. His "glittering generalities," as one observer called them, grew in importance as they were reharnessed to justify expansions of human rights—none more powerfully, perhaps, than Abraham Lincoln's Gettysburg Address. During the modern civil rights movement, the moral force of Jefferson's words was clearer than ever. What followed, including women's and gay rights, imbued the Declaration of Independence with new understanding and power.

U.S. CONSTITUTION

We the People of the United States, in Order to form a more perfect Union . . . When the Founding Fathers negotiated this stunning document, they created a government—and a country—based on the radical ideas of democracy, privacy, and freedom of personal conscience.

Fortunately for civil rights, they also created a document that could be revised, for U.S. democracy was imperfect in 1787. The issue of slavery split the Constitutional convention. In order to form a union at all, that is, to win ratification by southern states, delegates compromised on oblique language that never used the word "slave" but allowed the capture of African slaves to continue for at least two decades, allowed fugitive slaves to be arrested anywhere in the United States, and gave the South an edge in congressional representation by counting each slave as three-fifths of a person.

By 1787 Vermont, New Hampshire, Massachusetts, Pennsylvania, Rhode Island, and Connecticut had outlawed slavery. Yet the Constitution strengthened the institution of slavery south of the Mason-Dixon line where seven hundred thousand men, women, and children were enslaved as private property. Though an awful divide was visible, the politicians of North and South feared that dealing with it would threaten the newborn union. What historian Joseph Ellis calls "the silence" enveloped the Constitution, its institutions, and the nation until the imperfect union could no longer contain it. The Civil War settled what the Founding Fathers left unresolved.

BILL OF RIGHTS

Fearful of an all-powerful national government, the colonists who agreed to form the United States of America insisted that the new Constitution be balanced with a long list of specific protections for individual and states' rights. The first ten became known as the Bill of Rights and included such fundamental principles as freedom of speech and the right to bear arms. All of the amendments—there are twenty-seven to date—guarantee "civil rights." But three approved after the Civil War—Thirteen, Fourteen, and Fifteen—repaired a hole in the Constitution by outlawing slavery and giving blacks citizenship rights. Although the Fifteenth Amendment guaranteed black men the right to vote, many states gutted its enforcement for another century. Poll taxes, literacy, and property tests effectively denied black voting rights until the 1965 Voting Rights Act. Not until 1920 and the passage of the Nineteenth Amendment did women receive the right to vote. Amending the Constitution with another bill is difficult, requiring two-thirds' approval of Congress and three-quarters' approval of the fifty state legislatures. Two recent proposals—an equal rights amendment for women and an amendment granting the District of Columbia the congressional representation of a state—failed. Nonetheless, amendments remain a citizens' right to peacefully change the U.S. government.

EMANCIPATION PROCLAMATION

This three-paragraph paper is arguably the most revered document in African American history. Signed by President Lincoln on New Year's Day, 1863, it freed three million slaves living in eleven "rebel" states still fighting the Civil War. Written as a military order from the commander in chief, the proclamation contains none of the soaring prose of Lincoln's famous oratory. But it was a stunning psychological ploy, and the entire country, including illiterate slaves, understood its import. Two hundred and fifty years of slavery were at an end. Freedom was at hand. Bells rang, choirs sang, and blacks jubilantly left plantations and headed north, many to join the Union Army. Overseas, support for the southern nation vanished.

To this day, New Year's Eve is commemorated in many black churches to remember the excited anticipation of Lincoln's signature. Whenever the Emancipation Proclamation is put on display by the National Archives, waiting lines stretch for blocks—equal to crowds drawn to view the Declaration of Independence.

Lincoln issued the proclamation after failing to find a more politically expedient answer to slavery. At one point, he proposed buying slaves from their owners and shipping them to Africa or Haiti. In a pilot trial one year after the war began, the government offered three hundred dollars for each slave in the District of Columbia. The proclamation, drafted in July 1862, was politically sensitive to slaveholders in "border states" that had not seceded. It did not affect three hundred thousand slaves in border states.

The draft sat on his desk for two months, waiting, Lincoln said, for God to spell out his divine will. In late September at Antietam Creek, Maryland, Robert E. Lee's army was driven into retreat. Lincoln summoned his cabinet to the White House five days later: "God had decided . . . in favor of the slaves." The draft, read to the cabinet, was full of legalism but essentially warned the Confederacy that unless the rebel states returned to the Union in one hundred days, on January 1, 1863, their slaves "shall be then, thence forward, and forever free."

In Boston, where abolitionists waited until near midnight on New Year's Day, 1863, before word arrived of Lincoln's signature, bells pealed in victory. But news of emancipation spread slowly to the slaves in the South. The order was often read by Union officers after victories. Today, monuments and celebrations in many southern states recall that magical "first" reading of the Emancipation Proclamation. The African American holiday Juneteenth marks its reading two and a half years after it took effect, as the last of the Confederate forces surrendered in Texas.

The proclamation's lesser-known proviso, enlisting black soldiers in the Union Army, both shortened the war and advanced civil rights. The success of black soldiers and workers broke stereotypes and formed an early class of black leaders.

Civil Rights Row—The Jefferson, King, and Lincoln Memorials

This one-and-a-half mile stroll along the Potomac River spans two hundred years, beginning, as it must, with Thomas Jefferson, who wrote, "all men are created equal." At the other end sits Abraham Lincoln, the Great Emancipator who established Jefferson's word as the American creed. Halfway between is the site chosen to honor Dr. Martin Luther King Jr., the theologian who forced the nation to finally deliver the creed's promise.

The juxtaposition of Jefferson, King, and Lincoln is brilliant architecture, for the three men are connected across the centuries. Each stood on the shoulders, and honored the vision, of the previous man, each reinvigorated historical ideals while bending them to his own purpose. Each man was a civil rights hero of his time, and two died martyrs to the cause. Though the Lincoln and Jefferson memorials were struck in stone, their meanings have evolved as our understanding of the men deepened and the national conscience changed. The three memorials will create a picturesque and thoughtful anchor to the often chaotic real-time politics practiced at the other end of the National Mall.

2 | **THOMAS JEFFERSON MEMORIAL** *(East Basin Drive SW; 202-426-6841; www.nps.gov/thje)* Author of the Declaration of Independence and the third U.S. president, Jefferson was a landed aristocrat schooled in the lofty ideals of democracy and personal freedom. His phrase in the preamble of the Declaration of Independence, "We hold these truths to be self-evident, that all men are created equal," set a standard that, after two centuries, is far more powerful and inclusive than when he penned it. Jefferson was proudest of his stands for personal and religious freedom, liberty, independence, equality, and education.

As a human rights idealist, Jefferson was an enigma. He abhorred slavery but owned slaves. He loathed miscegenation but fathered children with one of his slaves, Sally Hemings. His optimism in Americans to make democracy work was unbounded. Yet he was persuaded by other Founding Fathers to let the issue of slavery slide in order to create an imperfect union of slave and "free" states. Jefferson lived a long life apparently at ease with these contradictions, and in some respects was a man best judged today not by what he did but by what he wrote.

His most famous lines are carved inside a structure patterned after the Greek Pantheon on white Georgia marble walls that surround an immense bronze statue. Because Jefferson thought of the Declaration of Independence as his crowning achievement, one early plan for his memorial placed it directly across from the National Archives. Instead, it was built among cherry trees on the Tidal Basin, and a copy of the Declaration was placed in the cornerstone.

After public life, Jefferson retired to Monticello, his Virginia estate, and spent the remainder of his life inventing, writing, and creating. He died on the fiftieth anniversary of the signing of the Declaration of Independence.

3 | **MARTIN LUTHER KING JR. MEMORIAL SITE** (*West Basin Drive near Independence Avenue*)   This waterfront spot between the Jefferson and Lincoln Memorials has been chosen to honor Dr. Martin Luther King Jr., the civil rights movement's leading figure and martyr. Shaded by the city's famous cherry trees, a ground plaque marks the spot where King's college fraternity, Alpha Phi Alpha, plans to erect the King memorial.

Memorial organizers have chosen as a design a large "stone of hope" to be sculpted with King's image, the stone surrounded by a "water wall" on which his memorable words will be washed by water.

"The memorial will embody the man, the movement, and the message," the fraternity said at its dedication December 4, 2000. "It will honor this twentieth century visionary who brought about change through the principles of nonviolence and equality for all. It will be a memorial symbolizing promise and hope for a brighter future for humanity."

King spent little time in Washington. His influence here came from national outrage stirred by his street strategy in the South. His work, beginning with the Montgomery bus boycott of 1955, took place on the front lines, in staged events designed to break segregation. But ultimate victory required federal intervention by the courts, the president, and congress. It was an uneasy partnership. The FBI spied on King and other civil rights leaders as possible communists. Yet the time was right. King's campaigns in Birmingham, St. Augustine, and Selma and his "I Have a Dream" speech led to the Civil Rights Act of 1964 and the 1965 Voting Rights Act.

4 | **LINCOLN MEMORIAL** *(West end of the National Mall; 202-426-6841; www.nps.gov/linc)* Day or night, no view in Washington is more inspiring than the one from below Lincoln's knees across the reflecting pools toward the U.S. Capitol.

Lincoln preserved the Union and Jefferson's ideals, and he ended slavery. Yet the Great Emancipator was more committed, initially, to the Union than the slaves, and his monument was originally built to honor that ideal—not civil rights. The transformation of the memorial's symbolism into a human rights mecca was the result both of its extraordinary vista and shrewd political and public relations strategy.

Lincoln was elected president in 1860 after campaigning cautiously on the issue of slavery. He opposed it, he said, but would not interfere. But his Republican victory so angered the South that secession and Civil War followed seven days after Lincoln took office. Even after a year of war, Lincoln approached slavery circumspectly. Only after assuring himself of broad support, and probable victory, did he sign the Emancipation Proclamation.

The Civil War ended on April 9, 1865. The Thirteenth Amendment abolishing slavery was winding its way through Congress and newly reelected Lincoln began working on Reconstruction "with malice toward none, with charity for all." Five nights later, on Good Friday, he was shot by John Wilkes Booth. Lincoln died the next morning. As his casket journeyed from the White House's East Room to the Capitol, black soldiers led the cortege and four thousand blacks marched behind. The rail ride home to Springfield, Illinois, wrung a weary nation.

Plans for a Lincoln memorial began immediately, but the first proposal, a gigantic figure surrounded by soldiers, was abandoned for all

Contralto Marian Anderson singing at the Lincoln Memorial

Martin Luther King Jr. at the 1963 March on Washington

the right reasons. Not until 1911, after the Civil War had passed into a mythologized contest of gallant white soldiers, and blacks had lost many of the war's original spoils, did Congress approve a memorial. At the 1922 dedication, the principal speaker, Dr. Robert Moton of Tuskegee Institute, had to sit in the "Colored Only" section and be escorted to and from the dais by a black White House usher.

In 1939, after Howard University and Marian Anderson were denied a concert at Constitutional Hall by its managers, the Daughters of the American Revolution, Harold Ickes, the interior secretary, offered the Lincoln Memorial. On Easter Sunday, April 9, 1939, Anderson's opening number, "America," sung from the top of the steps, sent chills through the integrated audience of seventy-five thousand. Overnight, according to the National Park Service, the Lincoln Memorial "was no longer a place to visit just to think about the past . . . the memorial had been transformed and given new meaning; it had become a special forum to address the problems and issues that divide us today."

And so it was that in 1963, leaders of the civil rights movement used the monument to focus national attention on work going on in

180 southern communities. Engineered by Bayard Rustin and A. Philip Randolph, the rally drew 250,000 people and featured virtually every major civil rights figure.

By the time Martin Luther King spoke late in the afternoon, the crowd was restless. Mahalia Jackson stirred them up with "We'll Never Turn Back." As King followed, according to historian Taylor Branch, someone heard Jackson say, "Tell them about the dream, Martin." King had often used the "I have a dream" sequence in his speeches, but here, in front of Lincoln, it soared across America for the first time. Standing where King spoke—a spot marked with an engraving—while listening to the speech is still a moving experience.

Other National Mall sites

NATIONAL MUSEUM OF AMERICAN HISTORY in the **SMITHSONIAN INSTITUTION** (*14th Street and Constitution Avenue NW; 202-357-2700; www.americanhistory.si.edu*)   A permanent exhibit describing the Supreme Court's 1954 decision to integrate public schools was scheduled to open in 2004. That court decision was widely viewed as the beginning of the modern civil rights era. Also included among the Smithsonian's collections are four seats and a portion of a lunch counter from the Woolworth's in Greensboro, North Carolina, where the sit-in movement began in 1960. The museum also has a pair of shoes worn by Mrs. Hosea Williams in the 1965 Selma-to-Montgomery voting rights march.

Off the mall in southeastern D.C., the Smithsonian operates the **Anacostia Museum and Center for African American culture.** Recently renovated, it includes changing exhibits and programs. Check the museum's Web site, *www.anacostia.si.edu,* or call *202-287-3306* or *202-336-2060.*

BLACK PATRIOTS MEMORIAL (*proposed*)   The best-kept secret of the American Revolution is that five thousand black soldiers—many of them slaves—fought against the British. Congress has approved a memorial to these patriots near the reflecting pool between the Washington and Lincoln Memorials. Sculptor Ed Dwight's design captures a long line of soldiers in bas-relief, the last looking at the Lincoln Memorial. The patriots memorial is in a fund-raising stage.

The best-known black patriot was Crispus Attucks, a rough-hewn Boston dockworker, born a slave of perhaps Indian and African heritage. On March 5, 1770, in the midst of rising tensions between British soldiers and colonists, Attucks and a group later described as "saucy boys, Negroes and mulattos, Irish Teagues and outlandish Jack Tars" began taunting British redcoats. During a shout-filled confrontation at the King Street Customs House, British Private Hugh Montgomery fired into the crowd and struck Attucks. During a melee, four others were killed, and a monument was raised in Boston to them. The real start of the Revolution, the "shot heard 'round the world," occurred five years later on Bunker Hill.

General George Washington initially refused to use black soldiers, until the British did by promising freedom in exchange for their service. As many as twenty thousand slaves fled to the British side, but worked mostly as laborers. Thousands left on British ships after the U.S. victory. After America's black patriots won their personal freedom, they soon learned that slavery would continue in southern states.

NATIONAL AFRICAN AMERICAN MUSEUM (*proposed*)   The idea of a black history memorial or museum on the National Mall dates back to 1915, and scores of bills to create one have come and gone. In 1923, during the Jim Crow era, one bill calling for a monument to "Faithful Colored Mammies of the South" passed the Senate, according to attorney and historian Robert Wilkins. After saner study, Congress authorized a black museum commission, which faded away in the Depression. Dr. King's death prompted a dozen bills and in 1991 the Smithsonian recommended its construction. To date, the concept has foundered, in part because of its depressing content. Yet the mall contains museums devoted to the Holocaust and the history of the American Indian. "It's as if there's a member of the family that no one really talks about," Wilkins told the *Washington Post*. In 2001 President George W. Bush signed bipartisan legislation to create another commission to decide how, not whether, to create a National Museum of African American History and Culture on or near the National Mall.

The U.S. Government

5 | THE WHITE HOUSE (*1600 Pennsylvania Avenue NW; 202-456-7041; www.whitehouse.gov/history/tours*) There is a reason that presidents are rarely remembered for their civil rights leadership. Except for a few, the forty-three most powerful leaders in U.S. history ranged from hypocrites and racists to men reluctant to get involved. By nature political animals who represented the entire country, they consistently subordinated minority rights to the political clout of whites.

Nine of the first fifteen presidents owned slaves. Abraham Lincoln "was the first to act his conscience on matters of race," Kenneth O'Reilly wrote in *Nixon's Piano,* a study of presidents and race. Teddy Roosevelt, a "progressive," held starkly racist opinions that blacks were a "stupid race" except for the "occasionally good, well-educated, intelligent and honest colored" man, like Booker T. Washington, who dined with Roosevelt at the White House. Woodrow Wilson loved the pro-Klan movie *Birth of a Nation,* his civil service fired and separated black clerks, and his administration posted WHITE and COLORED signs throughout federal buildings and the district.

Franklin Roosevelt was pressured by his wife, Eleanor, and civil rights groups to order black employment in defense industries during World War II. But he refused to integrate the military and his inaugurations maintained a Jim Crow "line" down Pennsylvania Avenue. President Harry S. Truman integrated the military and civil service with a stroke of his pen and is considered by some historians as Lincolnesque. Apparently motivated by postwar lynchings of black GIs, Truman delivered a breathtaking civil rights speech during the first-ever presidential visit to the NAACP and was the first to integrate an inaugural, according to historian Michael Gardner.

President Dwight D. Eisenhower is remembered for his stony silence on the 1954 Supreme Court ruling to integrate schools. But, pushed against the Constitutional wall by a rebellious Arkansas governor, Ike sent paratroopers to integrate Central High School in Little Rock in 1957. President John F. Kennedy's record remains debatable because of his death in office. He talked a good game and won black votes but privately told his brother Bobby to clear "this God-damned civil rights mess" off his desk, according to author William Doyle. Shamed by civil rights activists who were putting their lives on the line, Kennedy sent to Congress in 1963 a civil rights bill integrating virtually every aspect of American life. But, at the time of Kennedy's assassination, Doyle wrote in *An American Insurrection,* the bill was dead for lack of administration lobbying. Concludes O'Reilly: "John and Robert Kennedy remained civil rights minimalists for the whole thousand days."

A few days after Kennedy's death, President Lyndon B. Johnson's advisers reportedly asked him to pull the civil rights bill until after the 1964 election. "Johnson, to his great credit, said, 'What the hell is the presidency for if I can't use it for something like civil rights?'" historian Michael Beschloss told the *Des Moines Register.* "It seems so elemental, but in retrospect had he not spoken those words we might be a different country if those rights had not been put in place."

With the arrival of Ronald Reagan and his "states' rights" campaign—launched in, of all places, Philadelphia, Mississippi, where three civil rights workers had been murdered—the era of major civil rights advances in the United States came to an end.

6 | **U.S. Capitol** *(Eastern end of the National Mall; 202-225-6827; www.house.gov)*   Within the walls of this famous institution, Congress denied, waffled on, and eventually supported civil rights for all. Its legislative record recalls Martin Luther King's patient prophesy that the "arc of the moral universe is long but bends toward justice."

As bodies of compromise, congresses before the Civil War tried to maintain a middle road between the South's slavery and the North's push for abolition. When Jefferson's Louisiana Purchase of 1803 opened the West for settlement, the Missouri Compromise of 1820 admitted Missouri as a slave state and Maine as a free state, maintaining the political balance of twelve northern and twelve southern states. It also established a free-slave line at the northern boundary of Arkansas that was supposed to govern all future expansion west. When Congress left it up to Kansans to fight the issue out among themselves, they did just that, and the country divided into civil war.

Congress passed the Thirteenth Amendment, which abolished slavery in 1865, followed by the Fourteenth "due process" Amendment and the Civil Rights Act of 1866, which gave citizenship to blacks. Another civil rights bill in 1875 integrated public accommodations but was overturned by the Supreme Court. Congress would wait ninety years before integrating the country again.

Southern opposition to integration was brutal and frank during the first half of the twentieth century. According to *Quiet Revolution,* South Carolina's "Pitchfork Ben" Tillman bragged on the floor of the U.S. Senate: "We have scratched our heads to find out how we could eliminate every last one of them [blacks]. We stuffed ballot boxes. We shot them. We are not ashamed of it." In the 1940s, because of southern opposition, civil rights advocates "couldn't get anything through Congress," Thurgood Marshall told biographer Juan Williams. "You can't name one bill that passed in the Roosevelt administration for Negroes. Nothing. We couldn't even get the anti-lynching bill through . . . so you had to go to the courts."

Not until 1957 did Congress pass a modest civil rights act to create a prosecuting division within the Justice Department and launch the U.S. Civil Rights Commission. The crowning victories of the civil rights movement were the Civil Rights Act of 1964 and the Voting Rights Act of 1965, both pushed by President Johnson after violent resistance against protesters in Birmingham and Selma, Alabama. They passed during a period of unprecedented public support for civil rights sensitized by nearly one thousand civil rights demonstrations in 209 cities in a three-month period after May 1963, according to the Dirksen Congressional Center. That year, the center reported, the percentage of Americans favoring integration in neighborhoods and schools rose to nearly 75 percent: "Representatives and senators could not ignore the impact of social protest."

A bust of Martin Luther King Jr., installed in the Capitol in 1986, remains the only sculpture of a black American in the halls of Congress.

7 | **U.S. SUPREME COURT** (*First Street at East Capitol Street NE; 202-479-3000; www.supremecourt.us.gov*) The modern civil rights

(*left to right*) George E. C. Hayes, Thurgood Marshall, and James Nabrit Jr. standing in front of the U.S. Supreme Court after winning *Brown v. Board of Education* in 1954

era struck like a mighty storm at 12:52 P.M. on May 17, 1954, when Chief Justice Earl Warren announced an opinion called *Oliver Brown et al. v. Board of Education of Topeka*. In four pages, the court ruled that segregated public schools violated the Fourteenth Amendment's equal protection of the law. *Brown,* as the case became known, reversed more than a half century of court precedent in support of segregation, or "separate but equal" facilities for blacks and whites. The Warren court said that even if facilities were equal—and they weren't—segregating children by race deprived them of equal opportunities. "To separate them from others of similar age and qualifications solely because of their race generates a feeling of inferiority as to their status in the community that may affect their hearts and minds in a way unlikely ever to be undone," Warren stated.

Years ahead of any congressional or White House action, *Brown* set off an era of activist courts that dramatically improved and empowered the lives of blacks and other minorities, dismantled legal segregation in twenty-one states, and led to some of the bloodiest battles in the civil rights era, requiring the government to back up the court with paratroopers, National Guardsmen, and U.S. marshals.

Brown was an unprecedented reversal of court history. In the Supreme Court's 1857 Dred Scott ruling—Scott was a slave who had moved with his master to a free state and sued for his freedom—Chief Justice Roger Taney wrote that the Declaration of Independence never meant to include blacks, that a slave was not a citizen and, in fact, was "subordinate and inferior." As historian John Hope Franklin wrote: "The decision was a clear-cut victory for the South, and the North viewed it with genuine alarm. With the highest court in the land openly preaching the proslavery doctrine, there was little hope that anything short of a most drastic political or social revolution would bring an end to slavery." Civil war was inevitable. After the collapse of Reconstruction, the Supreme Court dismantled the new civil rights of freed slaves. Its 1896 *Plessy v. Ferguson* case approved "separate but equal" railcars in Louisiana and established legal segregation that stood until *Brown.*

A Matter of Law

The civil rights revolution, ultimately, was a movement of laws, not just marchers. During one thirty-year period, laws were reversed, struck down, and enacted, a legal tour de force matched only by the founding days of the Republic. As vital as protests were to draw attention to segregation and discrimination, it was the studious work of lawyers that legitimized human rights with the stability of law.

Their central assault was aimed at states' rights—the right of states to govern themselves. In the South, states' rights had come to mean legal segregation. Civil rights required a rollback of state primacy to federal authority under the Constitution.

Largely led by the NAACP, the legal battle began in the 1930s with lawsuits that demonstrated that "separate but equal" laws were a hoax. Facilities for blacks were, in fact, second class. But in the late 1940s legal strategy shifted to attack segregation as inherently unconstitutional. When the Supreme Court agreed, in *Brown v. Board of Education,* thousands of lawsuits and laws followed, dismantling a century of legal segregation.

Here is a select list of legal landmarks:

• 1896, *Plessy v. Ferguson:* In 1890 Louisiana passed an act "to promote the comfort of passengers," which required railway companies to divide their cars into black and white passenger sections. Outraged blacks in

New Orleans challenged the law by arranging for Homer Plessy to take a seat in the white section on June 7, 1892. His arrest and conviction (Ferguson was the convicting judge) were appealed directly to the Supreme Court, which in 1896 upheld what came to be known as the "separate but equal" doctrine. In short order, segregation became legal everywhere.

• 1938, *Gaines v. Canada:* In 1936 Lloyd Gaines, a twenty-five-year-old college graduate, applied for admission to the University of Missouri law school. He was denied by the registrar, a man named Canada. The Supreme Court ordered Missouri to either admit Gaines or provide a law school of equal quality. This led to the integration of graduate schools across the country.

• 1944, *Smith v. Allwright:* When Lonnie Smith, a black Texan, was refused a ballot in the "white primary" by election judge S. E. Allwright, the Supreme Court ruled it a violation of the Fifteenth Amendment, which guaranteed blacks the right to vote. With this case, African Americans came to "regard the Court as the most reliable safeguard of the rights of all citizens," wrote John Hope Franklin. This case alone raised black voter registration fourfold to one million votes. Thurgood Marshall of the NAACP described *Smith v. Allwright* as more important than *Brown v. Board of Education.*

• 1946, *Morgan v. Virginia:* When Irene Morgan, who was seated near the back of a Greyhound bus, was arrested for refusing to give up her seat to a white passenger, the Supreme Court outlawed segregated seating on interstate buses and trains. Her case stopped seat shifting on interstate transportation at state lines, but it did not change discrimination at bus terminals. That was left to law student Bruce Boynton who sat down in the white section of Richmond's bus station and was arrested. His 1960 Supreme Court case, *Boynton v. Virginia,* integrated bus station cafés, waiting rooms, and bathrooms. Both cases were tested by Freedom Riders.

• 1948, *Shelley v. Kraemer:* In 1945 J. D. Shelley, a black Mississippian who had moved to St. Louis to escape racial oppression, bought a modest, two-story row house on a street restricted by covenant to whites. In 1948 the high court ruled against Louis Kraemer, a neighbor who had sued to stop the neighborhood's integration. The case, argued by Thurgood Marshall of the NAACP, showed that the bench could force social change.

• 1954, *Brown v. Board of Education of Topeka:* One of five public school segregation cases consolidated by the Supreme Court, *Brown* reversed the fifty-eight-year-old separate-but-equal precedent by declaring segregated schools discriminatory and unconstitutional under the Fourteenth Amendment's equal protection. The ruling was extended two years later to end the Montgomery bus boycott. By 1966 the Supreme Court had extended the ruling to public parks, hotels, restaurants, libraries, and courtrooms.

- 1957, Civil Rights Act of 1957: Congress created a civil rights division within the Justice Department with the power to file voter registration suits. It also created the U.S. Civil Rights Commission.
- 1964, Civil Rights Act of 1964: This powerful act outlawed discrimination almost everywhere in America. It covered voting, public facilities, schools, public accommodations, and hiring. It empowered the Justice Department to file suits on behalf of individuals. The Supreme Court upheld the act in the case of a segregated Atlanta motel, *Heart of Atlanta Motel v. United States.* Over the next ten years, according to writer Richard Kluger, the government filed more than fifteen hundred lawsuits under the act.
- 1965, Voting Rights Act of 1965: Considered the most successful civil rights legislation, Congress outlawed virtually every trick used by states to prevent blacks from voting. It has been broadened by various acts and court rulings.

8   HOME OF FREDERICK DOUGLASS *(1411 W Street SE; 202-426-5961; www.nps.gov/frdo)*   Born Frederick Bailey, a slave, on Maryland's eastern shore, Douglass learned to read while working in a Baltimore household. Later, while working as a ship caulker he donned a sailor's suit and simply walked to freedom. In New England, he began speaking and writing about slavery, becoming a mesmerizing orator and face of the abolition movement with his signature mane of hair and Roman nose, likely inherited from his white master. His first autobiography, *My Life as a Slave,* named his owner, putting his family at risk under laws that allowed the recapture of slaves. Douglass fled to England while his friends raised two hundred dollars to buy his freedom.

In person and in his Rochester newspaper, the *North Star,* Douglass pushed President Lincoln to free the slaves and to enlist them as soldiers. After the Civil War, he was named U.S. marshal of the District of Columbia and purchased a "mansion on the hill" in Anacostia with a grand view of the Capitol. Because of opposition his move into the white neighborhood took two years to accomplish. After his wife of forty years, Anna Murray, died in the house, Douglass shocked society by marrying a young white assistant. The National Park Service runs a small visitors center and tours of Douglass's home.

Frederick Douglass home

9 | **LINCOLN PARK** (*Massachusetts Avenue SE at Twelfth Street;* 202-619-7222) This park a few blocks east of the U.S. Capitol contains two striking interpretations of civil rights, one now discredited, the other refreshingly optimistic.

Freedom's Memorial was the first monument erected to Abraham Lincoln after his assassination. Launched with a five-dollar donation from Charlotte Scott, an emancipated slave in Ohio who called Lincoln "the best friend colored people ever had," the monument was sponsored by the Western Sanitary Commission, a Civil War hospital and refugee camp in St. Louis. It was paid for largely by freed slaves. Sculptor Thomas Ball portrayed Lincoln standing over a kneeling black man, his shackles broken. The man's face is that of Archer Alexander, a slave who escaped in St. Louis, then was captured under fugitive slave laws, but rescued by U.S. troops in 1863 under the authority of the newly signed Emancipation Proclamation. William Eliot, a member of the Sanitary Commission who took in the illiterate Alexander, wrote that the sculpture represents Lincoln "in the act of emancipating a Negro slave, who kneels at his feet to receive the benediction, but whose hand has grasped the chain as if in the act of breaking it, indicating the historical fact that the slaves took part in their own deliverance."

At the monument's dedication, on April 14, 1876, President Ulysses S. Grant, accompanied by members of Congress and the Supreme Court, listened to an address by Frederick Douglass, who, according to historian Kirk Savage in *Standing Soldiers, Kneeling*

Slaves, didn't like the submissive position of the slave. Eliot, writing in the paternalistic tone of the time, said that Alexander—who apparently wasn't invited to the dedication—was shown a photo and exclaimed: "'Now I'se a white man! Now I'se free! I thank the good Lord that he has 'livered me from all my troubles, and I'se lived to see this.'" Though sculpted as a tribute to the Great Emancipator, the statue today is considered patronizing to the emancipated.

At the other end of the sunny park is a modern sculpture by Robert Berks of Mary Bethune, a delightfully uplifting figure of an old woman, cane in hand, handing the scroll of the "future" to two light-footed children. Bethune rose from a slave family to become a teacher, entrepreneur, and confidante of the Roosevelts. Bethune started a still-successful black college in Daytona Beach, helped buy a black beach, and, during the Roosevelt administration, headed an unofficial black cabinet that influenced the New Deal. Her Washington home *(1318 Vermont Avenue NW)* was headquarters to the National Council of Negro Women. Berks, famous for his John Kennedy bust at the Kennedy Center, sculpted the Bethune figure in his characteristic slabbed style and surrounded it by words from Bethune's will, delivered near the end of her life, that would serve any parent or grandparent. Among its wishes:

> *I leave you hope. I leave you the challenge of developing*
> *confidence in one another. I leave you a thirst for*
> *education . . .*

Robert Berks's sculpture of Mary Bethune

10 | **UNION STATION** *(50 Massachusetts Avenue NE)* Almost unnoticed in the busy Amtrak wing is a bust of A. Philip Randolph, who formed the Brotherhood of Sleeping Car Porters union, forced President Franklin D. Roosevelt to integrate wartime industry, helped with almost every significant civil rights battle of the 1950s, and conceived the 1963 Lincoln Memorial gathering.

In 1941 Randolph proposed a July 1 march of one hundred thousand on Washington to demand black employment in defense industries. Worried about world public opinion during the war against white supremacist Hitler, Roosevelt summoned Randolph and struck a deal. The march was called off, and on June 25 Roosevelt issued Executive Order 8802 banning discrimination in defense industries, unions, and government. As a result, antidiscrimination clauses were inserted in all defense contracts and a fair employment practices watchdog bureau was established. Randolph died in 1979, and the AFL-CIO commissioned this bust with a typically blunt Randolph quotation:

> *At the banquet table of nature there are no reserved seats.*
> *You get what you can take and you keep what you can*
> *hold. If you can't take anything, you won't get anything*
> *and if you can't hold anything, you won't keep anything.*
> *And you can't take anything without organization.*

11 | **HOWARD UNIVERSITY** *(2400 Sixth Street NW; 202-806-6100; www.howard.edu)* If civil rights were a body of work, its brain would have to be Howard University, the oldest black college and the fount for intellectual and legal advances for nearly one hundred and fifty years. It was named for Oliver Howard, the first commissioner of the Freedmen's Bureau during Reconstruction.

Howard's law school, once housed in Founders Hall, produced Nobel laureate Ralph Bunche and Supreme Court Justice Thurgood Marshall. Under James Nabrit and Charles Houston, the school developed civil rights law. In December 1952 Marshall and other lawyers gathered at the school and practiced for the lawsuit of their lives—*Brown v. Board of Education,* which in 1954 integrated public schools and ended legal segregation nationwide. A small museum in the archives of the building displays many historic photographs of these leaders.

Howard's graduates constitute an A-list of notables: civil rights activist and politician Andrew Young, opera stars Lillian Evans and Jessye Norman, writer Toni Morrison, and politicians Edward Brooke, Vernon Jordan, Douglas Wilder, and David Dinkins.

12 **U STREET NEIGHBORHOOD**
(*U and Fourteenth Streets*)

For more than half a century, the corner of U and Fourteenth was the heart of black Washington. Three hundred businesses thrived near here until the 1950s. A self-guided walking tour with a dozen markers describes historic entrepreneurship, activism, and good barbecue. Much of the U and Fourteenth area was destroyed in riots after the 1968 assassination of Martin Luther King. It is only now coming back, in part, because of gentrification.
Among notable sites:

HOME OF DUKE ELLINGTON (*1212 T Street*) and MURAL (*Thirteenth and U Streets*)   Ellington, the son of a butler, grew up with music ringing in his head, and composed the first of six thousand songs, "Soda Fountain Rag," while working as a soda jerk in the neighborhood, according to *Black Washington* by Sandra Fitzpatrick and Maria Goodwin.

HOME OF MARY CHURCH TERRELL (*326 T Street NW*)   Mrs. Terrell died in 1954 just as the fruits of her long civil rights labor were ripening. Well-educated and -traveled and the wife of the district's first black judge, she was radicalized by the lynching of a friend, whereupon she helped found the NAACP and the National Association of Colored Women, write the book *A Colored Woman in a White World,* and, at age eighty-six, integrate Washington restaurants.

HOME OF MARY MCLEOD BETHUNE (*1318 Vermont Avenue SW*)   Bethune rose from a South Carolina slave family to start a black college in Daytona Beach and become the highest ranking black government official under President Franklin D. Roosevelt. Her home is open as a National Park Site.

CARTER WOODSON HOUSE *(1538 Ninth Street NW)* The man most responsible for changing American opinion about the intelligence and potential of blacks, Dr. Woodson founded the Association for the Study of Negro Life and History at this house. In *The Journal of Negro History,* black scholars chipped away at mythologies dating back to Thomas Jefferson, including genetic inferiority and the "happy slave." He also founded Black History Month. An effort is under way to turn this home into a National Park Service unit.

Two other unmarked U Street businesses should be remembered for their pioneering civil rights roles. At the Hamburger Grill, down the street from the Lincoln Theater, white owners in 1933 fired black employees and hired an all-white staff to feed their all-black customers. Outraged, blacks picketed with signs that read, DON'T BUY WHERE YOU CAN'T WORK. Within days the Hamburger Grill hired back its black workforce. Their success, according to *Black Washington,* led to a string of successful hiring boycotts against white-owned stores. A lawsuit against Sanitary Grocery went to the Supreme Court in 1938 and set a precedent allowing boycotts.

At about the same time, U Street barber Gardner Bishop became fed up with the indignities forced on African Americans in Washington. His daughter Judine had been thrown out of a "white" park and was later forced to cut back her schooling because of overcrowding at a "black" school. He led a boycott to demand better treatment and then plotted integration of schools with Howard University's Charles Houston and James Nabrit. As recounted in *Simple Justice,* Bishop led eleven black children to the brand-new all-white John Philip Sousa Junior High School on September 11, 1950, and tried to admit them. When the school refused admission, their lawsuit became one of the five that integrated public schools in 1954.

13 | **AFRICAN AMERICAN CIVIL WAR MONUMENT** *(Vermont and U Street NW. A Green Line Metro stop is named for the monument; 202-667-2667; www.afroamcivilwar.org)* This modest memorial inscribed with more than two hundred thousand names of blacks who served in

Detail on the African American Civil War monument

the Civil War is a giant advance in rewriting America's history. The accompanying museum two blocks away (*1200 U Street NW; west down U Street*) contains framed photos of slave stories, but the main attraction is a computer data bank in which African Americans can search for their ancestors among the veterans.

Frederick Douglass had long urged President Lincoln to recruit black soldiers: "Once let the black man get upon his person the brass letters, U.S., let him get an eagle on his button, and a musket on his shoulder and bullets in his pocket, and there is no power on earth which can deny that he has earned the right to citizenship."

But northern commanders opposed the idea until the Emancipation Proclamation. Lincoln's order, writes historian James McPherson, "marked the transformation of a war to preserve the Union into a revolution to overthrow the old order."

The first authorized black soldiers joined the U.S. Army in Louisiana, South Carolina, Massachusetts, and Kansas. The first black casualties, ten dead, involved the Kansas soldiers. The most famous soldiers were those of the Fifty-fourth Massachusetts Regiment, the first northern unit, recruited and led by Robert Gould Shaw. Their martyrdom at Fort Wagner, South Carolina, is memorialized in the movie *Glory,* in the surrounding black neighborhood named for Shaw, and in the magnificent Shaw Memorial on the Boston Common. The original plaster cast created by sculptor Augustus Saint-Gaudens is in the National Gallery of Art on the National Mall.

In their service, black soldiers impressed white officers. In statements that seem naive and condescending by today's standards, whites "discovered" black competence. "Nobody knows anything about these men who has not seen them in battle," said Thomas Wentworth Higginson, a colonel from Massachusetts who led a South Carolina unit. The *New York Tribune* vouched that such positive reports "shake our inveterate Saxon prejudice against the capacity and courage of Negro troops."

Nonetheless, blacks were not treated equally as soldiers. The famous Fifty-fourth Massachusetts Regiment complained, as did the Third South Carolina Volunteers, that the promised thirteen dollars a month had been cut to seven. A former slave, William Walker, was court-martialed and executed for starting a strike. Pay was equalized in 1864.

When black soldiers were captured in combat, Confederate soldiers often executed them rather than treat them as prisoners of war. After bayoneting and burning several black soldiers, a North Carolina rebel wrote to his mother: "The men were perfectly exasperated at the idea of Negroes opposed to them and rushed at them like so many devils."

The Pioneering Military

The most successful integration story in America was written by its armed forces. Launched a few years before the civil rights movement began and affirmative action was invented, the program proved in time that equality is not just morally right, it also produces a superior institution.

Black soldiers fought in every American war. But when four hundred thousand blacks came home from World War I, some with French medals of honor, they were welcomed back with the Red Summer of 1919, when scores were lynched, burned alive, shot, and beaten in twenty-five race riots. The dead came home to segregated national cemeteries.

As World War II began, the black press and civil rights groups, notably the NAACP, launched the "double V" campaign: victory against fascism overseas and racism at home. When Congress opened World War II enlistment to blacks, the military put them in segregated units, a decision that essentially created a separate army and navy. Low morale was widespread and performance suffered, in large part because of ongoing discrimination on bases and the battlefield. Segregation was also grossly inefficient. One visible example was the first black fighter pilots' squadron in Tuskegee, Alabama—forty miles from the Army Air Corps' flying school at Maxwell Field in Montgomery.

Before the war was over, army officer training at Fort Riley, Georgia, was integrated, and both the navy and Coast Guard had begun integrating ships. The Coast Guard integrated the USS *Sea Cloud* with the first black officers at Manhattan Beach, New York, in 1943. The navy's first integrated ship was the USS *Mason*, a destroyer escort launched in 1944 at Norfolk, Virginia. Among the first petty officers was Ensign Samuel Gravely, later the first black admiral. Just after the war, the air force quietly closed Tuskegee and integrated aviation training at Randolph Field, Texas, "ending the last segregated officer training in the armed forces," according to *Integration of the Armed Forces 1940–1965* by Morris MacGregor Jr.

After World War II, attacks on black GIs shocked President Truman. One victim was Isaac Woodward who had fought in the jungles of the Pacific and was discharged in Georgia. Ten hours out of the army, on his way home to North Carolina, he was arrested while still in uniform and beaten blind by a policeman in South Carolina. The policeman was acquitted by an all-white jury in twenty-eight minutes. In a separate Georgia case, black veteran George Dorsey, his wife, and a companion couple were riddled with hundreds of bullets at a remote river crossing called Moore's Ford outside Atlanta.

These stories prompted Truman to send civil rights legislation to Congress. Blocked by southern congressmen, he issued Executive Order 9981 calling for "equality of treatment and opportunity" in the military. Confronted with this July 26, 1948, order, the military obeyed.

The navy and air force acted first, largely because the war had proven the silliness of separate segregated ships and planes. But it took the manpower demands of the Korean War for the army and Marine Corps to buy in. By July 1951 General Matthew Ridgway reported the Far East Army command integrated. Europe followed a year later.

Six years after Truman's order, in October 1954, the secretary of defense announced that the last racially segregated military unit had been abolished. Some quarter of a million black servicemen were now sleeping, eating, learning, and fighting shoulder to shoulder with white soldiers. This was a year before the Montgomery bus boycott, and only five months after the Supreme Court desegregated schools, an order that took years to implement.

The military's success helped push along civilian civil rights. GIs like Medgar Evers and James Meredith carried their expectations home. In the 1960s military personnel began demanding equal treatment of its men outside their gates. In Selma and Little Rock, for example, public schools attended by servicemen's children, and receiving federal support, quietly integrated.

Integrated military units were also called to put down militant stand-offs in Little Rock, Arkansas, and Oxford, Mississippi. The lead unit in the Ole Miss integration by James Meredith, according to author William Doyle, was the riot-trained 503rd MP Battalion from Fort Bragg, North Carolina. The unit was "a textbook example of the remarkable success of racial integration in the U.S. military," Doyle wrote in *An American Insurrection*. White privates reported to black sergeants, "yet there were absolutely no racial tensions in the battalion." Ironically, in both Little Rock and Oxford, commanders chose to segregate the troops and keep black soldiers at some distance from the action for fear of riling already angry white citizens.

Civil War Battlefields

The Civil War, which split the nation north and south, still divides white and black. Visitors to war battlefields and museums are largely white, in part because the story was interpreted for a century as a white man's war, its sites devoted more to tactics, soldier sacrifice, and military detail while barely mentioning the central moral conflict that cost 620,000 American lives and freed four million slaves. The National Park Service's "cannonball circuit" was a chief culprit. With new visitor centers and a radically different interpretation of the wars, the park service has begun a major revamping and balancing of the Civil War story throughout the South. From a civil rights perspective, three of the most important war sites are within a two-hour drive from Washington.

I **HARPERS FERRY, WEST VIRGINIA** *(US Route 340, 65 miles west of Washington, D.C.; 304-535-6298; www.nps.gov/hafe)* The Civil War, by most accounts, began at Harpers Ferry when John Brown, a fervent abolitionist, led a vigilante raid against a federal armory in 1859. He hoped that slaves would join him and begin a rolling revolt down the East Coast. Several people were killed here before a U.S. colonel named Robert E. Lee captured Brown and restored peace to the beautiful mountain schism where the Potomac and Shenandoah Rivers join.

Brown's raid, and his subsequent, unrepentant execution, shocked the nation. Southern planters, especially, believed that Brown's zeal was shared by Yankees, including Lincoln. It was only a matter of time, they feared, before their way of life would be attacked. One planter sent one of John Brown's "pikes"—bayonets on a long pitchfork handle—to every southern governor, reminding them that those pikes were forged for their hearts. In the North, Brown became a martyr and "John Brown's Body" became a favorite theme song of soldiers and slaves.

The National Park Service restoration of Harpers Ferry interprets the village's role as the Civil War's primary fuse and its importance to black Americans. Brown's story is told in a series of short films in one building, while the African American context is captured in another.

2 | **ANTIETAM BATTLEFIELD, MARYLAND** (*Route 65 in Sharpsburg; 301-432-4590; www.nps.gov/anti*) Rows of corn still fill the near horizon of bucolic hillsides above Antietam Creek. Redwing blackbirds warble in delight at harvest time when the stalks turn yellow and brittle. It was near this time, on September 17, 1862, when these cornfields and pastures ran red with American blood. Antietam, the single greatest one-day American war slaughter, with twenty-five thousand killed or wounded, turned back the northern advance of Robert E. Lee. Psychologically, Antietam was the day the Civil War began to be a battle about slaves, and not states' rights.

After backing and filling to find a politically suitable position toward slavery, President Lincoln discovered his backbone at Antietam. Two weeks after the battle, he announced that he would sign the Emancipation Proclamation on January 1, 1863. "Beyond whatever other purpose," Stephen Sears has written, "the dead of Antietam had died to make men free."

A mile away, in quiet federal groves of evergreens, the dead lie below rows of gravestones.

Casualties line a field in Antietam

3 | **GETTYSBURG BATTLEFIELD, PENNSYLVANIA** *(97 Taneytown Road in Gettysburg; 717-334-1124; www.nps.gov/gett)* In some ways, this famous Civil War battle is better viewed through the eyes of Ken Burns's PBS series or various good books. A serious civil rights visitor to Gettysburg could be offended by the crowds, tourist attractions named Pickett's Buffet, and the secondary, almost hidden role of the Gettysburg Address. The National Park Service promises a new visitors center and a major reinterpretation of the battlefield's role in human rights.

But even in the crowds, it is possible to step off the asphalt that crowns Cemetery Ridge and stand where Union artillerymen watched thousands of yelling rebel soldiers race toward them across an open field. Battlefield pockets that have become icons, such as the Bloody Angle, are mere corners of low stone walls. Yet here in hand-to-hand combat, the Civil War, and the rights of African Americans, were decided. Between July 1 and July 3, 1863, approximately 23,000 U.S. soldiers and 20,000 to 25,000 Confederate soldiers were killed, wounded, or went missing. Gettysburg marked the northernmost advance of the Confederate army, and began a slow two-year retreat toward Appomattox.

Later that year, President Lincoln was asked to say a few words to dedicate a federal cemetery for Union soldiers at Gettysburg. He drafted a short message in Washington and carried it in his pocket as he traveled by horse-drawn wagon to the northern edge of Cemetery Ridge. After a two-and-a-half-hour oration by a forgotten New York senator, Lincoln got up, read his few lines, and sat down to stunned silence. He feared he had disappointed them.

Today, the Gettysburg Address, carved into granite beside the statue of Lincoln in Washington, remains the single best distillation of the American dream and of human rights worldwide.

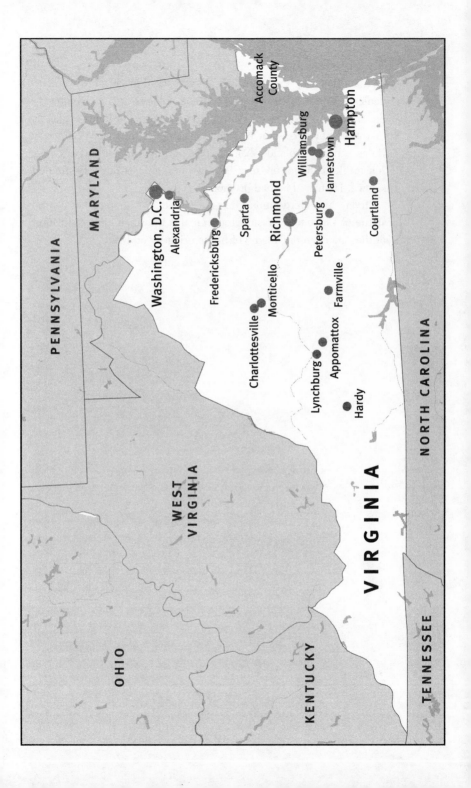

Virginia

AMERICA, IT IS SAID, was born in Virginia. Thus the saga of civil rights began here, too. In the verdant tidewaters off Chesapeake Bay three cultures—red, white, and black—met in the first half of the seventeenth century and set a pattern for what would become the United States.

From a "virgin" seedbed planted at Jamestown, Virginia produced both democracy and discrimination, policies that freed or shackled people according to race, a hypocrisy that took a civil war and a civil rights movement to reverse. The war ended in Virginia and one of the movement's first protests took place twenty-five miles from where Lee surrendered.

In the beginning, Virginia had more slaves than any other colony, but its leaders tried to abolish slavery at gatherings of Founding Fathers. George Mason, who wrote "all men are by nature equally free" in Virginia's 1776 Declaration of Rights, voted against the draft U.S. Constitution in part because it did not end the slave trade. Thomas Jefferson, whose antislavery clause was struck from his Declaration of Independence, voted for the compromise Constitution and went home to his slaves. As historian Joseph Ellis later wrote, "Virginia turned out to resemble the fuzzier and more equivocal picture that best describes the nation at large . . . whether they were living a paradox or a lie is an interesting question."

After four centuries, that "paradox or lie" still puzzles us. If only Thomas Jefferson were alive to question. He especially embodied the rift. His DNA, like his Declaration of Independence, is embodied in ancestors both black and white. If for no other reason, the legacy of Jefferson makes Virginia civil rights history worth exploring.

This "equivocal picture" may help explain Virginia's reputation as a moderate state in race relations. During the first half of the twentieth century, its segregation was just as strict but the state avoided the rash of Deep South lynchings. In the 1960s sit-ins and boycotts were generally peaceful. Virginia reportedly was the only state on the eastern seaboard that did not have to use the National Guard to quell racial confrontations.

Still, Virginia was among the most intransigent of states as "massive resistance" became its official response to court-ordered integration of schools, bus stations, and bedrooms. Integration, the state pleaded at the time, "will require a complete change in the feelings of the people [who] feel a sense of bewilderment that traditions and systems that have operated since 1619 can be so readily swept away."

Four hundred years after Jamestown, feelings have modified. In 1990 the state elected the nation's first black governor, who hopes to build the nation's first slavery museum. It would be fitting in a state that is only beginning to tell the whole story—red, white, and black—that stands for America.

Virginia and Civil Rights

In the space of fifty years, Virginia went from a "wilderness" controlled by Native Americans to a thriving British colony built on democracy, private enterprise, Indian conquest, and African slaves. This transformation, at once inspirational and violent, became the template for the developing nation.

One story is well told: In May 1607 104 Englishmen tied three ships to trees on an island and established Jamestown, the first lasting British colony in the New World. A dozen years later, in 1619, they established the first representative government, the House of Burgesses, elected by white men. Their first act set a minimum price for tobacco, already Virginia's most lucrative export. That same year, a boatload of unmarried women arrived, followed by a Dutch ship with "twenty and odd" African slaves who had been seized in the Caribbean.

They were not the first Africans in North America—the Spanish by then had founded St. Augustine—and though abducted as slaves from Angola, they were classified as servants in Virginia, a category that allowed them to earn their freedom. Yet from the beginning, blacks were distinguished by their color. In 1620 Virginia's census counted 892 Europeans and 32 Africans. Four years later, William Tucker, born to Anthony and Isabella, became the first known African American. By 1650 there were 400 blacks in a colony of 19,000.

Virginia's slide toward slavery may have been inevitable, given several factors: greed and the growing tobacco trade; one million slaves already in the Caribbean; a new and lucrative British slave trade; and white supremacy, what historian Howard Zinn calls "that special racial feeling—whether hatred, or contempt, or pity, or patronization—that accompanied the inferior position of blacks in America for the next 350 years." As tobacco boomed, huge plantations spread along the James River. The terms "Negro" and "slave" became interchangeable and slave labor became the norm.

In 1640 a court approved the first known case of racial profiling while sentencing three runaway servants. Two white men got four years of additional servitude while the third, John Punch, who was black, was sentenced to life. That same year, a white man who fathered a child with a black woman was forced to "do public penance" during church. The woman was whipped.

Virginia was not the first to legalize slavery—Massachusetts did in 1641—but Virginia developed a set of black codes that became a model in the South. In 1661 slavery became hereditary, depending on the status of the mother. In 1705 slaves were declared real estate. The same codes exonerated masters who might accidentally kill a slave while punishing him, and allowed them to dismember "unruly" chattel. Among the victims was Kunta Kinte, the African ancestor of *Roots* writer Alex Haley, who lost his foot while trying to escape near Fredericksburg. By casting slavery into a code, historian Gary Nash writes, Virginia crystallized negative racial feelings "into a deep and almost unshakable prejudice that continued to grow for centuries."

All the while—and this is the supreme irony—the same Virginians were perfecting the philosophies of liberty, equality, suffrage, individual opportunity, and the pursuit of happiness. One theory is that planters who grew wealthy on slaves could think of themselves as independent citizens rather than subjects of the king. When Jefferson wrote the Declaration of Independence, Virginia counted roughly five hundred thousand residents, about 40 percent of them slaves. "To a large degree," wrote Edmund Morgan, "it may be said that Americans bought their independence with slave labor."

This paradox was played out in the American Revolution's climactic battle of Yorktown, Virginia, when slaves promised their freedom by the British faced blacks fighting for American freedom. Afterward, two of the most serious civil rights rebellions in history occurred in Virginia: Gabriel Prosser's 1800 plan to arm one thousand slaves, sack Richmond, and kidnap Governor James Monroe, and Nat Turner's 1831 rebellion in Southampton County that killed sixty whites before being quelled. Both fueled tensions that led to the Civil War.

Although Virginia seemed to relish the Confederate rebellion, favorite son Robert E. Lee warned of "a terrible ordeal, a necessary expiation perhaps for our national sins." Embracing the contradictory refrains that slavery was evil but Virginia must be defended, Lee became an impossibly romantic hero and Virginia erected more monuments to the South's "lost cause" than any state.

Meanwhile, during the war, refugee slaves gathered at Fort Monroe near Hampton (thereafter known as Freedom's Fort) where they were declared Union contraband. Eventually recruited to fight, they helped wear down Lee's army at Richmond. Soon after, at the Hampton refugee camp, a school for ex-slaves was established. One of its early students was Booker T. Washington, a former slave who led America's black education into the twentieth century.

By that time, however, Virginia was undoing the freedoms supposedly secured by the Civil War and Reconstruction. Leading the South in voting chicanery, Virginia instituted five gerrymanders, a poll tax, and a complex ballot with a two-and-a-half-minute time limit. "Such requirements," wrote historian John Hope Franklin, "virtually disfranchised Virginia's illiterate voters, whether white or black."

As Jim Crow took root, black institutions arose in segregation's shadow, notably in Richmond's Jackson Ward. Insurance companies, banks, clubs, and churches fostered an affluent middle class. From this society came entrepreneur Maggie Walker, the first U.S. woman to head a bank, and lawyer Oliver Hill.

In a lifelong battle, beginning with a 1940 suit to equalize black teachers' pay in Norfolk, Hill filed scores of lawsuits to dismantle Virginia's legal segregation and discrimination. The state repeatedly fought him and other lawyers to the Supreme Court. Among the precedent-setting cases that came out of Virginia: integration of interstate bus terminals, integration of courtrooms, and legalization of interracial marriages. But it was in its public schools that Virginia made its staunchest defense of what it called its "way of life."

In the little town of Farmville, twenty-five miles from Appomattox, a 1951 boycott of classes led by a sixteen-year-old girl became one of five cases in the nation that convinced the Supreme Court to outlaw school segregation in 1954. Rather than comply, Virginia adopted "massive resistance," an official policy that closed any public school that had been ordered to desegregate. At one point the governor blocked twelve thousand students from schools in Arlington, Charlottesville, Norfolk, and Front Royal. Farmville's schools were closed for five years. It took several Supreme Court cases a decade later to force Virginia to integrate schools.

In 1990, after a steady increase in black voter registration, Virginians elected Douglas Wilder the first black governor in the United States. He pushed for a state Martin Luther King Day, laid plans for the first national slave museum near Fredericksburg, and tried to get rid of the state song, "Carry Me Back to Old Virginia," written by a black minstrel with its lines, "There's where this old darkey's heart am long'd to go / There's where I labor'd so hard for old massa." The song was voted the "state song emeritus" in 1997.

The memory of these civil rights struggles remains vivid as blacks propose monuments to their heroes and attempt to balance white history with the sacrifice and contribution of African Americans.

A Virginia Civil Rights Tour

Virginia encapsulates the whole long civil rights story from its colonial roots to its current effort, four hundred years after its founding, to memorialize this history in a meaningful way. This guide recommends three geographic areas.

The Tidewater/Hampton Roads

As much water as land, Virginia's Tidewater was a milk and honey paradise when the British came to stay in Jamestown in 1607. Along the James River, Powhatan Indians had cleared parklike meadows among old-growth forests filled with deer, nuts, and fruit. Today, this first American crossroads bristles with bridges and traffic and military might. Many historic spots are on military compounds. Only along Route 5's plantation row of canopied hardwoods does one get a sense of the wealth created by slaves and tobacco in this nursery of the United States. The plantations—Sherwood Forest, Martin's Hundred, Shirley Plantation, Carter's Grove—represent *old* money. Unfortunately, there is little said by way of monuments or tours about slaves who made up half the population. The one exception is "Other Half" walking tours at Williamsburg.

A short side trip to Southampton County takes you into Nat Turner country, still rural, where a small band of slaves turned Virginia into a terrorized and armed camp, a foreboding of civil war.

The Capitol and Mid-Virginia

Built on the "fall line" where Virginia's tidal rivers encountered rapids, Richmond, Petersburg, and Fredericksburg have retained historic districts in the midst of urban sprawl. History here, first and foremost, is about the Civil War. Battlefields and war museums are ubiquitous and second to none. Until recently, civil rights history had been "Jim Crowed" into black sections of town, which had seen better days during segregation. Those neighborhoods undergirded the movement of the 1960s. Today, black activists constantly push to share the historical stage with Robert E. Lee. The results are noticeable, if not quite equitable, in museums and visitors centers.

The Piedmont

These rolling foothills were the heart of Virginia's tobacco industry when slavery ended, and those days seem not so long ago thanks to historic preservation. It is an easy journey from Thomas Jefferson's plantation to Appomattox to the Farmville high school integrated by the Supreme Court. Lynchburg, one of scores of southern communities that overcame segregation without national attention, has taken steps to preserve its civil rights history.

Many of these sites are listed in "The Heritage and Culture of African Americans in Virginia: A Guide to the Sites," published by the Virginia Tourism Corporation. Call 1-888-4SOULVA.

City by City

Accomack County

(Eastern Shore on the southern tip of the Delmarva Peninsula)
This slender finger of Virginia's Eastern Shore, reachable by the Chesapeake Bay Bridge-Tunnel from Norfolk, was home to a number of freed slaves during the colonial period. Nothing yet marks this history, although archaeological digs are under way to find the homestead of Antonio the Negro, one of the few documented slaves to earn his freedom. His story illustrates the possibilities that blacks faced in coming to colonial Virginia—and their downfall as slavery took root.

Antonio arrived in 1621, perhaps from Angola, one of the first blacks in the British colony, and was sold as a servant to Edward Bennett. For his "hard labor and known service," Anthony Johnson, the name he took, was allowed to marry fellow slave "Mary," baptize four children, and earn his freedom. He followed the Bennetts across Chesapeake Bay, where, in 1640, he bought land. By 1651 Johnson sponsored five servants of his own, which entitled him to two hundred and fifty acres of land on Pungoteague Creek in present-day Accomack County. Ironically, in 1654, one of his black servants, John Casor, complained that Johnson had held him past his seven years' servitude. Court records show that Casor lost and was punished by being named servant for life—a slave to a former slave.

In 1665 Johnson moved north to Somerset County, Maryland, and leased three hundred acres for a farm called Tonies Vineyard. He then sold two hundred acres of his original farm to Edmund Scarburgh and deeded the remaining fifty acres to his son, Richard. According to court records, planter Scarburgh delivered more than half a ton of tobacco to the county sheriff to pay for the land, but he also produced a forged promissory note from Anthony Johnson—who could not write or read—for the value of the tobacco. By now, forty years after Johnson's arrival in Virginia, the court system had turned against equal protection of black citizens, and he lost. After he died in 1670, Virginia seized his land "because he was a Negroe and by consequence an alien" and gave it to Scarburgh. Son Richard's fifty acres were also confiscated.

Mary Johnson, Johnson's widow, lived at Tonies Vineyard until her death in 1680. Two years later, Virginia passed the first of many slave codes that prevented blacks from owning land.

Alexandria

FRANKLIN AND ARMFIELD SLAVE TRADING FIRM (*1315 Duke Street*) Long after the United States officially stopped importing slaves from Africa in 1808, slave trading remained a lucrative business because of the demand for slaves in the Deep South. Virginia, Maryland, and South Carolina became suppliers, even breeding slaves. The state's biggest trader was the firm formed by Isaac Franklin and John Armfield and based in this house. They sold thousands of slaves each year and controlled half the sea trade between Virginia and New Orleans. Slaves were held in pens until the Union army conquered Alexandria in 1861. The house is a National Historic Landmark.

ALEXANDRIA/BLACK HISTORY RESOURCES CENTER (*638 North Alfred Street; 703-838-4356; www.oha.ci.alexandria.va.us/bhrc*) A pioneering sit-in occurred in 1939 when five black men refused to leave Alexandria's segregated Queen Street library after trying to obtain library cards. The protest had been engineered by Alexandria native and lawyer Samuel Tucker, who successfully won their release. The following year Alexandria built this library for blacks, which was used until full integration of public accommodations in 1960. Tucker went on to partner with Oliver Hill in Richmond to create the state's leading civil rights firm. The library is now a gallery in Alexandria's Black History Resources Center.

Appomattox

APPOMATTOX COURT HOUSE (*Highway 24, two miles northeast of town; 434-352-8987; www.nps.gov/apco*) In this pastoral, rolling farm country, America's worst war and most barbaric institution came to

Grant's desk at the Appomattox Court House

an end when Robert E. Lee surrendered to Ulysses S. Grant. Frozen in time and captured for posterity, their every word and gesture—especially their civility after four grueling and deadly years—have become premier Civil War lore. The national historical park remains devoted to this single military moment, focusing especially on the gaunt, vanquished rebels, while paying scant homage to the end of slavery.

During the ceremonies, one of the most poignant lines occurred when Lee spoke to Eli Parker, a Grant aide and Seneca Indian: "I'm glad to see there is one true American." Parker, a lieutenant colonel, replied: "Sir, we are all Americans." The same could have been noted of four million Americans, slaves no more.

Just sixteen days before, Lee had issued an order, indeed a plea, for slaves to enlist in the Confederate army in exchange for their freedom. "To the slaves is offered freedom and undisturbed residency at their old homes in the Confederacy after the war," according to a newspaper account. "Not the freedom of sufferance, but honorable and self won by the gallantry and devotion which grateful countrymen will never cease to remember and reward."

By the time of Lee's surrender, few blacks had joined the South's fight. At Appomattox, Lee listed thirty-nine blacks—musicians, cooks, teamsters, and servants—who had been attached to units all along.

On the Union side, seven of the twenty regiments at Appomattox were black soldiers. Altogether, the Union had enlisted 179,000 black troops.

Charlottesville

Even this educated, upscale city had its share of divisive civil rights struggles. It took an NAACP–Thurgood Marshall lawsuit to force the University of Virginia to admit black law student Gregory Swanson in 1950, only to have him endure waving Confederate flags, the constant playing of "Dixie," and the university president (and former governor), Colgate Darden, declaring that Swanson's admission violated "Jeffersonian ideals." When a professor's wife, Sarah Boyle, penned "Southerners Will Like Integration," in the *Saturday Evening Post,* the Ku Klux Klan burned a cross in her yard. University students staged sit-in protests, including one at Buddy's Restaurant where Professor Paul Gaston was beaten by a white mob. Gaston later headed the Southern Regional Council, an influential think tank on racial issues.

Charlottesville's public school system, under court order to integrate, was closed several months by the governor, but began to integrate in 1959. When the Freedom Riders passed through in 1961, black rider Charles Person tried to get a shoe shine in the segregated terminal and was arrested. The attorney general let him go.

MONTICELLO (*From town, take Route 64 east to Exit 121A, and turn left on Route 53. Exit is 1¾ miles on right; 434-984-9800; www.monticello.org*)   Thomas Jefferson's mountaintop home, filled with the heritage of his brilliant mind and life, has become a must-see stop on a civil rights tour because of one recent revelation—DNA evidence that he fathered slave children with slave Sally Hemings. A visitor can use a Monticello stop to think deeply about the issue of slavery and the implication of America's color line. The story here literally runs in the family.

Jefferson confounded our modern sensibilities well before the Hemings affair became public knowledge. He abhorred slavery but kept two hundred slaves, selling them like cattle to pay off debts. He feared race mixing but fathered descendants that took both white and black identities. He perfected history's clearest human rights manifesto—all men are created equal—but really meant white men with property. For all his founding father qualities, Jefferson, according to Pulitzer Prize–winning author Joseph Ellis, had a "capacity for self-deception."

As taught in school, Jefferson's history is well-known: raised a patrician, he became a lawyer, drafted the Declaration of Independence, served as the third U.S. president. He founded the University of Virginia in neighboring Charlottesville and retired to Monticello, where he invented, remodeled his home, and wrote.

Less well known is Jefferson's attitude about African Americans, penned in his *Notes on Virginia,* that blacks were slaves because they were naturally inferior. His "scientific" analysis that included flatly racist observations about smell, color, musical rhythm, and nocturnal habits invested "racial prejudice with the gloss of pseudoscientific verification," according to historian John Chester Miller. These beliefs were widely held into the twentieth century.

The Jefferson-Hemings rumor was first published in 1802 by yellow journalist James Callender, and it remained part of the oral history of the Hemings descendants while mainstream historians rejected it. Sally Hemings, according to contemporary slave accounts, was "mighty near white," her father and grandfather having been white men.

In 1998 *Nature* magazine published the story of a DNA study showing a genetic link between Sally Hemings's youngest son, Eston, and Jefferson's uncle. After studying the evidence and collaborating information, the Thomas Jefferson Memorial Foundation announced a "high probability" that Jefferson fathered Sally Hemings's youngest son and "most likely" was father to all six of her children.

Long after Jefferson's death, U.S. society treated his children differently depending on their mother. While one side of the descendants became a revered American family, the other side stayed in the shadows, its whiter-looking members able to marry whites and enjoy the privileges afforded to whites in a segregated country, yet unable to attend family reunions of either the Hemings or the Jeffersons.

"I too would like to believe Jefferson never lied," said Lucia Stanton, a leading Monticello researcher on the Hemings issue who nonetheless led the foundation to the opposite conclusion and to a refreshing openness in research, publication, and Web resources. Since 1993, Monticello has collected slave oral histories. A year before the gene story broke, it sponsored a reunion of 150 slave descendants.

Mulberry Row, where Sally Hemings lived with other slaves, has both guided and self-guided tours. Inside the main house, some guides more comfortable with the old Jefferson story of his inventions and quirks acknowledge the Hemings affair in clipped tones. Others discuss it volubly. Books for sale in the bookshop and on the Monticello Web site explore the Jefferson-Hemings story thoroughly.

Courtland

NAT TURNER'S REBELLION *(U.S. 58)*   The bloodiest slave rebellion in U.S. history occurred in the cotton fields of Southampton County when sixty whites were slaughtered in thirty-six hours in the summer of 1831. But the real import of Nat Turner's rebellion was the panicked aftermath that helped bring on the Civil War.

Turner, handyman and lay preacher, convinced three fellow slaves to pursue a holocaust "vision," killing slave owners and setting slaves free. On August 21, after seeing a greenish-blue hue in the sky and taking it for a sign, they set off at night. Within two days, seventy slaves were moving toward Jerusalem (now Courtland), the county seat, killing men, women, and infants with swords, axes, and gunshots.

Slowed by exhaustion, alcohol consumption, and disjointed plans, the rebels scattered and were stopped by armed posses on the second day. Turner escaped for two months, while his men were executed along with more than one hundred other innocent blacks who were tortured, burned, and murdered during a violent backlash.

The rebellion set off panic among whites in several states, especially in places like Southampton County where whites were outnumbered 60 percent to 40 percent. The myth of the docile slave had been

U V 122
NAT TURNER'S
INSURRECTION
———◆———

On the night of 21-22 August 1831, Nat Turner, a slave preacher, began an insurrection some seven miles west with a band that grew to about 70. They moved northeast toward the Southampton County seat, Jerusalem (now Courtland), killing about 60 whites. After two days militiamen and armed civilians quelled the revolt. Turner was captured on 30 October, tried and convicted, and hanged on 11 November; some 30 blacks were hanged or expelled from Virginia. In response to the revolt, the General Assembly passed harsher slave laws and censored abolitionists.

Signpost in a cotton field near Capron

shattered. Every black was now a potential terrorist. "I have not slept without anxiety in three months," wrote one Virginian quoted by historian Herbert Aptheker. "Our nights are sometimes spent in listening to noises. A hog call has often been the subject of nervous terror, and a cat, in the dining room, will banish sleep for the night."

All over the South slaves were rounded up, jailed, and lynched. Those who had slept in the plantation house were locked out at night. Elderly whites suffered heart attacks at rumors of new rebellions that usually turned out to be sightings of slaves with tools on their shoulders. Wild rumors—that three thousand slaves were hiding out in nearby Dismal Swamp—flashed up and down the eastern seaboard.

Virginia Governor John Floyd blamed the insurrection on northern Yankees, especially preachers in Sunday schools where blacks were learning to read. He and other governors in the South called special sessions to issue a slew of new slave codes: All-black churches and black preachers were banned. Free blacks were banished. The idea of shipping slaves back to Africa gained new ground. What historians call "sectionalism" heated up through a combination of heightened fear of slave rebellion, northern influence, and a siege mentality. As historian Robert Watson put it: "Nat Turner put the South and the nation on notice that slavery would come to an end, one way or another. The [civil] war was bound to happen."

Turner's rebellion covered about thirty miles in a meandering, cross-country trek that began at the plantation of Turner's owner, Joseph Travis, and ended at the home of Samuel Blunt. The facts are known because of Turner's jailhouse confession (not the novelized William Styron version). Turner was hanged from a myrtle tree in Jerusalem on November 11, 1831, and most of his body buried in an unmarked pauper's grave near a railroad track and High Street. His head was shipped to the University of Chicago, where it was destroyed in a science lab fire.

It is not possible to follow the rebellion's path directly, but several roads still bear the names of victims. Blackhead Signpost Road got its name when a rebel's head was mounted on a stake. Six of the twenty-nine slave owner homes remain standing, one with a bullet hole from the insurrection. Two roadside markers have been posted near key events (*U.S. 58 at Quarter Road, near Capron; Virginia Road 35 at Cross Keys Road near Boykins*). Shiloh Baptist, a black church, leads an annual pilgrimage to one.

The Southampton County Historical Society has purchased victim Rebecca Vaughn's house, where she was killed as she prayed, with plans to move it into Courtland and restore it as a museum. The sword Turner used is on display in the county courthouse. The society offers a Nat Turner pamphlet and sells videotapes documenting key spots.

Farmville

ROBERT RUSSA MOTON MUSEUM (*Main Street and Griffin Boulevard; 434-315-8775; www.moton.org*) One of the most extraordinary civil rights stories occurred in this farming village in the spring of 1951 when blacks tired of second-class schools were spurred to action by a sixteen-year-old girl. Barbara Johns was one of 450 students at the segregated Moton High School, built in 1939 for 180 students. It was so overcrowded that tar-paper shacks had been built for overflow classes. Kids at other schools teased them about their "chicken coops."

Moton High School in Farmville

When Johns complained to a teacher, she replied, "Do something about it." Johns had grown up in a feisty family, one of many independent black farmers who owned land in Prince Edward County. They had long petitioned county officials for equality. Her uncle was Vernon Johns, the outspoken preacher of the Dexter Avenue Church in Montgomery, Alabama. After praying one night, young Johns said she awoke with a vision: "I would give a speech and we would march out of the school and people would hear us and see us and understand . . . and would grant us our new school building and our teachers would be proud and the students would learn more and it would be grand and we would live happily ever after."

On April 23, 1951, Johns tricked the principal into leaving the school and called an assembly where she asked students to join her in a strike. Within a day she had asked the NAACP for help. Within a month a lawsuit was filed and became one of five under the class action Supreme Court decision, *Brown v. Board of Education,* that integrated schools.

But the happy ending Johns envisioned was a long time coming. Coming one year after a new, improved but segregated school opened, the 1954 *Brown* decision infuriated the county. The local newspaper publisher and others formed the Defenders of State Sovereignty and Individual Liberty and became the core of Virginia's "massive resistance" policy toward school integration. "If Virginia surrenders, if Virginia's line is broken," said Senator Harry Byrd, "the South will go down too."

Governor Thomas Stanley broadcast an infamous radio address in which he envisioned a "livid stench of sadism, sex immorality, and juvenile pregnancy." He shut down school systems for several weeks, but Prince Edward County closed all schools between 1959 and 1964. White families built a private academy and set up schools in their churches. Blacks left town and attended various "freedom" schools, but many got no education. A "lost generation" suffered before another Supreme Court order forced schools to open ten years after *Brown*.

When the integrated school opened in September 1964, only eight whites were counted among the fifteen hundred students. Today the public schools are 60 percent black.

Moton High School, the scene of the boycott, is now a national landmark and local museum that houses many photographs, artifacts, and Barbara Johns's written memories. She died in 1991.

In 2003, in a moving reconciliation ceremony, members of the "lost generation" finally received their Moton diplomas. The Virginia legislature passed a resolution expressing "profound regret" at the closings, and the current editor of the *Farmville Herald* urged the creation of Virginia college scholarships for descendants of that generation.

Fredericksburg

Nominated by former Governor Douglas Wilder to host the nation's first major slave museum, Fredericksburg has a rich and sobering civil rights history dating from the days when Kunta Kinte, an African brought to Spotsylvania County in the 1760s, repeatedly ran away from his master. After several whippings failed to stop his rebellion, his foot was cut off with an ax, a story told in grisly detail by Alex Haley in his novelized family history, *Roots*. As a seaport on the Rappahannock River, Fredericksburg sported a slave mart and was home to many free blacks. Local history is dominated by the Civil War—both U.S. president Lincoln and Confederate president Davis spoke here while American Red Cross founder Clara Barton and poet Walt Whitman ministered to the wounded.

In 1962 a famous sit-in integrated Gorick's drugstore and the color-coded (whites in green area, blacks in tan) bus station. By 1963 accommodations here were among the most integrated in Virginia thanks to a biracial city commission. Members of the group prevented racial violence that struck other U.S. cities in 1963 and 1968. Jobs promised during these crises have put blacks in senior positions in the tourist industry. The city publishes an African American walking tour of the historic and (now) upscale downtown area along the river.

SLAVE AUCTION BLOCK *(Williams and Charles Streets)* This original block stands on a street corner with a plaque. At the time, one of the city's slave owners was a free black named De Baptiste. His family owned a large chunk of Charles Street, and at the corner of Amelia Street held a secret school for black students.

JAMES MONROE LIBRARY *(908 Charles Street; 540-654-1043; www.artcom.com/museums)* Before being elected governor and then president, Monroe was a lawyer and city councilman here. He cofounded the American Colonization Society, which sought to return slaves to Africa, a controversial method to end slavery. The society established the west African nation of Liberia, whose capital of Monrovia was named for Monroe.

THE SHILOH OLD SITE BAPTIST CHURCH *(801 Sophia Street)* Before the Civil War, this church became the first African Baptist church in Fredericksburg. Flooded and destroyed, the church was rebuilt by half of the congregation that wanted to stay at this location—the Old Site—while a "New Site" church was built a few blocks away. Minister Lawrence Davies almost single-handedly stopped a black riot after the 1968 assassination of Martin Luther King Jr. by confronting angry youths who wanted to burn and loot downtown. He formed a boys' club and, with the backing of the

Chamber of Commerce, promised them jobs. In 1976 Davies was elected Fredericksburg's first black mayor, a job he held for twenty years.

HOME OF JAMES FARMER *(U.S. 1, 100 feet north of Route 607)* A highway marker honors James Farmer Jr., who as head of the Congress of Racial Equality (CORE) organized the 1961 Freedom Riders bus tour from Washington, D.C., to Mississippi. A hulking man with a booming baritone voice, Farmer was a devoted disciple of Gandhi and nonviolence, and trained his riders to take abuse. The ride's intent was to goad Deep South racists into physical outrage. That, Farmer theorized, would press the Kennedy administration into enforcing a 1960 Supreme Court order to integrate interstate bus depots. At the first stop, in Fredericksburg on May 4, they found the WHITES and COLORED signs removed. But in Alabama, they were firebombed in Anniston and beaten severely in Birmingham and Montgomery. The violence forced Attorney General Bobby Kennedy to protect them with U.S. marshals. A force in major civil rights campaigns in Mississippi, Selma, and Washington, Farmer later became a federal official and a professor at Fredericksburg's Mary Washington College, where a bronze bust of him is on display. He lived in a house just east of the highway sign. President Clinton awarded Farmer the Medal of Freedom in 1998 and Farmer died the following year at age seventy-nine.

Hampton/Norfolk

The country's first true crossroads, Hampton Roads was traversed by generations of Americans, red, black, and white, as the Virginia colony took root. On the wild beach at First Landing State Park it is still possible to contemplate the origins of America and what became a four-century civil rights struggle. Ships bound for Jamestown stopped en route up the James River at Comfort Point, now Fort Monroe. During the Civil War, Fort Monroe took in thousands of runaway slaves. Many received their first book learning at a new school, now Hampton University.

The Hampton Visitor Center *(710 Settlers Landing Road, Hampton; 800-487-8778)* publishes a visitors guide with an African American heritage map.

FIRST LANDING STATE PARK *(Interstate 64–U.S. 60 toward Virginia Beach and Cape Henry Lighthouse; 757-412-2300; www. dcr.state.va.us/parks. The park is within Fort Story, an active military facility, open to the public except during training exercises or high alerts.)* Sticking like a thumb into the Atlantic, Cape Henry is the site of the earliest landing of English colonists who eventually established the first permanent colony at Jamestown. Protected as a natural area, the wild, windblown beach, covered with sea grass, offers a nice respite from sprawling Virginia Beach development. A cross marks the approximate spot where, on April 26, 1607, twenty-some colonists came ashore and were driven back to their ships by Chesapeake Indians. They spent the next two weeks exploring the entrance to the James River before settling sixty miles inland. Seashore State Park, on the adjacent north shore, has a tidy, child-friendly visitors center with environmental and cultural displays.

FORT MONROE *(U.S. 258 across the Hampton River; 757-727-3391; www.virginia.org. The historic fort and Casement Museum are part of an active military fort and open to the public except during maneuvers or high alerts.)* Fort Monroe was built on Comfort Point, a natural harbor and defensive position, and the first stop for settlers and slaves during the colonial period. The Union controlled Fort Monroe when the Civil War began on April 12, 1861. Within days, three runaway slaves, Shepard Mallory, Frank Baker, and James Townsend, came to the fort. On May 24, commander Benjamin Butler declared them "contraband," or confiscated enemy property, an act that became official U.S. policy. When word spread, thirty-five thousand refugees became squatters near the fort, thereafter nicknamed Freedom's Fortress. Many ex-slaves joined the army as laborers and soldiers and fought with Butler in the final defeat of Richmond. Jefferson Davis, the president of the Confederate states, was jailed here for two years after the war.

HAMPTON UNIVERSITY *(adjacent to downtown Hampton on the waterfront; 757-727-5000; www.hampton.edu)* During the Civil War, squalid conditions among black refugee camps prompted the American Missionary Association and the army to establish several schools for ex-slaves. Its official mission was to teach "civilization and Christianity, to imbue them with motives of order, industry and self-reliance, and to elevate them in the scale of humanity by inspiring them with self-respect." It was the first organized teaching of slaves in the country. Hampton Institute, founded by the Freedmen's Bureau after the war, was headed by teacher and soldier Samuel Armstrong, a Massachusetts native who had led two Colored Troop regiments during the war.

In 1872 a sixteen-year-old named Booker T. Washington showed up dirty and ragged but won admission by his willingness to work as a janitor. Washington embraced Armstrong's philosophy that combined physical labor with studies, became a Hampton teacher, and was later recommended to Alabama citizens who wanted to start a school for blacks at Tuskegee.

Hampton became a leading black university. Among its graduates are several military generals, federal and state judges, college presidents, and wealthy entrepreneurs. During the 1960s Hampton's students marched and organized sit-ins to break Hampton city's segregation.

Among the most notable sites on campus are the magnificent Emancipation Oak, under which Lincoln's proclamation was read to slaves in 1863, a Booker T. Washington memorial garden, and a museum of priceless artifacts and artwork. Among the museum's holdings is a vast collection of Kuba (African) artifacts gathered by Hampton missionaries and Henry Tanner's oil, *The Banjo Lesson*. Visitors are welcome. A campus tour can be arranged through the public affairs office.

Hardy

BOOKER T. WASHINGTON NATIONAL MONUMENT (*Virginia Road 122, twenty-two miles from Roanoke*)   Born to a slave cook and a white neighbor man, Booker T. Washington was listed on this plantation's 1861 inventory as a five-year-old boy, value four hundred dollars. He would become the most famous African American of his era, a counselor to presidents and founder of thousands of schools in the South. His autobiography, *Up From Slavery,* describes how a soldier arrived after the Civil War, "made a little speech and then read a rather long paper—the Emancipation Proclamation, I think. After the reading we were told that we were all free, and could go when and where we pleased." The National Park Service displays a bronze of this scene.

Washington later walked five hundred miles across Virginia to enter Hampton University. He founded Tuskegee Institute in Alabama and helped establish at least five thousand rural schools underwritten by the president of Sears, Roebuck, Julius Rosenwald.

Washington taught a combination of practical skills and education to black students at a time when white supremacy was regaining control of the South. In his public rhetoric, he seemed to abide by Jim Crow, urging blacks to improve themselves and assuring whites, among them Teddy Roosevelt and Tuskegee donors Andrew Carnegie and John D. Rockefeller, that agitation was "folly." As a result he became a darling to the white South and an Uncle Tom to black activists like Ida B. Wells and W. E. B. Du Bois, who described Washington as "safe and sure." Behind the scenes, Washington fought discrimination, and in the end, his one unblemished legacy was giving tens of thousands of freed slaves their first opportunity to "get into a schoolhouse."

Jamestown/Yorktown

When this famous former British settlement celebrates its four hundredth birthday in 2007, it ought to be a big triracial party. It was here, along the James River, that three cultures met. Initial accommodation collapsed and the British took control, crushing Indian culture and enslaving Africans. Because the English wrote the history, the stories told to visitors ever since have been largely Euro-white-centric.

When plans to celebrate the quadricentennial began, historians learned that many blacks consider Jamestown their Ellis Island. Some fifteen thousand slaves came up the James and other Virginia rivers. By the time the United States became a nation, 40 percent of Virginia was black, mostly slaves but about 4 percent, or twelve thousand people, free blacks.

Native Americans, on the other hand, could rightly think of Jamestown as the beginning of the end. They refused to be slaves and fought unending land grabs—they burned Jamestown twice—but were eventually decimated by war and disease. By 1700 there were fewer than one thousand Indians in Virginia. Today, seven remnant tribes are recognized by a state they once owned.

JAMESTOWN ISLAND *(Colonial Parkway; 757-898-2410; www.nps.gov/jame)* Operated by the National Park Service, this is the site of the original 1607 settlement. Largely made up of archaeological digs and foundations, the site includes a visitors center and a gigantic obelisk that marks the "birthplace of Virginia and the United States." On this island, in 1619, the first Africans and a boatload of unmarried women arrived, and the first representative assembly in the New World passed the first laws. The African and Native American stories are best told in a huge variety of books available for sale.

JAMESTOWN SETTLEMENT *(Colonial Parkway and Virginia 31; 888-593-4682 or 757-253-4838; www.historyisfun.org)* This is a state-run replica of Jamestown, complete with ships, an Indian village, and actors who portray colonists. Behind the theme park facade, however, is serious archaeology and history, and the best available displays on the three cultures that clashed at Jamestown. Panels include the story of Anthony Johnson, a slave who worked his way to freedom and owned slaves himself. The settlement plans an expansion of both Indian and African stories in new galleries.

Pocahontas

Lost in the four-hundred-year-old popularized fairy tale of this Indian girl is a poignant story of entwining fates and what might have been. When the English landed at Jamestown, Pocahontas was a twelve-year-old daughter of Powhatan, the Algonquin chief of the area. Named for her playfulness—she did cartwheels naked—she was a frequent and favorite visitor to the wood fort. After sporadic violence took place between Indians and settlers, Captain John Smith was captured by Powhatan and brought to his village on the York River. As Smith was stretched out to be clubbed to death, Pocahontas rushed in, embraced him, and, Smith reported, saved his life. Chief Powhatan then declared them friends. Some modern scholars believe the whole thing was a staged ceremony to show both Powhatan's strength and his willingness to live peacefully.

As historian Gary Nash writes, Pocahontas learned English and "became a kind of ambassador" between the two sides. But the following year, Smith decided to demonstrate his growing power with an Indian killing spree. Colonists squatted on more Indian land. Retaliation produced more death and destruction. In 1613 starving colonists kidnapped Pocahontas to barter for corn. While in custody for a year, she and widower John Rolfe fell in love.

They married a year later, bringing a temporary new peace with Powhatan. During a trip to England to see King James, Pocahontas, Rolfe, and their new son were darlings of London society. Pocahontas raised money and interest to send hundreds of new colonists to Virginia. Seven months later, en route home, Pocahontas contracted pneumonia, died, and was buried in Gravesend, England. She was twenty-two.

Five years later, displaced by the growing tobacco plantations, Indians attacked Jamestown and killed a third of the population, including John Rolfe. His son, Thomas, survived to father a daughter whose offspring counted themselves among the most aristocratic of Virginia families, which include the Randolphs, Blairs, and Bollings. Around Virginia, Pocahontas memorials are commonplace.

In 1924, at the height of Jim Crow segregation, Virginia's legislature passed "An Act to Preserve Racial Integrity," outlawing miscegenation and stripping rights from anyone with mixed blood. To ensure uninterrupted aristocracy, however, the legislature added what is known as the "Pocahontas Exception," declaring that those with one-sixteenth Indian blood were "white."

YORKTOWN (*Colonial Parkway and Virginia 1020; 888-593-4682 or 757-253-4838*) As U.S. colonists prepared to revolt against Britain, the hypocrisy of slave owners calling for "liberty" was not lost on anyone, including slaves. Here, where the decisive battle of the Revolution was won, the paradox was acted out by slaves themselves. In one of the least-known stories in American history, blacks who were promised their freedom by the British battled blacks fighting for American freedom. Some five thousand slaves fought for the Americans in the Revolution, and upwards of twenty thousand joined the British, fleeing with them in ships. A diorama at the Yorktown Victory Center tells the story of two African Americans, Jehu Grant and Boston King, who chose different sides.

Lynchburg

A tobacco and rail center with gorgeous old buildings, Lynchburg went through a nonviolent civil rights movement in the 1960s and is one of the few communities with a museum to commemorate it. Taking a cue from the Montgomery bus boycott, the Lynchburg transit company quietly integrated buses in the 1950s. In 1960 student and church sit-ins led to mass arrests but peaceful integration of stores. Court-ordered school integration was complicated by the Reverend Jerry Falwell, who built the private Lynchburg Christian Academy and in radio ads invited white parents to enroll their kids. The academy and Falwell's Liberty University now recruit black students.

HOME OF DR. WALTER JOHNSON (*Fifteenth and Pierce Streets*) Perhaps the most interesting Lynchburg civil rights story is the development of two black tennis pioneers—Althea Gibson and Arthur Ashe. Both were coached to greatness on a private tennis court next to the house of Dr. Walter Johnson, a black physician and tennis player with an eye for talent and enough money to support a string of black athletes during the Jim Crow era.

Gibson, who was raised in Harlem, New York, spent the school year with another black doctor-coach, Hubert Eaton, in Wilmington, North Carolina, and summers at Dr. Johnson's. After dominating the black American Tennis Association for a decade, she became the first black of either sex to enter the U.S. nationals in 1950. She won the singles competitions at Wimbledon and Forest Lawn in 1957, at a time when she was not allowed to stay in some hotels.

Ashe arrived in Lynchburg in 1953 as a ten-year-old, "so skinny he looked like he had rickets," Johnson later told *Sports Illustrated*. Aware of the racial mantle Ashe would have to shoulder, Johnson taught him over nine summers to keep his temper even after bad calls. Ashe went on to win the U.S. Open in 1968 and Wimbledon in 1975.

Johnson, according to writer Mike Brown of the *Roanoke Times,* supported more than one hundred kids at what became the center of black tennis for two decades. The athletes called him "Dr. J." although his nickname as a black collegiate All American was "Whirlwind" for football wizardry. He took up tennis as a medical resident in Texas and, after moving to Lynchburg, vowed to prove that blacks could become tennis champions. His home was in a once-affluent black section, a block from the house of Anne Spencer, a poet and hostess of luminaries from W. E. B. Du Bois to Thurgood Marshall. Both are designated historic homes. Johnson died in 1971, and the old clay court is an abandoned lot, marked only by a small stone monument. City tennis courts are named in his honor.

LYNCHBURG LEGACY MUSEUM *(403 Monroe Street; 434-845-3455; www.legacymuseum.org)* A large mural in the stairway honors Lynchburg's civil rights heroes. The museum hosts other changing exhibits.

Richmond

Virginia's capital seems at first glance to have one pastime—its Confederate history. With more Confederate memorials than Gettysburg, a renowned boulevard of Civil War monuments, a world-class Museum of the Confederacy that includes the Confederate White House, and the biggest Civil War museum in the South, Richmond does not seem to be a civil-rights-friendly stop.

Unless you take the view that the Civil War was the most important civil rights event in U.S. history. Then, Richmond is full of surprises, civil rights stories and lively debate over its mix of monuments.

Built on the James River, Richmond was a wealthy seaport and slave mart until the Civil War, and the industrial and spiritual heart of the Confederate war effort. One of the most touching scenes of the new postwar era occurred when President Lincoln, who had arrived by boat, walked into the city's burned-out remains, greeted by awestruck and kneeling newly freed slaves.

After the war, however, Richmond directed Virginia's spiritual and legal retreat into Jim Crow segregation—a 1900 ordinance required separate neighborhoods, which led to the rise of black-dominated Jackson Ward. Later, Richmond carried out a thirty-year battle against the civil rights movement. School desegregation was an exhausting marathon that closed schools, bused kids in and out of the city, and ultimately returned them to segregated neighborhood schools.

Today in Richmond, efforts to balance its history and public space result

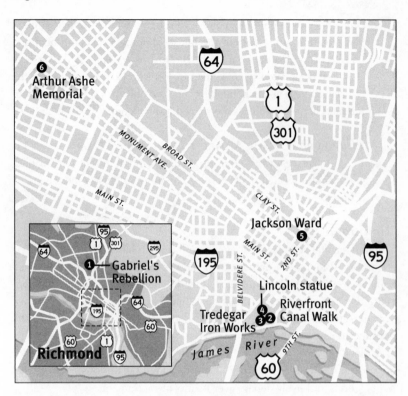

in heated exchanges, a process that, while messy, is rare among southern cities for its open and honest debate about human rights issues.

The following civil rights stops sample Richmond's history chronologically.

1 | **GABRIEL'S REBELLION** (*Three suburban sites have markers: Brook Bridge—Route 1 and Brook Run; Young's Springs—Lakeside and Bryan Park Avenue; Meadow Farm—Courtney and Mountain Road. A brochure is available. 804-672-5736*) In 1800 the largest slave conspiracy in southern history played out in Richmond and neighboring Henrico County when a slave named Gabriel Prosser enlisted several hundred slaves to take over Richmond, capture Governor James Monroe, and demand an end to slavery. Born in 1776, the year the United States declared liberty for all, Gabriel was keenly aware that he had been "born into a lie," according to biographer Douglas Egerton. A skilled blacksmith with rights to freelance around

Two Richmond riverfront sculptures: (*l*) *The Batteaux Man* and (*r*) replica of Henry "Box" Brown's container

Richmond, Gabriel, described as six foot three with a boney and scarred face, cached hundreds of swords and clubs.

On August 30, the day slaves were to gather at the stone Brook Bridge and march four miles into Richmond, an extraordinary thunderstorm filled creeks and made the bridge impassable. Gabriel postponed their rendezvous one night, enough time for two slave snitches to spread the word and alert Monroe. Filling the streets with militiamen, the governor then arrested and hanged more than thirty coconspirators, so many that Vice President Thomas Jefferson urged him to stop seeking revenge. Gabriel was later found in the hold of a ship about to leave Norfolk and was hanged in Richmond at Fifteenth and Broad.

Henrico County publishes a brochure and has marked key spots in the rebellion, including the brook rendezvous spot, the spring where Gabriel was elected leader, and the plantation park where slaves leaked the secret to authorities.

2 | RIVERFRONT CANAL WALK (*Downtown, along James River*) This old industrial canal along the James River has been developed for walking and boat tours of Richmond history. Slaves were traded here and many became watermen, depicted in Paul DePasquale's bronze sculpture *The Batteaux Man*. Not to be missed is a two-by-two-by-three-foot bronze box, an exact replica of the container in which Henry "Box" Brown, an enslaved tobacco worker, had himself nailed in and shipped to Philadelphia in 1849. His accomplice, Samuel Smith, a white shoemaker, was arrested but Brown became an anti-slave activist. Brown took the drastic action, during which he almost died, after his slave wife and three children had been sold. Brown later wrote, "My friends . . . managed to break open the box and then came my resurrection from the grave of slavery." A canal walk brochure is available.

3 | RICHMOND NATIONAL BATTLEFIELD PARK *(Tredagar Iron Works, Canal Walk)* Richmond's vast Civil War history is centered at this remodeled foundry, and the National Park Service has created a balanced interpretation between North and South. The contribution of black soldiers remains underrepresented and will until the Park Service better develops its satellite Fort Harrison interpretative center on the outskirts of Richmond.

At New Market Heights (Chapin's Farm) on September 29, 1864, three brigades of U.S. Colored Troops joined in an attack on a dug-in Confederate line protected by miles of tree piles, wood spikes, cannons, and some of Robert E. Lee's best riflemen. The black brigades lost 43 percent of their men in two suicidal assaults. When their white officers fell, black soldiers took command and captured a key fortification called Signal Hill. Many captured black soldiers were murdered by enraged Confederate troops. Two white and fourteen black soldiers won Medals of Honor for two and a half hours of combat. Among them, Corporal James Miles, whose commendation read: "Having had his arm mutilated, making immediate amputation necessary, he loaded and discharged his piece with one hand and urged his men forward; this within thirty yards of the enemy's works."

In 1999 Congress authorized an expansion of the national battlefield to include a monument to the battle, which it called "a premier landmark in black military history."

Bronze sculpture of Lincoln and his son Tad at the Tredegar Iron Works

4 | **LINCOLN STATUE AND TRAIL** (*Tredegar Iron Works and River-walk*) In what historian James McPherson calls one of "the most unforgettable scenes of this unforgettable war," President Lincoln strolled into Richmond, Virginia, on April 5, 1865, thirty-six hours after Lee and the Confederate government fled. Holding the hand of his twelve-year-old son, Tad, Lincoln was engulfed by freed slaves shouting "Glory!" and "There is the great Messiah . . . Come to free his children from bondage." They reached out to touch him and knelt at his feet. Thousands surrounded him, his stovepipe hat bobbing above them. From Rocketts Landing they walked two miles along the river, up Main, Seventeenth, and Broad Streets to the Confederate White House where he sat in Jefferson Davis's chair and asked for a glass of water. Through the day, one witness said, "his countenance was one of indescribable sadness," occasionally dampened with tears. Lincoln spent the night on a Union boat, met with Confederate soldiers the following day, and returned to Washington.

On April 9 Lee surrendered at Appomattox. On April 14 Lincoln was shot. He died the next day.

In 2003 a bronze of Lincoln and Tad on a bench was unveiled at the Tredegar Iron Works. The statue's sponsor, the United States Historical Society, views it as a reconciliation memorial, and plans to hold an annual April 5 reenactment of Lincoln's walkabout.

5 | **JACKSON WARD** (*Second and Clay Streets*) During Jim Crow segregation, this pocket of Richmond was known as "Little Africa" and "The Harlem of the South." With 93 percent of Richmond's blacks as residents, Second Street, or "The Deuce," was a rich and wild blend of business and bawdiness. The music was hot, secret black fraternities flourished, and there were three newspapers, a chain of beauty salons owned by a woman, and a tailoring school run by a man with fifteen hundred students. A number of black banks and insurance companies were established, including St. Luke Penny by Maggie I. Walker, the first woman to head a bank in the United States. Daughter to a black mother and Irish father, Walker had as her motto: "economic independence is the only independence in the world."

The history of Jackson Ward and Richmond's civil rights movement are concisely told at the **Black History Museum & Cultural Center** (*00 Clay Street; 804-780-9093; www.blackhistorymuseum. org*). A walking tour brochure will direct you to the **Maggie Walker National Historic Site** (*600 North 2nd Street; 804-771-2017*) run by the National Park Service, as well as to the statue of Bill "Bojangles" Robinson and other sites. Robinson, a renowned vaudevillian and Hollywood tap dancer who acted with Shirley Temple and owned an interest in a New York Negro League baseball team, is not the "Mr. Bojangles" of Jerry Jeff Walker's song about a down-and-out New Orleans street performer who happened to be white.

Richmond's civil rights movement involved daily sit-ins and arrests, but is best known for the legal work of Oliver Hill, whose law firm filled Virginia court dockets with discrimination cases. Bronze busts of Hill are mounted at the museum and the **Virginia Historical Association** (*428 N. Boulevard, 804-358-4901*).

Jackson Ward was gutted financially by desegregation and physically by "urban renewal," which led to the construction of an interstate highway through the neighborhood. Preservationists consider it Virginia's most threatened landmark.

6 | **ARTHUR ASHE MEMORIAL** (*Monument Avenue*) When tennis great Ashe died in 1993, more than five thousand people waited in line to view his casket at the governor's mansion. This Richmond native, who in the 1950s couldn't play tennis on the city's segregated courts, had returned a hero, the only black man to win the U.S. Open and Wimbledon. More than that, he was a man who had made it his mission to defeat all manner of injustice.

A descendant of a female slave traded for tobacco in 1735 in Yorktown, and a white governor named Samuel Ashe, Ashe was born in 1944, a skinny, quiet kid who learned tennis at a black playground. At age ten he was recommended to Walter Johnson, a black physician and tennis coach in Lynchburg who had helped develop Althea Gibson, the first black athlete of either sex to win the U.S. Open and Wimbledon. Known for his unflappable concentration, Ashe saw his career cut short by a heart attack and AIDS contracted in a blood transfusion. He raised millions for AIDS and various nonprofit groups, founded the tennis players' union, authored a three-volume study of black athletes in America, *Hard Road to Glory,* and led a boycott of sports against apartheid-ruled South Africa. When Nelson Mandela emerged from twenty-seven years in prison and was asked whom in the U.S. he wished to have visit, he named Arthur Ashe.

Arthur Ashe Memorial on Monument Avenue

But when a black-controlled city council voted to honor Ashe with a monument on this city's historic Monument Avenue, many considered it an affront to symmetry and heritage. Monument Avenue is famous for its gigantic memorials to Confederate heroes—Lee, Jackson, Davis, et al.—each intersection of the expansive boulevard punctuated by heroic figures standing erect and on horseback. Many liberals realized how much they'd taken for granted the city's Confederate milieu. Not all blacks liked the idea of putting Ashe with the generals either. But Richmond did, and you can judge for yourself. Ashe is shown holding a tennis racket in one hand and books in the other above the heads of several children. His was only the second black monument in the city, the first being the statue of Bill "Bojangles" Robinson, the entertainer from the black Jackson Ward.

Petersburg

Petersburg's civil rights history is one of gritty perseverance, not unlike the famous Civil War siege that wore Robert E. Lee's Confederate forces into submission on the city's outskirts. Most tourists coming off Interstate 95 turn east toward the national battlefield to learn more about its siege and Crater stories. Both involved heroic black contributions. Turning west, Petersburg's black neighborhoods tell quieter but deeply abiding tales.

The oldest black congregation in America, First Baptist, is still here. So are neighborhoods settled before the Civil War by free blacks—Petersburg was home to the largest free-black population in the South. Many were watermen operating on Pocahontas Island in the Appomattox River, and some, no doubt, helped slaves escape on a waterborne underground railroad. The first president of Liberia, Joseph Jenkins Roberts, was a prominent black merchant. During Jim Crow, these neighborhoods thrived and provided foot soldiers for the civil rights movement here and in Richmond. The city publishes a detailed brochure of African American heritage sites.

PETERSBURG NATIONAL BATTLEFIELD (*Virginia Road 36 off Interstate 95; 804-732-3531; www.nps.gov/pete*) Even Civil War haters ought to drive through this park to take a look at the mere piles of dirt that separated Union and Confederate soldiers during the horrific ten-month Petersburg siege. You can also walk the Crater, the brilliant but flawed effort to burrow five hundred feet beneath the South's lines and blow up Confederate forces. The bomb worked, but

Union soldiers who poured into the pit couldn't get out. Black reinforcements were mowed down. The Union's 3,500 casualties were double the Confederate's. The Twenty-ninth U.S. Colored Infantry went in with 450 men and came out with 128. One black soldier and twenty whites won Medals of Honor.

FIRST BAPTIST CHURCH *(236 Harrison Street;* 888-355-8602; *www.fbcrichmond.org)* This is the oldest black organized congregation in America, tracing its roots to rural gatherings in Prince George County in 1756. Organized as the First African Baptist Church in 1774, two years before the Declaration of Independence, it later moved to this location. This stolid church was not built until 1870. The church publishes a history brochure and gives tours on request.

GILLFIELD BAPTIST CHURCH *(209 Perry Street)* Petersburg's second-oldest church, originally a rural congregation that later would be moved to Pocahontas Island, has been home to politically active preachers. In the 1950s it was led by Wyatt T. Walker, a sharp-dressing seminary classmate of Martin Luther King, who had dabbled with communism in high school. Walker made headlines in 1958 when he led a group into the segregated Petersburg Public Library ("wearing a clerical collar for the first time in his life," according to historian Taylor Branch) and asked for a biography of Robert E. Lee. His ironic protest was not lost on reporters tipped off ahead of time. Walker, his wife, and their children spent three days in jail. After leading Richmond's first large civil rights march, Walker joined King as field director for the Southern Christian Leadership Conference and was involved in key protests from Albany, Georgia, to Birmingham.

PETERSBURG PUBLIC LIBRARY *(137 South Sycamore Street;* 804-733-2393; *www.ppls.org)* Still lending out books, this library was segregated by floors until the 1960s. The color barrier was broken after two black ministers, Wyatt Tee Walker and R. B. Williams, walked into the main (white) room and asked for a biography of Robert E. Lee. After they were arrested, a mass protest was held at the Zion Baptist Church on Byrne Street.

Sparta

In 1958 one of the South's biggest taboos, interracial marriage, reared its head in the private bedroom of Mildred and Richard Loving. At 2 A.M. they were awakened by flashlights in their eyes and the sheriff beside their bed. He demanded that Richard identify the woman beside him. Loving, a bricklayer, was struck dumb with fear.

"So I spoke up. I said I was his wife," Mrs. Loving, seventeen at the time, recalled years later. They had broken a 1924 law that made it a felony for a white person to marry anyone with any "discernible" black blood.

A judge suspended a year's prison term—if the couple left Virginia. They moved to Washington, D.C., where they had married, but they remained unhappy and unable to travel because of Jim Crow laws. Six years later, according to the *Richmond Times-Dispatch,* Mrs. Loving wrote to Attorney General Robert Kennedy. She wanted to know if the Civil Rights Act of 1964 would protect them in Virginia. It would not, he wrote back, but he urged them to contact the American Civil Liberties Union.

Their pro bono attorney, Bernard Cohen, lost the case, *Loving v. Virginia,* before the state supreme court but won a landmark decision in the U.S. Supreme Court in 1967. Their case ended miscegenation laws in sixteen states. The couple moved back to Sparta and into a new home built by Richard Loving. He was killed in 1975 by a drunk driver.

"I didn't know it was against any law," Mildred Loving said in 1992. "We were just happy. We weren't out to change nothing [but] I believe that's why we were put here. That's why we were married."

Williamsburg

COLONIAL WILLIAMSBURG *(Interstate 64, exit 238, follow the signs to the visitors center; 757-229-1000; www.history.org)* More than any other national site, Williamsburg tries to tell complex stories of human conflict in the eighteenth century. At the time it was the capital of Virginia and 52 percent of the population was black, a statistic noted by the park in its two-hour walking tour called "The Other Half." Costumed interpreters throughout the site are eager to discuss black history if questioned, and on any given day, several slave stories are listed in the Visitor's Companion.

Beginning in the 1980s, Williamsburg mounted cutting-edge historical interpretation, including an estate auction that featured actors posing as slaves for sale. The NAACP picketed. Carter's Grove, a satellite plantation, was opened with Virginia's best interpretation of the three-culture milieu (Indian, African, English). Among the stories discussed: master-slave miscegenation, free blacks who owned slaves, blacks choosing sides in the American Revolution, slaves paying for freedom by selling their children.

But when Carter's Grove used period-costumed interpreters, both black and white, many tourists wanted to hear only from the black staff, whom they considered more authentic. A play with simulated whipping called "Broken Spirit" evoked tears and sober discussions. The programs were especially tough on black actors who often found slave reality depressing.

In 2003 budget cuts and public reaction forced Williamsburg to reduce its slave program. Carter's Grove was closed for a two-year reevaluation and upgrade. Most of the staff was transferred to the main Williamsburg village, but a spokeswoman said "high-risk" programs would not continue. A new slave section, Heart's Hope, would focus instead on rural slaves and their poor white neighbors.

The Role of the Media

Without the press, the civil rights movement may not have unfolded as it did. Certainly, our memory of it would not be the same. Events covered in remote places like Selma, Alabama, and Philadelphia, Mississippi, jarred a nation. Those pictures and stories, fifty years later, still have power to move us.

Until the Supreme Court decision to integrate schools, blacks were largely invisible in America's mainstream press. Black issues were printed only in black-owned newspapers, such as the *Chicago Defender,* whose founder Robert Abbott, beginning in 1910, covered lynchings, race riots, and other injustices with headlines such as WHITE GENTLEMAN RAPES COLORED GIRL. The *Pittsburgh Courier,* Baltimore's *Afro-American,* New York's *Amsterdam News,* and the *Atlanta World* reached more than a half million readers.

Brown v. Board of Education came like a thunderclap in 1954, forcing even racist white papers in the South to print news about integration. This sudden awareness of race issues is one reason why seventy-five reporters covered the Emmett Till lynching trial in Sumner, Mississippi, the following year. It was, wrote David Halberstam, "the first great media event of the civil rights movement."

When Rosa Parks was arrested in 1955, word of a bus boycott was spread through Montgomery the old-fashioned way—by hand-cranked mimeographed sheets and word of mouth, including announcements from black pulpits. As an added measure, E. D. Nixon of the NAACP called an editor at the *Montgomery Advertiser* who printed an advance story. Over the next decade, movement leaders would show savvy use of the media to broadcast their messages and convey the brutality of the resistance.

On their way to Woolworth's in 1960, four students in Greensboro, North Carolina, stopped to alert a photographer. The following year Freedom Riders secured coverage of their confrontations to force a reluctant President Kennedy into enforcing integration regulations for interstate travel. Their opponents eventually realized this. A Montgomery mob destroyed cameras before attacking the riders. "We learned from Montgomery the value of the camera and the value of the press," said John Seigenthaler, a Department of Justice aide who was knocked out while trying to rescue fleeing women.

In *The Children,* David Halberstam recalled the effect of his reporting of the 1960s Nashville protests on the protesters themselves: "When they had been beaten up downtown, they would sometimes wonder whether they could go on, and then there would be the morning story in the *Tennessean* giving the details of exactly what had happened. The fact that the rest of the community now had to witness the price of segregation helped them to keep going."

The southern press, by and large, resisted racial change. It covered events, but rarely quoted black activists and usually took white authority as gospel, according to David Davies in *The Press and Race.* Headlines often gave the impression that protesters were outsiders, not neighbors: CHANTING NEGROES STAGE MASS RALLY, read one headline in the *Charleston News and Courier,* a newspaper picketed for its biased coverage. Some newspapers published the names and employers of black parents whose children integrated white schools. In Mississippi, voter applicants found their names in the paper, soon to be followed by layoffs, reprisals, or other acts of terror.

A half dozen southern editors bucked the trend and won Pulitzer Prizes for moderate voices that reduced strife and led to peaceful change, such as in Tupelo, Mississippi, where editor George McLean's support of *Brown* led to a rare school integration success, still evident today. But that was the exception. In most communities, local newspapers delayed acceptance of the new order and, whether intended or not, promoted division and violence.

The national press and network television made the difference. Studies of network news, such as Sasha Torres's *Black, White and in Color,* conclude that TV—which had only achieved national coverage and prominence in 1952—prompted millions of viewers to identify with protesters. While southern TV stations sometimes blocked these news feeds, network coverage brought more social change in ten years than in the previous one hundred, Halberstam argued.

At the same time, southern politicians, sheriffs, and cops also used the media to play to their constituents. But to national audiences, they came across as racist rubes. Montgomery's attempt to bankrupt the *New York Times* with a libel suit over a partially erroneous fund-raising ad backfired. *Sullivan v. New York Times* established a firewall around the media to report on public figures. Anthony Lewis writes that when the court decided *Sullivan* in 1964, "Southern officials had brought nearly three hundred million dollars in libel actions against the press."

If there was a downside to press coverage, it was the focus on a few leaders that made Rosa Parks, Martin Luther King, and a handful of others the "stars" of a movement that involved masses. To this day, events heralded as "famous" are those that were covered in the national media. Similar actions in other cities remain unknown because they were not covered prominently.

Ultimately, pictures and stories of police states trying to deny citizens their rights brought down the walls of segregation. Film of Bull Connor's hoses and dogs attacking young people in Birmingham shocked the nation. The next summer in St. Augustine, Martin Luther King staged a confrontation with the Ku Klux Klan to push through the Civil Rights Act of 1964. The following year, film of "Bloody Sunday" in Selma interrupted ABC's Sunday Night Movie, *Judgment at Nuremberg,* and bowled over southern opposition to the Voting Rights Act of 1965.

"Without the press," John Lewis has said, "the civil rights movement would have been like a bird without wings."

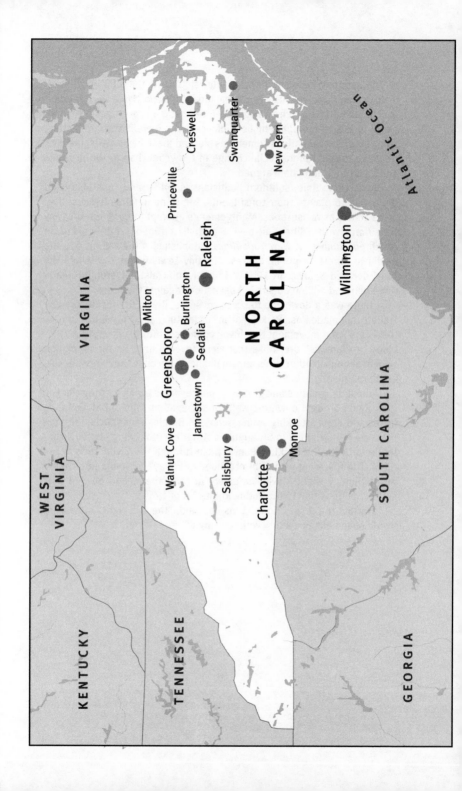

North Carolina

NORTH CAROLINA HAS a reputation for being a progressive southern state. Truth is, in matters of race, North Carolina has always displayed both tolerance and bigotry.

Born a slave state with a harsh slave code patterned after Virginia's, North Carolina from the beginning was home to religious organizations, especially the Quakers, that lobbied against slavery. But when they tried to release their own slaves the legislature forbade it. As the country moved toward civil war and North Carolina reluctantly went along, the Quakers ran stations of the Underground Railroad, and some three thousand white North Carolinians enlisted on the Union side.

During the war, 10 percent of the state's slaves escaped to Union camps along the coast, mingling there with free blacks in thriving centers such as New Bern and Wilmington. Their progress in business and politics over the next half century so enraged white supremacists that they engineered in Wilmington the only known coup d'etat in U.S. history. Within a year of the coup, the legislature disenfranchised blacks and in 1900 established a segregated state.

During much of the twentieth century, North Carolina's leaders took a "moderate" stance between what they called "extremes"—the Ku Klux Klan on one side and the NAACP on the other. This peculiar brand of temperance grew from the ruling majority's "progressive mystique," what historian William Chafe describes as a mix of civility, paternalism, and unspoken resistance to change.

What cracked Jim Crow was classrooms that for a century had been steadily educating black North Carolinians. From one-room schools built by money from the president of Sears, Roebuck to a collection of black universities—more of each than in any state—young minds were encouraged to imagine a better life. On February 1, 1960, in a Woolworth's store in Greensboro, they sat down at a lunch counter to demand it.

The governor at the time, a Kennedy-styled moderate named Terry Sanford, created a "good neighbor council" and "appealed to the consciences of Carolinians to do the right thing," according to a state-published history. "Sanford helped produce a positive atmosphere in the realm of race relations by recognizing the legitimacy of black aspirations for freedom and equality. His policies, however, had little substantive effect. Hiring practices in state government did not change." North Carolina took just as long as its Deep South neighbors to change its segregated way of life.

North Carolina has become an enviable center for the study of civil rights. Scholars at the state's universities have written blunt histories that expose the racism and preserve important stories. As a result, North Carolina stands with Mississippi as well-examined southern states. Like Mississippi, the state has learned that study alone does not translate into tolerance.

North Carolina and Civil Rights

North Carolina was chartered by the King of England on behalf of Virginia and Barbados planters who used slaves to raise rice, indigo, and tobacco. Their struggles to clear and drain coastal swamps amid snakes and malaria took countless black lives, while slave codes permitted a master to kill runaways. Planters' dreams of many large plantations were thwarted by a coastline without good harbors or deep rivers. As a consequence of this geologic accident, the state's concentration of slaves was smaller than in its charter-sister, South Carolina, and produced a difference in race relations down through the years. After the American Revolution, North Carolina counted

100,000 slaves, which composed about one-quarter of a population dominated by small farmers. By contrast, South Carolina's 107,000 slaves accounted for 43 percent of that state's population.

The salt marshes and waterways of North Carolina's serrated coast became a storied haven for blacks—free, pirate, and slave—and the ports of New Bern and Wilmington became majority black. Many had maritime jobs—stevedores, harbor pilots, rowing crews, watermen—whose proximity to the sea bred independence, if not rebellion. They formed a waterborne underground railroad, ferrying runaways to outlying islands, north to New England and south to St. Augustine. No image was more frightening to whites than runaways hiding in the Dismal Swamp. Near Wilmington a "General of the Swamps" was hunted and killed.

Freedom was also implicit in the teachings of Baptist, Methodist, and Quaker churches that during the Great Awakening taught slaves to read the Bible. In 1776 Quakers, aware of the inherent hypocrisy raised by the American Revolution, called on its members to "cleanse their hands" of slaves, an action that brought censure from the North Carolina General Assembly for corrupting the minds of slaves. In the 1820s and 1830s North Carolina passed a rash of laws to tighten control on blacks and their minds—no schooling, no preaching, and no voting, even for more than ten thousand free blacks.

Despite the presence of 361,000 slaves at the start of the Civil War, North Carolina remained a state of small farmers who were not dependent on slave labor. They tried to avoid war and were the last to secede on May 20, 1861. Once committed, they sent more volunteer soldiers to fight for the South, 125,000 men, than any other southern state. Some 40,000 died.

During Reconstruction, seventy-seven blacks were elected to the state legislature and gained real power in the coastal counties where the Second District sent three black congressmen to Washington.

By 1868, however, white supremacists were fighting back. White Republican John Stephens was stabbed to death. Black Republican Wyatt Outlaw was hanged. Hundreds were whipped, schools were burned, and farmers were chased from their land. By 1870 the Democrats were back in control. They impeached the Republican governor. They also crushed a populist movement through a combination of organized smears and violence, the latter carried out by two gangs of bullies called the Red Shirts and Rough Riders.

In 1898, in an American first, whites staged an armed coup in Wilmington and overthrew the black power and business structure. Alfred Waddell, a white politician who seized power, told supporters that if they found a Negro voting, they should "kill him, shoot him down in his tracks." A black newspaper was burned, black businessmen were escorted to a waiting train, and nearly two thousand blacks left town. Within a year North Carolina had disenfranchised blacks, never to relinquish this power grab.

North Carolina's last black congressman, George Henry White— the last of twenty-two southern black congressmen until the civil rights movement—bid a poignant farewell in a 1901 speech in the House of Representatives:

> *This is perhaps the Negroes' temporary farewell to the*
> *American Congress; but let me say, Phoenix-like, he will*
> *rise up some day and come again. These parting words are*
> *in behalf of an outraged, heart-broken, bruised, and*
> *bleeding, but God-fearing people, faithful, industrious,*
> *loyal people, and rising people, full of potential force. The*
> *only apology that I have to make for the earnestness with*
> *which I have spoken is that I am pleading for life, liberty,*
> *future happiness, and manhood suffrage for one-eighth of*
> *the entire population of the United States.*

Back home segregation became the law of his state. In 1915, the state senate barely defeated an amendment to the state constitution to divide agriculture land into black and white districts. However, many cities were separated into racial residential zones.

Yet this was the time that North Carolina began to carve a reputation as a moderate state. Measured in lynchings, the state's 101 murders sat between Virginia's 100 and South Carolina's 160. Among black leaders, peer and political pressure muffled protest. Exposing conditions in schools or admitting that blacks wore a hypocritical smile was considered ungracious. Whites, for their part, agreed both with a *Raleigh Times* editorial that North Carolina was "exceptionally free from race oppression, enmity and malice" and with Governor Thomas Bickett's 1920 declaration: "In North Carolina we have definitely decided that the happiness of both races requires that white government shall be supreme and unchallenged."

A Rosenwald school in Walnut Cove

Behind this curtain of white supremacy black Carolinians forged their own businesses, churches, and, especially, schools. Education became their polestar. With backing from churches, philanthropists like Sears, Roebuck president Julius Rosenwald, and a state office for black education, North Carolina established more black schools and colleges than any southern state at the time. Thirteen black colleges trained business and church leaders and others who began to agitate for change.

Between 1938 and 1957, a dozen marches, sit-ins, and boycotts were staged. Voter registration increased to the point that in 1947 the first black won a seat on the eight-man Winston-Salem city council. The city responded with a restriction that one black was enough. North Carolina's response to desegregation rulings from the U.S. Supreme Court was cordial but token, although the state university at Chapel Hill became the first state school in the South to integrate undergraduates in 1955.

Integration of public schools, which the state's own studies showed to be unequal in quality, was delayed for years by the Pearsall Committee's freedom-of-choice plan, which essentially maintained the status quo until it was struck down in 1969. Ten years after *Brown,* historian Timothy Tyson writes, only one in two hundred black children attended a desegregated school.

The *Brown* decision revived the North Carolina Klan, this time under James "Catfish" Cole, who held semireligious tent revivals around Charlotte that drew as many as fifteen thousand. Crosses were burned and people harassed, and one couple was shot to death in their home. When Cole's Klan made repeated shooting raids led by a police chief into Monroe's black neighborhoods, ex-marine Robert Williams led a dug-in unit in shooting back. His militant stand, however, was assailed both by the NAACP and the FBI, and he fled to Cuba where he broadcast *Radio Free Dixie* back to the States on Radio Havana. When Cole tried to burn a cross in a Lumbee Indian community, the Indians, again led by a World War II veteran, surrounded the Klan and scared them away with war whoops and harmless shots. For their stand, North Carolina Indians—who make up 1 percent of the state population—were applauded.

By 1960 the yearning for equal rights had reached a critical mass. On February 1, four young black men from North Carolina A&T University sat down at the Woolworth's lunch counter in Greensboro and asked to be served. Within a week, sit-ins had spread to Winston-Salem, Charlotte, Durham, Fayetteville, Raleigh, Elizabeth City, and High Point.

A sit-in at the Woolworth's counter on February 2, 1960

In April student leaders from across the South met at Shaw University with the Reverend Martin Luther King Jr. and Ella Baker, and created the most dynamic and courageous civil rights organization of the period, the Student Nonviolent Coordinating Committee. By July blacks were being served at Woolworth's in Greensboro, and within a year stores in more than one hundred southern cities were integrated.

The euphoria of sit-in victories combined with the election of Governor Terry Sanford brought North Carolina a couple of years of racial calm. But in 1962–1963, new rounds of protests targeted discrimination at shopping centers, theaters, and restaurants in every major city. In May and June 1963 thousands of students marched and hundreds filled jails in Greensboro, among them Jesse Jackson, by then the student body president of A&T. As a result the mayor led a citywide integration and hiring effort. By 1964 Charlotte integrated hospitals and most public accommodations, and Durham and Raleigh desegregated restaurants and motels.

Under the 1965 Voting Rights Act, the poll tax, literacy tests, and other restrictions were lifted. Nearly 46 percent of black adults registered to vote, and the first blacks in sixty years were elected to the state legislature.

Through all this, the North Carolina Klan remained a shrill voice for white supremacy and segregation. In 1965 the homes of four NAACP leaders in Charlotte were bombed. In eastern North Carolina, Klan rallies were held nightly. White Citizens Councils and segregationists in general "were influential in determining the status of race relations," according to a state archive's history.

In 1969 Greensboro erupted again over a high school student election. Within days, tear gas and shots were fired, A&T student Willie Grimes was shot and killed, and the National Guard, with armoured personnel carriers, swept through A&T dormitories searching for weapons. Guardsmen found three.

In 1971 Wilmington erupted over the closing of a black school. Police were sent to keep order, a boycott was organized, and eventually a race riot broke out in the neighborhood around the school and led to arson and two shooting deaths. The Reverend Ben Chavis of a church-based civil rights group and nine young people were convicted of shooting at firemen. The Wilmington Ten became a cause célèbre, their long prison sentences eventually overturned by a federal court.

By the 1970s North Carolina was winning high marks for school deseg-regation plans. But there remained the occasional outbreak that undercut the state's mantle of moderation. In 1973 three black men in Tarboro were sentenced to death for the rape of a white woman, a case that civil rights attorney Morris Dees eventually overturned. In 1979 in Greensboro, five members of a communist group were shot dead in a bizarre face-off with members of a Klan group. The shooters were acquitted. In the early 1980s Dees prosecuted a militant Klan group near Raleigh that had vowed racial cleansing. The leader, Glenn Miller, was jailed with evidence that active-duty marines at Fort Bragg were involved as trainers. In 1995 three sol-diers from Fort Bragg were convicted of killing two blacks in Fayetteville. As late as 2002 radical right and supremacist groups operated in western North Carolina, their targets ranging from abortion clinics in Greensboro to a racist takeover of the Sons of Confederate Veterans.

Meanwhile, blacks were winning elections—some five hundred posts, including state house speaker, the first in the South in modern times, plus mayoralties in majority-white Charlotte and Chapel Hill and a number of judgeships. When Harvey Gantt, the former black mayor of Charlotte, won 47 percent of the vote in a run against U.S. Senator Jesse Helms in 1990, civil rights activists cautiously looked forward to the day when North Car-olina's actions spoke as loudly as its mystique.

North Carolina Civil Rights Tours

North Carolina's civil rights heritage divides easily into an early coastal history, and modern movement stories in centrally located cities.

A drive along the beautiful tidal flats should include a stop at Somerset Place near Creswell, where slave history is preserved alongside the "big house." New Bern has a good African American walking tour that portrays a sense of the black middle class in the nineteenth century. Wilmington is beginning to tell the story of its 1898 coup with a brochure, a planned me-morial, and ongoing citizen discussion.

The role of education in the civil rights movement is well marked in the central corridor. Greensboro is home to the sit-in movement and Raleigh has a city museum that describes its lesser known transformation. Historically black colleges like Shaw, Bennett, St. Augustine, and A&T are open to visitors. Small black Rosenwald schools and Quaker settlements also have been preserved.

City by City

Burlington

MCCRAY SCHOOL (*North Carolina Route 62, fifteen miles north of Burlington*)   Two miles beyond McCray Crossroads, beneath an old hickory tree, sits a one-room schoolhouse, a testament to the thirst for education among blacks in the South. This school, now on the national register of historic places, was typical of rural schools used by blacks after the Civil War and into the twentieth century. Its faded paint, rusted school bell, and outhouse tell of another time. But look inside the windows and one can imagine the kids at work. Artifacts include a dunce's hat, iron stove, benches, a weed broom, and oil lamps. The calendar reads 29 MAY 1915.

Charlotte

Missing from most civil rights histories, Charlotte should be remembered for pioneering the most controversial solution to school integration—busing kids between black inner cities and white suburbs. The practice evolved from a 1965 desegregation case called *Swann v. Charlotte-Mecklenburg Board of Education*. The Swanns were one set of black parents represented by attorney Julius Chambers and the NAACP. Charlotte-Mecklenburg is the countywide school system that at the time had more than one hundred schools and eighty-four thousand students. Under a 1970 federal judge's order, Charlotte largely accepted busing—in contrast to cities like Boston that fought it violently. Charlotte's goal was to achieve a 40 percent black population in every school, and through the years a citizens committee moved kids like checkers to accomplish it. In 1992 the school board replaced busing with a series of magnet schools and parent choice.

Charlotte had its share of civil rights sit-ins and marches and was one of the first North Carolina cities, in 1963, to peacefully integrate its public accommodations. The credit goes first to two brothers, Fred and Kelly Alexander. Kelly resurrected the NAACP, and served as state chairman for forty years. In 1965 Fred became the first black city councilman in the twentieth century.

On the "other side" was white mayor Stanford Brookshire who, between 1961 and 1969, guided desegregation with a moderating hand. On November 22, 1965, bombs damaged the homes of both Alexander brothers, attorney Chambers, and dentist-activist Dr. Reginald Hawkins. The city seemed outraged by this damage to its reputation, and volunteers rebuilt the homes while the mayor established a relief fund.

One infamous racial profiling case occurred in July 1972 when three black men—the Charlotte Three—were convicted of setting fire to a barn that killed fifteen horses. Their sentences, up to twenty-five years each, were later reduced after their cases received international notoriety, including criticism from Amnesty International.

Segments of the **Levine Museum of the New South** (*200 East Seventh Street; 704-333-1887*) describe the modern civil rights movement in Charlotte.

Creswell

SOMERSET PLACE STATE HISTORIC SITE (*North Carolina Route 64, seven miles south of Creswell, 919-797-4560*)   Many southern plantations attempt to tell the "slave story" out behind the mansion but none as authentically as this state park. Dorothy Redford, a descendant of Somerset's slaves who was inspired by *Roots,* dug out her own history. When she became site manager, she turned it into an honest portrayal of the slavery system, perhaps the best in the South.

Bushwhacked out of impenetrable swamps by slaves, Somerset was a sprawling, 100,000-acre rice plantation. A six-mile canal was dug to drain the land, a two-year ordeal beset by malaria, insects, and other swamp creatures. Visitors approaching the plantation through cleared tidal flats barely above sea level will notice an occasional, huge stump that provides a hint at the primeval land set to by a clearing party of twenty-seven whites, thirty-two enslaved locals, forty-nine purchased slaves, and eighty Africans. To prevent the slaves from running away, the Scottish foreman built cages around each man as he dug, "forcing them to pass the dirt and mud out through the bars," Redford wrote in *Somerset Homecoming*.

The plantation was written up in agriculture journals for its self-sufficiency. Slaves even had their own "hospital." But families were broken, bought and sold, the death rate was high, and runaways common. At one time, more than three hundred slaves served a "family" of ten, which included a minister and tutors, an overseer, and the owner. The main house (seven thousand square feet, with fourteen rooms) is restored to period appearance. The state is reconstructing slave quarters (each seven hundred square feet, housing fifteen slaves). The first half hour of guided tours typically is spent in the slave area.

Except for old men, blacks left Somerset after the Civil War. The state took over the property in 1939. In 2000 Somerset held its first annual homecoming of descendants of slaves and plantation owners. The reunion has continued every year on Labor Day. It is open to the public.

Greensboro

In the mid-1950s downtown Greensboro contained a classic collection of businesses along a main drag called Elm Street: department stores and drugstores, hardware and ice cream shops, insurance and bank buildings of classic Italianate and art deco design. On its eastern edge were two colleges for black students—North Carolina Agricultural and Technical State University and, for women, Bennett College. The students, like all blacks, were treated like pariahs downtown. They could buy food but they could not sit at the main lunch counters. They could buy clothes but not try them on—except at the store of Ralph Johns, a white NAACP supporter who encouraged the kids to rebel.

In the late 1950s attempts were made to integrate the city's golf course and swimming pools, to no avail. When Martin Luther King Jr. came to speak in 1958, A&T refused to let him use an auditorium for fear of being linked to him. Bennett's president offered a hall, and King's speech "brought tears to my eyes," remembered A&T student Ezell Blair Jr. Two years later, after many discussions in their dorm rooms, Blair and three friends walked downtown and entered Woolworth's—and history.

While Woolworth's began serving an integrated lunch counter five months later, the city of Greensboro resisted widespread change. Bigger and more violent demonstrations occurred in 1963 and 1969. Greensboro's schools were not integrated until 1971—seventeen years after the Supreme Court ruling.

The original Woolworth's, minus the company sign, has been preserved to honor the sit-in movement. The nearby city museum also has a substantive sit-in display. For walking tour guides, maps, and other brochures, stop at the **Greensboro Visitor Information Center** (*317 South Green Street; 800-344-2282*).

❶ | **F. W. WOOLWORTH CO. STORE** (*132 South Elm Street, corner of February One Place; 336-274-9199*) One of the three most important civil rights campaigns of the 1960s began on a Monday morning, February 1, 1960, in a college dorm room with this prosaic exchange:

"We might as well go now."

"You really mean it?"

"Sure, I mean it."

With that, according to historian Taylor Branch, four students— Joseph McNeil, Franklin McCain, David Richmond, and Ezell Blair Jr.—sat down at Woolworth's lunch counter. The manager refused service but let them sit until closing. The next day, another nineteen students, including women from Bennett College, sat down at the same counter. On Wednesday, eighty-five joined them and filled the store's sixty-five seats.

On Thursday, as white hecklers arrived, three white women from Woman's College in Greensboro stood behind the protesters and said, "We don't agree. Serve the blacks." On Saturday when white gangs with Confederate flags surrounded and blocked protesters, members of the A&T football team formed a wedge to allow protestors in and out. "Who do you think you are?" one of the hecklers asked the team. "We the Union Army," one of them responded, according to historian William Chafe. On Saturday, Greensboro counted nine hundred student protesters at Woolworth's and Kress's dime store down the street.

The four A&T college students had started a fire that could not be put out. On July 25 the first black was served sitting at Woolworth's, and Greensboro became the third city in North Carolina to "break with tradition" after Winston-Salem and Charlotte.

Of the Greensboro Four, Blair became a teacher, McNeil an air force general, and McCain a bank vice president. Richmond, who dropped out and became a janitor, died in 1990.

The store closed in the early 1990s and was sold to Sit In Inc., the nonprofit organization designated to develop a museum.

With black-and-white terrazzo floor and marble stairways, the store remains virtually intact inside—though the original L-shaped lunch counter in the northwest corner was later replaced with U-shaped counters and the original black vinyl and steel seats were replaced with four-color vinyl. But much of the equipment, including a milk dispenser, dishwasher, blender, and toasters, remains.

In 1999, in a vote along racial lines, Greensboro citizens rejected a bond to support a national civil rights museum in the famous store. In 2002, A&T took it over as a university project. The store-museum will include figures at the counter, sound effects, and a section on the sit-in's impact around the world.

Outside, at the corner of February One Place, a "walkway of history" chronicles local African American history. Bronze footsteps honor pioneers, including the four A&T students.

2 | **GREENSBORO HISTORICAL MUSEUM** (*130 Summit Avenue; 336-373-2043; www.greensborohistory.org*) This city museum has a substantial display on the sit-in movement, with life-sized photos of the groundbreaking four students, and many news photos and newspaper stories of the time. The time line explains how the movement spread across the South.

Jamestown

MENDENHALL PLANTATION (*U.S. 29A and 70A; 336-454-3819*) This Quaker farm outside Greensboro was a stop on the Underground Railroad. Richard Mendenhall was a local founder of the Manumission Society, which tried to release slaves before the Civil War. Thwarted by the legislature, he and other Quakers devised various ways to secret slaves north, including badges assigned to "free" blacks and wagons with hidden compartments. One wagon is on display at this period-preserved farm.

Milton

THOMAS DAY HOUSE (*North Carolina Route 62, south of Danville, Virginia*) A renowned furniture maker whose pieces became museum quality, Day possessed skills and wealth that preserved his freedom during North Carolina's antebellum period. Born a free black in Virginia, Day came of age just as the state began stripping free blacks of personal liberties. They had to wear badges, they lost their right to vote, and they couldn't preach or go to school. After 1826 North Carolina forbid free blacks from moving into the state, a problem for Day three years later when he married a Virginia woman. White friends including the state attorney general petitioned the legislature on his behalf. Day also owned slaves, which violated a legislative edict. A local legend claims Day traded new church pews for the right to sit with whites in the main sanctuary (and not the "black" balcony), but historians now discount it. Toward the end of his life, he lost his business, and he died in 1861. The house—later a tavern and now a National Historic Landmark, is being restored as a museum to Day.

Monroe

GRAVESITE OF ROBERT WILLIAMS (*Adams and Wiatt Streets, off U.S. 74 and Stafford Street*) In 1936 an eleven-year-old boy watched a police officer beat and drag a woman off the streets of Monroe. The cop was Jesse Helms Sr., father of the future senator, and the boy was Robert Williams, who grew up to become the father of the black power movement. Both an ex-GI and ex-marine, Williams headed an NAACP chapter that used guns to scare the Klan away—once at a funeral of a GI and once at the home of a doctor, Albert Perry. In 1957 Williams, Dr. Perry, and a group of youths tried to

Robert Williams's gravestone in Monroe

integrate the country club pool, a public entity open only to whites. To prevent it, the pool was filled in and covered with a putting green.

When "Catfish" Cole sent a swarm of Klansmen on another shooting rampage into Williams's black neighborhood on the night of October 5, 1957, Williams and other military veterans met them with gunfire from behind bunkers. The raids stopped. After a series of outrageous injustices against blacks in 1959, Williams declared hotly that it was time to meet violence with violence, a statement that ruptured his ties with the national NAACP. Thurgood Marshall even urged the FBI to investigate Williams, according to Williams biographer Timothy Tyson. Williams and Dr. Martin Luther King Jr. traded published salvos over the need for armed defense.

As shootings and arson escalated in Monroe, a white couple caught in the crossfire one night took refuge in Williams's home. Williams led his family out of town, but was charged by the FBI with kidnapping the couple. With the help of supporters, he slipped into Canada and then Cuba. For many years on Friday nights, Radio Havana broadcast Williams's *Radio Free Dixie*. From there he also published *Negroes with Guns,* which influenced Huey P. Newton, a founder of the Black Panther Party in Oakland, California. After breaking with Castro, Williams left for Beijing, and in 1969 returned to the United States. He died in 1971 and was buried in Monroe. Rosa Parks spoke at his funeral. The inscription on the family gravestone reads INTERNATIONAL FREEDOM FIGHTERS.

Nonviolent? Not Always

The power of the civil rights movement stemmed in large part from its philosophy of nonviolence. Through gunshots, beatings, fire-hose spray, and dog attacks, the soldiers of peace persevered. In the years since, with memorials focused on Martin Luther King Jr., and his emulation of Gandhi, nonviolence is perceived as the movement's only strategy.

It wasn't. Blacks with guns and a willingness to use them were widespread in the South.

Take, for example, E. W. Steptoe, a wiry dairy and cotton farmer in Amite County, Mississippi, where no black dared vote. Steptoe agreed to house the first SNCC voter registration worker, Bob Moses, in 1961 and introduce him to black citizens. As recounted in *Local People* by John Dittmer, the pioneers were beaten by bullies, and two farmers, Herbert Lee and Louis Allen, were murdered. But Steptoe wasn't cowed. His remote farmhouse was an arsenal with guns under pillows and chairs, and a .45 caliber automatic in the bed stand.

In Mississippi's Tallahatchie County, SNCC worker Margaret Block remembered arriving at the door of an elderly black woman who agreed to take her in: "Are you nonviolent? We ain't," said the farm woman, raising a shotgun. When night riders threatened, the family shot back and was never bothered again.

In southwest Georgia's Lee County, SNCC worker Charles Sherrod told of the gumption of eighty-year-old Mama Dollie Raines, who ran her own farm, took SNCC workers in when everyone else was scared to death, and stood watch at night with her feet out the window and a twelve-gauge shotgun in her lap.

Hosea Williams, the SCLC leader who was beaten and arrested scores of times, once said, "Nonviolence as a way of life was just as foreign to blacks as flying a space capsule would be to a roach." The wonder is that, given their history, blacks did not resort to violence more often.

Fear of armed blacks had been an American nightmare since the seventeenth century, when rules were created to prevent slaves from assembling, owning guns, and traveling at night. The Haitian revolt of 1791, in which thousands of slaves, summoned by drums, rampaged across plantations hacking and burning, spread widespread fear of slave uprising in the States.

Historian Herbert Aptheker counted 250 revolts or conspiracies. The most famous was Nat Turner's rebellion that killed sixty whites in Virginia in 1830. Two failed conspiracies, by Gabriel Prosser in Richmond and Denmark Vesey in Charleston, led Southern states to crack down on civil liberties by blacks, slave and free.

After the Civil War, when white supremacists terrorized blacks, "it is remarkable in how few instances blacks attacked whites," wrote historian Eric Foner. Black-on-black crime was common, but in Freedmen's Bureau records, violence or even threats against whites "were all but unknown."

As the Jim Crow era of lynching began, Ida B. Wells urged that a Winchester rifle have a "place of honor in every home." Quoted by Timothy Tyson, she wrote, "When the white man . . . knows he runs as great a risk of biting the dust every time his Afro-American victim does, he would have a greater respect for Afro-American life." Even intellectual W. E. B. Du Bois, who bought a shotgun to defend his family against mobs in Atlanta in 1906, later wrote, according to the Yale–New Haven Teachers Institute, "If we are to die, in God's name let us not perish like bales of hay." Robert

Moton, who succeeded Booker T. Washington as head of Tuskegee Institute, bought shotguns to fend off the Klan in the 1920s.

Trained black soldiers home from world wars defended themselves in Columbia, Tennessee, and thereafter were left alone, according to Carl Rowan. Robert Williams, an ex-GI and ex-marine, trained a squad to shoot back at the Klan in Monroe, South Carolina. Drummed out of the NAACP for his militancy, and railroaded by the FBI, he escaped to Cuba, where he broadcast a show called *Radio Free Dixie.*

The literature of the civil rights movement is salted with accounts of self-defense and gun carrying. In Little Rock, Arkansas, the mother of one of the Little Rock Nine kept a gun by her bible. In Birmingham, after Fred Shuttlesworth began his activism, his church was guarded by what he called "nonviolent Winchesters." In Mississippi and Louisiana, the Deacons for Defense, armed with shotguns, rifles, and CB radios, kept the peace in Jonesboro, Bogalusa, and along James Meredith's "march against fear."

Martin Luther King and Medgar Evers owned guns. But they knew that shooting back was not the answer, and that blacks would lose a shooting race war. Both men were assassinated by white men with rifles.

New Bern

New Bern was once a village of black aristocracy, the biggest and most sophisticated free black population in the South before and after the Civil War. Just enough of their grand neighborhoods remain to remember a time, not unlike today, when affluence created its own equity.

An African American walking tour guides visitors to sites such as St. Peter's church, the first AME church in the South, and to opulent homes owned by free black businessmen. Following the Civil War, the city's black community "was poised to make the most of the opportunities," according to a local history. Blacks were elected to the city council, the state legislature, and Congress. With their success came white backlash.

The state legislature subsequently passed the Disfranchisement Amendment, which made it almost impossible for a black to vote. It also dissolved New Bern's city government. On the eve of a local 1868 vote, Rough Riders and other white supremacist gangs turned New Bern into a shoot-'em-up frontier, frightening black voters into staying home. Jim Crow segregation followed.

New Bern stores were desegregated in the early 1960s after student sit-ins. The schools integrated in 1965 and the city elected its first black mayor in 1977.

New Bern today is gentrified, upscale, and beautifully planted along the Neuse River, a gateway to the Outer Banks. A sparkling visitors center carries thousands of brochures, but you'll hear more about the invention of Pepsi-Cola here than the fate of the black elite.

Princeville

The first all-black incorporated town in America fell onto hard times just as it was trying to create a historic trail to attract tourists. Hurricane Floyd in 1999 devastated the village with floods and contaminated water. Rebuilding took priority over a planned heritage district with a guided trail between the original 1865 freed-slave settlement, Freedom Hill, and such buildings as the Old Town Hall, first built as a Rosenwald schoolhouse.

Raleigh

Though its capitol ground crawls with Confederate monuments, Raleigh has done a nice job of memorializing the victory of civil rights. In a historic building just a few steps from the capitol, the city museum is largely devoted to the integration struggle that began nine days after the Greensboro sit-in. Students from Shaw University and St. Augustine sat down at lunch counters at the local Woolworth's, Kress, McClellan, Walgreens, Eckerd Drugs, and Hudson Belk stores. By and large, the well-dressed and polite demonstrators were met with cold indifference. Students also marched on the Cameron Village shopping center, where forty-one of them became the first protest arrests in North Carolina. By the end of February 1960 the Kress store had removed seats and begun serving blacks and whites while they were standing. In April 1960 the SNCC was organized at Shaw University.

Raleigh was also home to John Chavis, an attorney's servant who won his freedom for fighting in the American Revolution. He became a minister and teacher to blacks and whites in Raleigh. "I am free born American and a Revolutionary soldier," he once exclaimed, yet he had to teach the black kids at night. A park is named for Chavis but the story of his life is not described there.

Raleigh publishes an African American heritage sites brochure, available at the **Greater Raleigh Convention and Visitors Bureau** (*421 Fayetteville Street Mall, Suite 1505; 800-849-8499*).

NORTH CAROLINA MUSEUM OF HISTORY (*5 East Edenton Street; 919-715-0200; www.ncmuseumofhistory.org*) A major exhibit, "A Change Is Gonna Come—Black, Indian and White Voices for Equality," is scheduled to open by late 2004. The gallery will focus on the struggle for racial equality in North Carolina between 1830 and 1980. The starting date was chosen to include the state constitution of 1835, which restricted rights for free blacks. The end date makes room for Indian rights won after the civil rights movement.

RALEIGH CITY MUSEUM (*220 Fayetteville Street Mall; 919-832-3775; www.raleighcitymuseum.org*) Curators of this small collectibles museum recognize that "no other national event impacted Raleigh more profoundly than the civil rights movement of the 1950s and 1960s." A substantial portion of its displays focus on the local sit-in movement, which struck like thunder on February 10, 1960. The mayor, speaking for his race and time, called it regrettable that "young blacks would risk endangering race relations in the city by trying to change a long-standing custom in a manner that is all but destined to fail."

Frustrated by the city's resistance, college students from Shaw and St. Augustine marched and picketed again in 1963, at theaters, the Sir Walter Hotel, the city newspaper, and Governor Terry Sanford's North Carolina Symphony Ball. By 1964 downtown Raleigh was largely integrated.

Raleigh's twenty-year resistance to school integration is detailed here, including the story of seven-year-old William Campbell, enrolled as the first, token student to comply with the U.S. Supreme Court ruling. He was alone among white students for five years. The city finally integrated its schools in 1976. Two years later, John Baker Jr. was elected Wake County's first black sheriff in North Carolina since Reconstruction.

Shaw University in Raleigh, birthplace of the Student Nonviolent Coordinating Committee (SNCC)

The museum also has an exhibit on Ella Baker and the birth of SNCC at Shaw University.

SHAW UNIVERSITY (*188 East South Street; 919-546-8200; www.shawuniversity.edu*) A historic highway sign is the only monument to one of the most exciting events in civil rights history—the creation of the Student Nonviolent Coordinating Committee. Herding the spontaneous sit-in movement under way in dozens of cities and campuses, Ella Baker, a Shaw alumna and executive director of the Southern Christian Leadership Conference, organized a gathering at Shaw on April 15, 1960. This, she told the students, "is bigger than a hamburger."

Virtually every civil rights leader, past and future, was present. Inspired by Dr. Martin Luther King and James Lawson, the students moved away from the staid style of the NAACP and the leader-heavy SCLC to form a nearly leaderless group of shock troops that pushed civil rights into the darkest corners of the South. SNCC, noted Taylor Branch, combined religious fervor with boisterous student politics.

Marion Barry, a Lawson disciple from Fisk University and a future mayor of Washington, D.C., was its first head.

According to news accounts at the time, the SNCC meetings were held at Memorial Auditorium, now remodeled as the BTI performing arts center on Wilmington Street, and in the old Rex Hospital on Salisbury Street.

Prior to SNCC, Shaw was known as the "mother" college for blacks in North Carolina. Estey Hall, its oldest and most distinguished-looking building, was built in 1873 as a dorm for women.

MLK MEMORIAL PARK (*Martin Luther King Boulevard and Rock Quarry*)   Reminiscent of the Civil Rights Memorial in Alabama, this black stone and flowing water memorial honors local heroes in the civil rights movement. Among those named: Ralph Campbell Jr., the parent of the first child to integrate city schools; and Joseph Holt, whose court suit on behalf of his son Joe eventually integrated city schools. A life-sized statue of King stands near the fountain.

ST. AUGUSTINE'S COLLEGE (*1315 Oakwood Avenue; 919-516-4000; www.st-aug.edu*)   Founded two years after the Civil War by the Episcopal Church, St. Augustine has one of the more beautifully preserved campuses in the South. The unusual medieval chapel is the oldest building, complete with a lych-gate, an ancient sacred gateway marking the boundary to sacred ground. Beginning in 1960, students from this historically black school joined in sit-ins and marches to integrate many downtown stores.

The library contains a memorial to famous graduates Sarah and Elizabeth "Bessie" Delaney, sisters who published *Having Our Say* when they were both over one hundred years old. The Delaney sisters were born on the campus. Their father, a former slave, and mother were both administrators. Bessie became the second black woman dentist in New York City and Sarah became a teacher in New York public schools. They lived quietly in New York until a reporter, Amy Hill Hearth, discovered them, and collaborated on a book that became a 1993 best-seller, a Broadway play, and a TV film. The authors donated $1 million to St. Augustine for scholarships.

The Thirst for Education

Imagine, if you can, a law forbidding you to learn. No reading. No books. No schools. No future. For many generations of African Americans in the South, such a law was in force in every state except Tennessee.

The laws were enacted in the 1830s after two notorious slave rebellions. White rulers reasoned that education was a dangerous thing in an oppressed people. They were right.

By the time of the Civil War, after thirty years of prohibition, less than 10 percent of southern blacks could read. The thirst to learn was overwhelming. As Booker T. Washington described later, "I had the feeling that to get into a schoolhouse and study . . . would be about the same as getting into paradise."

The first known "organized" education of slaves occurred at the start of the Civil War in 1861 in Hampton, Virginia, when Mary Peake, a freeborn black, set up a school for slave refugees. As soon as the war ended, the Freedmen's Bureau and churches rushed in to establish hundreds of schools across the South. According to historian Richard Kluger, the Freedmen's Bureau opened 4,000 schools attended by 250,000 people.

In North Carolina, where religious organizations established 250 schools, a teacher described arriving at his new post to find 300 people, old and young with multiple generations in a family, lined up to learn. "I never knew anything like the craving," he said.

"It was a whole race trying to go to school," Washington remembered in his autobiography, *Up From Slavery*. "As fast as any kind of teachers could be secured, not only were day-schools filled, but night-schools as well. The great ambition of the older people was to try to learn to read the Bible before they died."

During Reconstruction black legislators led the way to establish state-funded public schools, a new concept in the South where planters had sent their kids to academies and believed that school "spoiled a good field hand," wrote James Anderson in *The Education of Blacks in the South*. Yet by 1900, under Jim Crow, more than half of black children remained unschooled.

The migration of blacks out of the South to better opportunities convinced southern states to build more schools, aided by a partnership between Booker T. Washington and Julius Rosenwald, the president of Sears, Roebuck & Co., who spread seed money across the South to encourage communities to build schools. Their first "Rosenwald" school was built in 1914 at Loachopoka, Alabama, near Tuskegee. By the 1930s more than five thousand Rosenwald schools housed nearly seven hundred thousand black children.

Each school project produced moving scenes of poverty-stricken tenant farmers donating their only money—in one case, a single copper penny—to give their children a chance, according to Anderson. In Hobson City, Alabama, children carrying tobacco cans formed a "snuff box brigade" to raise an unheard of $200. Families with no shoes gave a dollar. In Boligee, Alabama, an ex-slave pulled his life's savings out of a greasy bag and announced, "I want to see the children of my grandchildren have a chance, and so I am giving my all." In that village where organizers expected to raise $10, they collected $1,365. "They shouted and they cried and applauded" and eventually built a five-room school that cost more than $6,000, wrote Anderson.

Scenes such as these were repeated all over the South, where nearly a quarter of all black children were taught in Rosenwald schools. North Carolina led the region with 813 structures, Mississippi built 633, and Texas communities constructed 527.

By this time, North Carolina's first superintendent for black education—a white man—was calling black schools disgraceful: "To one who does not know our history, these schoolhouses, though mute, would tell in unmistaken terms a story of injustice, inhumanity and neglect on the part of our white people."

North Carolina also led the nation in building black colleges, most of them church-supported. Children of leading black families went to the prep school Palmer Institute outside Greensboro, and then to college. Some pushed to enter the state's leading, but segregated, universities. Floyd McKissick, for example, one of the first four blacks to enter the University of North Carolina law school in 1951, became head of the CORE in time to lead protests in the 1960s.

In general, the student protesters who broke the back of Jim Crow came out of black colleges such as Fisk University in Nashville and North Carolina A&T in Greensboro. The four young A&T men who sat in at Greensboro's Woolworth store in 1960 had been steeped in black pride and protest from teachers, literature, and parents. In their dorm rooms weeks before their sit-in, the four had talked about black life and what they could do to improve it. William Chafe, in his study of Greensboro, *Civilities and Civil Rights,* quoted protester David Richmond: "We used to question, 'Why is it that you have to sit in the balcony? Why do you have to ride in the back of the bus?'" When they left Woolworth's that first day, Franklin McCain recalled: "I felt as though I had gained my manhood."

Their sit-in at Woolworth's inspired students across the South. In fifty-four cities in nine states, sit-ins were staged over the next two months. In a year, Chafe reported, "more than one hundred cities had engaged in at least some desegregation of public facilities in response to student-led demonstrators. The 1960s stage of the freedom movement had begun."

A wall divides a segregated cemetery in Salisbury

Salisbury

OAK GROVE–FREEDMAN'S CEMETERY MEMORIAL (*Liberty and Church Streets*) A mowed lawn next to a cemetery is a stark reminder that Jim Crow followed blacks to the grave. Some 150 slaves and ex-slaves were buried here, but their gravestones were removed, bodies disinterred, and boundaries reduced. A tall wall erected in 1855 remains a sharp divide between the unmarked burial sites and the "white" cemetery with its many stones and Confederate flags. A citizens group plans to build a memorial plaza and reconciliation "gateway" on the property.

Salisbury publishes an African American heritage trail brochure that includes Livingston College, a historically black school that retains its brick beauty beneath spreading elm trees. Livingston was the site of the first intercollegiate football game between two black colleges, Livingston versus Biddle. A marker near the brick administration building denotes the event.

Sedalia

CHARLOTTE HAWKINS BROWN HISTORIC SITE *(U.S. 20 east of Greensboro; 336-449-4860; www.chbfoundation.org)* The Palmer Institute, one of North Carolina's most distinguished schools and the first prep school for blacks, was built on this site from humble beginnings by Charlotte Brown, an eighteen-year-old black scholar. Schooled in Boston in the classics, Brown was reading *Virgil* while pushing a pram through a park when she was noticed by Alice Palmer, the president of Wellesley College. Palmer became her mentor, and Brown later named her school for Palmer.

In 1901 Brown stepped off a train in the woods of Guilford County to start a school for the American Missionary Association. When the church withdrew support a year later, she stayed at the request of the students' parents. Starting with one hundred dollars and a blacksmith's shop, she built a facility that became the private school of choice for elite black families on the East Coast, plus many from Bermuda, Haiti, and Liberia. She married academics with the practice of social graces, compiled in her small textbook, *The Correct Thing to Do, to Say and to Wear*. Women students had to serve a tea before they could graduate. She also exposed them to symphony music and Latin. Ninety-five percent of graduates went on to college and professional lives. Brown died in 1961, and the school survived ten more years. The state historic site was the first created to honor an African American or a woman. Buildings are being restored, and a visitors center shows a historical video.

Swanquarter

O. A. PEAY SCHOOL *(North Carolina Route 45)* School desegregation in the South was almost always a one-way street. Black schools were most often closed and the students shipped out of their neighborhoods to white schools. Equality for them meant starting as outsiders. In the process, black principals and teachers lost out and black communities lost a core glue. The story of Swanquarter's historic fight to resist this change in 1968 and 1969 was notable for its short, sweet success. Historian David Cecelski single-handedly preserved the story in his book *Along Freedom Road*.

In a town of oyster shacks surrounded by water, Swanquarter's black families kept their children out of school for a year rather than lose their local, all-black schools and be forced to bus the children to the Mattamuskeet central school. The federal government pushed for integration, and black families found themselves in agreement with the segregationist school board that two black schools ought to remain open under parental freedom of choice. In a referendum, the black parents won, and the school board then worked to integrate the entire system, including school activities. A year later a black principal was named for Mattamuskeet.

Cecelski details daily demonstrations, marches on the state capitol in Raleigh, alternate schools, and a gunfight with the Ku Klux Klan. The stand by blacks in Hyde County was echoed in subsequent integration struggles throughout the South.

An annual Memorial Day gathering of the boycott is celebrated in Swanquarter, although the Peay School has been turned into the school system headquarters. A plaque at the school honors O. A. Peay, the first black principal, who said, "We will find a way or we will make a way."

Walnut Cove

WALNUT COVE SCHOOL *(U.S. 311 north of Winston-Salem)* Lovingly preserved as a community center, this former Rosenwald school is one of the finest remaining in the South. Some eight hundred Rosenwald schools—named for Julius Rosenwald, the president of Sears, Roebuck & Co.—were built in North Carolina. Five thousand were built across the South from common plans, using Rosenwald seed money and local fund-raising and labor. The Walnut Cove Colored School, which opened in 1921, was one of the larger schools, with five classrooms. It operated until the 1950s. Former students restored the school in the mid-1990s as a community center, and won a place on the National Register of Historic Places.

Wilmington mob after burning Alex Manly's newspaper during the 1898 coup d'état

Wilmington

In the entire history of southern racial tragedies, few stories top the 1898 Wilmington coup d'état. A city that had developed a remarkable racial mix in both government and business was gutted in a murderous political rampage by white supremacists. The black leadership, largely Republican, was run out of town by white Democrats who stole property and installed themselves in power. Wilmington never recovered its equanimity, although the city has now memorialized the event in an attempt to heal old wounds.

As a seaport and the turpentine capital of the South, Wilmington was once North Carolina's largest city. Blacks outnumbered whites eleven thousand to eight thousand and held a fourteen hundred voting majority. One-third of city council seats and several federal posts were held by blacks. City and fire departments hired both races and some of the better neighborhoods were integrated. "Never before and never since had blacks occupied such a central place in a city's political and economic life as they did in Wilmington from 1865 to 1897," wrote H. Leon Prather in *We Have Taken a City*. Some blacks flaunted their positions, threatening many whites, including Irish immigrants competing for jobs.

As part of a statewide effort to regain power, Democrats mounted an openly racist campaign against blacks, based in large part on the old southern specter of black domination, and black men raping white women. A cabal of Democrats called the Secret Nine planned an election day takeover and filled newspapers and stirred up public debate with fear-fanning lies. In the heat of the campaign, the editor of the black *Daily*

Record, Alex Manly, himself an octoroon, penned a blunt rebuttal that noted that white men raped black women without consequence, suggested that white women found black men attractive, and warned readers: "Don't think ever that your women will remain pure while you are debauching ours."

The editorial poured gasoline onto an inflamed city. Manly fled town. On November 9, after Democrats won the election, the Secret Nine declared a "White Man's Declaration of Independence" and seized power rather than wait until inauguration day in the spring. An armed Klan-like group called the Redshirts burned Manly's newspaper and went on a shooting rampage in the black neighborhood of Brooklyn. Most of the violence occurred around Fourth and Harnett Streets. As the Wilmington Light Infantry gunned down fleeing blacks, the Secret Nine forced the sitting mayor and board of aldermen to resign. The head of the mob became mayor.

The known death toll was around twenty, but rumors suggested many black bodies were found in surrounding woods or floating in the Cape Fear River. The Red Shirts also rounded up leading black businessmen and officeholders and forced them onto a train leaving town. As many as two thousand blacks abandoned Wilmington, never to return, their property snapped up for taxes. Although the coup got President McKinley's attention, organizers escaped punishment and took over abandoned property and government jobs. The coup—thought to be the only one in U.S. history—was the crowning victory for North Carolina Democrats who, forty-five years after the Civil War, established a Jim Crow state. In the next session of the legislature blacks were disenfranchised under a bill written by a white Wilmington attorney.

Wilmington made civil rights news again in the 1970s when a black protest of a school integration plan erupted in violence. The Wilmington Ten, including leader Ben Chavis, were imprisoned.

The city is also known for black sports heroes, among them Michael Jordan, Meadowlark Lemon, Althea Gibson, and Gibson's mentor, Dr. Hubert Eaton, who trained her on a grass court behind his house.

Wilmington publishes several brochures on black history with clear maps. **The Visitors Information Center** (*Third and Princess Streets; 800-222-4757*) is open daily.

1 **1898 MEMORIAL PARK** (*U.S. 421, Third and Davis Streets*)   In 1998, one hundred years after the infamous overthrow of Wilmington's integrated power structure, the city of Wilmington reopened the painful event in an extraordinary attempt to air it, rewrite it, and reconcile race relations. A mayor's committee sponsored a yearlong commemoration with historical studies and guided dialogues that made it possible for the first time to talk about the century-old crime and its legacy. One result was a memorial to the 1898 coup, to be built at a northern gateway to the city adjacent to the Brooklyn neighborhood where many residents were murdered.

2 **ALEX MANLY HISTORIC MARKER AND SITE OF NEWSPAPER FIRE** (*Marker is on Third Street between Nun and Church Streets. The*

Alex Manly marker in Wilmington

fire site is four blocks east, at a vacant lot next to St. Luke's Church between Nun and Church Streets.) The 1898 coup began when a mob of one thousand gathered at the city armory on Market Street and marched six blocks to the *Daily Record* and set fire to it. The black-owned *Record* was edited by Alex Manly, who fled town before the coup. The historic marker was unveiled as part of the centennial reconciliation. Manly's newspaper was on Seventh Street but the empty lot is unmarked. Across the street is the office of the *Wilmington Journal,* a black newspaper founded twenty-nine years after the arson attack. Manly settled in Washington, D.C., and worked for a congressman. His granddaughter returned to Wilmington for the centennial event.

3 | **GREGORY CONGREGATIONAL CHURCH** (*609 Nun Street*) Built by the American Missionary Association for freed slaves shortly after the Civil War, Gregory and an adjacent school were safe harbors for neighborhood blacks during the Jim Crow era. In 1971 the church and the neighborhood were in the eye of a tragic race riot.

Trouble erupted when the city's refusal to honor the memory of Martin Luther King exacerbated an unresolved standoff over school integration. Unrest of students at the leading black school, Williston High, prompted school officials to close Williston and bus the students to two white schools.

Isolated and rejected in their new surroundings, black kids began a boycott to reopen Williston, which was three blocks away from the church. Gregory became boycott headquarters for the Reverend Ben Chavis, a young civil rights organizer with the United Church of Christ's Commission for Racial Justice. His arrival fired up both the kids and the Ku Klux Klan. Beginning February 2, 1971, shots were fired into the church. Two days later, fire destroyed Mike's Grocery, a white-owned store across the street. Firemen were shot at while fighting the blaze. In the melee, a policeman was shot, a black teenager was killed by police, and a white man was found shot to death in his pickup. The riot lasted until February 11 when the National Guard arrived. The Wilmington Ten—Chavis, eight black students, and a female antipoverty volunteer—were convicted of arson and shooting at the firemen and sentenced for up to thirty-four years, startling punishments that prompted Amnesty International to list them as political prisoners. Chavis later made headlines while attending Duke University in leg irons. After a witness admitted lying, the ten were paroled. In 1980 an appeals court overturned their convictions. Chavis later headed the national NAACP for one year before being fired for paying hush money to stop a sexual harassment suit.

4 | **HOME OF DR. HUBERT EATON** (*1406 Orange Street*)   A black physician, tennis coach, and civil rights activist, Dr. Eaton began suing the city in 1950 to improve black schools. He returned to the courts in 1964 when it became apparent the school system was not going to bow to the Supreme Court's *Brown* decision integrating schools. In 1957 he and other black physicians, who had to practice at the segregated and inadequate Community Hospital, sued to force James Walker Memorial Hospital to admit black doctors to its staff.

Eaton also had a lifelong interest in tennis. He was president of the black American Tennis Association (ATA), and both hosted and trained Althea Gibson at a tennis court still visible behind his house.

Born on August 25, 1927, Gibson learned to play tennis in Harlem. After bitterly losing the ATA women's singles in 1946, she was approached by Walter Johnson, a physician and tennis coach from Lynchburg, Virginia. He and Eaton persuaded her to finish high school and undertake intensive coaching at their homes. During the school year, she lived with Dr. Eaton and played on his court here, and spent her summers with Dr. Johnson in Virginia. In 1947 she won nine ATA tournaments. She graduated from high school in 1949, and, with the help of former tennis star Alice Marble, won admission to Forest Lawn. Marble, in a famous letter, called organized tennis "sanctimonious hypocrites."

Gibson became the first black player at Forest Lawn in 1950, and won the U.S. Open in 1957. Never able to profit from endorsements, she later played professional golf, toured with the Harlem Globetrotters, and settled down to a teaching job in New Jersey. The Williams sisters, Venus and Serena, call her their role model.

5 | CAPE FEAR MUSEUM *(814 Market Street; 910-341-4350; www. nhcgov.com/CFM)* A balanced story of Wilmington's development is told here, although the civil rights story is given short shrift. Sports fans will enjoy a panel devoted to basketball superstar Michael Jordan who played high school ball here and worked in a fast-food restaurant before gaining fame and fortune. Meadowlark Lemon, one of the most famous members of the Harlem Globetrotters, also played basketball in Wilmington's schools, but left before college to play professionally with the Globetrotters.

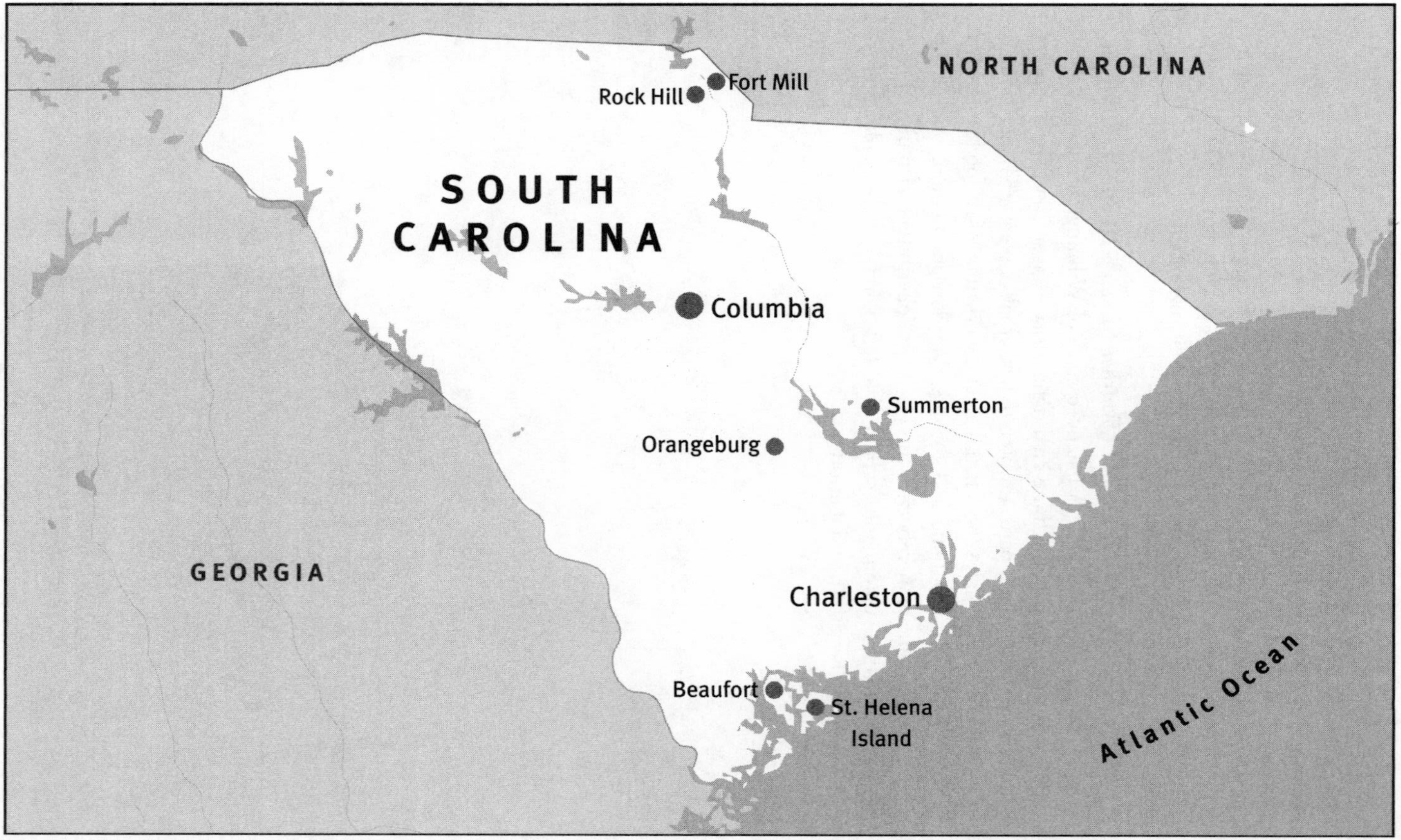
NORTH CAROLINA
Fort Mill
Rock Hill
SOUTH CAROLINA
Columbia
Summerton
Orangeburg
GEORGIA
Charleston
Beaufort
St. Helena Island
Atlantic Ocean

South Carolina

Without the story of race, any state history of South Carolina would be a slim volume.

From the beginning, rulers were blunt about the role of black people who outnumbered whites for two centuries. "South Carolina," said founding father Charles Pinckney, "cannot do without slaves." He struck from the nation's charter documents, the Declaration of Independence and the Constitution, any reference that might threaten chattel. Pinckney was followed by a long line of South Carolinians who seceded from the Union, started and fought in the Civil War, crushed black hope during Reconstruction, instituted segregation, and resisted civil rights from the 1940s to the 1970s.

Even the state's favorite icons—Charleston plantations, the Citadel, Fort Sumter, the Confederate flag, Strom Thurmond—owe their fame to black history. Yet until recently, written histories distorted or hid the role of African Americans, becoming, in I. A. Newby's words, another "blunt instrument of racial repression." He cited a 1932 textbook that stated: "Slavery had many features which commended itself to Negroes" but "freedom was forced upon them."

That same year, an NAACP survey of blacks described widespread lethargy, a "timorous" people who thought voting unimportant. Historian

Newby blamed the attitude on "defeat, poverty, frustration and failure." In 1951 psychologist Kenneth Clark demonstrated that black children in one rural county preferred white dolls and thought of black dolls as "bad." In the 1960s, native-born black activist Cleveland Sellers said, "Their minds are chained."

Which makes the scene today remarkable. Bowed by an NAACP tourism boycott, the state legislature in 2000 removed the Confederate battle flag from the capitol dome. The following year, South Carolina built the first state capitol memorial to black history.

In Charleston, the tired old story of the Civil War and Lost Cause have been dramatically rewritten to focus on the real cause—slavery. With its first memorial to an African American hero, Gullah tours led by blacks, and a proposed international black history museum, Charleston almost overnight has become a civil rights destination. Black history, so long hidden in the mythical "Catfish Alley," will soon be more accessible here than anywhere in the South.

The change did not happen overnight. "Somebody didn't just flip a switch," historian Walter Edgar told *The State* newspaper at the start of an unprecedented civil rights conference at the Citadel in 2003. "That didn't happen without people on both sides of the racial divide saying that things were going to change."

Indeed, the freshest breeze in South Carolina today is the rediscovery of black history. From slaves and their African rice, which helped to make the state the country's richest colony, to dirt-poor farmers who, in the 1950s, challenged the South's most aristocratic, paternalistic, and suffocating system of segregation, stories of a gentle fierceness smoldered for a long time. Malaise, it turned out, was not a permanent condition.

South Carolina and Civil Rights

South Carolina's first constitution in 1669 stated: "Every freeman of Carolina shall have absolute power and authority over his Negro slaves." That line set the state's tone for the next three hundred years.

Though the Spanish had explored the coastline in the 1500s, they did not realize that "Carolina gold" would turn out to be a strain of rice imported from Africa with kidnapped farmers. Within decades of South Carolina's founding by English charter, huge plantations were carved from swamps and sea islands, the land reclaimed by countless black hands. By the Revolutionary War, nine of the ten richest men in the United States were planters from South Carolina.

They were addicted to slaves—75,000 in 1770, some 60 percent of the population, the only state where blacks outnumbered whites. Along the coast the ratio was more like ten to one. Charleston became the country's largest slave port, selling roughly half the Africans that came to America, some 250,000. During peak years, seven humans on average were sold every day on an auction block somewhere in the city. According to advertisements that survive, blacks from Africa's "rice coast" of Sierra Leone brought premium prices.

The state's reputation for cruelty was not unique but it is documented: whippings, dismemberment, brandings, use of rings and muzzles, being burned alive, and castration were all punishments used by overseers. Runaway slaves called maroons, who hid in the swamps and islands, became an almost mythological force to be feared, hunted, and defended against. A southbound waterborne underground railroad using ships and other watercraft carried runaways to Florida, where the Spanish offered freedom in exchange for baptism into the Catholic Church or service in the militia. Charleston, according to Ira Berlin, became a wild port where runaways mixed with sailors, free blacks, and artisans.

The first major slave uprising in North America occurred southwest of Charleston in 1739 when an Angolan named Jemmy led twenty men to a bridge across the Stono River. They broke into a store of guns, killed the owners, and headed south beating drums and shouting "Liberty." Their group grew to seventy-five and killed twenty-five whites before militiamen stopped them. Fourteen were shot, their heads posted on poles, and about forty others were hanged or gibbeted as a warning to other slaves. The next year, new slave codes prohibited group gatherings, learning how to write, and beating of drums.

By the Revolution, South Carolina's politics were controlled by a relatively few planters who owned 75 percent of slaves. The state's delegation to the founding conventions led efforts to preserve slavery. Among the compromises written by delegate Charles Pinckney: postponing for twenty years, until 1808, a vote on banning the slave trade from Africa, and a guarantee that runaways would be returned.

By the 1800s, however, the spread of slavery was clashing with a growing abolition movement in the North. After a particularly slanderous speech against slave owners by abolitionist Senator Charles Sumner of Massachusetts, South Carolina Congressman Preston Brooks walked onto the Senate floor and beat him bloody until his cane broke apart. Brooks became a hero at home, showered with dozens of canes inscribed with "Hit Him Again."

As early as 1847 Senator John C. Calhoun warned that the South might revolt unless the North was willing to let slave owners travel west into new states. Congress, he said, "could no more prevent a slave owner from taking his human property to the territories than it could prevent him from taking his horses or hogs there," according to historian James McPherson. In 1851 the governor flatly predicted that South Carolina would secede from the United States.

Meeting in Charleston in April 1860, the national Democratic convention displayed the rebellion for all to see. Candidate Stephen Douglas said a slave guarantee wouldn't fly in the North. To which South Carolina delegate J. S. Preston replied: "Slavery is our King. Slavery is our Truth. Slavery is our Divine Right." He and other southern delegates walked out. The split guaranteed Lincoln's election and civil war.

"Not surprisingly," wrote McPherson, "South Carolina acted first." On December 20, 1860, the legislature voted to leave the Union. Within a month, six states followed. Charleston Harbor happened to have federal forts. In April 1861 the president of the new Confederate States of America ordered Pierre Beauregard to fire on Fort Sumter. The Civil War was under way.

After the war, South Carolina turned upside down as the black population controlled the state legislature for a decade. They sent more black congressmen to Washington (eight) and more black legislators to the state capital (eighty-seven) than any other southern state. Their legislature enacted a sweeping civil rights law for equal access to public accommodations, set up integrated schools with compulsory attendance, and created programs to protect small farmers, the elderly, the sick, and the poor. The University of South Carolina even opened its doors to more than two hundred black students, faculty, and staff.

In reaction, the new Ku Klux Klan, imported from Tennessee, rose to crush black gains. In 1868 in York County, Klansmen killed several Republican leaders. When the Republicans won again in 1870, Klansmen rode through several counties "almost nightly" for a year, whipping hundreds, killing thirty-eight blacks—including three state legislators—and torturing women and children. President Grant sent in the army.

Among the atrocities reported to Congress and compiled in *The Great South Carolina Ku Klux Klan Trials* were these stories: Hot tar was poured into the vagina of a white woman on suspicions that she had slept with a black man. Spartanburg's first black magistrate, Anthony Johnson, was hanged in front of his mother. In Laurens County, a "Negro chase" drove 150 blacks from their homes. Thirteen died. In York County alone, nearly every white male joined the Klan and participated in 600 whippings and eleven murders. Thousands of blacks took to sleeping in the woods. The military investigator, Major Lewis Merrill, called it a "carnival of crime not paralleled in the history of any civilized community." He took 600 suspects into custody but key Klan leaders fled to Canada. Fifty-some Klansmen were convicted, but more than 1,200 cases went unprosecuted.

Though crushed as Klansmen, white supremacists in other guises continued terrorism in 1876. In Hamburg, a former Confederate general and hundreds of armed men ambushed a black militia, executed six, and razed the town. Antiblack "rifle clubs" were organized in three hundred towns. "Red Shirts" on horseback took control of Edgefield County's courthouse and kept blacks from voting. Grand Dragon Wade Hampton was elected governor and South Carolina followed Mississippi in creating a white supremacist state.

This was the era of "Pitchfork Ben" Tillman, a Democratic politician who led repeal of all civil rights laws and created a single black district called a "boa constrictor" that curled across the state, encompassing black neighborhoods from Columbia to Charleston. With blacks contained in one district, the rest of the state reigned white supreme. "We have scratched our heads to find out how we could eliminate every last one of them," Tillman bragged on the floor of the U.S. Senate. "We stuffed ballot boxes. We shot them. We are not ashamed of it," according to the book *Quiet Revolution in the South*. Few totalitarian states, wrote historian I. A. Newby, "have done so well."

By the dawn of the twentieth century, more than half of blacks still couldn't read, infant mortality was three times that of whites, and 80 percent of blacks were poverty-stricken tenant farmers. In 1916, when Septima Clark began teaching at Promise Land School on Johns Island outside Charleston, she found people listless and "primitive." People cared little about improving themselves, she said. Half of the schoolchildren came from homes without windowpanes and three out of four had no toothbrushes.

But when tens of thousands of black South Carolinians returned from World War I—some decorated with the French croix de guerre for bravery—they yearned for something better. The NAACP started two small chapters, but many blacks left for the north. In 1922, when fifty thousand blacks moved away, whites regained the population lead. By 1950 the exiting flood had reached six hundred thousand African Americans.

During World War II, James Hinton of the NAACP and John McCray of the South Carolina Negro Citizens Committee launched an attack on the all-white Democratic primary, which, in the absence of a strong GOP, guaranteed election of Democrats. In a seismic decision in 1947, U.S. District Judge J. Waties Waring of Charleston ruled that South Carolina's all-white primaries were unconstitutional. Thirty-five thousand blacks voted in 1948.

In 1948 WWII navy veteran Harry Briggs lent his name to a lawsuit against the Clarendon County school board to improve black schools. At the time South Carolina spent $43 on each black student, compared to $179 for each white student. The case, *Briggs v. Elliott,* would be the first filed as part of the landmark Supreme Court decision to integrate schools.

Governor Strom Thurmond, fuming at civil rights gains, including President Truman's decision to integrate the military, rounded up southern racists in a new Dixiecrat party. Between 1957 and 1965, the state's congressional delegation "resolutely opposed every civil rights bill proposed in Congress," according to *Quiet Revolution in the South.*

Not until 1963 did a new governor, Donald Russell, signal a change when he invited "everyone" to his inaugural barbecue—the first integrated public social event since Reconstruction. In July of that year, a federal court integrated state parks, and the Francis Marion Hotel in Charleston allowed black guests to check in during the day—although they could not yet drink at the bar. That fall, Charleston let the first few blacks into white public schools, and Harvey Gantt broke the color line at the state college, Clemson. Still, ten years after the Supreme Court edict, only ten black kids were in public school classes with whites.

Continued resistance escalated out of control in 1968 when state troopers shot into a crowd of college students who previously had tried to integrate a bowling alley in Orangeburg. Three were killed and twenty-seven injured.

In 1971 the first black legislators in the twentieth century were elected. In 1982 blacks took control of Edgefield County, the home of "Pitchfork Ben" Tillman and Strom Thurmond, seating themselves in the same courthouse that Red Shirts seized in 1876 to prevent blacks from voting. By 2000 the number of black elected officials statewide had risen to 540.

As the twenty-first century began, South Carolina took down from its capitol dome a Confederate flag that had flown as a civil rights battle flag since 1962. The following year, schoolchildren and churches raised $1 million for the nation's first black history monument at a state capitol.

A South Carolina Civil Rights Tour

South Carolina's civil rights story spans four centuries, but only a few hours of driving. Charleston is the place to begin the journey, just as slaves did on Sullivan's Island. There are no markers to indicate the "modern" movement, but thanks to the National Park Service and Mayor Joe Riley, Charleston will soon be unmatched for interpreting slave and Civil War history from a balanced point of view.

Beaufort and a glimpse of the sea island Gullah story make for a beautiful ride along the coast.

The state's three other significant civil rights stops are ninety minutes up Interstate 26 from Charleston. The Columbia capitol, one of the most beautiful in the nation, shelters a unique African American monument. In Orangeburg, South Carolina State University remembers the massacre of 1968 with several memorials. And in little Summerton, off Interstate 95, are a couple of small markers to one of the bravest acts of civil rights history— the first lawsuit to integrate and equalize black education.

City by City

Beaufort

ROBERT SMALLS MEMORIAL AND GRAVE SITE *(907 Craven Street)*
One year into the Civil War, Charleston harbor pilot and slave
Robert Smalls heard rumors that an army general in his hometown of
Beaufort had declared slaves emancipated. Sneaking his family and
friends aboard the Confederate *Planter,* he steamed past Fort

Sumter and its Confederate soldiers and
directly into the Union blockade, where
he threw up a white bedsheet and the
Stars and Stripes. By nightfall he had
reached Beaufort (BYOO-fert) and was a
hero. In March 1865, two weeks after
Charleston surrendered, Smalls sailed the
Planter back into Charleston Harbor in a
triumphant return. He later served five
terms as a congressman, and lived out his
years as a customs collector in Beaufort.

Smalls is buried in the small courtyard
of the Tabernacle Baptist Church. A
bronze statue, showing an animated face

Robert Smalls bust and
gravesite in Beaufort

with swept-back hair, carries the inscription: "My race needs no special defense,
for the past history of them in this country proves them to be the
equal of any people anywhere. All they need is an equal chance in the
battle of life."

Charleston

Charleston's devotion to anything old has preserved, more by accident than
design, a fair amount of civil rights history. A number of sites remain, juxtaposed against the city's vaunted antebellum grandeur. So closely bound is
this history, all one needs is a reinterpreted road map to appreciate both the
suffering and contributions of blacks to the city's history.

Its many plantations reek of duality—slaves raised the cash crops, built
the mansions, and lived out back. The inauguration of Charleston's modern
civil rights movement took place in the shadow of monuments to the city's

historic racism. Richly ironic, a civil rights tour of Charleston reminds us how separate black and white histories of southern cities could be entwined.

At the start of the Civil War, Charleston had more than seventeen thousand blacks, free and slave. One out of five was an artisan engaged in mansion building and ship carpentry. Some owned slaves of their own. Many were sailors, such as Robert Smalls of Beaufort, a slave pilot who stole the Confederate steamer *Planter* at the start of the Civil War.

At the war's end, Charleston was a bombed-out shell, "a city of the dead," and freed blacks put on tableaus that illustrated how life had changed. On March 29, 1865, for example, four thousand blacks, including eighteen hundred children, marched through the streets pulling floats, one with an auction block with a real auctioneer "selling" two women and children. Another carried a coffin marked SLAVERY.

On May 1, 10,000 former slaves paraded to a former prisoner of war camp in an antebellum race course where 257 Union soldiers were buried. They labeled the gate "Martyrs of the Race Course." Women and children walked through the graves singing "John Brown's Body" and dropping rose petals until the mounds were covered. It was the first Decoration Day, soon copied all over the country. For years after, the only people who paraded in Charleston on July 4 were blacks.

After white supremacists regained control of South Carolina, Charleston maintained Jim Crow with a grim paternalism. In 1962, eight years after the Supreme Court integrated the nation's schools, J. Arthur Brown, who headed the NAACP, sued to integrate local schools on behalf of his daughter Millicent. Charleston mounted the crudest defense, claiming black children were degenerates, unstable, illegitimate, and infected with VD. In August 1963 the federal judge ordered delays to stop, although schools didn't really comply until 1970.

Charleston saw its first modern sit-in protest in April 1960 at Kress's five-and-dime, when twenty-four high school students peacefully endured verbal assaults, even from blacks who were shocked to see such behavior. The kids were arrested and turned over to their parents. With little progress toward integration, however, a summer assault in 1963 included "boycotts, blacklists, sit-ins, wade-ins, theater stand-ins, kneel-ins, picketing and marches," according to the *Avery Review.* The most effective protest was a pedestrian gridlock at the commercial center of King and Calhoun Streets. As all four walking lanes filled with hundreds of people, traffic came to a standstill.

This intersection was ripe with historic irony as protesters marched beneath the stony gaze of John C. Calhoun, father figure of South Carolina secession. Behind his monument is the pink facade of the original Citadel, the military school created to ward off a black revolution.

With rare exceptions—one was a brick-throwing melee outside the then-racist newspaper, the *News and Courier*—protests were almost genteel. In the summer of 1964 Rudy Cornwell, a black dentist's wife, dressed in hat and gloves, hired a limousine to drive her and her friends to the Fort Sumter Hotel, and asked to be served. "We knew we were breaking the law. Our purpose was to be arrested," she said later at age one hundred. When the manager politely turned them down, a paddy wagon arrived with a police captain who apologized for the law, and warned the arresting officers: "No funny stuff. These are respectable people." By September, a slow integration was under way.

Charleston saw more street violence in 1969 in the midst of a ninety-nine-day strike by black hospital workers during which time the Reverend Ralph Abernathy was jailed. It ended with concessions to rehire a dozen workers and improve race relations. Today, blacks hold half or a majority of positions on public boards, but power remains with old money and class.

As for civil rights history, professional personnel at the airy **visitors center** (*Ann and Meeting Streets; 843-853-8000*) speak comfortably and knowledgeably about early events. They offer many brochures, walking tours, and driving tours.

Jim Crow in a Nutshell

Under Jim Crow segregation laws and practices, which began in the 1870s and lasted in many parts of the United States until the 1970s, African American citizens could not:
  Eat with whites
  Check out a book at the public library
  Go to the state fair except on "colored day"
  Try on clothes or shoes in a store
  Live in white neighborhoods
  Drink from public fountains

Swim in city pools
Sit in the main bus terminal
Use the front door at city hall
Go to a white hairdresser
Go to a white dentist
Get a blood transfusion from a white donor
Give blood to a white GI
Sit with white churchgoers
Ride in a railroad car with whites
Ride in an elevator with white people
Ride in the front of public buses
Play pool with whites
Wash their clothes in a "white" machine
Have their tax records filed next to whites'
Marry a white
Make love to a white
Go to school with whites
Be jailed as a delinquent within a quarter mile of a "white" delinquent facility
Call a white person by his or her first name
Shake hands with a white
Wait to see a doctor in the same waiting room with whites
Ride in a "white" taxi
Swear to testify in court except on a "colored" bible
Be committed to a "white" mental institution
Play baseball in a vacant lot within two blocks of a white baseball team
Buy beer or wine in a "white" liquor store
Be committed to a reform school for white children
Rent an apartment if one white lived in the building
Work as a policeman
Run for election
Vote
Teach white children
Use "white" telephone booths
Be medicated by a white nurse
Work in the same chain gang as white prisoners
Fight and die alongside a white soldier in the U.S. Army
Get treated, even near death, in a "white" hospital
Be embalmed by a white undertaker
Be buried in a cemetery alongside whites

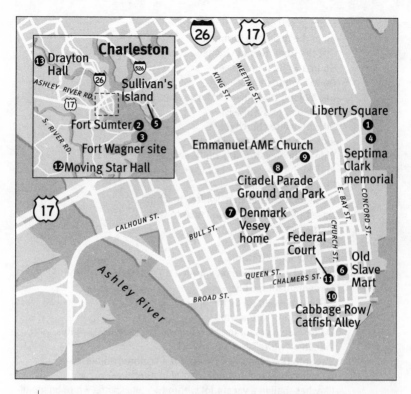

I | **LIBERTY SQUARE** (*Calhoun and Concord Streets*) Gateway to Charleston, South Carolina, and the Civil War, this visitors center represents an extraordinary sea change in southern history. For the first time at any Civil War site or southern city, the cause of the war is plainly stated—slavery. That it happened in the birthplace of secession is due to a decision by the National Park Service to move away from its "cannonball circuit" focus on military maneuvers and toward a new interpretation that describes the origins and legacy of the war. As recently as 2001, park brochures avoided the word "slavery." A visitor today cannot miss these opening lines: "Underlying all the economic, social and political rhetoric was the volatile question of slavery."

Liberty Square is a good starting point for a deep look at South Carolina. One can see across the harbor Sullivan's Island, where slaves first arrived; Fort Sumter, where the Civil War started; and Fort Wagner, where black soldiers of the Fifty-fourth Massachusetts Regiment are buried.

The theme of the outside plaza is liberty, and a dozen panels quote people who expanded on its meaning. The Septima Clark fountain is Charleston's first public memorial to an African American.

Charleston has committed to a major African American history museum on the square by 2007.

2 | **FORT SUMTER** *(by ferry from Liberty Square; 843-888-3123; www. nps.gov/fosu)* When Lincoln was elected, South Carolina seceded from the United States, an act that essentially seized four federal forts around Charleston harbor. Six days after South Carolina's vote, the local U.S. commander, Major Robert Anderson, snuck his troops onto this island where he thought they would be safer. When outgoing president James Buchanan refused to give up the fort, the new Confederate army tried to starve them out. On April 4, 1861, one month after he was inaugurated, President Lincoln sent an armed convoy to resupply the fort. Eight days later, before relief arrived, Confederate artillery began blasting the fort apart. Anderson abandoned the fort after thirty hours. The Civil War had begun. Fort Sumter displays the U.S. flag flying at the time of the surrender, which was raised again when Charleston fell two months before Appomattox. Displays at the fort also tell the story of nearby Fort Wagner.

3 | **FORT WAGNER SITE** *(visible from Liberty Square and Fort Sumter)* One of the Civil War's most memorable tragedies occurred on a sandy spit of island that separated the sea from Charleston Harbor. The land has long been washed away, but the story of black soldiers and their white commander who died there has become immortal. The Fifty-fourth Massachusetts Regiment, composed entirely of free blacks recruited around Boston, was one of the first black companies from the north to see action.

Led by pale, slight Robert Gould Shaw, son of an established New England family, the Fifty-fourth was chosen to lead the attack on Fort

Wagner on Morris Island. Less a fort than a sand-bermed artillery unit, the structure could only be reached across three-quarters of a mile of exposed, wave-washed beach. But it was defended by 1,700 riflemen. On the evening of July 18, 1863, Shaw led 650 troops over the parapet where he was shot to death. Two hundred and seventy-two men died with him before the attackers fell back. Shaw was stripped of his uniform and jewelry and buried in a common grave with his soldiers. The Confederates lost eight men.

Sergeant William Carney, a twenty-three-year-old black who raised the unit's fallen banner and carried it across the fort's moat, up and over the bodies of his fellow soldiers, was wounded several times but kept the U.S. flag upright. "We continued to fight for the freedom of the enslaved and for the restoration of our country," he said later. He was awarded the Congressional Medal of Honor, but not until 1900.

According to historian Richard Bailey, an army board of inquiry later learned that the Union assault commander, Major General Truman Seymour, had said, "Well, I guess we will put those damned niggers from Massachusetts in the advance. We may as well get rid of them one time as another."

The movie *Glory* tells the story of the Fifty-fourth. The name "Shaw" may be second only to "Martin Luther King" on honorific street signs and institutions in black communities across the South.

4 | **SEPTIMA CLARK MEMORIAL** (*Liberty Square*)   This fountain honors Septima Poinsette Clark, a quiet revolutionary and wellspring of civil rights. As a teacher, activist, and counselor she nurtured and inspired generations of blacks—including Rosa Parks and SNCC leaders—to press for their rights.

Born in Charleston in 1898, daughter of former slave Peter Poinsette (named after the master who introduced the Christmas plant to the United States), Septima Poinsette began teaching Gullah children on Johns Island when it was still reachable only by boat. She married a sailor, Nerie Clark, who died four years later. After moving to Columbia, where she taught and worked toward her master's degree, Clark joined an NAACP agitation for better teacher pay. In 1954 South Carolina prohibited teachers from belonging to the

Septima Clark (*l*) sitting with Rosa Parks (*r*) at the Highlander School in Tennessee

NAACP and she quit at age fifty-seven to direct integration and voting rights workshops at the Highlander Folk School in Tennessee. Among the "students" that first year was Rosa Parks, who was arrested four months later in Montgomery, Alabama, for refusing to give up her bus seat to a white man. Later, Clark returned to Johns Island to establish "citizenship schools" for adults wishing to vote but stymied by literacy tests.

In 1965, coming full circle in a city that denied her the right to teach in 1916, Septima Clark was elected the first black to Charleston's school board. President Carter named her a Living Legacy, Charleston College named an auditorium for her, and Taylor Branch dedicated his Pulitzer Prize–winning book on the civil rights movement to her. She died in 1987 on Johns Island.

5 | **SULLIVAN'S ISLAND** (*terminus of South Carolina Route* 703) At least half of all African slaves shipped to the United States landed on this island, numbering nearly a quarter of a million between 1619 and 1808. They were placed in quarantine pens to check for disease before being sold in Charleston auctions. A large sign outside Fort Moultrie describes this history, as do displays inside the visitors center.

6 | **OLD SLAVE MART** (*6 Chalmers Street*) Through the stone arch of this small, dark edifice an untold number of chained Africans arrived to begin their lives as slaves in America. The last sale here was in 1863. It became the city's first and only black history museum in 1937. A pair of sisters, Judith Chase and Louise Graves, saved the property from the wrecking ball in 1960.

7 | **HOME OF DENMARK VESEY** (*56 Bull Street*) Around 1820, slave carpenter Denmark Vesey, who had purchased his freedom with a lottery jackpot, began to plot a revolt to lead slaves to Haiti. According to testimony, the conspiracy was hatched in this clapboard house and was spread through his church, Emmanuel AME. Among his deputies were Gullah Jack, a sorcerer; Blind Phillip, who saw ghosts; and a barber who fashioned Caucasian wigs. Hundreds of slaves were informed of the plan, and they stockpiled 250 pike heads and 300 daggers. But the plot was tipped off to authorities by a slave, and dozens of men were rounded up. During two months of trial, people were shocked to learn of Vesey's plot to kill thousands of Charlestonians. He and thirty-five others were hanged in the summer of 1822. Others were deported. In the aftermath, Charleston spied on black churches, opened slave mail, and built the Citadel to train militia to guard against slave uprisings.

Efforts to create a Vesey memorial have bogged down over whether he was a mass murderer or a freedom fighter.

8 | **CITADEL PARADE GROUND AND PARK** (*King and Calhoun Streets*) This expansive park in downtown Charleston is layered with South Carolina's long racial struggle. The original Citadel, whose castle wall faces the park, was built in 1842 after the Vesey uprising to train militia for slave uprisings. The towering statue of Senator John C. Calhoun pays homage to South Carolina's leading effort to maintain slavery in the South—even to the point of snapping the United States in half to do it. According to unconfirmed black oral history, Calhoun was put on the tall pedestal to curtail vandalism by black women as they passed by.

In 1963 the adjacent intersection of King and Calhoun Streets was a gridlock of marching protesters who walked in a "square" on all four pedestrian lanes and blocked traffic for days. Suffering from losses, King Street businesses opened their lunch counters to blacks and ended demeaning practices like not allowing blacks to try on clothing they intended to purchase.

9 | **EMMANUEL AME CHURCH** (*110 Calhoun Street*) The oldest AME church in the South, its congregation organized by Charleston's free blacks in 1791, Emmanuel was later closed after authorities discovered that Denmark Vesey's proposed insurrection had been discussed here between 1818 and 1822. As soon as the Civil War ended, the congregation re-formed. The present church and the Halson-Boags Funeral Home across the street were staging areas for civil rights protests in the 1960s.

10 | **CABBAGE ROW AND CATFISH ALLEY** (*89–91 Church Street*) Between the planter homes of old Charleston there once thrived earthy black camps that inspired the opera *Porgy and Bess,* with its mythical setting "Catfish Alley." Today, there is only a sense of hidden wealth behind iron privacy gates and alleys prettied by lattice and ferns. Catfish Alley, in fact, was one of the greatest whitewashes of the South. Conditions in the real alleys were dreadful—"Probably the vilest human habitations in a civilized land," wrote W. E. B. Du Bois in 1908. There were no bathrooms and the alleys were filled with petty thieves and prostitutes preying on each other.

11 | **FEDERAL COURT** (*Meeting and Broad Streets*) This beautiful building, named for Fritz Hollings, should be dedicated to its one true heroic occupant: U.S. District Court Judge Julius Waties Waring. A blue-blood Charlestonian, Waring dragged South Carolina into the twentieth century with a series of civil rights rulings in the 1940s. In

1948 he outlawed the state's whites-only primary, pointing his finger at county registrars before him, warning them that he would sit in his courtroom all primary day and find them in contempt if they did not register blacks. Thirty thousand blacks voted, an act that made Waring an outcast in Charleston's private clubs and earned him the epithet, "the guy who let the nigger vote." Because Waring upheld the law, crosses were burned on his lawn and shots were fired into his house. Waring lashed out at Governor Strom Thurmond for creating the Dixiecrat movement—"the dying gasp of white supremacy and slavocracy."

A month after the attack on his home NAACP lawyer Thurgood Marshall appeared before Waring and two fellow judges to argue the first of five school integration cases that would change the South, *Briggs v. Elliott* from Summerton. At the trial, hundreds of blacks lined up to see both Marshall and Waring, who was outvoted in the initial decision two to one. In the 1954 Supreme Court decision, *Brown v. Board of Education,* Waring's dissent became the law of the land. Waring left the bench and lived in exile in New York. His 1968 funeral in Charleston was attended by a handful of whites and two hundred blacks.

12 | **MOVING STAR HALL** (*South River and Hunter Roads, Johns Island*)   Though unmarked as such, this one-room building is a monument to the thirst for equal rights and full American citizenship. Inside, in the 1950s, illiterate residents like Rosa Wine memorized the U.S. Constitution, even though she couldn't read or write, in order to qualify to vote. Hundreds like her succeeded. The hall is now used by a church.

Reachable today by bridges and modern highways, Johns Island in the 1930s was considerably more difficult to access. Charleston was nine hours away by boat. Residents spoke Gullah, a Creole mix of African dialects and English. When Septima Clark arrived to teach school in 1916, she found blacks leading "indifferent lives . . . [they] cared little, in fact, about improving themselves."

Clark and another teacher had 132 students. But in the evening, she began to teach adults to read and write and to improve their sanitation situation and personal hygiene. Her students wrote on the only paper she could find—dry-cleaner bags. Years later she returned, invited by

Moving Star Hall outside of Charleston

Esau Jenkins, who drove a vegetable truck—later a bus—to Charleston and picked up hitchhiking maids and laborers. He had begun passing out voter registration cards and reading the Constitution aloud so they could memorize it for the voting test. At the time, only one in ten blacks could read. Jenkins attended the Highlander Folk School in Tennessee, where he invited Clark and a local beautician, Bernice Robinson, to set up a "citizenship school." At this one-room hall, and the Progressive Club down the road (now a bar), Clark and Robinson taught islanders how to read such things as road signs and voting forms. In the first year, one hundred people registered to vote. By 1959 the citizenship school model had spread across the South.

Esau Jenkins died in 1972. His grave, at the **Wesley United Methodist Church** (*2726 River Road*), reads, "Love is Progress. Hate is Expensive."

13 | **DRAYTON HALL** (*3380 Ashley River Road; 888-349-0588; www. draytonhall.org*) Charleston has the South's greatest array of stately antebellum mansions, which still stand as monuments to America's richest families. Incrementally, estate tours are paying homage both to the slave labor that produced the wealth and skilled slave artisans who crafted the ornate buildings. Drayton Hall provides the most thoughtful "slave tour."

Rice farming, based on imported strains of rice and skilled workers from Africa, was at the root of Charleston's affluence. John Drayton, who owned fifty properties, paid premium prices for "grain coast" slaves stolen from the Sierra Leone and Congo areas. In 1810

125

Drayton Hall was home to two white people and ninety-six slaves. After the Civil War, Drayton couldn't afford to grow rice with paid labor. But many former slaves helped him mine phosphate on the plantation grounds, a mineral that allowed the Drayton family to recover its fortunes. The plantation now is owned and operated by the National Trust for Historic Preservation.

Columbia

The state capital has reflected the state's racial turmoil since its founding. A month after President Lincoln's election, a convention met at First Baptist Church and voted to secede. In 1871 the famous Ku Klux Klan trials jailed more than fifty white terrorists. Columbia's wide streets contain so many markers and monuments that every house seems important—for wildly contradictory reasons. Within a mile of each other, for example, sit segregationist Wade Hampton's mansion, built with slave labor, and the modest house of Modjeska Simkins, who helped draft *Briggs v. Elliott,* the South Carolina lawsuit that helped end school segregation. Historic Columbia publishes an African American heritage site tour guide *(1601 Richard Street; 803-252-1770).*

A panel from the Capitol's African American history memorial

SOUTH CAROLINA CAPITOL *(Main and Gervais Streets)* One of the most beautiful capitols in America sits in the middle of an expansive grounds littered with monuments to racists. But it also contains the first state memorial to African American history. The state's original secession ordinance is on display on the second floor.

A striking monument to Strom Thurmond captures him in full stride and honors a lifetime of public service. As governor in 1947, Thurmond hired the first black and the first woman in government. But he called President Truman's civil rights program a communist plot and created the segregationist Dixiecrat party in 1948. In 1957, as a U.S. senator, he filibustered for twenty-four hours against the first modern civil rights bill.

In 2000 the capitol grounds was the site of the South's hottest debate, which was over the flying of the Confederate battle flag, atop the dome since 1962. Under pressure from an NAACP boycott, which cost the state one hundred conventions, and the state's largest civil rights rally led by David Swinton, the first black chair of the Columbia Chamber of Commerce, the flag came off the dome and was repositioned in front of the capitol. During the debate a state senator, Arthur Ravenel, called the NAACP "the National Association of Retarded People." He then apologized to retarded people.

The African American monument, sculpted by former astronaut Ed Dwight, captures in thirteen large bronze panels the entire sweep of black history, from slave ships to civil rights.

RANDOLPH CEMETERY (*adjacent to Elmwood Cemetery, Elmwood Avenue at Interstate 26*)   This segregated, all-black cemetery is named for state senator Benjamin Randolph, the chair of the Republican state central committee during Reconstruction. Randolph's obelisk describes his assassination in 1868, one of the first during the Ku Klux Klan age of tyranny that crushed Reconstruction and ushered in a century of white supremacy. Also buried in this cemetery is George Elmore, whose lawsuit in 1947 opened the white primary to black voters. Other headstones tell of loved ones, accomplished professionals, and military veterans who endured segregation throughout life and after death.

Fort Mill

The nation's only "faithful slave" monument sits in a prominent place in this former mill town. Built by a local businessman at the height of Jim Crow, it depicts a mammy with children and a subservient black male. The monument is a fair representation of attitudes of that time. It is part of a collection of monuments to the war that depict soldiers, women who stayed at home, and other Lost Cause elements.

Orangeburg

SOUTH CAROLINA STATE UNIVERSITY (*300 College Street;* 803-536-7000; *www.scsu.edu*)   One of the worst unresolved acts of official violence in the civil rights era took place on the campus of South Carolina State on February 8, 1968. State police, riled by three

Three victims of the Orangeburg massacre, (left to right) Henry Smith, Samuel Hammond Jr., and Delano Middleton

days of angry protests over a segregated bowling alley, opened fire on defenseless, fleeing students. They killed three and wounded twenty-seven, with all but two shot in the back or side, and were acquitted of any wrongdoing.

Orangeburg was a conservative town, even by South Carolina standards. The state John Birch Society was based here. When black parents petitioned the school board to integrate schools in 1955, the town saw to it that they lost their jobs. When students boycotted, they were expelled. Segregation remained in place until black college students from SCSU and Claflin, another local university, led sit-ins and other mass actions between 1960 and 1963. Police used tear gas and fire hoses to break them up and arrested hundreds. The local newspaper refused to list protesters' demands. Nevertheless, downtown stores began to integrate.

In 1967 students at State protested the lack of good teachers and the firing of two white professors who had been agitating about the school's poor quality. The governor, Robert McNair, helped negotiate the end of a class boycott and change in administrations. A new student organization, Black Awareness Coordinating Committee, also pushed for more black studies. One adviser was SNCC activist Cleveland Sellers, a South Carolina native who came to town to organize students. Because he allied himself with more militant activists, including Stokely Carmichael and H. Rap Brown, and had refused to sign up for the draft to Vietnam, the FBI spied on him.

The bowling alley incident began February 5, 1968, when student-bowler John Stroman led a protest to the All Star Bowling Lanes, which had refused years of polite requests to integrate. The next night, crowds grew and a melee led to arrests and beatings. The governor called in state troopers and the National Guard. On February 8, after dark, and with Orangeburg an armed camp, students built a bonfire in the street at the edge of campus, taunted state police who were lined up with guns, and threw debris.

When a state patrolman was struck by a stair banister, knocking him down with blood pouring from his mouth, a rumor spread that he had been shot. Five minutes later, cops opened fire on a large crowd on a campus knoll, striking students cringing on the ground and at a dormitory a quarter mile away. The governor refused to investigate and nine patrolmen were acquitted in a federal trial. In their book, *The Orangeburg Massacre,* Jack Bass and Jack Nelson claimed a cover-up of crucial information by the FBI, which Director J. Edgar Hoover denied. Cleveland Sellers was charged with rioting and sentenced to a year in prison.

While the bowling alley protests were the spark for the Orangeburg massacre, "the fundamental causes were the continuing unwillingness of white Orangeburg to treat blacks equally and the growing resentment of blacks," wrote historian I. A. Newby.

The college honors the three young men killed, Delano Middleton, Henry Smith, and Samuel Hammond Jr., and the twenty-seven wounded students with several plaques and a garden memorial. The school's main sports and events arena is named for the three men, and their photographs and story are prominently displayed at the entrance. An annual memorial service is held on campus.

ALL STAR BOWLING LANES (*559 East Russell Street*) The Orangeburg Massacre was sparked by student protests to integrate this segregated holdout in a shopping center near campus. While owner Harry Floyd maintained that he would lose white customers, he didn't believe that the 1964 Civil Rights Act applied to him, according to *The Orangeburg Massacre.* One month after the massacre, Floyd bowed to Justice Department pressure and opened his bowling alley to blacks. John Stroman, who led the initial protest, was the first to bowl. Floyd reported that his business increased and white customers did not flee. One college bowling league is named Smith, Hammond, and Middleton for the three slain students.

Terrorism—Now and Then

For most Americans, September 11, 2001, was a tragic introduction to terrorism. For black America, terror is an old, familiar story.

Africans arrived in the United States traumatized and their enslavement for two centuries rested on "black codes" that got progressively worse. Dismemberment, murder, whippings, being sold, being bred—America's brand of slavery was the worst in the world.

Their new citizen status after the Civil War was soon crushed when the South, as Stetson Kennedy wrote, "reverted from open warfare to mass terrorism." President Grant told Congress of five thousand cases of terrorism, with Louisiana's "Negro hunts" among the worst.

But even after whites regained control, blacks endured another one hundred years of lynchings. Nearly five thousand Americans were lynched between 1882 and 1951, an average of more than one a week, according to the Yale–New Haven Teachers Institute. This included twelve hundred whites, most often punished for voting Republican or being perceived as friendly to blacks. Only rarely did blacks lynch whites—in one case, three Arkansas men died at the hands of a black mob after the men allegedly killed a black lawyer.

Since its formation in 1865, the white-robed Ku Klux Klan has been the leading symbol of American terrorism. The Klan and groups with similar methods—Regulators, night riders, Red Shirts, Rough Riders—visited upon southern blacks a reign of terror reminiscent of the Taliban in Afghanistan. They broke into homes and told whole families to run for their lives while they shot them. They cut off fingers and other body parts and took them home as souvenirs. They slit throats. They hanged people by their thumbs and whipped them until blood ran down like rain. They fired hundreds of bullets into hanging bodies. Pictures of lynchings became postcards.

However, most lynchings were committed by unorganized mobs, stoked with fear and hatred over issues ranging from voter registration to owning land to crime. Murder suspects were the most punished victims, although the rumor of a black man's rape of a white woman triggered some of the worst rage. In South Carolina, Lou Falkner Williams wrote, mobs castrated men in at least one case and poured tar in the vagina of a white woman found with two black men in her house. According to the Yale–New Haven Teachers Institute, rape or attempted rape was the alleged crime in 25 percent of lynchings.

Beyond lynchings, the first quarter of the twentieth century saw dozens of massacres, usually called "race riots," that were started when white mobs attacked black neighborhoods. During the Red Summer of 1919, when twenty-six cities erupted, one hundred blacks were killed, thousands were wounded, and many were left homeless. Mobs emptied and obliterated black neighborhoods in Rosewood and Ocoee, Florida. The 1921 Tulsa massacre, sparked by a charge that a black man attacked a white woman, killed ten whites and twenty-six blacks, although black gravediggers claim to have buried 150 black victims. Up to forty blocks of a thriving black community were destroyed, including more than 300 homes.

The modern civil rights era began with attempts to stop this mayhem. Ida B. Wells and W. E. B. Du Bois, the NAACP and the *Chicago Tribune* kept logs of lynchings, as did Monroe Work and Irene McCoy of the Tuskegee Institute. But antilynching laws always died in Congress under filibusters by southern senators who claimed the legislation infringed on states' rights. Southern governments sanctioned murder and intimidation, even during the course of the 1954–1968 civil rights movement, when at least forty-one people were killed. But terrorism was not only physical. White Citizens Councils closed businesses, foreclosed on homes, got people fired, and trumped up charges to force innocent blacks into prison. Lives were ruined.

Today, the occasional horrific race crime receives major news coverage. Church burnings and the dragging death of a man in Texas are signs of isolated terror. But black activists argue that police brutality, racial profiling, and a justice system that disproportionately punishes blacks are still terror by other names.

Rock Hill

McCRORY'S LUNCH COUNTER SITE *(135 East Main Street, Vantell's Variety)* White supremacy had been taken for granted so long in this former Klan county that the first black boycott in 1959 shocked everyone. The Local Committee for the Promotion of Human Rights, led by the Reverend C. A. Ivory, drove the segregated city bus line out of business.

On February 12, 1960, Friendship Junior College student Leroy Johnson led a sit-in of 100 students at McCrory's, a department store. Four days later, 350 people joined a new White Citizens Council to resist integration.

A year later, ten students were arrested after they sat down at McCrory's. But instead of posting bail, they opted for thirty days of hard labor. The "Rock Hill Jail-in" created a new strategy for the civil rights movement. Four SNCC workers including Diane Nash joined them in jail, where they sang and preached so loudly to the chain gangs that jailers complained. Two weeks later, Ivory called a mass meeting and began a downtown boycott. Police arrested seventy. Ivory called the "Rock Hill Seventy" "the finest looking group of criminals you've ever seen." At times the boycott crowds in Rock Hill reached one thousand protesters.

Three months later when the Freedom Riders bus arrived, John Lewis and Albert Bigelow were beaten by thugs at the Rock Hill bus station, the first violence of their trip.

St. Helena Island

Long before Lincoln decided that the Civil War was even about slavery, the problems and promises of emancipation were thrust upon South Carolina's sea islands. In November 1861, little more than six months after the start of the war, the U.S. Navy captured Port Royal Sound, including the antebellum village of Beaufort. Plantation owners fled, leaving ten thousand slaves behind with cotton in the fields and mansions full of furniture. While Lincoln avoided the issue, Treasury Secretary Salmon Chase launched the Port Royal Experiment, a joint military and missionary project that started schools, drafted slaves as soldiers, and wrestled with issues that later confounded the South during Reconstruction. For the newly freed men and women, the experiment introduced new relationships with white folks ranging from condescension to unheard-of respect and brotherly love. At their first Fourth of July celebration in 1862 a parade of blacks marched through St. Helena singing a stirring "Roll Jordan, Roll." The scene, according to historian Willie Lee Rose, had an "oceanic grandeur" to it.

Under Philadelphia teacher Laura Towne and her friend Ellen Murray, the Penn School began classes in a church until a prefabricated school arrived by boat. Both women stayed until their deaths in the 1900s. A monument to Towne was erected in the yard of the brick church.

During the experiment, blacks took control of Beaufort city hall, and bought nearly three-quarters of the surrounding land. As South Carolina fell back into the control of white supremacists in the 1890s, St. Helena remained a shining example of what could have been. Thousands of former slaves could read, write, and run their own farms and businesses. In 1903, according to Rose, literate males outnumbered white voters thirty-four hundred to nine hundred—but were no longer allowed to vote. By the 1920s, despite Jim Crow and because of their isolation, the sea islands had become self-governing. Citizens made decisions in town meetings, supported their churches, and escaped much of the harsh realities of Jim Crow segregation that swept over the rest of the state.

PENN SCHOOL HISTORIC DISTRICT AND MUSEUM *(Land's End Road, Frogmore; 843-838-2432; www.penncenter.com)* This pioneering school became a retreat and think tank for the Southern Christian Leadership Program in the late 1960s. Septima Clark ran a voter education program, and Martin Luther King and his strategists met to discuss economic issues and chart the civil rights movement into northern cities. King stayed at Gantt Cottage, a modest white clapboard with tin roof. At one point, the Nobel laureate sat in the cottage and told folksinger Joan Baez he "couldn't take the pressure anymore and he just wanted to go back . . . and preach in his little church, and he was tired of being a leader." He was assassinated a few months after his last visit to Penn.

The museum publishes a booklet on the retreats, and conducts a walking tour of buildings beneath spreading live-oak trees that includes sites from the Civil War and modern civil rights eras. The school continues as a community center focused on preserving Gullah culture, history, and the environment. A national historic site, Penn is a rustic respite from the frenetic "plantation" developments in nearby Beaufort–Hilton Head.

Summerton

SCOTT'S BRANCH SCHOOL SITE *(Fourth Street, one-quarter mile past intersection of U.S. 15 and U.S. 301. Briggs-DeLaine Foundation; 803-485-8164)* and **LIBERTY HILL AME CHURCH** *(Liberty Hill Road three miles outside town)* On the western edge of this inauspicious village stand two roadside markers to civil rights triumph and sacrifice. They honor a black minister and twenty parents who dared challenge South Carolina's apartheid policies of the 1940s. Though they paid a terrible personal price, their lawsuit, *Briggs v. Elliott,* integrated America's public schools and, ultimately, every other institution. *Briggs* was the first of five cases in what became known as *Brown v. Board of Education.* Harry Briggs, the first plaintiff in alphabetical order, worked at a gas station. R. W. Elliott was the white school board chairman, who, when asked for a school bus for black children, replied: "We ain't got no money to buy a bus for your nigger children," according to historian Richard Kluger.

The leader of the Summerton movement was the Reverend Joseph DeLaine, a preacher and teacher who lived across the street from the black Scott's Branch school where his wife taught. In 1947 he persuaded Briggs and other black parents, fourteen of them members of his Liberty Hill AME Church, to petition the school system for equal treatment for their children. Thurgood Marshall of the NAACP transformed the case into an assault on segregation itself. At the time more than eleven thousand school districts across the country had legally segregated schools.

It was at Scott's Branch that psychologist Kenneth Clark presented white and black dolls to several children between the ages of six and nine. Ten out of sixteen black children preferred white dolls. Eleven said the black dolls looked "bad." When asked to pick the doll most like themselves, seven picked the white doll, according to Richard Kluger in *Simple Justice*. The pioneering study helped persuade the Supreme Court that segregation was inherently unconstitutional.

While pursuing their case, the black plaintiffs lost their jobs and credit, their homes were firebombed, and they were jailed on trumped-up charges. DeLaine's church was burned to the ground and his wife was fired. When someone shot into his home, he fired back and was convicted of a felony. He became a fugitive until his death in 1974. His arrest warrant was dropped in 2000.

Though Summerton has new schools today, white parents have largely moved their children to private academies. The county erected a commemorative marker at the site of the Scott's Branch School, now a middle school. A state historical marker stands outside the Liberty Hill church. The Briggs-DeLaine Foundation plans markers at the Briggs home and other sites. Foundation members conduct personal tours with advance notice.

About the Gullahs

The Gullah or Geechee culture on the sea islands of South Carolina and Georgia developed from a unique combination of isolation and immigration. African slaves brought to these islands to cultivate rice also carried malaria and yellow fever, which they had some resistance to because of their sickle-cell blood. Their masters were susceptible however, and built homes away from the islands, leaving the slaves to themselves under a foreman's watch. With slaves arriving periodically over two hundred years, these communities developed a culture that was part English and part African with a unique creole language, rituals, and cosmology that included Islam.

The Gullahs' isolation continued after the Civil War when plantations were abandoned, according to anthropologist Joseph Opala. "The first bridges were not built until the 1920s and a decade later there were still adults on the islands who had never visited the U.S. mainland."

Opala and others have found songs, words, rituals, and habits used on both sides of the Atlantic. Recent emotional exchange trips with residents of African countries have been made.

Today, Gullah culture is kept alive in traditional basket weaving, cuisine, van tours, festivals, books, and TV shows. Pat Conroy's *The Water Is Wide* and the movie adaptation, *Conrack,* is based on his work as a teacher among Gullahs on Daufuskie Island.

Today's Gullahs are not preserved in time-forgotten villages. What remained of Gullah land holdings at Hilton Head and Daufuskie have largely been developed into plush resorts by corporations. Remaining Gullah families face the usual pressures of any indigenous people: lack of jobs, discriminatory economics, and children leaving the islands for better opportunities.

South Carolina Gullah tours are available in Charleston, Hilton Head, St. Helena, Beaufort, and Daufuskie, and in Georgia at Savannah and Sapelo Island. Penn Center at St. Helena is a center for Gullah cultural preservation. Look for brochures at local visitors centers.

Georgia

GEORGIA HAS COME SO FAR from its dark racist past that it is news when Coca-Cola or the Augusta Country Club is accused of discriminating. This is a state notorious for chain gangs, backwoods sheriffs, and lynchings that burned victims over fires—in the *twentieth* century. Yet out of this pyre grew the intellectual and spiritual core of the civil rights movement. More than any state in the South, Georgia has demonstrated that change is possible and that tolerance is preferable and profitable.

The makeover occurred rather recently, as Georgia history goes. But it was not sudden. Behind the state's most famous son, Martin Luther King Jr., stood a line of unbent aspiration stretched back to the shores of the Savannah River where the first slaves set foot. And though blacks here withstood the most brutal regimes, fraud and torture and trampling of their rights, Georgia led the South in creating strong black institutions.

Leadership seems to have made the difference, from clergymen who ran for office, to intellectuals like W. E. B. Du Bois who created a black think tank, to entrepreneurs who led the state away from tenant farming to create the South's greatest concentration of black wealth. Their churches, colleges, and businesses served as bulwarks behind which educated, self-assured, and independent men and women blossomed. By the 1940s they could not be ignored.

Alone among southern states, Georgia and its white leaders share the credit for this turnaround. Even before integration changed Atlanta's downtown, the city's mayor, William Hartsfield, adopted the slogan, "A city too busy to hate." Coca-Cola company chairman Robert Woodruff added, "Coca-Cola cannot operate from a city that is reviled."

As the civil rights movement rolled across the state, the old order collapsed before a moral weight and left men like Warren "Gator" Johnson, a hick sheriff, and Lester Maddox, the ax-handle governor, as mere caricatures from the movie *Deliverance*. With some vicious exceptions, Georgia desegregated peacefully.

Three years after Martin Luther King was laid to rest, Georgia elected as its governor Jimmy Carter, who declared at his inauguration, "the time for racial discrimination is over." Two years later, Atlanta elected as mayor Maynard Jackson, a black attorney whose vision transformed the "too busy" city into the business and affirmative action capital of the South. It's now almost expected that a black candidate will run the city.

Which is not to say that all is peachy in Georgia. Highly visible among the one million visitors to the boyhood neighborhood of Martin Luther King are many homeless people. Statewide, black income remains one-tenth that of whites, a reflection of economic inequality and the divide between Atlanta and the rest of the largely rural state. With 26 percent of the population, only 9 percent of elected positions are held by blacks.

And in 2003 a rural governor was elected largely on the pledge of allowing a vote to refly the Confederate flag over the state capitol—a reminder that prejudice can never disappear if it is periodically pulled out of the closet and exploited.

Georgia and Civil Rights

Georgia's founding legend is built on two yarns: that the state was settled by prisoners and that slavery was outlawed. Well, yes and no.

There were a dozen convicts among the hundreds of Englishmen who came to seek their fortune with James Oglethorpe in 1733. His initial rules did forbid drinking, lawyers, and slaves. But no one ejected the slaves that had been slipped across the Savannah River from South Carolina. And Oglethorpe, a former slave owner himself and an investor in the Royal African Company, which shipped slaves to America, soon created a leasing system that allowed Georgia planters to rent slaves for up to one hundred years. Though Oglethorpe's utopia envisioned Jefferson-like yeoman farmers, the job of clearing the hot, swampy wilderness into paying plantations was so onerous that farmers began abandoning Georgia for Charleston. It took only eighteen years for Georgia to join the slave states.

Busy with setting up rice and indigo plantations, Georgians were lukewarm about revolting from England and only belatedly joined the Continental Congress where they opposed any ban on slavery. By then, slaves amounted to 45 percent of the state's population and Georgia became one of two states, the other being South Carolina, in which blacks were not allowed to fight for independence for fear of insurrection. Historian John Hope Franklin estimates that during the Revolution, three-quarters of Georgia's fifteen thousand slaves ran away, many of them joining Indian tribes in western Georgia and Florida—there to form the Seminole band. Several thousand sailed away with the British.

Nothing changed Georgia—or the South—like the cotton gin, invented near Savannah by Eli Whitney. The number of slaves quadrupled in twenty years to 105,000. Forget *Gone With the Wind*—and southern gentility—

Eli Whitney marker outside of Savannah

Georgia developed a reputation in the trade as one of the rougher states on slaves. One law in the 1850s stopped masters from "cruelly and unnecessarily biting or tearing with dogs." Ibo Landing on St. Simon's Island is said to be haunted by Ibo tribesmen from Nigeria who, preferring death to slavery, walked into Dunbar Creek and drowned themselves.

Another casualty of Georgian greed were the Cherokee Indians, a "civilized" tribe with a written language, a newspaper, and a government. In 1830, in defiance of federal treaties,

Georgia and Congress expelled the Cherokees and put their land up for lottery. Historians directly link the "Trail of Tears" to Oklahoma with the thirst for slaves and large plantations.

At the same time, Georgia produced melancholy tales of marriages and relationships that challenged the racial order. In Macon, for example, a merchant and cotton broker, Solomon Humphries, known as "Free Sol," hired white clerks and convinced the legislature to free his wife and father. But when he had white guests in his house, he served them dinner in the role of waiter and did not sit down with them. When he died Macon declared a day of mourning. Just outside Macon, Michael Healy, an Irish immigrant who married slave Mary Eliza and raised ten children, was unable to free them. So Healy sent his children north where, despite discrimination in schools, one became the first black bishop of the Catholic Church and another the first black president of Georgetown University.

Miscegenation was so common in Georgia that in 1840 the legislature ruled that anyone with a black ancestor three generations back was considered "black," a ruling that remained on the books until 1927 when it was broadened to include any black blood. Historian Donald Grant called it a "skeleton-rattling" law, which allowed neighbors to take people to court to prove their ethnic purity. But Ellen Craft's features were such that she was able to dress like a white man and ride a train with her "servant" husband to Philadelphia where they were feted by abolitionists.

By the time of the Civil War, there were 465,000 blacks and 591,000 whites in Georgia. Forty percent of families owned slaves. Yet Georgia was divided about leaving the union. The vote for delegates to a secession convention was 44,000 to secede and 41,000 to wait and see. The chosen delegates were mostly slave owners who then voted 166 to 130 to join the Confederacy.

Georgia suffered most of its war losses in one attack, General William Sherman's siege of Atlanta and "march to the sea." His capture of Atlanta on September 2, 1864, ensured Lincoln's reelection. A week later, with fifty-five thousand troops trailed by nineteen thousand freed slaves, Sherman slashed and burned his way to Savannah, presenting the city to Lincoln as a Christmas gift.

Sherman didn't much like blacks but he was forced to deal with them forthrightly when Secretary of War Edwin Stanton called a conference of black leaders. Asked their opinion—a startling act in its own right—the ex-slaves requested land. Sherman issued Field Order Number Fifteen, which set aside a huge swath of the southeast coast from Florida's St. Johns River to Charleston. But their dreams vanished a month after Lincoln's assassination when President Johnson returned most of the land to the original owners.

Forced by Congress to allow black voting, the state elected thirty-two blacks to the legislature. But as soon as the state was readmitted to the Union, they were kicked out. A small monument to their loss stands behind the Capitol.

To ensure white supremacy's reign, groups such as the Regulators, the Black Horse Cavalry, and the Ku Klux Klan rode through small Georgian towns murdering, whipping, and mutilating blacks and white Republicans. After Democrats regained control in 1870, the *Atlanta Journal* bragged, "Georgia takes her place among the enlightened and progressive states which have announced that the white man is to rule." In the coming century, no state did more to defraud blacks of political power, and only Mississippi surpassed Georgia's 531 lynchings.

Of countless horror stories, one deserves telling because of its effect: In April 1899 Sam Hose, a black man accused of rape, was dismembered while still alive. His fingers, ears, and genitals were handed out as souvenirs before he was set afire. His body was then chopped into pieces and distributed. It turned out that Hose had killed a farmer in a quarrel and had not raped at all. Seeing one of Hose's knuckles on display in a store so upset W. E. B. Du Bois that he turned activist and later launched the NAACP.

A 1906 race massacre in Atlanta and the 1915 resurrection of the Klan on Stone Mountain outside Atlanta prompted thousands of blacks to leave Georgia. "In some counties the Negro is being driven out as though he were a wild beast," reported Governor Hugh Dorsey. In 1919 the AME church issued a report that one million blacks had left the South since 1915, more than one hundred thousand from Georgia alone.

The exodus prompted whites, who saw their cheap labor vanishing, to try to stop black families at train stations. Jackie Robinson's mother, Millie, was one of them but she slipped away from Cairo to California with Jackie in her arms. Georgia even outlawed distribution of the *Chicago Defender,* the leading black newspaper edited by Robert Abbott, a native of the state who regularly ran lynching stories from Georgia.

Those who stayed began building institutions—black colleges, businesses, and clubs—that trained leaders and pressured for equal rights. Farmers joined the Council of Laborers and a Colored Farmers' Alliance. Women formed the Georgia Federation of Colored Women's Clubs and the Georgia Equal Rights Association, which opened more than one hundred schools teaching reading, writing, arithmetic, and human rights. At one time Georgia, according to Donald Grant, had twenty-three black newspapers, more than any other state.

Churches, the oldest of black institutions, prayed and plotted for better days. The Reverend A. D. Williams, a slave preacher's son and head of Ebenezer Baptist Church, became the first chairman of the NAACP's Atlanta chapter. A few years later, Williams took an unschooled son-in-law named Mike King under his wing and into his pulpit. King later changed his name and that of his son, born in 1929, to Martin.

In the 1930s and 1940s Georgia's white leaders uttered rhetoric that, read today, is stunning. Governor Gene Talmadge once drew laughs by praising the state's infamous black-dominated chain gangs that "kept men out of doors in God's open country where they could enjoy the singing of the birds and the beautiful sunrises and sunsets." Meanwhile, U.S. Senator Richard Russell introduced a bill to appropriate $4 billion to ship southern blacks north and bring whites to Georgia.

In 1946 the Reverend Primus King of Columbus won a Supreme Court decision that opened the Democratic primary to black voters. It made a difference in urban elections with heavy black registration, but it could never overcome the influence of rural white Georgia in statewide elections. In 1954, six months after the Supreme Court integrated public schools, Marvin Griffin was elected governor on the motto, "Come hell or high water, races will not be mixed in Georgia's schools." Two years later, the legislature added a Confederate battle flag symbol to the state flag. As late as 1958, Governor Ernest Vandiver's campaign slogan was "No, Not One," meaning no blacks in white schools.

By then, however, the tide was rising against white supremacy. The Southern Christian Leadership Conference, founded in 1957 by the Reverend Martin Luther King Jr. and other ministers, began to build on the success of the Montgomery bus boycott. Atlanta's bus service was integrated in 1959. The following year, students began sit-ins. It took more than a year in both Savannah and Atlanta to break the will of downtown merchants. In 1961, under federal court order, the University of Georgia in Athens admitted its first two black students, Charlayne Hunter and Hamilton Holmes.

But when Student Nonviolent Coordinating Committee workers pushed into southwestern Georgia in 1962, they found another Mississippi. Webster County had not registered a single black. And in Terrell County, only fifty-one blacks were registered out of more than eight thousand residents. During SNCC's campaign, churches were burned and SNCC workers were jailed. In Americus, later home to Habitat for Humanity, officials used an 1871 anti-insurrection ordinance—with a death penalty—to jail SNCC activists.

Such trench warfare took place in virtually every Georgia county, much of it out of sight. Savannah's large and eventually successful civil rights movement did not receive national publicity because it was peaceful. Columbus integrated peacefully, although Augusta held out until two days before the 1962 Masters Golf Tournament, when lunch counters were integrated to avoid bad publicity during the televised event.

Yet one day after President Johnson signed the Civil Rights Act of 1964, Lester Maddox stood at the door of his Pickrick restaurant with an ax handle to keep blacks out. On the basis of that he was elected governor. After the federal Voting Rights Act was passed in 1965, black registration in Georgia tripled, but it still took nearly one hundred lawsuits to change at-large elections to district elections that would reflect black populations, according to *Quiet Revolution in the South.* Julian Bond, elected that year to the statehouse from Atlanta, was not allowed to swear in after he criticized the Vietnam War. It took a second election, another legislative rejection, and a Supreme Court decision to seat him.

The most dramatic change in racial politics happened in 1970 with the gubernatorial election of Jimmy Carter, the peanut farmer and state senator who ran on a ticket with Maddox as lieutenant governor, and who sidled up to pro-segregationists until the day after balloting. He appointed dozens of blacks, just as he would later when he became president in 1976. The election of former King aide Andrew Young to Congress in 1972 in a majority-white district bucked the historic odds. The following year, Maynard Jackson became Atlanta's first black mayor. At the urging of Coretta King, President Carter in 1980 created the Martin Luther King Jr. National Historic Site.

For all of Atlanta's progress, however, Georgia continued to demonstrate that race as an issue was never far away. As late as 1987, blacks were told to leave lily-white Forsyth County, an Atlanta suburb. When SCLC's Hosea Williams led marchers into the town of Cumming they were met and attacked by hundreds of Klansmen. They returned with twenty-two thousand marchers and two thousand National Guardsmen. Integration could also still make headlines in 1994 when the *Savannah Morning News* recorded, BLACK DOCTOR ADMITTED TO YACHT CLUB.

And in 2002, seventeen years after the legislature approved a Martin Luther King holiday and eliminated its annual Jefferson Davis day, and one year after Governor Roy Barnes got rid of the Confederate battle emblem on the state flag, a rural politician named Sonny Perdue defeated incumbent Barnes with a pledge to hold a referendum on the rebel flag.

A Georgia Civil Rights Tour

Georgia has three distinct civil rights destinations: urban Atlanta, rural Albany, and Savannah. All three have good museums that describe their civil rights story.

Savannah is a tourist town under any circumstances, and the addition of black heritage tours, a civil rights museum, and visits to nearby Midway or Sapelo Island, and nearby St. Helena Island, South Carolina, make it a destination for human rights study.

Albany, pronounced All-BIN-y and surrounded by rural Georgia, endured one of the civil rights movement's toughest battles. The story is told in a local museum and commemorative park.

Atlanta is black America's favorite tourist destination, in no small part because of the Martin Luther King Jr. National Historic Site. Dr. King's boyhood home, his tomb, the King family center, Ebenezer Baptist Church, and the National Park Service's visitors center require a full day or more.

City by City

Albany

In 1961 the largest city in southwest Georgia was surrounded by peanuts, pecans, and the past. Terrorized by so many acts of brutality, blacks couldn't even think of asking for rights being won elsewhere in the South. As one rural sheriff famously told the *New York Times*: "We want our colored people to go on living like they have for the last hundred years."

Into this darkness walked three young men from the Student Nonviolent Coordinating Committee—Charles Sherrod, Charles Jones, and Cordell Reagon—to organize demonstrations and register voters. At first, residents of the "Harlem" neighborhood crossed the street to avoid them. But starting with knots of young people on basketball courts, they gathered groups at the Shiloh Baptist Church for singing and antisegregation "sermons." On November 1, 1961, the day that federal interstate rules integrated bus terminals, they led a demonstration to test the Albany bus station. Police chief Laurie Pritchett, vowing that no "nigger organization" was going to "take over this town with mass demonstrations," began arresting and distributing demonstrators to jails in surrounding rural counties. By mid-December, seven hundred had been arrested, the first mass arrests in the civil rights movement.

Attracted by the standoff, Dr. Martin Luther King Jr. spoke at Shiloh on December 15, was arrested the following day, and was mysteriously bailed out under "concessions" that turned out to be lies. King's preferential treatment fractured the Albany Movement and, despite two more arrests, he never regained moral leadership there. Because of this, the Albany Movement has gone unheralded for the extraordinary gains ultimately made and for pioneering efforts that taught organizing lessons to subsequent civil rights campaigns such as Birmingham and Selma.

Albany's outreach into neighboring counties was shadowed by vicious white supremacists such as Sheriff "Gator" Johnson in "Bad" Baker County who shot prisoner Charlie Ware three times in the neck as he sat handcuffed in the seat next to him, and Dougherty County Sheriff "Cull" Campbell who beat black attorney C. B. King bloody when he arrived to represent a prisoner. When a pregnant Marion King, wife of Albany Movement leader Slater King, took food to prisoners in the Mitchell County jail, she was knocked down and later miscarried.

In one of the most charged scenes in Georgia civil rights, the sheriff of "Terrible" Terrell County, Zeke Mathews, led fifteen white deputies into tiny, remote Mount Olive Church during a voter registration meeting coordinated by Sherrod on July 25, 1962. Mathews interrupted the singing of "Jacob's Ladder" to take names and announce that whites were "fed up with this registering business." Blacks began humming "We Shall Overcome." Claude Sitton described in the next day's *New York Times* how lawmen stalked around the pews rubbing their guns and whacking flashlights in their palms and barking to members of the cowering group, "I know you." The church was later firebombed, along with several other black churches. Baseball great Jackie Robinson visited the church ruins and raised money for the movement. After several more church burnings in Georgia, the Justice Department moved in, convicted white men for arson, and filed suits to stop voter harassment.

Long after King and the *New York Times* left Albany, Sherrod and local folks persevered, registering voters while enduring arson, shootings, and countless indignities. Official segregation ended in 1963 and schools began to integrate in 1964. Thirty years later, Albany had a black police chief, and every elected board was controlled by black members. Sherrod, the only one of the three original SNCC workers to settle down in town, served on the city council between 1976 and 1990. In surrounding areas, Baker and Terrell Counties had black sheriffs in 2003.

One of the most telling changes in Albany was the logo on police cars—altered to display something like SNCC's clasping black and white hands. The courthouse was named for C. B. King, and the city created a small civil rights district that includes a memorial park and the two key churches, one of which was transformed into a museum.

Another enduring legacy was the Freedom Singers, a group that grew out of the musical talents of SNCC members and local students, who subsequently entertained and inspired the movement, and made singing synonymous with civil rights. Activist Cordell Reagon married student Bernice Johnson, and Ms. Reagon went on to found the women's group Sweet Honey in the Rock and become the leading musicologist of the era.

ALBANY CIVIL RIGHTS MOVEMENT MUSEUM AT OLD MT. ZION CHURCH (*Jefferson and Whitney Streets; 229-432-1698; www. albanycivilrights.org*)   Set up in a sanctuary that once rocked with mass meetings and song, Albany's museum provides a good representation of events that transformed southwestern Georgia. Simply told with photographs, newspaper clips, and signage, the story of the Albany Movement is one of perseverance over years. Most events took place outside the glare of national publicity, and success occurred in spite of the early failure of Dr. Martin Luther King Jr. to solidify the movement.

The displays begin with quotes from the chamber of commerce, which bragged in 1962 that in Albany, "tolerance is an outstanding attitude" because the city contained two Catholic churches and a Jewish synagogue.

The Freedom Singers entertain once a month.

SHILOH BAPTIST CHURCH (*325 Whitney Avenue at Jefferson*) Without the sign outside that reads "The Albany Civil Rights movement started here" and the footprints in the concrete sidewalk, this simple wood sanctuary would not stand out from the thousands of black churches in the South. The first mass meetings led by SNCC workers convinced timid Albany blacks to challenge Jim Crow segregation. They walked out of the church toward Jackson Street and into lines of waiting police. One thousand were arrested and many were brutalized.

Although his efforts in Albany were divisive and personally unsuccessful, Dr. Martin Luther King Jr. is remembered for his first, electric

Shiloh Baptist Church in Albany

appearance in this church on December 15, 1961. Hours before his arrival, pews were filled at Shiloh and Mt. Zion across the street, and people hung out the windows to watch for him. Both churches rocked with song from the newly organized Freedom Singers. Taylor Branch recounted in *Parting the Waters*, "As . . . King was sighted on his way down to the pulpit, the sound exploded into cascades of rapture . . . FREE-DOM, FREE-DOM . . . they thought the Lord Himself had arrived . . ."

CHARLES SHERROD CIVIL RIGHTS PARK *(Jackson and Highland Streets)* A black granite memorial is inscribed with highlights of the Albany story, important national civil rights events, and a quotation from Dr. Martin Luther King Jr. Sherrod was a young SNCC worker who arrived in a terrorized city in 1961 and stayed for the rest of his life, winning incremental equal rights for black people in southwest Georgia and a seat on the city council for himself. In 1968 he and several colleagues purchased a five-thousand-acre plantation to create New Communities, envisioned as a utopian farm for five hundred families. The plan collapsed in 1985 when the federal government foreclosed. Sherrod was honored with a tribute gathering in 2000.

Atlanta

If the civil rights movement can be thought of as a body of work, its central nervous system would have to be black Atlanta. The nascent seeds that became the NAACP sprouted here and much of the leadership of subsequent campaigns was based in Atlanta. Nelson Mandela in a 1990 visit called Atlanta the center for civil rights in America.

Atlanta became a city during the Civil War, doubling in size when coastal planters fled inland with their slaves. Allegorized in *Gone With the Wind*, the city was destroyed by Sherman, and a regenerated Atlanta became home to freed blacks, who, through education, ambition, and activism, created a lively black capital. Thirty thousand blacks settled around Auburn Avenue, nicknamed "Sweet Auburn," which ran due east from the center of the city. Two thousand black-owned businesses, including a bank and eighty-three barber shops, arose here. Alonzo Herndon, born a slave, turned a barber shop empire into the Atlanta Life Insurance Company,

headquarted on Auburn. He later joined a natty intellectual at Atlanta University, W. E. B. Du Bois, to start the NAACP.

Atlanta's segregation was as bad as any in the South—neighborhoods separated by law, only three of the twenty-four parks open to blacks, and blacks dug up to be reburied in "black" cemeteries—according to historian Donald Grant. In September 1906 rumors of widespread rapes of white women by black men prompted ten thousand whites to burn and loot black neighborhoods, including Sweet Auburn. Twenty-five blacks and one white were killed, two hundred were injured, and hundreds were arrested. Scavengers hacked off fingers and toes from bodies as souvenirs. When it was over, a mayor's committee could find no one who had been raped, but an estimated one thousand blacks fled Atlanta. Margaret Mitchell, the author of *Gone With the Wind,* remembered as a child hiding under her bed from "Negro mobs." Thirty-three years later, at the Atlanta premiere of *Gone*

With the Wind, Hattie McDaniel, who played the mammy, was not allowed to attend. She won an Oscar for the role.

Into this world on January 15, 1929, was born Michael Luther King Jr., renamed Martin when he was six, the son of the preacher at Ebenezer Baptist Church. Except for his Ph.D. years at Boston College and six years in Montgomery, Alabama, King lived in Atlanta all his short life. Largely because of him, the Southern Christian Leadership Conference, the Student Nonviolent Coordinating Committee, and other civil rights organizations based their operations here.

In the 1950s Atlanta adopted the slogan "The city too busy to hate" even as it took its sweet time to treat its citizens equally. A federal lawsuit integrated schools beginning in 1959. In March 1960 Morehouse College students Julian Bond and Lonnie King organized sit-ins at segregated lunchrooms and at the state capitol. Dr. King joined them and was arrested at the Magnolia Room of Rich's Department store. A famous call by presidential candidate John Kennedy to King's wife, Coretta, helped Kennedy win the White House with black votes.

In 1962 the Peachtree Manor Hotel opened its doors to integrated major league baseball teams, and singer Harry Belafonte received the key to the city. His integrated band was allowed to sleep in a downtown hotel but could not eat at the restaurant. It was another local motel called Heart of Atlanta whose unsuccessful Supreme Court challenge of the 1964 Civil Rights Act assured open public accommodations everywhere.

In sports, meanwhile, Hank Aaron of the Atlanta Braves broke Babe Ruth's home-run record, and despite death threats went on to hit 755 home runs. An Aaron statue sits outside Turner Field, named for owner Ted Turner who, in a historic act of affirmative action, named Bill Lucas the first black general manager in major league baseball. Turner Field was built for the 1996 Olympics, a plum that rightly can be attributed to former King aide Andrew Young, who in 1972 became Georgia's first black congressman since Reconstruction and later U.N. ambassador.

Atlanta has elected three black mayors since Maynard Jackson in 1973. John Lewis, a former SNCC leader, has represented the Atlanta area in Congress since 1986.

Atlanta's civil rights story, told in once-segregated neighborhoods, is a major tourist draw. The Martin Luther King Jr. National Historic Site is busy year-round, but especially during February, Black History Month.

Hank Aaron statue at Atlanta's Turner Field

MARTIN LUTHER KING JR. NATIONAL HISTORIC SITE *(450 Auburn Avenue NE; 404-331-5190 [Visitors Center]; 404-331-6922 [Visitor information recording]; www.nps.gov/malu; www.thekingcenter.org)* This streetscape preserves both the story of Dr. Martin Luther King Jr. and his hometown Sweet Auburn neighborhood. King was born here and lived here until his assassination in 1968. Between the tribute sites by the National Park Service and the King family, King's legacy as the leader of the modern civil rights movement is thoroughly described. The Park Service focuses on the movement in a well-done multimedia visitors center that could take a day to absorb. The King family center across the street is the site of King's tomb and a museum of personal effects, including his Nobel Peace Prize, the key to the Lorraine motel room in Memphis where he died, and other artifacts. Less impressive are rooms devoted to King's hero, Gandhi, and to Rosa Parks, the Montgomery woman responsible for the bus boycott that first made King famous.

King's life and death have come to symbolize the civil rights movement, though King himself resisted the hero worship that often

151

Dr. Martin Luther King Jr.'s tomb in Atlanta

surrounded him. Many considered him a modern-day Moses, and his martyrdom, at age thirty-nine, and the subsequent honor of a national holiday on his birthday have made him the movement's star. But King called himself a drum major, not the leader, of a huge army of black Americans who rose up in the 1950s and 1960s to demand their constitutional rights.

Briefly told, King went to Morehouse College, received a Ph.D. in theology from Boston College, and won his first pastor's job in 1954 in Montgomery. Settling in with wife, Coretta, and the first of four children, King was elected by fellow pastors to lead a yearlong bus boycott. Its success made him *Time* magazine's Man of the Year and a national figure. In 1960 he moved back to Atlanta as head of a new organization, the Southern Christian Leadership Conference, which, with deputies like Ralph Abernathy, took on desegregation in the South's most racist cities. Campaigns in Albany, Georgia, and St. Augustine, Florida, failed to win decisive victories. But those in Birmingham and Selma, Alabama, led to federal civil rights laws that ended segregation and eliminated barriers to voting. In the late 1960s King began attacking economic racism and the Vietnam War. In Memphis in 1968, while supporting a garbage collector's strike, he was assassinated. His body, carried in a mule-drawn wagon that was symbolic of poverty and humbleness, traveled through the heart of Atlanta. In his absence, the movement split over personal rivalries and black power tactics, and no one ever dominated civil rights issues as King had.

His many speeches, preserved on audiotape and CDs, remain wonders of eloquence, inspiration, and prophecy. His 1963 "I Have a Dream" speech at the Lincoln Memorial in Washington is probably his most famous. King was the undisputed oracle of the nonviolent campaign that broke the back of southern segregation and legal white supremacy.

2 | **AUBURN AVENUE**   Nicknamed "Sweet Auburn" for its nurturing embrace of African Americans during the twentieth century, Auburn Avenue has seen better days. The King site is a tourist destination sandwiched by poverty and gentrification.

Dr. King's modest boyhood home (*501 Auburn Avenue*) is open for free tours. Park rangers describe a mischievous boy growing up in a middle-class home presided over by an activist father. Period furniture includes King's childhood crib.

The entire length of Auburn is labeled with historic signs to the glory days during segregation, and a walk to the center of Atlanta is an easy, revealing look at change after integration. The black newspaper, *Atlanta Daily World,* is still in business at the corner of Piedmont Avenue. But restaurants have disappeared and the Southern Christian Leadership Conference has moved off the street.

3 | **EBENEZER BAPTIST CHURCH** (*407 Auburn Avenue;* 404-688-7263)   Activism fairly seeped from the bricks of this church built at the height of Atlanta's Jim Crow era. The Reverend Adam Daniel Williams was a founding member of the NAACP. When Williams died in 1931, his son-in-law, Martin Luther King Sr., took over and served until 1977. King encouraged voter registration throughout his career and helped public school teachers win equal pay. He also attacked city hall segregation by himself, integrating both elevators and water fountains.

King Senior outlived his son by sixteen years and his wife Alberta by ten. He retired from preaching shortly after she was murdered by a mentally disturbed black man while she sang the Lord's Prayer during a service. The church's congregation has built a new sanctuary across the street, and the old church is open to the public except on Sunday morning.

4 | **MOREHOUSE COLLEGE, KING STATUE, AND "I HAVE A DREAM" SPEECH IN BRONZE** (*Westview Street, at Morehouse College and Atlanta-Clark University Center*) Ed Dwight's giant sculpture of King, backed by King's most famous speech, forged in bronze on a brick wall, marks the center of King's alma mater and what has been called the Cambridge of black America. This consortium of black colleges has turned out the best and brightest, including many civil rights leaders. Atlanta began modestly as a missionary elementary school in 1869, gradually adding grades as students required. Its first college graduates left in 1876. The school was eventually joined by Clark, Gammon Technological, Morris Brown College, Spelman, and Morehouse College.

The president of Atlanta, John Hope, was called the "maker of college presidents" for his students who later headed many major black schools. Atlanta University also became a black think tank under W. E. B. Du Bois, who in 1896 began hosting an annual Conference on Negro Problems that in its research and histories attacked the prevailing white supremacist view of people of color. Du Bois taught at Atlanta University between 1897 and 1910, and again in the 1930s. A scholar by nature and training, he encouraged the top 10 percent of educated blacks, the "talented tenth," as intellectual leaders. While in Atlanta, Du Bois wrote *The Souls of Black Folk,* the first major work detailing the reality of black life in the South.

Benjamin Mays, the president of Morehouse, grew up watching his father and other blacks bow and scrape to white mobs in South Carolina. After gaining a doctorate in theology from the University of Chicago, he set out to use the black church to break inequality. The scholars Mays brought to Morehouse would later teach a young Martin Luther King Jr. the tactics of nonviolence as espoused by Mahatma Gandhi. Other notable Morehouse graduates include Atlanta's first black mayor, Maynard Jackson, and movie director Spike Lee.

Spelman graduates include Alice Walker, a daughter of sharecroppers from Eatonton, Georgia, whose novel *The Color Purple* was awarded the Pulitzer Prize.

Monroe

MOORE'S FORD (*roadside marker on U.S. 78, six miles east of Monroe; 706-769-0988 [Moore's Ford Memorial Committee]; www.mooresford.org*) On July 25, 1946, a black GI, his wife, and a related couple were lynched at a fording point on the Apalachee River by a gang of white men. News of their murder reached the White House, prompted an unprecedented FBI investigation, and ultimately led to the integration of the U.S. military by President Truman. But the men responsible were never caught.

The story began with a pitchfork and knife fight between sharecropper Roger Malcolm and his white boss at a nearby farm. Malcolm wounded the man and was thrown in jail. His pregnant wife,

Signpost outside of Monroe

NON SIBI SED ALIIS

GEORGIA HISTORICAL SOCIETY

Moore's Ford Lynching

2.4 miles east, at Moore's Ford Bridge on the Apalachee River, four African-Americans - George and May Murray Dorsey and Roger and Dorothy Dorsey Malcom (reportedly 7 months pregnant) - were brutally beaten and shot by an unmasked mob on the afternoon of July 25, 1946. The lynching followed an argument between Roger Malcom and a local white farmer. These unsolved murders played a crucial role in both President Truman's commitment to civil rights legislation and the ensuing modern civil rights movement. In 1998, a biracial memorial service honoring the victims was held at Moore's Ford Bridge.
Erected by The Georgia Historical Society and the Moore's Ford Memorial Committee, Inc.

1995

147-1

Dorothy, her brother George Dorsey, and Dorsey's wife, May, bailed Malcolm out. Dorsey had just returned from World War II service in the Pacific. According to an investigation by NAACP field investigator John LeFlore, the two couples were taken by the farm foreman to a river bottom where a gang of twelve to fifteen white men waited. The couples were beaten and shot hundreds of times.

Their friends didn't dare come to the funeral, but the case—and others like it involving assaults on black GIs—so upset President Truman that he became a civil rights advocate. He sent twenty-five FBI agents to join the efforts of seventy-five agents of the Georgia Bureau of Investigation who came up empty handed. When Truman sent to Congress several civil rights bills they were killed by southern senators. Acting as commander in chief, he ordered the military integrated in 1948. By 1952, every branch had integrated and the military became the leading U.S. institution in race relations.

A ten-year-old witness to the Moore's Ford shooting, Clinton Adams, came out of hiding as an adult in 1991 to tell what had happened. In 1998 a biracial committee revisited the lynching site, held a service at the crossing—now a bridge—and erected a roadside marker. They also found three of the four graves, and restored the cemeteries with new monuments. Dorsey was honored in a 1999 Memorial Day service. Ongoing reconciliation efforts include a scholarship fund to promote racial justice.

Sapelo Island
(Darien Visitor Center: 912-437-3224; Cornelia Bailey: 912-485-2206; www.sapelonerr.org)
Reachable only by boat, Sapelo is one of the few Atlantic sea barrier islands that have not succumbed to modern "plantation" and golf-course development. Now a state preserve with a resident Gullah community, it is in many ways a living laboratory for cultural preservation amid greed, racism, and inevitable change.

Set up as a sugar and cotton plantation in 1802 but abandoned during the Civil War, the island was repopulated by ex-slaves who, in isolation, created several communities of a unique African-English culture and language called Gullah or Geechee. Local residents and scholars have compared Sapelo traditions with those in Sierra Leone, Africa.

Large portions of the island remained in the hands of wealthy owners, however. Through attrition, land swaps, and pressure from the tobacco magnate R. J. Reynolds, who owned a huge tract, the Gullah community shrank to a group of seventy in Hog Hammock. The remaining families have fought to preserve culture and land rights, find jobs, and maintain privacy amid an uneasy relationship with the state and thousands of annual visitors. Some tourists arrive hoping to "see the natives" still speaking Geechee, unaware that Gullah families have evolved with the times. Children now head to school on the ferry each morning and most leave permanently for jobs.

Those who have enough time for a two- or three-day visit to Sapelo can combine nature walks with conversations with people like Cornelia Bailey, a writer, activist, and grandmother who owns Wallow's Lodge. A local "eco-tour" shows off wildlife as well as historic structures such as the first African Baptist church established the year after the Civil War.

Savannah

Made famous by John Berendt's modern tale of murder and mojo, *Midnight in the Garden of Good and Evil,* Savannah is a city with an equally compelling story to tell about its struggle for human rights. The black community has been unusually strong-willed since slaves first stepped foot on the south bank of the Savannah River.

As a seaport and Georgia's founding city, Savannah became an early stewpot of newly arrived Africans, free artisans, ministers, mariners, and entrepreneurs. Even before slavery was allowed by the state, slaves were sold openly on the waterfront. As late as 1858, fifty years after being outlawed by the United States, kidnapped Africans were unloaded by pirates. The thirst for slaves was driven in large part by a Yankee invention on an area plantation—the cotton gin—that made Savannah a leading cotton port.

But blacks conspired when they could, often in the sanctuary of church. When General William Tecumseh Sherman took control in December 1864, he met with a group of black leaders, most of them ministers, who persuaded him that freed slaves wanted land. His war order handing over the entire South Carolina and Georgia coastline in forty-acre plots to ex-slaves would have remade the South had it not been reversed by President Andrew Johnson after Lincoln's death.

During the Jim Crow era white Savannah invented extraordinary measures to separate themselves, including the use of "black" and "white" bibles

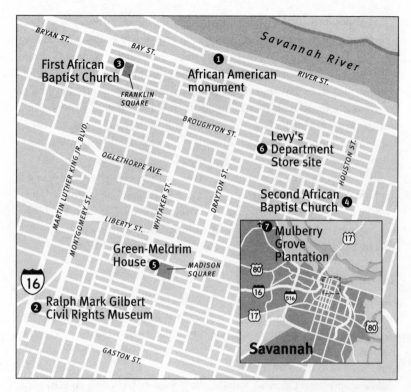

to swear in witnesses in court. Cemeteries were segregated by ordinance in 1888.

Beginning in 1960 with lunch counter sit-ins and a yearlong boycott of the leading department store, black activists transformed Savannah. There were beatings, use of tear gas, and burnings of Sears and Firestone stores before a business group called the Committee of 100, led by businessman Mills Lane, steered the city toward integration. Savannah's civil rights museum was one of the first in the country to tell a local story.

Savannah has a state-of-the-art **visitors center** (*301 Martin Luther King Jr. Boulevard; 877-SAVANNAH*) with informed clerks, thousands of brochures, and a parking lot full of tour operators, including Johnny Brown and others who specialize in black history. Not all the stories they tell are true, but part of Savannah's attraction seems to be its moss-hung mixture of myth, fact, and the occult.

1 | **AFRICAN AMERICAN MONUMENT** *(Rousakis Plaza/River Street, between the Savannah River and City Hall)* Standing above broken chains of slavery, a bronze African American family looks out over the Savannah River in this monument to struggle, survival, and civil rights. In a city famous for forty-two statues, this one was the first to honor African Americans. Its central location places it between city hall, where Georgia founder James Oglethorpe first camped, and the Savannah River, which transported tens of thousands of slaves to the thirteenth colony.

The monument's dedication in July 2002 ended a ten-year battle that reflected the many facets of race in America. Professor Abigail Jordan, who proposed the memorial in 1992, withstood repeated delays and heated debates over its central location, its meaning, the hiring of white sculptor Dorothy Spradley, and even the inscription, which poet Maya Angelou had to modify to please the city council. A few months before the dedication, she added a last optimistic line:

African American monument in Savannah

"We were stolen, sold and bought together from the African continent. We got on the slave ships together. We lay back to belly in the holds of the slave ships in each others excrement and urine together, sometimes died together, and our lifeless bodies thrown overboard together. Today, we are standing up together, with faith and even some joy."

2 | **RALPH MARK GILBERT CIVIL RIGHTS MUSEUM** *(460 Martin Luther King Jr. Boulevard; 912-231-8900; www.savannahcivil rightsmuseum.com)* This well-researched and presented museum preserves a civil rights chapter that escaped the attention of national media. With only isolated incidents of violence, black

Savannah integrated public facilities and the workforce between 1960 and 1963.

Sit-ins at downtown lunch counters began in March 1960. The fifteen-month boycott of Levy's ended in June 1961. The following year, buses were integrated, and schools began to integrate in 1963. In between, Tybee Island beach, golf courses, and playgrounds were targeted and integrated. A museum map shows the "battleground": nineteen demonstration sites and thirty-two segregated facilities.

The movement was led by three men: Ralph Gilbert, W. W. Law, and Hosea Williams. Gilbert arrived in 1942 to pastor First African Baptist. He resurrected the local NAACP chapter and boosted its membership of under two hundred to three thousand. Upon his death in 1956, W. W. Law took over the chapter and led it through the 1960s. His assistant, pugnacious Hosea Williams, had been a government chemist, who went on to join Dr. Martin Luther King Jr. and set a protest record of one hundred arrests. Williams was in the front lines at the "Bloody Sunday" protest in Selma, Alabama.

In Savannah, sporadic violence occurred years later. James Floyd of the NAACP was killed in his Savannah office in 1970, and NAACP attorney Robert Robinson was killed by a mail bomb in December 1989. Williams died in 2000. Law died in 2002, the day after the dedication of the riverside slave memorial.

3 | **First African Baptist Church** (*Franklin Square*)   If not the country's oldest, this congregation, established in 1773, is among the pioneer black churches in the United States. This structure was built at night by slaves when they were released from day jobs. Founding pastor George Liele was succeeded by Andrew Bryan, who took in badly abused slaves and expanded the church. Its thirteenth pastor, between 1942 and 1956, was Ralph Gilbert, who revived the NAACP and set the stage for the civil rights movement. He persuaded Savannah to hire black police in 1947. During the two-year boycott and sit-in movement of 1960–1961, hundreds of people filled the sanctuary and balcony, many hanging out the windows.

Tour guides repeat tales of an Underground Railroad depot beneath the church, and Arabic-like scratchings by Africans during slavery, both stories disputed by longtime civil rights historian W. W. Law.

Black Institutions Led the Way

The civil rights movement grew from a garden with deep roots—black institutions that stretched back to slavery. Colleges, businesses, and especially churches gave birth to philosophy and strategy, as well as leaders and foot soldiers that attacked and defeated segregation. Most civil rights "hot spots" occurred in cities with strong black churches and schools.

The irony, of course, is that these institutions were created because of segregation, and grew to prominence in its shadow. Slavery and Jim Crow had the unintended consequence of creating a distinct African American culture. Out of isolation and segregation, George Rawick summarized from oral histories, "came black pride, black identity, black culture, the black community and black rebellion in America."

What counted during the movement years was economic independence from the white-controlled system. Black funeral homes and barber shops became sanctuaries rarely invaded by "the man." Many leaders emerged from the ranks of garage owners, pharmacists, farmers, federal postal workers, railroad porters, and teachers.

The first black college, Howard University, taught the lawyers who later won the 1954 Supreme Court case integrating public schools. Students from many black colleges, including North Carolina A&T, Florida A&M, Fisk University, Tougaloo, and Morehouse, led the sit-in movement in the 1960s.

But nothing matched the role of churches, America's first black institution. During segregation, hundreds of churches became the anchors of vibrant black communities. "All roads converged at the Negro church," Taylor Branch wrote. "It served not only as a place of worship but also as a bulletin board . . . a credit union . . . and even a kind of people's court."

Because preachers could read, write, and talk on their feet, they were influential both inside and outside of church. During Reconstruction, "every AME preacher in Georgia was said to be actively engaged in Republican organizing," according to Eric Foner. "Political materials were read aloud at churches, societies, leagues, clubs, balls, picnics and all other gatherings."

After a century of Jim Crow segregation, black churches became the staging arenas for the final assault on inequality. Mass meetings, fiery calls to action, strategy sessions, and prayer fueled the legions who took to the streets and lunch counters of the South. They created the moral climate, nurtured assemblies with prayer and fried chicken, and provided thousands of foot soldiers for the battleground in a movement that finally forced the nation to deliver its founding promise.

4 | **Second African Baptist Church** (*127 Houston Street*)   The minister of this church was one of twenty black leaders who met with General Sherman in January 1865 and asked for land for freed slaves. Sherman's war order, providing forty acres for every slave family, was announced at a mass meeting here, but his promise was not kept. Nearly a century later, according to historian Taylor Branch, Martin Luther King Jr. delivered the New Year's emancipation speech before this congregation on the eve of John Kennedy's presidential inauguration. King, who reused favorite phrases and stories in his many speeches, is said to have delivered a version of his "I Have a Dream" speech.

5 | **Green-Meldrim House** (*Madison Square; 912-233-3845*)   At the end of his march to the sea, General Sherman arrived in Savannah with thousands of freed slaves in his wake. At his headquarters here on January 12, 1865, Sherman and Secretary of War Stanton met twenty black leaders and asked their advice in dealing with the freed men and women. It was land they most desired. Four days later, Sherman issued Special Field Order Number Fifteen, which set aside the sea islands and a thirty-mile swath of coastline from Charleston to Florida for slave settlements of up to forty acres each. Thus was born the concept of "forty acres and a mule," adopted by the Freedman's Bureau during Reconstruction. By the end of the war, forty thousand freedmen had new farms. Sherman later said he didn't mean land ownership, and the coastal program was canceled after only a fraction of land was deeded to blacks. As writer Lerone Bennett Jr. put it, "Without the means to realize or validate their freedom, most freedmen were driven back to the plantations by hunger and violence."

The mansion is open for tours by docents who share old gossip about the house and its belongings. Charming as they appear, the docents don't seem as well briefed about the extraordinary meeting where, perhaps for the first time, blacks influenced the government. It was an early milestone along a long road to freedom.

6 | **Levy's department store site** (*Broughton Street*)   On March 16, 1960, three young adults—Sage Brown, Sarah Townsend, and

George Shinhoster—sat down at the Levy's department store lunch counter and asked to be served. Their action launched Savannah's civil rights movement, which finally brought Levy's—and every other segregated facility—to its knees.

Shinhoster, a dishwasher at the segregated Anton's Restaurant, had been asked by his boss what he wanted to do when he grew up, and replied: "I used to think that I wanted to be able to come in this restaurant and eat." Still in high school, he picketed by day and worked at night, until his boss fired him for his activism.

Sage Brown also integrated Savannah's high school, but didn't dare use the bathroom for fear of being beaten behind closed doors. When President Kennedy was assassinated, a high school student shouted at her: "Who's going to protect you now that your nigger president is dead?"

Savannah's NAACP organized a fifteen-month shopping boycott of Levy's, demanding integrated service, jobs, and courtesy titles. Levy's charge cards were turned in by the hundreds and dropped at the door. At Easter, rather than buying the traditional new dress, bonnet, or suit, people brought hand-me-downs to exchange at mass meetings, held every Sunday at 4 P.M. If blacks were caught shopping at the store their names were read aloud at the meetings. The store agreed to integrate in June 1961. Years later, civil rights leader Hosea Williams called it "the most successful boycott in all of America."

The old Levy's store is now the library for the Savannah College of Art and Design.

7 | **MULBERRY GROVE PLANTATION** (*highway markers on Georgia Route 21 west of city; www.mulberrygrove.org*) One of the most important, but unappreciated moments in civil rights history occurred in 1793 when a tinkering tutor named Eli Whitney invented the cotton gin at Mulberry Grove, a plantation along the Savannah River. The gin remade the South into a cotton empire, entrenching slavery for sixty more years.

The plantation upstream from Savannah had been granted to a Revolutionary general, Nathanael Greene of Rhode Island, who had led the southern campaign. His original intent had been silk production, with silkworms dining on mulberry leaves, but rice and indigo became the main crops, followed by cotton.

Greene had married a woman with four children who needed a tutor. When Greene died of heat stroke, the tutor, Phineas Miller, became the foreman, then later Mrs. Greene's husband. As a replacement teacher, she hired a young Yale graduate whom she had met on a boat, Eli Whitney.

Whitney heard planters complain about the difficult task of separating sticky seeds from cotton bolls. After watching slaves card cotton by hand, Whitney tinkered for several days in an upstairs room and produced a hand-cranked rotary contraption that simulated the hand process. In correspondence with Thomas Jefferson, Whitney claimed that his "engin," if powered by horses or water, could do in a day the work of one hundred laborers. But rather than replace people, it increased the need for slaves.

The invention swept the South and pushed cotton farming—and slavery—into Alabama, Mississippi, and Texas. U.S. production jumped from nine thousand bales in 1791 to seventy-nine thousand in 1800, and doubled every decade thereafter. By the time of the Civil War, the South produced five million bales a year, three-quarters of the world's cotton. The number of slaves jumped from seven hundred thousand in 1790 to four million by the beginning of the war. As the price of a "prime" worker jumped to $1,800, slave breeding, which historian John Hope Franklin called "one of the most fantastic manipulations of human development in the history of mankind," became a big business in Maryland, Virginia, and the Carolinas. Although imports from Africa were banned in 1808, pirates as late as 1858 brought slaves to Savannah, Mobile, and New Orleans.

Mulberry Grove's original foundations and property, owned for years by the Georgia Ports Authority, are off-limits to the public. Three road markers at the edge of the original plantation describe the history briefly. Plans are to transfer the property to the U.S. Fish & Wildlife Service, to save this wild portion of the river, and interpret the history for visitors.

8 | **DORCHESTER ACADEMY** *(U.S. 84, two miles west of U.S. 17 in Midway, Georgia, thirty miles south of Savannah)* If walls could speak, this stately building might share a century-long tale of civil rights dreams. Built as a Congregationalist missionary school for freed slaves after the Civil War, it remained a black school until 1941 and thereafter a community center. In 1961 Septima Clark opened an adult "citizenship school" for the Southern Christian Leadership Conference. The goal was voter registration, Clark wrote in *Ready From Within,* but the skills of blacks who arrived by bus for weeklong seminars required her to start with the fundamentals—writing their names, reading street signs, adding and subtracting numbers on bank accounts, and figuring seed orders for their fields. Writing lessons on dry-cleaner bags because she had no blackboards, Clark eventually taught them state constitutions, government hierarchy, and voting procedures. Better students became teachers who went home to establish dozens of similar schools. The classes here during a four-year period prepared ten thousand teachers who registered seven hundred thousand blacks to vote.

In January 1962 Dr. Martin Luther King Jr. and his closest advisers met here to plan their assault on Birmingham, Alabama, later that year. Wyatt Walker of SCLC laid out a four-stage plan that began with sit-ins, boycotts, mass marches, jail-ins, and national publicity. It would be called Project C for *confrontation.*

A caretaker's cottage has been remodeled into a visitors center and museum. The boys dormitory, built in 1934, is on the national registry of historic places.

The Women of the Movement

In 1851 a former slave stood before a women's rights forum in Ohio and made her case for equal rights: "I have plowed, I have planted . . . And ain't I a woman? I could work as much and eat as much as man—when I could get it—and bear the lash. And ain't I a woman?"

A century later, Sojourner Truth's lament resonated for all women of the civil rights movement. In leadership and organizational skills, sheer physical courage, and a range of disciplines ranging from music to communication, women were the equal of men.

And yet in the male-dominated church, the father-dominated 1950s, and the plantation South, women didn't receive their due. Worse, they were patronized or objectified, as in Stokely Carmichael's infamous response when asked about the position of women in the movement: "Prone." So they suffered doubly, against the prejudice of whites and the sexism of black men.

Rosa Parks was not the first woman to be mistreated on public transportation. Refusing to accept segregated transportation was a time-honored protest for black women. Sojourner Truth, Ida B. Wells, Charlotte Hawkins Brown, and Septima Clark protested in their time. Wells won a five-hundred-dollar court judgment (later reversed) after a conductor wrestled her out of a first-class section of a Memphis train. This was during a period when ninety women were lynched in the United States. In 1955 men looking for a test case in Montgomery passed over other women equally wronged but whose characters they judged to be lacking.

The Montgomery bus boycott, in fact, was a woman's idea. Jo Ann Robinson, an English teacher at Alabama State University, had been humiliated by a bus driver the year before. When word of Mrs. Parks's arrest reached her, she and members of the Women's Political Council stayed up all night to mimeograph a boycott letter that was distributed to every black church and business in town. A day later, a reluctant Martin Luther King Jr. agreed to head up the movement. In time, Robinson lost her teaching job for her leadership.

Women's "traditional" roles in the movement ranged from cooking fried chicken to keeping minutes of NAACP meetings. Less apparent was the spunk women showed, like Mother Pollard, who was quoted when she declined a lift in Montgomery: "My feets is weary, but my soul is rested." In many Deep South communities, elderly black women had the guts to take in young activists, and be first to face the white registrar down at the courthouse.

This fortitude may have grown out of a peculiarly southern attitude, described by activist Modjeska Simkins, that "the only two classes of people free in the South are white men and black women." Historian Simon Cuthbert-Kerr argues that black women could get away with actions and attitudes that black men couldn't or wouldn't dare.

Yet, after all their work and sacrifice, deliberate rebuff by male activists was unforgivable. Ella Baker, the founding mother of SNCC, was essentially pushed out of King's Southern Christian Leadership Conference in favor of another black minister, Wyatt T. Walker. Septima Clark, who also worked for SCLC, blamed Ralph Abernathy, King's trusted deputy, who led a male attitude that "a woman didn't have any sense."

At the 1963 march on Washington, male leaders barred Coretta King and other wives from marching with their husbands, according to Taylor Branch's *Parting the Waters*. Instead, there was a brief "Tribute to Women" on the podium, with bows from half a dozen women. In the three-hour program, Branch recorded, "The committee scheduled no female speakers."

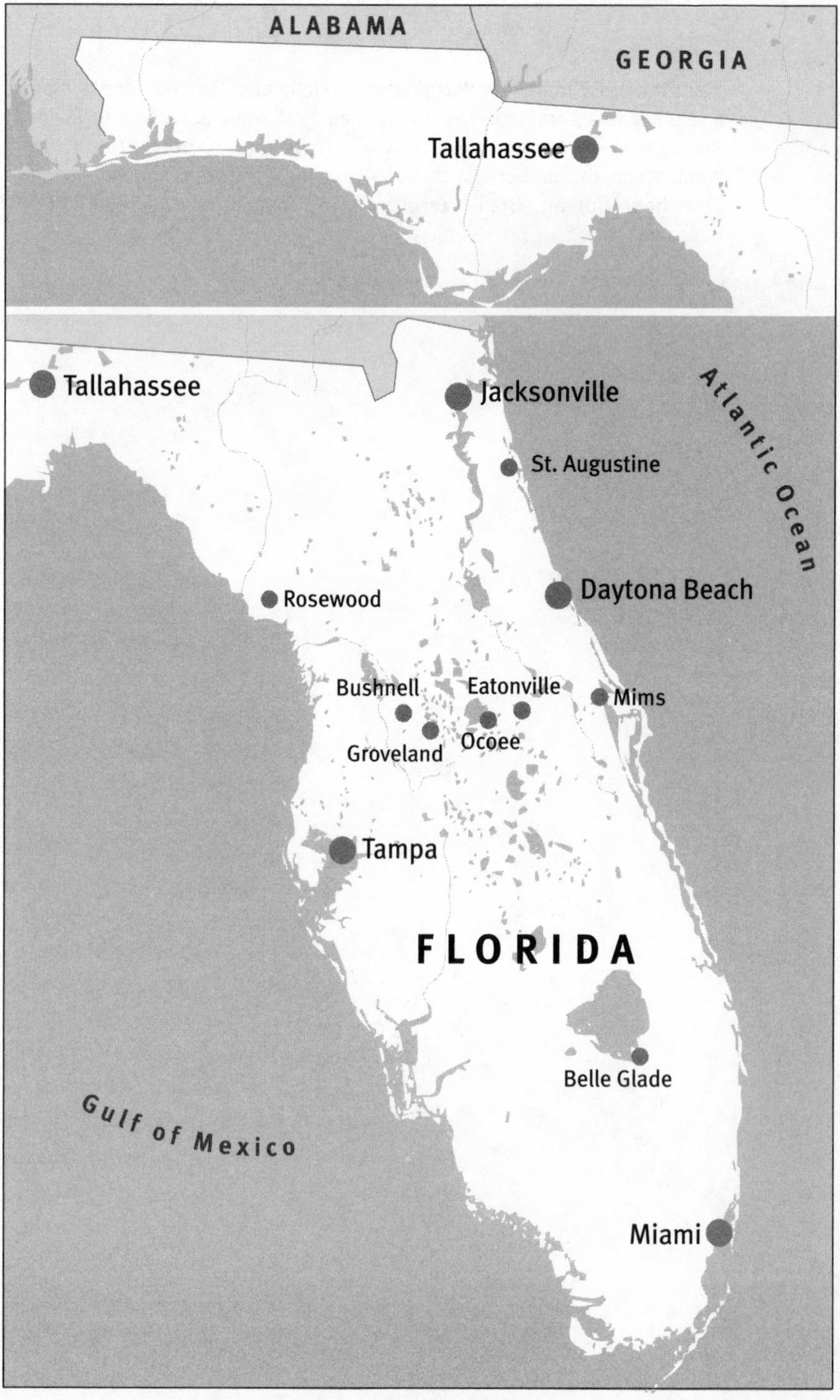
ALABAMA
GEORGIA
Tallahassee
Tallahassee
Jacksonville
Atlantic Ocean
St. Augustine
Daytona Beach
Rosewood
Bushnell
Eatonville
Mims
Groveland
Ocoee
Tampa
FLORIDA
Belle Glade
Gulf of Mexico
Miami

Florida

FLORIDA COULD BE CALLED the birthplace of American diversity—it has the oldest African American heritage in the United States and some of the most poignant and painful civil rights stories to tell—but it is not known as a "civil rights" state. The problem is, Florida has suffered the bias of histories that consign the original Spanish colony to a footnote, and blacks there to virtual nonexistence.

In 1600, nineteen years before the first Africans arrived in Virginia, Spain's royal census counted nineteen slaves in Florida. With St. Augustine already populated by Indians, Spaniards, Bahamians, then black Seminoles and mestizos, the arrival of the British there created a unique hybrid society that three hundred years later would reassert itself by way of Cuba.

When the United States took over this tropical appendage in 1821, Rachel Jackson, the feisty wife of military governor (later president) Andrew Jackson, was horrified, according to historian Gary Mormino: "The inhabitants all speak Spanish and French. Some speak four languages," she wrote. "Such a mixed multitude . . . Fewer white people by far than any other . . . Jamaican blacks bearing prodigious burdens on their heads; a fish peddler filling the street with incomprehensible cries . . . And must I say the worst people here are the cast-off Americans."

By the Civil War, slaves made up half the population of Florida, yet blacks became a forgotten people, their disappearances staining Florida's human rights saga. In the 1920s three black communities were purged by white mobs. In 1928 thousands of black farmworkers died or disappeared in a hurricane. Years later, thousands of blacks were "removed" from downtown Miami by an interstate highway.

Florida's civil rights activists have been forced to overcome not only racism but this peculiar blankness of existence. As the editors of a state history put it in 1995, "For centuries the African American heritage in Florida has been ignored by a white population unwilling to acknowledge that people of color had been instrumental in the creation of this state."

Indeed, blacks were involved in the foundational industries of Florida, recruited or sentenced as cheap labor to build railroads and harvest turpentine, fruits, and vegetables. Until the 1980s, the majority of migrant workers were African Americans.

Their struggles for equal rights against an entrenched white establishment took decades, but began to bear fruit just as the first group of Cuban refugees arrived during the Cold War. In South Florida, new cultures came in waves—Haitians, Mexicans, Guatemalans, Columbians, each group with its own civil rights story, each wave stirring up racial tension among people of color who came before.

Today, Florida is wildly diverse, and civil rights is daily news fare. Away from Miami, Key West, and Disney World, there are pockets of a Deep South past. The interior is full of cowboys, "crackers," and cattle not far from Babel fields of farmworkers fresh from half a dozen countries.

Florida and Civil Rights

When Juan Ponce de León happened upon Florida in April 1513 and claimed it for Spain, Indians who fired arrows at him were subject to enslavement. But African slavery was virtually unknown in the New World. One of his staff, in fact, Juan Garrido, was a free black, the first identified African to set foot in North America.

By the time the Spanish came back to stay in St. Augustine in 1565, Indian harassment was illegal and black slavery was entrenched. Yet, thanks to the soul-seeking Catholic Church, even slaves had moral standing and redress in court, and could free themselves by joining the church or military. Such convolutions in human rights became a Florida pattern.

Under Spain, Florida became a haven for runaway slaves from the Carolinas and Georgia. Their numbers were thought to be in the thousands. Spain established a "free" town for one hundred runaways just north of St. Augustine called Mose. When Spain lost Florida to Britain, many blacks, free and slave, left with the Spanish for Cuba. Spain regained Florida after the Revolutionary War, but it was only a matter of time before the newly formed American nation wanted Florida, too, in part to stanch the runaway problem, in part to create a new slave state.

By then, Florida also sheltered Creek Indians who'd been pushed out of Georgia and Alabama. They had settled along the Suwannee and Apalachicola Rivers and become known as Seminoles, a word meaning runaways. Later, "Seminole" denoted both Indians and ex-slaves who commingled as masters, slaves, colleagues, and couples.

As America, in the representative of Andrew Jackson, raided Florida, the runaway slaves served as interpreters between the Seminoles and the U.S. Army, and eventually joined them as guerrilla fighters in the costliest Indian war in U.S. history. Jackson drove the Seminoles out of the Panhandle, made and broke various treaties, and then removed most of them to Oklahoma.

With the Seminoles gone, an antebellum society sprang up overnight on the red soil of northern Florida. Wrote historian Mark Derr: "The central fact of Florida society in the years 1821 to 1865 was human bondage." Plantations named Casa Bianca, Belmont, and El Destino were built in the north, while on the Miami River, William English ordered slaves to clear land and plant lime and orange trees. The state's first constitution prohibited the General Assembly from emancipating slaves. In 1850, five years after statehood, a law was passed that forced all blacks to "belong" to someone. True to the motto on its first unofficial flag—"Let Us Alone"—Florida, barely sixteen years into statehood, voted in 1861 to secede from the United States. At the time, Florida had just fifteen hundred farms with more than one hundred acres, and only five thousand people who owned slaves.

During the war, the U.S. Navy easily controlled Florida's ports and coastline, while the interior remained a Confederate hideaway connected to the war in spirit. Word of Lee's surrender at Appomattox was never embraced, according to Marjory Stoneman Douglas, and the state's center—"proud, secretive, unlettered, suspicious"—remained unreconstructed.

In the port cities of Jacksonville, Tampa, and St. Augustine, ex-slaves settled in large numbers to enjoy freedom. Voting as Republicans, they elected themselves to city councils and school boards, and became cops and judges. Josiah Walls, a black, was elected to Congress, and Jonathan Gibbs, a black minister's son who'd studied the classics at Dartmouth, became secretary of state and state school superintendent, during which time he expanded the public school system.

War debris was still smoldering when Francis Fleming and his wife reopened Hibernia, their St. Johns River plantation, to northern visitors who enjoyed, at $2.50 a day, "the lavish Southern meals in the great dining room, cooked and served by returning house servants, sometimes paid," wrote Douglas. By 1900 Jacksonville was the winter getaway home to fifteen thousand Yankees, doubling the city's population then dominated by black maids, cooks, and others in service. Downriver, writer Harriet Beecher Stowe, author of *Uncle Tom's Cabin,* hired black labor to plant orange groves, vegetables, and strawberries. Ostracized by local whites as Mrs. Uncle Tom, she turned to writing frothier fare that gushed over Florida.

The state, so ripe, appealed to all. Frost-free below Tampa, Florida was full of exotic birds and water creatures—a buffet for hunters and birders—and became a smorgasbord for speculation and exploitation. Along the coast, wreckers legalized a kind of piracy. All the while blacks began losing their new freedoms.

Between 1868 and 1871, 235 people died in political violence, the worst of which occurred in Jackson County on the Alabama border after Freedmen Bureau agents promoted black voting. A war that broke out between blacks and the Klan lasted for weeks, and killed one person every day. By February 1869 the death toll was seventy-five, including ten white Republicans. "This is where Satan has his seat," a black clergyman was quoted in *Reconstruction* by Eric Foner.

At the time, Foner wrote, Florida had more black landowners than other southern states and the Klan demanded blacks give up their land and work for white men. On election days, "regulators" on horseback patrolled roads to keep blacks from voting, and murdered white Republican senators. With

Democrats back in control, the legislature instituted barriers to black voting: a poll tax, a complicated ballot with a voting time limit, and, later, a whites-only primary. Two-thirds of black votes disappeared.

In 1877 the Florida legislature approved slavery by a new name: convict leasing, a system made possible by vagrancy laws that could scoop up any black on the street and sentence him or her to a year. Blacks were jailed for trying to vote, for homesteading, or for speaking up. Leg irons "were never taken off," wrote Marjory Stoneman Douglas. "In the turpentine woods the gangs had to move all day . . . in a queer hopping run." They built railroads, cut wood, made bricks, cleared land for what would become Palm Beach and Miami—at a cost to developers of twenty-six dollars a year per convict. They were punished, wrote Mark Derr, by flogging, being sealed in a sweatbox, having their stomachs filled by force with a water hose, and being hung by their thumbs, which left grotesquely stretched thumbs a mark of their servitude. "They died by the hundreds and no one, not even the Freedmen's Bureau, paid any attention," Douglas wrote. Florida's convict leasing was known as the American Siberia and lasted until 1923, longer than any state except Alabama.

Around 1900 blacks streamed into Florida, mostly from Georgia, but also the Bahamas and West Indies, for farmwork and developer Henry Flagler's various projects. They helped extend his railroad down the East Coast to Palm Beach and Miami. Once there, they couldn't share in the wealth. In places like Palm Beach, they periodically performed a "cake walk," part parody, part demeaning minstrel show, dressing in their best clothes to parade and dance before white patrons. Then they went back to their jobs changing beds. As late as the 1980s blacks were required to present ID cards before they could enter the rich enclave.

In 1915 English settlers established Moore Haven near Lake Okeechobee and brought in the first black farmworkers. Marian O'Brien had to arm vigilantes to protect her workers from racist neighbors. Douglas, in her history of the Everglades, recounts the finding of an old woman's body—gutted and floating in the swamp. A truck farm foreman named Watson, it seemed, simply shot, buried, or gutted blacks when they came to be paid. In 1920 the Klan ganged up on Mose Norman, an orange grove owner, and July Perry, an influential land owner, for trying to vote in Ocoee. When Perry killed two Klansmen, Klan members went on a rampage, killing thirty-five blacks, burning homes and churches, and running five hundred blacks out of town. In Perry, Florida, when a white school teacher was found dead a month before Christmas, 1922, three black men were lynched, including one burned at the stake. On New Year's Day, 1923, in the most infamous of Florida's lynchings, whites searching for an alleged black rapist drove blacks from the sawmill town of Rosewood and killed an unknown number.

Between 1900 and 1930, Florida's lynching rate led the South. As late as the 1930s, black labor seemed little more than peonage as WPA folklorist Stetson Kennedy found at a turpentine camp.

"Why don't you leave and get out of it?" Kennedy asked one worker.

"The onliest way out is to die out," the worker replied. "If you tries to leave, they will kill you, and you will have to die, because they got peoples to bury you out in them woods."

Some black families, working together, managed to buy homesteads, and a few, like the Robinson family of Fort Pierce, built their own fruit and vegetable empires. There were also pockets of black wealth in Jacksonville and Miami's Overtown. A number of beaches were purchased by black entrepreneurs for their segregated use: American Beach on Amelia Island, and Butler or Bethune Beach near Daytona Beach.

Blacks began voting again when the poll tax was eliminated in 1937. Miami hired five black cops in 1944. They worked Colored Town and could not arrest whites until 1963. But with beach "wade-ins" as early as 1945, black Florida began to demand equal rights. Harry Moore, operating from his home in Mims, raised to one hundred thousand the number of black voters and openly criticized racist officials, work that cost him his life and that of his wife. The Christmas, 1951, bombing of his home is now considered one of the first assassinations of the modern civil rights era.

In 1950 Virgil Hawkins won Supreme Court backing to enter the University of Florida law school, but the school defied the court and he was never admitted. Instead, he was dragged before a McCarthy-like legislative committee headed by state senator Charley Johns and questioned about communists in the movement. Hawkins finally was admitted to Florida's bar in 1975, at the age of seventy.

Florida's official reaction to the 1954 Supreme Court decision to integrate public schools was to build more segregated schools. At the time, according to historian David Colburn, Florida was one of only four states without at least some school integration, and it would take a decade of lawsuits to enforce compliance. For his lawsuit to integrate Miami's schools and other activism, Father Theodore Gibson was hauled before the Johns Committee and sentenced to six months in prison for refusing to give up NAACP membership rolls. When the Supreme Court threw out the case, Johns went after gays and lesbians, and 110 college teachers lost their jobs.

The civil rights movement arrived in Tallahassee in 1956 with a bus boycott. Four years later, sit-ins at lunch counters quickly spread from Tallahassee to several other Florida cities including Daytona Beach, Jacksonville, Tampa–St. Petersburg, and Sarasota. Governor LeRoy Collins, in a historic about-face of southern leadership, said: "We can never stop Americans from struggling to be free." But his energies largely went to keeping the reactionary legislature from closing schools. By 1962 Miami, Tampa, St. Petersburg, and Jacksonville had integrated lunch counters and parks. Still, two years later, with Tallahassee and St. Augustine remaining as segregated holdouts, the U.S. Civil Rights Commission called Florida a "tight-white" state.

As the movement crept across Florida, farm labor underwent a seismic change, beginning with the recruitment of Mexican labor. Working for less, they forced out blacks who had not benefited from civil rights gains. The arrival of Cuban refugees created new competition, one with government support, and they soon dominated southern Florida.

In the 1990s blacks made up 15 percent of the state population. Yet black unemployment was twice the state average. Nearly half the prison population was black, and by 2000 there were so many felons that 525,000 Floridians couldn't vote—including 24 percent of Florida's black men.

No one has ever put a figure on the number of black votes that were discounted, lost, or somehow disenfranchised during the 2000 presidential election. But there is deep suspicion in the black community that it cost Al Gore the White House. According to the U.S. Civil Rights Commission, "voter disenfranchisement appears to be at the heart of the issue." Among the infamous ballot problems, black voters "were nearly ten times more likely than white voters to have their ballots rejected." In Jacksonville, where the worst problems occurred, twenty-seven thousand ballots were rejected, the bulk of them in Democratic precincts, including nine thousand in black precincts that voted nearly unanimously for Gore. After President Bush won by 537 votes, Evangeline Moore, the daughter of martyr Harry Moore, commented, "They killed my father. Now they just throw out black votes."

A Florida Civil Rights Tour

Florida has only recently begun to preserve its black history, and most civil rights stories remain unrecorded. At this writing, not a single museum includes the civil rights story as part of its history. Visitors must be imaginative to find in the blankness of Rosewood or the glitz of Miami the hardships and heroism that created a state where diversity is an attraction. Indeed a visitor from other southern states may be surprised at the number of colors and languages of the people of Florida. The civil rights movement made this possible, and established an ideal that Florida strives for.

Florida's **Division of Historical Resources** publishes large "trail" guides focusing on black history, Cuban history, and women's history. Each is available at visitors centers or through the division (*500 South Bronough Street, Tallahassee, FL 32399; 850-487-2344*).

The state divides easily into three tours:

North

St. Augustine, Jacksonville, and Tallahassee each had difficult and protracted civil rights movements with deep roots in their antebellum and colonial periods.

Central

Harry Moore's assassination in Mims and Jackie Robinson's first scored run in Daytona Beach are memorialized on the eastern shore, while the state's three most infamous lynching villages are located on the western side: Groveland, Ocoee, and Rosewood. Eatonville was home to Zora Neale Hurston, and the black Seminole story is told both in Bushnell and Tampa.

South

Though they appear very different, Belle Glade's fields and Miami's fiesta have in common diversity, economic disparities, and the state's toughest ongoing human rights issues.

City by City

Belle Glade

Any notion that the struggle for human rights is in the past will be disabused by a visit to this village of workers who put vegetables on America's tables. Though not a tourist town, Belle Glade is historic, and the ongoing issues of corporate-farm labor are in plain view. The town's motto is "Our soil is our fortune," referring to the peatlike ground known as "muck" that once was the northern Everglades.

The parking lot where laborers board buses headed to the fields has remained essentially unchanged for decades, except for the languages of the workers. *Harvest of Shame,* Edward R. Murrow's 1960 CBS documentary, was shot here and led to the first federal protection act for migrant workers. But periodic media updates have a sameness that is depressing. NOBODIES was the headline of a 2003 article in a national magazine, followed by the subtitle: DOES SLAVERY EXIST IN AMERICA?

Farms were developed here before World War I, when the Everglades were drained and a low dike built around Lake Okeechobee. Central Florida became home to tens of thousands of African Americans. Marjory Douglas wrote that Belle Glade slums were among the worst in America: "Thousands sleep packed together in sordid rooms, hallways, tar-paper shacks, filthy barracks . . . the patched and peeling walls seem saturated with their heavy smell of dirt and fatigue and disease and misery." In sharp contrast, notes black activist Robert Hazard, "These folk helped make Palm Beach County one of the richest agriculture counties in the nation."

Today, Belle Glade refuses to annex a black section that could shift white control of elections, but it takes pride that Belle Glade High has become the single leading source of black athletes in the National Football League. The civil rights movement opened opportunities for blacks, including crew leadership, but many were replaced by unskilled laborers recruited from Mexico and Central America. They work hard for a few thousand dollars a year. Because many are undocumented immigrants, they labor in a shadowy world of virtual peonage. Government prosecutions and lawsuits by advocacy groups periodically expose violations ranging from nonpayment of taxes to sex slavery. According to migrant lawyer Greg Schell, two-thirds of peonage prosecutions are against black crew leaders who, acting as independent contractors, insulate corporations from liability.

MIGRANT PARKING LOT (*Fifth Street and S.W. Avenue D*) Morning and night, the scene in this square has been unchanged since the 1920s, except for languages and nationalities. Farm laborers are picked up and driven to fields each morning, and deposited here at night after a day of seeding, weeding, and harvesting winter vegetables, sugarcane, and other crops. *Harvest of Shame* followed workers from this parking lot north with the crops. In 2003 workers whose boots, hats, machetes, and crates of green vegetables made the scene feel foreign were largely Haitian, Guatemalan, and Jamaican. Yet, it is only an hour from the wealthy enclaves of Palm Beach and Miami.

Not until 1966 did farmworkers have a minimum wage, and not until 1978 was unemployment insurance a possibility. At the end of the twentieth century, there was still no overtime, health benefits, or a pension plan. "It's a lousy job," said migrant advocate Schell. "It is populated by people with no other options." In 2003 a bucket of tomatoes fetched the same price as in 1979: about forty cents.

HURRICANE MONUMENT AND MUSEUM AT BELLE GLADE LIBRARY (*530 South Main, Florida Route 80; 561-996-3453; www.pbclibrary. org/branch-bg.htm*) In September 1928 a major hurricane crossed Florida, bashing Palm Beach and obliterating a huge migrant population that lived in shacks around Lake Okeechobee, which rampaged out of its shallow bed with a fifteen-foot wall of water. The death toll will never be known but estimates range to five thousand. Bodies were everywhere: "tangled in shrubbery, floating in water, hanging in trees," Zora Neale Hurston wrote in *Their Eyes Were Watching God*, a novel based on the storm. In the heat and decay, hundreds had to be buried in trenches, separated by race when possible and covered with lime. According to *Killer 'Cane* by Robert Mykle, the shores of the lake were lined with cremation pyres, and farmers plowed up bones for decades.

"The storm did not kill equitably," Mykle wrote. "More than three-quarters of the people killed in the 1928 storm were black. Living in

Belle Glade memorial to the 1928 hurricane

flimsy shanties, many built of tarpaper and scrap wood near the least desirable areas (below sea level) they were the first to feel the water's wrath." The storm has been called by a memorial coalition "the greatest single natural disaster ever to happen to African Americans."

Belle Glade's dramatic sculpture of a family fleeing the storm is noticeably "white." The small museum inside the adjacent library contains newspaper clippings and an old display on the migrant path from Belle Glade to the Mohawk Valley of New York.

PORT MAYACA MASS GRAVE (*Florida Route 76, five miles east of Hoover Dike*) After the 1928 hurricane, thousands of bodies lay about like logs. Because of heat, insects, and disease, sixteen hundred were cremated and buried here. They are memorialized with a waterfall, fish pond, and plaque. Another mass grave at Miami Locks was apparently obliterated when new dikes were built in the 1940s.

WEST PALM BEACH MASS GRAVE (*Tamarin Street and Twenty-fifth Street, West Palm Beach*) For years, this mass grave of 674 black victims of the 1928 hurricane went unnoticed as West Palm Beach expanded. Kept alive by oral history in the black community, the graveyard story was authenticated in 2000 by ground-penetrating radar. Now a state historic site marked with a roadside stand and a graceful line of old banyan trees, the grave site will eventually include a museum and a memorial garden in the shape of a hurricane warning sign.

Victims both of the hurricane and of Florida racism at the time, blacks were unceremoniously buried in a trench before relatives or friends could identify or retrieve them, a privilege granted to white victims who were on view for up to two days. According to site historians, this grave was just one of several burial sites for some three thousand recovered bodies. Sixty-nine other bodies, including eight blacks, were buried together in coffins in Woodlawn Cemetery.

Bushnell

DADE BATTLEFIELD (*7200 County Road; 352-793-4791; www.floridastateparks.org/dadebattlefield/default.asp*) Tranquil but for one fateful day, this hammock of oak, pine, and palmetto was the ignition point for the costliest military campaign in U.S. history against Indians and African Americans. In February 1835 President Jackson ordered the Seminoles out of Florida. Some agreed to leave, but younger warriors showed their contempt with attacks on settlers. On a cold, rainy December 28, a band of nearly 200 blacks and Indians ambushed a U.S. Army column of 107 men led by Major Francis Dade. The infantry fashioned pathetic "breastworks" of pine logs, but eventually the men were massacred but for three survivors. The event made Dade a national martyr, his name a common Florida approbation, and hastened Seminole removal.

The Second Seminole War involved ten thousand troops at a cost of fifteen hundred U.S. lives and $40 million. When it was over in 1841, after seven years, four thousand Seminoles were shipped and marched to Oklahoma. Counted that way, wrote Isa Bryant, the cost for each black Seminole was roughly $80,000.

The Seminole wars brought to an end a two-hundred-year siege to open the eastern U.S. to white settlement. Altogether, eighty-one thousand Indians were moved and 100 million acres made available for western expansion. Jackson believed he saved the Indians from extermination. But Jackson biographer Robert Remini concludes, "It was one of the unhappiest chapters in American history."

In Oklahoma, the U.S. government reneged and made black Seminoles slaves again, subject to capture and return. Many fled to Mexico. After the Civil War, they became scouts for the U.S. Army's efforts to clear Texas of Indian renegades, work that earned four of them Medals of Honor. Denied land of their own, they remained attached to the Seminole nation for two hundred years—until 1999 when courts awarded the Seminoles $56 million for the tribe's losses in Florida. The Seminole chief then announced that two thousand blacks were not members and could not share in the award.

The state historic park shows an excellent video on the Seminole history, and hosts an annual, narrated reenactment of the Dade massacre in December.

Daytona Beach

JACKIE ROBINSON BALLPARK AND MONUMENT (*105 East Orange Street; 386-258-3106*) Jackie Robinson broke the color barrier in major league sports at this ballpark on March 17, 1946. He was a player with the Montreal Royals, a minor league team owned by the Brooklyn Dodgers. The game, against the Dodgers, was the first racially integrated exhibition game.

Jackie Robinson sculpture in Daytona Beach

Four thousand fans, including one thousand blacks, watched Robinson score a run but go hitless in five innings. Playing in a fishbowl he then went into a three-day slump until March 30 when a headline reported, ROBINSON GETS A HIT. ROYALS LOSE, according to biographer Arnold Rampersad. In the season opener in New Jersey, he hit a home run, stole two bases, and scored four runs including two on balks that had the crowd—white and black—roaring with delight.

Robinson had to endure humiliating experiences in Florida. He and his wife, Rachel, were shoved to the back of a bus en route to Daytona, where they stayed at the Spruce Street home of a black pharmacist because Robinson couldn't room with the team at the Riviera Hotel on the beach. During one game, someone threw a black cat at Robinson. They were run out of Sanford during tryouts, and despite the open welcome from Daytona's mayor, had to eat at black cafés and Rachel had to sit in the black section of the ballpark. In subsequent weeks, Jacksonville, Savannah, and Richmond canceled games against the Royals.

Branch Rickey, the president of the Dodgers, soon signed two other black players, catcher Roy Campanella and pitcher Don Newcombe. After a season with Montreal, Robinson was called up to the Dodgers. He was enshrined at the Baseball Hall of Fame and died in 1972. In the estimation of Arthur Ashe, a groundbreaker himself in tennis and a sports historian: "Jack Roosevelt Robinson was the single most significant athlete—black or white—after World War II. He made possible the introduction and participation of other black athletes in all team sports."

The ballpark, a national historic site, is home to the Daytona Cubs, a minor league franchise of the Chicago Cubs.

Sports Heroes and Civil Rights

What civil rights hero refused to give up a seat on a bus and was arrested?

This same person went on to break a national color line eight years before Rosa Parks became a heroine in Montgomery. In fact, two months before she launched the bus boycott, this man and his integrated Brooklyn Dodgers won the World Series and became "America's team."

Jackie Robinson, the first African American in major league baseball, was a civil rights pioneer. Signed to the Dodgers organization in 1945, he played under the intense glare of worldwide publicity and paved the way for black athletes in every sport.

Sports provided America's first level playing field where people were judged by the same rules—civil rights' ultimate goal—and where achievement counted, not birth. Given a chance, blacks succeeded and became role models for kids of all colors while capturing the hearts and changing the minds of the dominant society.

The man behind baseball's integration was Branch Rickey, the president of the Brooklyn Dodgers. In 1904, as coach of a college baseball team, he had watched in horror as his one black player, barred from a hotel room, tried to peel the flesh from his hands. "Damned skin," he cried to Rickey. "If I could only rub it off." As head of the Dodgers, Rickey vowed to break baseball's color bar.

His top choice was Robinson, a good player in the Negro Leagues and an ex-army officer with poise, intelligence, grace, and a burning hatred of segregation. In 1942, on an army bus in Texas supposedly integrated by military regulation, Robinson had refused the driver's order to move to the back. After a shouting match, MPs arrested him, but a court-martial freed him. In their first meeting in New York, in an office with a portrait of Lincoln on the wall, Rickey play-acted the foulest-mouthed racist that Robinson would encounter. When Robinson began to boil, Rickey said, "I'm looking for a ball player with guts enough *not* to fight back." Like Martin Luther King a generation later, Rickey invoked Mahatma Gandhi's policy of "active nonviolence." Robinson triumphed, while enduring epithets from fans, the skepticism and disparagement of teammates, and attention that magnified every double play, home run, and fielding error into a civil rights event.

He began play in 1946 on the Dodgers' farm club, the Montreal Royals, during spring training in Daytona Beach, Florida. A statue of Robinson marks the spot. A year later he joined the Dodgers for a ten-year career that included six world series, including Brooklyn's only win in 1955. By then, Rickey had fully integrated the Dodgers. The World Series team of nine included four black players—Robinson at third base, catcher Roy Campanella, Sandy Amoros in left, and Jim Gilliam at second base—and at least two black pitchers. By then, blacks were playing on all but three major league teams. In 1962, when some of the worst turmoil of the civil rights era still lay ahead, Robinson was inducted into baseball's Hall of Fame.

Robinson's hiring burst a dam in sports. The same month he reported to Montreal's training camp, the National Football League hired its first black player—Kenny Washington with the Los Angeles Rams. During Robinson's first year, the National Basketball Association hired its first black players, William King and William Gates.

Robinson was the idol of "every black kid in America in the late 1940s and early 1950s," wrote tennis pioneer Arthur Ashe in his *A Hard Road to Glory,* a three-volume history of black sports. But Robinson acknowledged standing on the shoulders of men like Olympic runner Jesse Owens and boxers Joe Louis and Jack Johnson, stars in the only integrated sports at the time.

"The Jack Johnson–Jim Jeffries fight in 1910 was the most awaited event in black American history," Ashe once told *Sports Illustrated*. "It took months for word of the Emancipation Proclamation to circulate through the land, but eighty percent of black Americans knew of that fight, knew why Jim Jeffries unretired from his alfalfa farm—so he could be the Great White Hope. No other event had such immediacy for black Americans." Johnson, fighting in trunks emblazoned with the American flag, crushed Jeffries and set off thirteen racial murders across the country.

Owens dominated the 1936 Olympics in Germany with four gold medals, and "Brown Bomber" Louis beat German Max Schmeling in 1938, both events seen by the world as pitting American democracy against Hitler's white supremacy.

After Robinson, all sports opened to black players. Among the highlights:

- 1947: First game between a white and black college, Bergen College vs. Wilberforce (Wilberforce, the oldest black college, won 40–12).
- 1948: Alice Coachman of Tuskegee became the first black woman to win Olympic gold, with a five-foot, six-inch high jump.
- 1950: Althea Gibson was the first black tennis player to play at Forest Lawn. She lost but went on to win the French Open in 1956 and both the U.S. Open and Wimbledon titles in 1957.
- 1958: Oklahoma Coach Bud Wilkinson signs Prentiss Gault, the first black player in a big "southern" school.
- 1967: Charlie Sifford becomes the first black to win a PGA tournament, the Hartford Open.
- 1968: Arthur Ashe becomes the first (and only) black man to win the U.S. Open.

Many black athletes became civil rights activists off the court, marching in picket lines and boycotting events, including the Olympics. Those who chose not to get involved politically, among them Althea Gibson, Hank Aaron, and Willie Mays, were criticized. But so, too, were outspoken leaders like Robinson. *Ebony* magazine once chided: "Jackie is a baseball player and not the executive secretary of the NAACP."

After retirement from baseball in 1957, Robinson raised money for civil rights and spoke in hotbeds such as Albany, Birmingham, and St. Augustine. Throwing out a World Series ball on the twenty-fifth year of his entry into major league baseball, he said: "I am extremely proud and pleased. I'm going to be tremendously more pleased and more proud when I look at that third base coaching line one day and see a black face managing in baseball." Two years later, Frank Robinson of the Cleveland Indians was named the first black manager in the major leagues.

HOME OF MARY MCLEOD BETHUNE *(Bethune-Cookman College, 640 Second Avenue; 386-481-2000; www.bethune.cookman. edu)* Simple frames on the walls of this modest house capture a glimpse of Mary Bethune's world—letters from and pictures of presidents and prominent Americans. Born one of seventeen children to South Carolina slaves, Bethune rose to become companion and confidante of important people, her life a testament to her most famous phrase: "Invest in the human soul—who knows, it may be a diamond in the rough."

After the Civil War, when her parents collected their brood from various plantations where they had been sold as slaves, Bethune begged to read. In a one-room school, and later at missionary schools, she became a star student and then a teacher herself. After her husband's death she moved to Daytona Beach and opened a school for black girls. She had $1.50, an old cabin, and the pluck to both scour dumps and approach philanthropists who wintered nearby. Soon her school was a college, and Bethune was known among northern matrons, most notably Eleanor and Sara Delano Roosevelt, for her wise and fearless views about education and equal rights. During Franklin Roosevelt's years, Bethune moved in and out of the White House as chair of an unofficial "black cabinet" that persuaded the first president in U.S. history to prepare a place at the table for blacks.

A savvy investor, Bethune also cocreated a Daytona resort for blacks, Bethune–Velusia Beach. Bethune's second home in Washington, D.C., which became the headquarters for the National Council of Negro Women, has been preserved. After her death in 1955, the council erected a dynamic sculpture of Bethune in Washington's Lincoln Park, which excerpts her will, written in this home as a challenge to future generations of black students.

HOWARD THURMAN HOUSE/CULTURAL PARK *(614 Whitehall Street; www.howardthurmanbooks.org)* Howard Thurman's grandmother couldn't read or write, but during their twenty years together in this home she encouraged him to reach for the stars. As mystic, theologian, and mentor to Martin Luther King Jr., Thurman succeeded beyond his grandmother's expectations. Born in 1900, Thurman went to a public school supported by white visitors down for the winter, and became the first black in Florida to pass the high school entrance exams. After graduating as valedictorian at Morehouse College in Atlanta, he moved among the top ranks of black chapel deans at Howard University and Boston University, arriving there as King was pursuing a Ph.D.

Legend has it that King sometimes traveled with a copy of Thurman's *Jesus and the Disinherited*, a series of essays written after a 1935 trip to India and visit with Mahatma Gandhi. One historian called it the handbook of the civil rights movement. Yet Thurman, who was a spellbinding preacher, was criticized for not becoming the Moses of the movement himself and for remaining aloof from the dirty work of southern integration. He pioneered in leading integrated churches in the north and San Francisco, and later became a favorite of New Agers.

Eatonville

ZORA NEALE HURSTON ART MUSEUM (*227 East Kennedy Boulevard; 407-647-3307*) A quiet town not ten blocks long, Eatonville brims with pride over its heritage as the oldest black incorporated city in America and the hometown of writer Zora Neale Hurston. The annual Hurston festival every January turns Eatonville into Florida's black cultural capital.

Established in 1887 by ex-slaves, the "town that freedom built" was actually the happy result of racism exhibited by a band of Union veterans who planned a colony of their own at Maitland. Because they needed thirty men to charter a town, the soldiers invited local blacks to register and vote. They did and elected a black mayor—not quite what the soldiers had in mind. So they bought another property for blacks and it took its name from one of the white sponsors, Captain Josiah Eaton.

Today, Eatonville remains an all-black village in the midst of frenetic metropolitan Orlando. The Hurston festival, in fact, grew out of local efforts in 1987 to stop Orange County from paving a five-lane road through town. The village seal commemorates farmworkers who helped establish the citrus industry.

Through her novels, her autobiography, *Dust Tracks on a Road,* and the files of the WPA Writers' Program for whom she collected Florida folklore, Hurston preserved history, vernacular, tragedy, and the spirit of black Florida in the 1920s and 1930s. Among her topics and locales were Eatonville, including the storytelling "lying porch" of Joe Clark's store; Ocoee, where blacks were lynched for trying to vote; and Lake Okeechobee and its migrant workers lost in the 1928 hurricane (*Their Eyes Were Watching God*). A star of the Harlem Renaissance, Hurston nonetheless died in poverty in Fort Pierce in 1960. Writer Alice Walker resurrected interest in Hurston's life and works, and placed a gravestone in the Ft. Pierce Garden of Heavenly Rest with the inscription: A GENIUS OF THE SOUTH, 1901–1960, NOVELIST, FOLKLORIST, ANTHROPOLOGIST.

Eatonville publishes a walking tour brochure, available at **town hall** (*307 East Kennedy Boulevard; 407-623-1313*), that includes the sites of Hurston's childhood home and Joe Clark's store.

Orlando's **visitors bureau** publishes the "African-American Travel Guide" (*407-363-5872*).

Groveland

Groveland is the "Scottsboro" of Florida because of an infamous 1951 lynching performed by the sheriff himself. Nothing in the area memorializes this story, but the case eventually involved two governors, the Supreme Court, NAACP attorney Thurgood Marshall, and the assassination of Florida's best-known civil rights hero, Harry Moore.

As a rural citrus center west of Orlando, Groveland relied on cheap labor to harvest crops. Lake County Sheriff Willis McCall, a paunchy former fruit inspector, rounded up blacks who were expected to work. When local black scofflaws Walter Irvin and Sam Shepherd were discharged dishonorably from the U.S. Army, they avoided the groves. On July 16, 1949, a white man and his estranged wife, Norma Padgett, claimed that four black men—Irvin, Shepherd, Charles Greenlee, and Ernest Thomas—had beat them and raped Mrs. Padgett. A posse killed Thomas during a chase, after which a mob ransacked, shot up, and burned Groveland's black neighborhood. In an overheated atmosphere fanned by the press—the *Orlando Sentinel* ran a front-page cartoon of four electric chairs with the headline NO

COMPROMISE—the remaining three were convicted, and Irvin and Shepherd sentenced to death. Greenlee, age sixteen, got life.

The U.S. Supreme Court overturned the case as a "menace" to justice. No rape had been proved, plaster "footprints" at the scene were pathetic fakes, and the suspects had been beaten and cut with broken glass around the clock to win "confessions." As Florida readied for a second trial in November 1951, Sheriff McCall drove Irvin and Shepherd along a back road and shot them while they were manacled together. He claimed they jumped him. Shepherd died immediately. When Irvin was found to be alive, he later testified, McCall and a deputy shot him again as he lay on the ground. Even that neck wound didn't kill him. So outrageous was this lynching that state NAACP chair Harry Moore called for McCall's resignation. A month later, Moore and his wife were blown up in their Mims home.

With Thurgood Marshall as his new attorney, Irvin was convicted and sentenced to death again, but a new governor, LeRoy Collins, commuted the sentence to life. Greenlee was paroled in 1962 and a paroled Irvin died in 1968. Sheriff McCall resigned in 1973 after kicking another black prisoner to death.

Jacksonville

Jacksonville's civil rights history began on May 3, 1901, when a disastrous fire destroyed the entire city. It was rebuilt as a Deep South city of the times—segregated. Gone was a city "known far and wide as a good town for Negroes," wrote Russ Rymer. It became, in the words of James Weldon Johnson, "a one hundred percent Cracker town." Johnson, a black lawyer and poet, had written a poem a year before the fire, "Lift Every Voice and Sing," which extolled the emergence of blacks from the "gloomy past [to] stand at last where the white gleam of our bright star is cast." The poem, set to music by his brother, became in time the "Negro national anthem." But a few days after the fire, Johnson was beaten on the street by a white mob.

Under Jim Crow segregation, black Jacksonville retreated to an area northwest of the wharves along the St. Johns River, in neighborhoods that included LaVilla, Sugarhill, and Hansontown. Along "The Bricks" was built one of the first independent black business and cultural centers in the United States. At its heart was Bethel Baptist, Mount Olive AME, Stanton High School, and the Afro-American Life Insurance Company, headed by

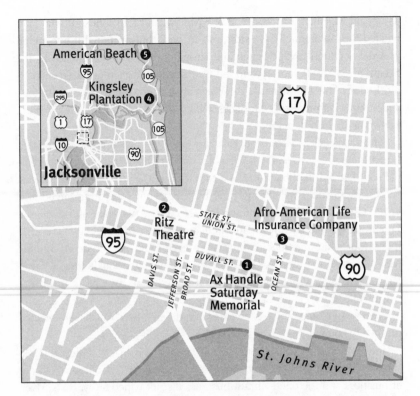

former cobbler Abraham Lincoln Lewis. Along Ashley Street, black Jacksonville partied in the Ritz, the Strand, and the Two Spot. Ray Charles began his career here after learning music at the St. Augustine School for the Deaf and the Blind. To visit the ocean, black Jacksonville traveled north to American Beach, a two-hundred-acre resort on Amelia Island purchased by Lewis. There, wealthy black families bought oceanfront property and built summer homes.

In the 1950s token civil rights gains were made in Jacksonville—the first swimming pool for blacks and the hiring of the first black cops (who could not arrest whites). Not until April 1, 1959, under an NAACP federal lawsuit, did the first golf course allow blacks to play. However, within a month, bombs exploded at a Negro school and a Jewish synagogue.

In December 1960 Sadie Braxton sued the Duval County school system to integrate her children in the better white schools. With NAACP attorneys

Thurgood Marshall, Constance Baker Motley, and Earl Johnson (who later headed the city council), Braxton won in 1962, but meaningful integration was delayed until 1970. When the sit-in movement bloomed across the South, an NAACP youth group led by Rutledge Pearson and sixteen-year-old Rodney Hurst launched a campaign against downtown lunch counters. Three weeks of protests led to Jacksonville's day of infamy, August 27, 1960, known as Ax Handle Saturday.

More violence occurred on February 16, 1964, when a bomb exploded under the house of Iona Godfrey, a black civil rights worker whose six-year-old son, Donald, had been the first to integrate a white elementary school. Kitchen appliances fell through the blast hole but Iona and Donald survived. On March 23, a downtown protest rally by two thousand people at Hemming Square became a riot. Police arrested two hundred. Later that night, four white men decided to "get a nigger" and gunned down Johnnie Mae Chappell, a thirty-six-year-old domestic who was looking for her wallet along U.S. 1. Only one of the men served time, two years in prison. Meanwhile, all over the city, black kids rioted for a week. A biracial commission was created, and three years later, the first two blacks were elected to the city council.

Integration and "urban renewal" devastated the black center of Jacksonville. By the 1990s the Afro-American Life Insurance Company was out of business and the once-vibrant business district wiped away. Russ Myer, in *American Beach,* described present-day Ashley Street as a "midtown tundra."

I **AX HANDLE SATURDAY MEMORIAL** *(Hemming Square, Downtown)* A state historic marker blandly titled CIVIL RIGHTS DEMONSTRATION identifies the vicinity where on August 27, 1960, several hundred white supremacists, Klansmen, and neo-Confederates chased and beat a smaller group of NAACP youths trying to sit in at segregated lunch counters. The men used ax handles, bats, and golf clubs and injured dozens; the event thus became known as Ax Handle Saturday. When the lunch counters closed, the kids were met outside by the thugs who beat everyone they could catch. When the melee entered black neighborhoods, black gangs attacked the Klan, using guns, sticks, and Molotov cocktails. It took two hundred cops to quell the violence. Fifty people were wounded, and sixty-two were arrested, mostly blacks.

The sit-in targets are now gone—W. T. Grants at West Adams and North Main, and Woolworth's on Hogan Street—but after the Saturday demonstration, the Jacksonville Chamber of Commerce negotiated an integration plan. Still, many restaurants remained segregated for years, while Hemming Square witnessed another riot in 1964. "Within the decade," the marker reads, "lunch counters were integrated, Duval County public schools began to desegregate, four African-Americans were elected to City Council, and segregation of public accommodations, including parks, restrooms, and water fountains, ended."

2 | **RITZ THEATRE AND LAVILLA MUSEUM** (*829 North Davis Street at State Street; 904-632-5555*)   This was not the fanciest club in the LaVilla neighborhood, but it is one of the few surviving buildings, and has been remodeled into a small museum to black Jacksonville's heyday. Special exhibits cover the civil rights movement, but the centerpiece of the museum is an animatronic display featuring James Weldon Johnson and John Rosamond Johnson, brothers who wrote "Lift Every Voice and Sing." A multitalented Jacksonville native, James Johnson was variously a poet during the Harlem Renaissance, a teacher, the first black to pass the Florida bar, an international diplomat under President Wilson, and the founding secretary of the Jacksonville NAACP. He left Jacksonville because of segregation.

Interstate construction and urban "redevelopment" scraped much of the deteriorated black neighborhood clean. Another museum is proposed in the building that once housed Emanuel's Tap Room, a club famous for its nightlife during segregation.

3 | **AFRO-AMERICAN LIFE INSURANCE COMPANY** (*Ocean and Union Streets*)   This old building doesn't do justice to the company that once pumped millions of dollars and immense pride into black Jacksonville. Founded under segregation in 1901, it provided burial and other insurance to black families across the South. Abraham Lincoln Lewis, the founding secretary, created many wealthy black executives,

Ritz Theatre (now LaVilla Museum) in Jacksonville

and purchased the only remaining black resort in Florida—American Beach on Amelia Island. The company closed in 1987, a victim of competition from giant insurance companies. Its last office now houses the district office of the AME church.

4 | KINGSLEY PLANTATION *(Florida Route 105, Fort George Island; 904-251-3537; www.cr.nps.gov/nr/travel/geo-flor/21.htm)* The most interesting story at this plantation is unseen: the meaning and morality of race and slavery, and how it played out in ambiguous and powerful ways in one mixed-race family. The physical setting—an old house and the ruins of slave quarters—provides only a backdrop for an American drama as interesting and ongoing as *Roots,* but this one revolving around women.

In 1806 Zephaniah Kingsley, a Scottish slaveholder, said to be brilliant and rich and a hunchback, purchased in Cuba a kidnapped African teenager named Anta. By the time they reached his plantation on the St. Johns River, she was pregnant with the first of their four children. He had other slave mistresses and children, but Anna, as she became known, he claimed as his wife. He formally freed her in 1811 and she had slaves and property of her own granted by Spain. This plantation, operated by the National Park Service, is the only surviving plantation from the Spanish Colonial period in Florida.

The difference in Spanish and U.S. attitudes about slaves and race became immediately clear when Florida was traded to the United States in 1821. The territorial legislature passed laws that made the Kingsley marriage illegal, and the family moved to Haiti. After Kingsley died in 1843, his sister challenged Anna's inheritance, though Florida courts upheld it. Returning after the Civil War, Anna lived until 1870 and was buried behind her daughter's house on the St. Johns River south of Jacksonville. One of her grandsons was elected to the state senate, and her bloodline extended seven generations to MaVynee Betsch, the matriarch of American Beach north of the plantation, and her sister, Dr. Johnnetta Cole, who became president of Spelman College in Atlanta.

5 | AMERICAN BEACH *(Florida Route 105, Amelia Island; www.cr.nps. gov/nr/feature/afam/2003/florida.htm)* Caught in a time warp, this rustic oceanfront property is a remnant of segregated America now facing inexorable change. Purchased in 1935 by black millionaire A. L. Lewis, it was one of the few places in Florida where blacks could enjoy the beach. Executives with Lewis's Afro-American Life Insurance Company bought property, and vacations were awarded as sales incentives.

The 1964 Civil Rights Act ended segregated beaches in the South, which left American Beach a historical curiosity. Most beach businesses are closed and whites now own several dozen of the oceanfront lots. Still, owners are seeking protection as a historic district from encroachment by neighboring, megaresort "plantations" that can be seen over the sand dunes.

For years, a great-granddaughter of Lewis, MaVynee Betsch, has lived a colorful and controversial existence on the beach, inveighing against and donating her fortune to fight creeping development, environmental racism, and economic disparity. Approachable, witty, and passionate, the former opera singer turned "beach lady" is a remarkable figure with her seven-foot-long hair full of political pins and her visitors center trailer covered with bumper stickers on behalf of butterflies, feminism, and freedom.

Miami

Civil rights as practiced in Miami is not a black-and-white story. A city renowned for its Latin immigrations and Cuban domination, the subplot among blacks is not as cheery. After securing civil rights for all minorities, some African Americans perceive that the arrival of each new refugee creates another rung above them.

Miami was carved out of mangroves by black men—twelve, to be exact—handpicked by John Sewell, the supervisor for Henry Flagler's Royal Palm Hotel. They cleared the land, notably a Tequesta Indian mound, and used dynamite to break the hold of mangrove and ironwood rooted in coral. But after the dozen workers built the city, they couldn't participate in its growth. Many women washed clothes for tourists who, according to the fashion of the time, wore "Palm Beach white." In a 1915 tourist booklet, rich northern travelers were advised to leave their black chauffeurs home because Miami garages wouldn't accept cars driven by blacks. Thus began a

habit of changing to white drivers at the city line. A near riot occurred over the issue in 1917, before blacks finally broke the chauffeur color line.

Blacks, who made up 42 percent of the population in 1910, lived in Colored Town, later called Overtown, fifty blocks of cultural hotbed and "squalid, congested" slum, according to historian Marvin Dunn. Efforts in the 1930s to clean the slums for health reasons allied with thinly disguised efforts to eradicate blacks from the city center. As early as 1936, the Dade County Planning Board targeted Overtown for a "Negro resettlement plan," and real estate magnate George Merrick once proposed "a complete slum clearance effectively removing every negro family from the present city limits."

Historian Raymond Mohl described how real estate "redlining" and official government housing projects created black neighborhoods outside Miami—Liberty Square in Liberty City included a wall to separate it from a white neighborhood—and how the construction of Interstate 95 finally did the trick. "Some forty thousand blacks had made Overtown home before the interstate came, but less than eight thousand now remain in what is an urban wasteland dominated by the physical presence of the expressway," Mohl wrote.

As middle-class blacks sought better lives, they ran into suburban racism. Coconut Grove, which had been originally settled by black Bahamians, objected when two black families tried to move into a "white" section. The planning board built a dividing wall. In 1945 residents of Opa-locka came within six votes of an ordinance prohibiting black homes and businesses. Blacks began moving in, and Opa-locka now is considered a historic black community, its Moorish architecture a tourist attraction.

Miami Beach hotels and restaurants that were owned by Jews (who had been shunned earlier in the century) integrated in 1956. Four years later, after a brief sit-in at Burdine's by CORE and the NAACP, business leaders led by John Turner desegregated stores en masse on August 1, 1960. Miami thus became the first city in Florida to integrate lunch counters. Beaches, golf courses, parks, and swimming pools followed. The school system led the state—Orchard Villa elementary integrated in the fall of 1959—but it would take more than a decade to fully integrate.

Although Martin Luther King Jr. visited Miami several times, the city's civil rights movement was a local revolution led by Fathers Theodore Gibson and John Culmer, the Reverend Edward Graham, Dr. John Brown, and attorney G. E. Graves. In 1965, Athalie Range became the first black on the city commission. Their work helped pave the way for Cuban refugees, who were welcomed as cold war refugees and awarded some $50 million in federal small business loans. As Latinos took control of the city, they also won the bulk of minority contracts, according to *Black Miami*.

Beginning in 1968, numerous black riots exploded over police brutality. The first erupted after officers dangled a naked seventeen-year-old from a bridge over the Miami River. In December 1979 a black insurance agent, Arthur McDuffie, was handcuffed during a traffic infraction and beaten to death by a gang of police. Their 1980 acquittal on manslaughter charges filed by Janet Reno led to a four-day riot that killed eighteen and left $100 million in damage. Ten years later, the *Miami Herald* reported that most of the postriot money aimed at revitalizing black areas went to Hispanics.

By the 1990s many blacks were tired of widespread busing used to achieve school integration in a city with segregated housing patterns. Of the twenty-three thousand kids bused, nineteen thousand were black. The school board was asked to try magnet schools. Blacks made up 30 percent of Miami in 2003, and held seats on the city and county commissions and school board.

Black Miami's long and traumatic history, including groundbreaking civil rights work, has not been memorialized well. The single best source is the **Black Archives, History and Research Foundation of South Florida** (*305-636-2390*) but it requires advance notice to schedule tours or open its properties.

1 | **OVERTOWN** (*between Sixth Avenue and the railroad tracks and Fifth to Twentieth Streets*)   Gutted by Interstate 95, weakened by integration, and damaged during the 1980s riots, Miami's original black neighborhood never recovered. Once known as Colored Town, it apparently took its less obvious name from the phrase "I'm going over town." From the 1920s to the 1960s, Overtown was full of small neighborhoods with thriving bars, bakeries, clubs, churches, schools, and hotels. Second Avenue was the "Great Black Way" where every major black entertainer, athlete, and civil rights leader came to play and socialize. Overtown also had Miami's worst slums.

There are long-range plans to tie together several historic buildings, including the home of millionaire Dana Dorsey and the Lyric Theater, into an Overtown Folklife Village. One roadside marker denoting Overtown stands at the corner of Fourteenth Street and Third Avenue.

2 | **LYRIC THEATER** (*Second Avenue and Eighth Street*)   Built in 1917, the Lyric hosted vaudeville acts, silent movies, and black bands as the entertainment center of black Miami. Second Avenue remained vibrant until the 1970s, and included clubs such as Rockland Palace, the Harlem Square, and the Zebra Lounge, which were as popular with whites as with blacks.

The theater has been restored, and an addition is under way, scheduled to open in late 2004, to house the city's Black Archives,

History and Research Foundation. Inside, the Urban League of Greater Miami will create a time line of civil rights events.

3 | **BOOKER T. WASHINGTON HIGH SCHOOL** (*Sixth Avenue and Twelfth Street*) The first high school in Miami to offer a diploma to blacks, this institution challenged widely held white supremacist views in the 1920s that blacks were genetically inferior and unworthy of classes beyond grade school. Its construction so upset Miami whites that black residents of Colored Town stood watch every night with bonfires and guns. With a courtyard and large meeting rooms, the school became the intellectual and social center for black Miami. According to *Black Miami,* the school produced doctors, nurses, scientists, attorneys, clergy members, business and military leaders, "and legions of black educators." Among its graduates were Garth Reeves, who owned the *Miami Times,* and insurance agent Arthur McDuffie, whose beating death by white police led to the 1980 riot. The original school was torn down and replaced by a new campus with the same name.

4 | **MOUNT ZION BAPTIST CHURCH** (*Third Avenue and Ninth Street*) and **GREATER BETHEL AME CHURCH** (*245 Eighth Street*) These two churches have been fortresses in Miami's black community since their construction in 1896. "Big Bethel" is a beautiful Mediterranean Revival church. Mount Zion, rebuilt after the 1926 hurricane, was led in the 1960s by the Reverend Edward Graham who headed the Miami NAACP. In 1959 Graham and Father Theodore Gibson were sentenced to six months in prison for refusing to hand over the NAACP membership list to a state legislative committee snooping for "subversives." The Supreme Court ruled on their behalf in February 1963. The black-owned *Miami Times* wrote, "Lesser men would not have stood as firm and as courageously as these two men have done."

5 | **VIRGINIA KEY BEACH** (*Key Biscayne Toll Road; 305-361-2749*) Miami's beaches—its most attractive feature—were closed to blacks until June 6, 1945, when Dade County opened Virginia Beach as "colored only" and began running boats from downtown Miami. The first public ocean beach open to blacks in Florida, it was a "separate but equal" beach with first-class facilities, including a bathhouse, merry-go-round, tourist train, and concession stand. At the time, Virginia Key was not connected to the mainland by the Key Biscayne toll road. But within two weeks, four thousand blacks had visited the beach by boat, according to Marvin Dunn in *Black Miami*.

The beach was developed after a small group of activists led black swimmers onto Baker's Haulover Beach, a whites-only beach, and demanded to use it. Three months later, the county opened Virginia Beach.

Although the beach was closed for many years, a citizens group is planning to reopen Virginia Beach as a black historic and environmental landmark with permanent displays by 2005.

6 | **HISTORICAL MUSEUM OF SOUTHERN FLORIDA** *(101 West Flagler Street; 305-375-1492; www.historicalmuseum.org)* Miami's central museum has permanent exhibits on Florida's history and a large photo montage mural, "The Vanguard," memorializing black pioneers. The Urban League of Greater Miami commissioned the mural on the twenty-fifth anniversary of the 1965 Voting Rights Act. The museum's displays and programs pay particular attention to Caribbean immigration, which continues to create civil rights issues for Miami.

Mims

HARRY T. MOORE HOMESITE *(2180 Freedom Avenue; www.nbbd.com/godo/moore)* The first civil rights assassinations of the 1950s occurred in this quiet coastal village on Christmas night, 1951, when white supremacists blew up the house of NAACP state director Harry T. Moore and his wife, Harriette. It was their twenty-fifth wedding anniversary.

Moore, a schoolteacher, became a one-man crusader against racism. As *Ebony* magazine said at the time: "Harry Tyson Moore . . . ground out handouts about equal education on his mimeograph machine in his small six-room cottage, drove his new Buick around the state to talk about civil rights and attended NAACP meetings where he became so active he was named state head of the organization." He and his wife lost their teaching jobs for their activism.

Moore doubled black voter registration in Florida to 116,000, he got the first black deputy sheriff named in the state, and he openly challenged Lake County Sheriff Willis McCall, who had shot two black prisoners while they were handcuffed together. Moore raised money to free the men, and just as that case was coming to trial, a bomb exploded at Moore's house. He was killed instantly and his wife died nine days later. *Ebony* reported that a white man who came to see the wreckage in the town of one thousand remarked: "That's one coon who will keep his mouth shut." The FBI investigated three members of the Ku Klux Klan; one committed suicide after an interrogation, but no one was ever arrested.

In 1989 the county government bought the Moore homesite, and the state legislature appropriated $700,000 to build an interpretative center and museum scheduled to open in late 2004. Plans also call for a replica house to be built on the ten-acre site.

Ocoee

When two black men tried to vote in this central Florida agricultural village on November 2, 1920, whites went on a rampage, killing dozens, burning homes, and driving the entire black population of five hundred out of town. Voting activist July Perry was lynched but not before he killed two attackers. Mose Norman was beaten and run out of town. An NAACP investigator reported thirty to sixty dead along with eighteen homes, a school, and church burned down. Many blacks settled in nearby Apopka, and Ocoee remained a "white" town until the 1980s. By 1998, with black professionals moving into what had become a pleasant suburb of Orlando, the incident was revived and a reconciliation committee worked to create a memorial, and preserve an unmarked African American graveyard.

Rosewood
(Florida Route 24, 10 miles northwest of Cedar Key)
It is not hard to find Rosewood—a wide spot on a lonely two-lane highway cut through tall pines like a tunnel. If someone hasn't stolen it again, a

Rosewood, site of an infamous 1923 massacre

small sign marks the boundary. But it is nearly impossible to find someone willing to talk about Florida's most infamous racial lynching.

On New Year's Day, 1923, in a community built around a sawmill, the wife of the mill's manager claimed a black man attacked her in her home. Bloodhounds following a scent led a white mob into neighboring Rosewood where, over the next week, black men and women and their children were shot, beaten, and burned out of their homes. Families fled into the piney woods, never to return, and a full accounting of death and destruction has never been made. Oral histories from white men tell of mass graves of twenty-six here, thirty-five there. Oral history among blacks begin with eyewitness accounts that the man who started it all, the one who attacked the white woman, Fannie Taylor, was white. These stories were resurrected after Gary Moore of the *St. Petersburg Times* published a 1982 account. The story was subsequently explored in the book *Like Judgment Day* by Michael D'Orso, and the movie *Rosewood*.

"Rosewood was a tragedy of American democracy and the American legal system," concluded a study team commissioned by the Florida legislature. In 1994 a $2 million compensation act was passed providing $150,000 to five survivors of the attack and $500,000 for lost property. College scholarships were created for descendants. The law also set in motion a criminal investigation that eventually named sixteen white men, all dead or unable to be found.

The one remaining landmark in Rosewood is the two-story home of John Wright, a white man who hid several blacks from the mob. Privately owned, the house faces away from the highway toward what was the Rosewood railroad depot. One nearby sign memorializes five white men who reportedly kept the mob from killing everyone. A memorial to the massacre has been talked about for years.

St. Augustine

Being the oldest city on the continent is St. Augustine's claim to fame, and the city's ancient walls have witnessed Florida's entire human rights chronicle. But a visitor must scratch through the city's slick patina of marketed history to find this story.

Established by the Spanish in 1565, St. Augustine was also home to some of the first Africans on the continent. Their status varied from free baptized soldiers to slaves who did the dirty work of carving a colony from wilderness. The establishment of the British slave colony of Charleston, South Carolina, in 1670 created an international conflict, and fifteen years later, the first runaways arrived in St. Augustine seeking sanctuary. It was granted, and the ex-slaves helped finish the massive San Marcos fort to defend against the English. "Liberty to all," declared the Spanish king in 1693, and Florida became a hated refuge among slave owners in the states.

In 1738 St. Augustine established the first settlement for free blacks in the Americas, grandiosely called Gracia Real de Santa Teresa de Mose, two miles north of the San Marcos fort. It was a short-lived but shining dream. Twenty-five years later, after the British took over Florida, the Spanish sailed for Cuba with the entire village of Mose. When the Spanish regained control following the Revolutionary War, Florida again became a slave refuge, which led to Andrew Jackson's infamous "defense" attacks that persuaded Spain to sell Florida to the United States. Again, several colonies of free blacks left for Cuba and Mexico.

As part of the antebellum cotton kingdom, St. Augustine followed the familiar Deep South trajectory: Civil War, Reconstruction, segregation, and a paternalistic order based on unspoken white supremacy. Blacks and whites knew their place and somehow expected that nothing would change. After the Supreme Court integrated public schools in 1954, for example, St. Augustine decided to go ahead and build a new segregated high school for blacks, according to historian David Colburn.

In 1961, more than a year after the sit-in movement swept southern states, college student Henry Thomas tried a solo sit-in at the Woolworth's and was committed to a mental institution. For the next two years, anyone who tried to integrate a St. Augustine store was "put away," according to Colburn. Not until 1963 did St. Augustine's NAACP youth council, led by dentist Robert Hayling, begin to picket and sit in at downtown stores and the tourist center, holding signs that read, "America's oldest city unfair to Negro citizens." At that point St. Augustine's civility ended.

Klansmen from Jacksonville and members of the local John Birch Society burned crosses and demonstrated against integration as local officials maintained a hands-off attitude. At one Klan rally, a speaker said of the 1963 Birmingham bombing that killed four girls in a church: "If there's four less niggers tonight, then, I say, 'good for whoever planted the bomb.' We're all better off."

Into this atmosphere, in April 1964, marched Dr. Martin Luther King Jr. and the Southern Christian Leadership Conference. Their agenda was twofold: confrontation and publicity to integrate St. Augustine and to push through Congress the 1964 Civil Rights Act. They got what they came for. Scores were arrested, including King and Mrs. Malcolm Peabody, the mother of the Massachusetts governor who lived in St. Augustine. A riverfront motel, the Monson Motor Lodge, was the stage for a bizarre "swim-in" that included diving cops, and acid, and alligators thrown in the water. On St. Augustine's beach, cops trying to defend swim-in protesters ended up bashing white supremacists.

The ugliest scenes took place in the downtown square where nightly marchers ran into the clubs and fists of five hundred Ku Klux Klansmen shouting "kill the niggers." After a night of brutality on June 25, King called St. Augustine "the most lawless city SCLC had ever worked in." The following day, Florida's governor announced the creation of a biracial commission and King exited the scene. The commission was a hoax, Colburn wrote in *Racial Change and Community Crisis,* and St. Augustine went down as one of King's failed campaigns.

St. Augustine later integrated, blacks were elected to the city commission, and a black became head of the school system. But several civil rights leaders left town—Dr. Hayling cited threats and loss of business—and the black Florida Memorial College moved to Miami, in part because its graduates couldn't find work in St. Augustine. In a 1990 update to his book, Colburn wrote: "Despite the passage of time, economic data reveal that black residents remain in a subservient position."

FORT MOSE *(Saratoga Boulevard off U.S. 1, two miles north of St. Augustine; www.cr.nps.gov/nr/travel/underground/fl2.htm)* A long boardwalk that dead-ends in a quiet marsh is as close as anyone can get to the site of North America's first free black community. Fort Mose was a modest village but a powerful symbol of hope for escaped slaves from the Carolinas and Georgia. Granted asylum, they became fierce defenders of both the main fort in St. Augustine and their own little village two miles north. The log-and-earth fortress, home to one hundred ex-slaves, was headed by a Mandingo native, Francisco Menendez, who had escaped from the Carolinas in 1724. During the 1740 war, Georgia's governor, James Oglethorpe, attacked the site but was repulsed by a black force from Mose. The black population then built a second fort and village with homes for twenty-two families.

In 1746, Ira Berlin reports, blacks made up one-quarter of St. Augustine, and they were baptized, married, and buried under church sanctity. When Spain ceded Florida to the English, most of the blacks in St. Augustine and Fort Mose moved to Cuba.

Archaeologists have found the foundations of both forts, but they are surrounded by saltwater marsh. A visitors center is planned.

LINCOLNVILLE HISTORIC DISTRICT *(Martin Luther King Street)* One year after the Civil War, free blacks created a neighborhood called Africa just off St. Augustine's main square. Renamed Lincolnville, it became a proud, segregated enclave as Jim Crow ruled Florida for the next century. Victorian houses, palms, and live oaks give it an air of Caribbean ease. But in 1964 Lincolnville was the staging area for courageous, nightly civil rights marches to the town square where demonstrators were met by club-wielding members of the Ku Klux Klan. When Klan members drove through Lincolnville firing guns, residents shot back and killed a white man. The arrest of four black men for murder brought Dr. Martin Luther King Jr. and his SCLC staff to town. For months, Hosea Williams held nightly rallies at **St. Mary's Missionary Baptist Church** (*69 Washington*), and then led a nonviolent crowd down Cordova Street, right on King Street, and two blocks to the town square. There they were beaten, spat on, and arrested. On June 25 King spoke to more than three hundred at the nearby **St. Paul's AME church** (*85 Martin Luther King Street*), and sent them downtown.

While in St. Augustine, King stayed at several houses and moved between them for security. Two houses that hosted him (*81 and 83 Bridge Street*) are marked with signs. A historic marker at the **home of Frank Butler** (*87 Martin Luther King Street*) honors the black businessman who purchased Butler Beach, a historic black beach south of St. Augustine.

PLAZA DE LA CONSTITUCIÓN (*Martin Luther King Street and Cathedral Place*)   This peaceful park has seen all during St. Augustine's long history, but tour guides rarely mention the old slave market, and never the ugliest night in the city's history, June 25, 1964, when the Ku Klux Klan beat civil rights demonstrators.

That morning the demonstrators had conducted a large "wade-in" at St. Augustine's segregated beach, which turned into a melee. As angry whites waited in the water to jump waders, cops chased both sides. That night King inspired a large crowd in Lincolnville to march on the square again.

As more than 300 marchers came down King Street, some 500 Klansmen and their supporters waited at the slave market pavilion. About 150 police tried to keep them separate, but the Klan rushed at them with bricks, firecrackers, and epithets. Tear gas was fired. The marchers, many of them bleeding, scattered.

Tallahassee

Born a frontier capital with a log house for the legislature and Indians peering in the door, Tallahassee soon adopted an antebellum veneer with slave labor. The red soil was good for cotton, and large plantations sprang up, creating in thirty years a Deep South mentality not unlike neighboring Georgia and Alabama. When the civil rights movement intruded, Tallahassee had to be dragged into the twentieth century.

Blacks comprised 34 percent of the city's population, but it took eight years of entreaties by a delegation of ministers before the city hired its first black cop in 1952. Even though the Montgomery bus boycott touched off a Tallahassee version, it took another fourteen years of boycotts, sit-ins, pickets, marches, and voter drives amid violence and intimidation to finally bring a semblance of equal rights to Florida's capital.

The movement ignited on Saturday, May 26, 1956, when two black college students boarded a crowded city bus and sat in the front row. When the driver told them they couldn't sit there, Wilhelmina Jakes responded, "Why? If I can't sit where I want to, then I'd like to have my money back, please." The driver called police, who charged Jakes and her roommate Carrie Patterson with inciting a riot. When they were released, the bondsman asked if they were communists. The next day, after they were front-page news, a cross was burned on their lawn.

On Monday, according to historian Glenda Rabby, student government leader Broadus Hartley held a mass meeting on the Florida A&M campus and declared a boycott. Students ran to bus stops and asked black riders to get off. They did, and within a day a citywide boycott was under way. An organization of ministers, patterned after the Montgomery Improvement Association and called the Inter-Civic Council (ICC), was coordinated by the Reverend Charles K. Steele, pastor of Bethel Missionary Baptist Church. Nicknamed "Preacher" as a child for his tabletop efforts to spread the gospel to his own family, Steele was a graduate of Morehouse College in Atlanta and later a founding vice president of Martin Luther King's Southern Christian Leadership Conference.

The Montgomery boycott, Steele later said, was "the handwriting on the wall for the South" and Tallahassee's boycott, coming five months after Montgomery's, was "a little David who came along and interpreted that handwriting." ICC set up car pools, as in Montgomery. And like Montgomery, negotiations with the city quickly deteriorated into a long contest of wills. Loans were called on participants. Insurance was canceled. The car pool was ruled illegal. The city also pried into Steele's background. After Montgomery won its bus case in December 1956, Tallahassee tried an informal integration scheme, but violence flared. Steele, according to Rabby, left the bullet holes in his home window blinds unrepaired for years as a reminder of the violence. After a year, the financially hurting bus company phased out segregated seating by simply ignoring a city ordinance.

The next wave of activism was prompted by the 1960 sit-in movement. Twelve days after the February 1 sit-in at Woolworth's in Greensboro, North Carolina, Patricia and Priscilla Stephens, sisters and students at A&M, sat down at the Woolworth's in Tallahassee. Nothing happened, but they were arrested on a subsequent day for "riotous conduct." In the ensuing days there was tear gas and arrests and state police called to keep students on campus. Supported by the Reverend Steele and white students from Florida State University, the Stephens sisters became local CORE leaders involved in many civil rights actions.

Governor LeRoy Collins, who had once compared demonstrators to communists, changed his rhetoric during the sit-ins. On March 20 after a tear-gas attack by police, Collins declared that blacks had the moral right to be seated at a lunch counter. This was a first for a governor in the South. By the end of 1962, Tallahassee had quietly joined Florida's other major cities in serving blacks.

That same year, the Reverend Steele and four other parents filed to integrate Leon County schools. Under federal court order, three kids entered Leon High School on September 8, 1963. But Harold Knowles, Phillip Hadley, and Marilyn Holifield were the only blacks out of two thousand students and the experience was brutal. "I just wanted to get out of the South," Knowles told Rabby. When they graduated only five other black students were at Leon High.

After watching her son go through the experience, Knowles's mother, Christene, took a typewriter and went door to door in black neighborhoods, filling out student applications. "I just had my dog and I was frightened, but I always lived by the philosophy of Martin King. He said if you live on earth and you don't do anything, you're dead anyway. . . . That is how we really began to integrate the schools of Leon County." It took sixteen years after *Brown* and eight years after the Steele court case to create a unitary school system, Rabby wrote in *The Pain and the Promise*.

In the summer of 1963, A&M students went after segregated swimming pools, but the city closed them. Not until five days after the 1968 assassination of Martin Luther King Jr., on a day "when riots engulfed the city," did Tallahassee reopen its swimming pools to all citizens.

Charles Kenzie
Steele sculpture

CHARLES KENZIE STEELE MEMORIAL AND BUS STATION *(111 West Tennessee Street)* Frail looking but with the temperament of bronze, the monument of Reverend Steele is a fitting tribute to the man who led the Tallahassee civil rights movement and became a trusted lieutenant to Dr. Martin Luther King Jr. When two black college students spontaneously refused to move from a "white" seat on a Tallahassee bus in May 1956, Steele headed up a boycott committee in one of the most recalcitrant cities in the South. For the next fourteen years, Steele was in the forefront of Tallahassee civil rights, along with students at Florida A&M and Florida State. When a car-pool system was gutted by legal action, the sight of black maids walking to work inspired Steele. "I'd rather walk in dignity than ride in humiliation," he said. The boycott wore down the bus company, though the city government resisted longer than any other city in the South to prevent integration of restaurants, pools, theaters, and schools. Steele died in 1980.

FLORIDA A&M UNIVERSITY *(Gamble Street and Boulevard Street; 850-599-3000; www.famu.edu)* Without the students at this historically black college, there would not have been a civil rights movement in the state capital. Founded in 1887 as the first black public school, Florida Agriculture and Mechanical became a land grant college in 1890 and created a campus on a former plantation. The Black Archives Research Center and Museum displays a wide variety of black history totems, but little about the civil rights movement.

Tampa

LA UNION MARTI-MACEO *(1226 East Seventh Avenue, Ybor City)* The story of Cuban cigar makers in Tampa is preserved in the bricks of old Ybor City, at the eastern edge of the city. Here, cigar rollers of all shades came together in a multiethnic civil rights model. Then state law forced mutual aid societies to segregate along race or color lines. The darkest workers were lumped with the city's blacks in schools and other second-class categories. A new mutual aid club, La Union Marti-Maceo, opened for their support.

St. Paul AME Church *(506 East Harrison Street)*   On February 29, 1960, fifty-seven members of an NAACP youth group staged Tampa's first sit-in at Woolworth's lunch counter. Shots were fired into the home of the Reverend Leon Lowry of St. Paul's for helping lead the protest. But within days, Tampa business leaders negotiated a settlement to avoid the violence of St. Augustine and Jacksonville. It became known as the "Tampa Technique." Small groups of black "testers" checked out compliance at stores. Tampa's movie theaters resisted integration for years, and for a long time, the area beaches were a dangerous place for blacks to be seen.

Contanchobee Park *(East Tampa–Hillsborough Bay)*   A "weeping wall" fountain with historic plaques describes the story of Fort Brooke, a nexus of the Second Seminole War, which crushed Indian resistance and opened Florida to white settlement and statehood. The seven-year, $40 million conflict was the costliest Indian war in U.S. history, with 1,500 U.S. soldiers dead and some 4,000 Seminoles, including 500 black Seminoles, relocated to Oklahoma. The war began here with the departure of Major Francis Dade and his 107 soldiers, who were ambushed and slaughtered on December 28, 1835, by Seminoles near Bushnell. At various points during the war, groups of Seminoles were shipped west from this fort. Remnant bands of Seminoles remained in Florida. Now based in Hollywood, outside Miami, the Seminole tribe developed Big Cypress museums in Tampa and Hollywood.

Alabama

WHEN PEOPLE THINK of the civil rights movement, they picture Alabama. Mass meetings, mass marches, demagoguery, fire hoses, beatings and bombings. From images captured during a decade of struggle, Alabama stands at the epicenter of America's second revolution.

The battle, at times, seemed biblical—pitting the powers of the state against the unarmed, resolute will of black people. Officials Bull Connor and George Wallace became arch villains while Rosa Parks and Martin Luther King Jr., unknown citizens, emerged as heroes. Behind both sides stood small armies of supporters whose clashes, caught on film, constituted one of the great dramas of human history.

Before 1955, Alabama's race relations were typical of Deep South states. Whites were in charge—period. Black Alabama endured, the vast majority locked in poverty, and its middle class unwilling to rock a carefully constructed, if segregated, boat. Any number of possible ignition points came and went until Rosa Parks was arrested. What erupted then, a yearlong bus boycott, had as much to do with white resistance as black fortitude. Members of the power structure refused to offer the slightest concession or measure of dignity to their fellow Alabamans. Similar hostilities sparked the infamous clashes years later in Birmingham and Selma.

Rosa Parks riding the bus in Montgomery in 1956

Protest tactics learned in the Montgomery movement spread across the South. Combined with court orders, progress was steady in many states. Yet eight years after the bus boycott, newly elected Governor George Wallace bellowed from the capitol steps, "Segregation forever!" Not long after, Birmingham erupted with dogs and hoses against children, and the bombing of a church that killed four girls.

Ten years after the bus boycott, in a march for voting rights, thousands of people, black and white, walked past the spot where Rosa Parks had been arrested and advanced on Wallace's capitol. By then, the movement had reached unimaginable heights—federal legislation and court rulings outlawing discrimination in virtually every public accommodation. Four months later, a voting rights act would mark the movement's zenith.

For a long time after, shame and exhaustion silenced Alabama. Not until the 1980s did anyone honor the memory of a movement that had brought the state so much notoriety. Books and movies and TV shows began to describe the movement years. An annual reenactment of the Selma-to-

Montgomery voting rights march was launched. Birmingham built a museum, and on the spot where the act was photographed, erected a bold sculpture of a police dog attacking a young man. As tourists began to arrive, pride replaced injury.

Today, without a whiff of irony, Alabama is making a name for itself promoting this history of race relations. Two dozen sites, museums, monuments, and visitors centers are open, under construction, or promised. There still are pockets of defensiveness and unresolved racial differences, but they are sublimated to a new reality. Alabama again has become a civil rights destination.

Alabama and Civil Rights

Alabama's origins are not romantic. The state emerged from a river-soaked wilderness peopled by Indians to a cotton kingdom peopled by slaves, one pushed out to make room for the other.

The first cotton gin reached Alabama twelve years before Andrew Jackson crushed the Creeks to officially open the Mississippi Territory to white settlement. Two years later, in 1816, on a high bluff overlooking the Alabama River, Montgomery was founded. Within three years, Alabama was born an antebellum state—"a land of cotton with stately mansions and Negroes singing in the hot sun," so went the common picture described by the federal writers' project in the 1930s. A *Gone With the Wind* social fabric remained in place, more or less, until the civil rights revolution.

Though there were many independent yeoman farmers, big planters of the fertile black belt drove Alabama economically and politically. Markets in Selma and Montgomery sold slaves by the hundreds. They arrived by steamboat up the Alabama River and overland from Virginia and South Carolina and were put in warehouses until picked over by buyers. John Hardy, quoted in Harvey Jackson's *Rivers of History,* saw "blacksmiths, carpenters, bright mulatto girls and women for seamstresses, field hands, women and children of all ages, sizes and qualities."

On the eve of the Civil War, Alabama counted 565,000 whites, of whom only 33,000 owned the state's 435,000 slaves. The typical planter view, expressed by W. G. Robertson in a book about early Montgomery settlers, was: "the slave was not only satisfied and contented with his lot in life, but he was a happy being."

Threatened by the northern abolitionist movement and wedded to slavery for its livelihood, Alabama pushed for federal guarantees of its "way of life." Congressman William Yancey, the first of a long line of strident racists, even called for the reopening of the African slave trade. Antislave sentiment, Yancey ranted, denies "the people and their states the rights that they so dearly love . . . if it continues there will be no other resource than to split the nation in half." States' rights, as defined by this "oracle of secession," meant the right to own slaves. At the time, only thirty-four Alabama men owned more than two hundred slaves.

On January 11, 1861, two months after Lincoln's election to the White House, an Alabama convention in the starch-white capitol in Montgomery voted for a Yancey motion to secede, the fourth southern state to do so. The strongest objection came from hilly Winston County, which threatened to secede from Alabama and form a "northern" state called Nickajack. After the vote, deafening cheers filled the galleries. Bells rang, cannons were fired. A minister called it a "thrilling" scene.

Such scenes were repeated a month later as secessionist states gathered in the same building, now the capitol of the Confederacy. Observers described the mood as "a prairie fire." Using language that today seems ridiculously ironic, U.S. Senator Jefferson Davis of Mississippi demanded, "Will you be slaves or will you be independent?" Beneath the columned portico, he took the oath as the first president of the new southern nation. The band played "Dixie." People danced in the streets. Two months later, on April 11, Davis telegraphed Charleston to fire on Fort Sumter. William Yancey, who died before the war ended, left a fitting epitaph: Montgomery, he said, is "above all else the cradle of the Confederacy, a splendid town filled with beautiful people who believe in The Cause."

For the next century, those heady days would be remembered by white Alabama. After a war that took perhaps 40,000 young white Alabama men and freed 439,000 slaves, the lost cause would be glorious baggage. Whites buried their dead and mourned for the good old days, while blacks from plantations poured into squatter camps—one in Montgomery was called Hard Times—looking for the promise of emancipation. The idea of giving these ex-slaves freedom, citizenship, *and* the vote was, from a white southern perspective, a "radical" notion pushed by local Republican sympathizers (scalawags) and outsiders (carpetbaggers). Yankee teachers working in new black schools were especially hated.

When the first postwar legislature refused to share democracy with freed blacks, a federal military governor took control and allowed ex-slaves to vote. In March 1867 blacks all over the state met in their first, hopeful political meetings. By 1869 blacks controlled a third of the seats in the state legislature and soon sent black congressmen Benjamin Turner, James Rapier, and Jeremiah Haralson to Washington.

The promise, however, was not to be. With little economic clout or experience, blacks were defrauded, terrorized, and voted out of power. Some were accused of taking bribes. They were abandoned by their supposed friends among scalawags and carpetbaggers who didn't really believe in equal rights.

The Ku Klux Klan, formed on Christmas Eve, 1865, in Pulaski, Tennessee, played a major role in ending the dream of shared power, especially in northern and western Alabama. One of the Klan's first targets was a black man in Athens who had been seen with a white northern schoolteacher. He was kidnapped, taken to a wooded cove outside of town, and dunked into icy water. Later, an Irish teacher and four black men were lynched in Cross Plains. In Huntsville, three hundred Klansmen rode through on a Sunday, driving blacks from their churches. As the 1870 elections neared, Klansmen raided a GOP rally in Eutaw, and killed four blacks and wounded fifty-four. In Mobile, Democrats rolled a cannon in front of a polling place, aimed it at one thousand waiting black voters, and scattered them.

The fear drove blacks and their supporters from the polls, so much so that Democrats regained control in 1870, based almost entirely on the sudden drop in black Republican votes in Greene, Sumter, and Elmore Counties. According to congressional investigations, the Klan killed 109 Alabamans between 1865 and 1870, the worst violence in the South.

It was this atmosphere that Booker T. Washington faced when he arrived—invited by a slave and a former slave owner—in Tuskegee in 1881 to create a school for blacks. His goal was practical, industrial education that would, in time, allow white southerners to accept equality between the races. Progress, he said in a famous Atlanta speech, "must be the result of severe and constant struggle rather than of artificial forcing." For the next eighty-five years, behind the COLORED signs of a segregated Alabama, the struggle was indeed constant. In 1908, after Montgomery's city council segregated the city, including its trolley system, the private bus company shut down for two days to protest the burden of creating "black" and "white" buses. As a compromise the city allowed trolleys to carry both races, but forced the blacks to ride in back, a system passed on to city buses.

By the 1930s more than 80 percent of black farmers were sharecroppers, a system little better than peonage. They were actually outnumbered three to two by poor whites stuck in the same cycle, their plight brought to national attention by writer James Agee and photographer Walker Evans in *Let Us Now Praise Famous Men*. While poor folks, both black and white, might have been allies, politicians and industrialists drove a race wedge between them.

The quick dispatch to death row of eight black men accused of rape by two white women in Scottsboro in 1931 was a crude mirror of Alabama human rights at the time. The Scottsboro Boys (a ninth was sentenced to life) were saved eventually by a communist-led defense. Hosting secret meetings of the National Committee to Defend Scottsboro Boys in Montgomery was one Raymond Parks, whose new wife, Rosa, was both frightened by the guns the men laid on the table, according to biographer Douglas Brinkley, and radicalized by the issue. Mrs. Parks, a graduate of Miss White's Industrial School for Girls and employed at Maxwell Air Force Base, began taking umbrage as she transferred from Maxwell's integrated trolley to Montgomery's segregated bus. "You might just say Maxwell opened my eyes up," Mrs. Parks told Brinkley. In 1943 she was kicked off a city bus by driver James Blake for refusing to reenter through the back door after paying her fare. They would meet again twelve years later.

Mrs. Parks volunteered as secretary of the NAACP branch led by E. D. Nixon, a rough-hewn railroad porter and union leader who wanted a legal case to challenge the bus system. In March 1955, when Claudette Colvin, a rebellious high school student, refused to give up her seat to a white passenger, Nixon declined to use her as a test case. In August of that year, Mrs. Parks attended a desegregation and voting rights workshop at the Highlander Folk School in Tennessee. "I was 42 and it was one of the few times in my life up to that point when I did not feel any hostility from white people," she told Brinkley. In October another woman, Mary Louise Smith, was arrested for refusing to give up her bus seat. Nixon again declined her case because of her background. Three months later, Rosa Parks gave Nixon a defendant he could be proud of.

The yearlong boycott survived every violent and legal obstruction Montgomery and the state could throw at it—including the banning of the NAACP, the drafting of the boycott's lead attorney into the army, and arrests and lawsuits against its leader, Dr. Martin Luther King Jr. It ended only after the U.S. Supreme Court extended its school desegregation ruling to buses. By then King had been crowned the new movement's national chief.

But rather than diffusing racial differences, the 1956 boycott victory sharpened them. The White Citizens Council formed in Selma and grew to eighty thousand members statewide. Race politics became the norm in Alabama, and years of resistance and violence followed. Between 1958 and 1980 the Supreme Court decided fourteen landmark cases involving racial discrimination in Alabama, according to historian Wayne Flynt. "It is fair to say that the bitter resistance of Alabama whites played a major role in the success of the civil rights agenda," he concluded in *Alabama: The History of a Deep South State*.

In Birmingham, so many homes and black churches were bombed in 1957 that the city was nicknamed "Bombingham." In 1959 Montgomery's city commission closed all fourteen city parks rather than comply with a federal court order to integrate. It sold the animals in the zoo and filled in the swimming pool. When ordered by the same judge to integrate its library, the city removed all desks and chairs. In 1961 Birmingham closed thirty-eight playgrounds and six swimming pools rather than integrate. When the Freedom Ride buses arrived that year, Alabama greeted them with three sets of beatings in Anniston, Birmingham, and Montgomery.

Governor George Wallace's "segregation forever" pledge during his inauguration in January 1963 was followed by Birmingham's year of infamy. The Southern Christian Leadership Conference opened Project C (for *confrontation*) with daily mass marches and sit-ins. Police commissioner Bull Connor met them with fire hoses and police dogs. A month later, Wallace stood "in the schoolhouse door" to symbolically stop court-ordered integration of the University of Alabama. In September, just as public schools were about to integrate, the Klan exploded the bomb killing four girls, an event that brought everlasting notoriety to Birmingham and helped push through the Civil Rights Act of 1964.

The following year, the focus shifted to voting rights in the black belt. After state troopers shot and killed Jimmie Lee Jackson during a mass march in Marion, organizers decided to confront Wallace, a demonstration that led to the Bloody Sunday beatings and, ultimately, the biggest mass march of the civil rights era, from Selma to Montgomery. That march, and four protester deaths surrounding it, persuaded Congress to pass the last great piece of civil rights legislation, the Voting Rights Act of 1965.

As Birmingham moved toward reconciliation, Selma and Montgomery maintained leadership reluctant to sharing power with blacks. Yet, blacks slowly won elections—a Birmingham mayor, a sheriff in Lowndes County. In 2000 Alabama was second only to Mississippi in the number of black elected officials, with 731.

Given this history, it is not surprising that on almost any issue, race matters. A divide remains in neighborhoods, schools, and economic and political clout. Alabamans, black and white, concede that this legacy has helped keep the state near the bottom in national indices, and yearn for a way past it.

An Alabama Civil Rights Tour

The vast majority of civil rights spots lie along Interstate 85 through what is known as Alabama's "black belt," a term that referred to the soil. The forced presence of slaves on this soil set up the conflicts of the twentieth century.

A state-designated civil rights trail runs from Tuskegee through Montgomery, Selma, Marion, and Greensboro. It includes the Selma-to-Montgomery National Historic Trail. Visiting the sites and museums could take a visitor one to four days.

Birmingham, with its unique civil rights district, is one hundred miles to the north of Montgomery. A visitor should plan a day's trip.

The cities of Tuscaloosa, Muscle Shoals, and Mobile, while separate from the main trail, contain important landmarks in the state's human rights struggle.

Alabama's Bureau of Tourism and Travel publishes a substantial black heritage guide and trail pamphlet. Additional pamphlets are available at museums and visitors centers (**Alabama Bureau of Tourism, P.O. Box 4927, Montgomery AL 36103; 800-ALABAMA; *www.touralabama.org*).**

City by City

Anniston

This Appalachian industrial town halfway between Birmingham and Atlanta was the site of two bizarre acts of violence during the civil rights movement, though nothing marks either event. The first was the firebombing of a Greyhound bus carrying Freedom Riders in 1961. Their trip, from Washington, D.C., to Mississippi, had been largely uneventful until they met a mob here with clubs, pipes, and knives that slashed tires and tried to get inside. Two undercover agents inside the bus ordered the driver to pull away and they raced west on U.S. 78 followed by fifty cars and two hundred men. Just outside of town, the tires went flat. The driver pulled over and ran for his life, leaving nine Freedom Riders and five uninvolved passengers inside, as the mob used axes and bricks to smash windows. Someone threw a firebomb inside. As seats caught fire, the mob held the door shut. Waving his gun, one of the undercover agents forced the crowd back and the passengers spilled out to a savage beating. Firing state troopers broke it up. An hour later, a second bus with more Freedom Riders pulled into Anniston and a second mob boarded, beating the passengers in the aisle.

Two years later, an Anniston mob beat two black ministers who were the first to integrate the city's public library. Federal courts in Alabama and Virginia had desegregated libraries, and both the Anniston city commission and library board had ordered the library open on Sunday, September 15,

The Freedom Riders' firebombed bus in 1961

1963. With city approval, the Reverend W. B. McClain and the Reverend Quintus Reynolds were to make the ceremonial first entry. But before they reached the door, a group of seventy attacked with chains and sticks, injuring both men. The attack was buried beneath the news of that morning's bombing of Birmingham's Sixteenth Street Baptist Church that killed four girls. According to Patterson Graham's *A Right to Read,* the attack was "one of the most disturbing events in the history of American public libraries." The library, with city police protection, was integrated the following day.

Birmingham

Created in the fire of steel blast furnaces in the late 1800s, Birmingham's birth coincided with Jim Crow's, and the city began life segregated. Racial attitudes were institutionalized by the city's "Big Mules," the industrialists who built company towns in the shadows of smokestacks. Steelworker unions integrated in the 1940s, but among the working white miners were Ku Klux Klansmen who handled dynamite in their work and lashed out at anyone they considered a threat to their jobs. When blacks began activism in the 1950s, Klansmen blew up dozens of homes and churches. Nat King Cole was attacked on stage at the Municipal Auditorium. Just a few days after the Montgomery bus boycott ended, a bomb exploded at the Reverend Fred Shuttlesworth's church, prompting deacons to set up an armed guard. In September 1957 Klansmen abducted black handyman Edward Aaron and castrated him with a razor. Four men were sent to prison for it, but the Klan's terrorism would keep Birmingham in the news for years thanks to an unofficial alliance with police commissioner Bull Connor.

In May 1961 a mob beat Freedom Riders in the city's bus station. When a federal judge desegregated city parks, the city council closed all thirty-eight, going so far as to pour concrete in the golf holes. The decision also closed Rickwood Field, the city's popular minor league baseball park used by black and white pro teams.

Blacks began an Easter-buying boycott in the spring of 1962, and the Southern Christian Leadership Conference arrived to begin mass protests in 1963. Dr. Martin Luther King Jr. needed a confrontation to expose Birmingham racism, and he got it from newly elected Wallace and Bull Connor, who had just been defeated in a city election but remained in office pending appeal.

Dogs were used against marchers on Palm Sunday, 1963. King and Ralph Abernathy were arrested during a Good Friday march. When local "mainstream" ministers urged King to leave town, he penned his famous "Letter from Birmingham Jail." When attempts to rally adults failed, SCLC's Jim Bevel reached out to children through local disc jockeys who, in coded chatter, informed them about mass meetings at the Sixteenth Street Baptist Church. "Kids, there's gonna be a party at the park," said DJ Shelley the Playboy. "Bring your toothbrushes because lunch will be served."

More than one thousand children jammed the church on May 2 and began a march downtown. Buses hauled them away. On Friday, May 3, fifteen hundred children marched and were met by high-pressure fire hoses. Blown and rolled by the force, they cowered wherever they could. With another one thousand onlookers booing, Bull Connor ordered six police dogs and their handlers into action. They bit and tore. A picture was taken of K-9 officer Dick Middletown restraining his dog, Leo, as he lunged at a tall high school sophomore, Walter Gadsden. "Why didn't you bring a meaner dog?" Bull Connor said later. Connor, wrote Diane McWhorter in *Carry Me Home,* did not "understand that his show had just entered the realm of myth."

Seven days later, Birmingham agreed to desegregate stores, hire blacks, and create a commission on race relations. But the next day, the Klan tried to blow up King's "war room" at the Gaston Motel. Blacks rioted and President Kennedy sent seventeen thousand troops. That fall, just as Birmingham schools were about to integrate, the Klan blew up a bomb at the Sixteenth Street Baptist Church, killing four girls on September 15. It was Birmingham's forty-seventh bomb since 1947. The event was the final blow to a city's shattered ego. But it would be 1966 before the first black policeman was hired, and 2002 before all the church bombers would be convicted.

Today the space around Kelly Ingram Park is a civil rights district, and a day can be spent in the park and visiting the two major attractions that border it, the Civil Rights Institute and Sixteenth Street Baptist Church. Fourth Street, the once vibrant black neighborhood a block to the south, is undergoing a revival. The former Gaston Motel has been purchased by the city for Institute expansion.

BIRMINGHAM CIVIL RIGHTS INSTITUTE (*520 Sixteenth Street North; 866-328-9696; www.bcri.bham.al.us*) A life-sized statue of the Reverend Fred Shuttlesworth greets visitors to this large museum dedicated to the Birmingham and Alabama civil rights movement. Shuttlesworth worked at high personal risk (arrests, beatings, bombings, jailings) to mobilize a reluctant black population to attack Birmingham's segregation. In 1961 he moved to a Cincinnati church, but returned to join Dr. Martin Luther King Jr. and his Southern Christian Leadership Conference team that took on Birmingham in the spring of 1963. The museum is designed metaphorically to go from the darkness of segregation to the light of a reconciled city. Among the many stories told in the museum is that of James Armstrong, a barber whose children attempted but failed to integrate schools in 1957 under the Supreme Court's *Brown* ruling. His younger children finally won admittance in September 1963 after the brutal Birmingham clashes. The actual jail cell where Dr. King wrote his "Letter from Birmingham Jail" is preserved. Written in the margins of a newspaper and on scraps of paper and smuggled out of city jail, the statement was pieced together at the Gaston Motel (adjacent to the Institute) by King aide Wyatt Walker. The letter condemned apathy among clergy and other good-hearted citizens.

Alabama events are described in detail, including the Montgomery bus boycott, Freedom Rider violence, and the Selma voting rights march. Visitors emerge into a bright gallery overlooking Kelly Ingram Park to signposts of progress: 1968, the city's first black councilman, Arthur Shores; and 1979, its first black mayor, Richard Arrington, who created the civil rights district.

SIXTEENTH STREET BAPTIST CHURCH (*Sixteenth Street and Sixth Avenue; 205-251-9402*)   This was the first black church in Birmingham, organized eight years after the Civil War. The building, erected in 1911, contains a large sanctuary, balcony, and royal red carpet sweeping down to an altar and pipe organ. The basement contains a central meeting room, classrooms, and bathrooms. Built in the heart of a thriving black community in segregated Birmingham, it became the center of mass meetings during civil rights activism. Most marches began here with stirring speeches and lessons in nonviolent protest. Among the most important in breaking the back of the "most segregated city" were children's marches into fire hoses and police dogs May 2–3, 1963. Afterward, the city agreed to integrate downtown stores and hire blacks, a détente that was shattered on September 15, 1963, at 10:22 A.M. when a dynamite bomb went off under the church's entrance stairwell. Below, in a corner women's lounge, were several girls dressed in white for Youth Day. Four were killed: Cynthia Wesley, Addie Mae Collins, and Carole Robertson, all fourteen, and Denise McNair, eleven. The blast sent a streak of fire above the church, knocked people out of cars, and sent fragments of the church throughout the neighborhood. It blew the clothes off the girls who were found piled together under bricks. One girl survived, Addie's younger sister, Sarah Collins. Repaired, the church basement today contains a Memorial Nook with photos and mementos of the blast and the marches.

Although the suspects were identified by the FBI within days, their conviction waited for a change in Alabama's political wind. It came with Attorney General William Baxley, who, on the day of the bomb, was a student at the University of Alabama. He vowed then to see justice done. Later, on his state phone card he wrote the names of the girls to remind him, according to *Carry Me Home*. In 1977 Baxley convicted Robert "Dynamite Bob" Chambliss of murder. Chambliss died in prison in 1985. Two remaining living suspects, Thomas Blanton Jr. and Bobby Frank Cherry, were sentenced to life in prison in 2001 and 2002. All were members of the United Klans of America.

Sculpture depicting jailed children in 1963

KELLY INGRAM PARK *(the block between Sixteenth and Seventeenth Streets and Fifth and Sixth Avenues. Walking tours can be arranged with Urban Impact Inc., a city agency: 205-328-1850)* Dotted with bold sculptural reminders of the 1963 Armageddon between the city and its citizens, this park today is a unique American civil rights space. A "freedom walk" guides a visitor past depictions of leaping police dogs, water cannons, and jailed children. A statue of Martin Luther King Jr. and one of three praying ministers bracket the park. Described as a "place of revolution and reconciliation" by the city's first black mayor, Richard Arrington, the park today hosts events ranging from Easter egg hunts to Christmas parades.

RICKWOOD FIELD (*1137 Second Avenue West; 205-458-8161; www.rickwood.com*) America's oldest baseball park, Rickwood served as a unique biracial home to the Birmingham Barons, a white minor league team, and the Black Barons of the Negro National League. The teams played alternating dates to segregated crowds drawn from the steel mills and coal mines. Right-field bleachers were used for the "minority" fans—blacks during white-team games, and whites during Black Baron games. Among the stars who passed through: Ty Cobb, Satchel Paige, Jackie Robinson, Babe Ruth, Hank Aaron, and local favorite Willie Mays, who as a sixteen-year-old center fielder helped the Black Barons win the 1948 Negro League championship. The black team played from 1923 to 1963, the original Birmingham Barons from 1910 to 1987. In 1953 white baseball fans forced the city to temporarily lift its ban against integrated games so that the Barons could play against an integrated Texas rival in the playoffs. Less than a year later, after the Supreme Court school desegregation order, voters reinstated segregated play. In 1961, after an ultimatum by the major leagues, the Barons folded for three seasons. They returned as an integrated team in 1964 playing to integrated audiences.

Willie Mays, who was born in nearby Westfield, was the third black player in the 1951 New York Giants outfield. Criticized for not taking part in civil rights activism, he said, "I don't picket in the streets of Birmingham. I'm not mad at the people who do. Maybe they shouldn't be mad at the people who don't."

Rickwood Field, on the national register of historic places, is open for a self-directed tour that includes brochures and historic photographs. Guided tours can be arranged by telephone. The field's shared history is described in Christopher Fullerton's *Every Other Sunday*.

Florence–Muscle Shoals

Some combination of black and white and country and gospel came together in this remote corner of Alabama to create a veritable music fountain. W. C. Handy, the father of the blues, was born here, picking up rhythms from lock workers along the shoals of the Tennessee River. Much later, after the shoals were flooded by a reservoir, a small group of musicians and producers created a unique fusion of black and white music—rhythm and blues, soul, and rock 'n' roll. Muscle Shoals today remains a hot spot of studios and musicians, with two museums.

W. C. Handy Birthplace Museum (*620 West College Street, Florence; 256-760-6434. Closed Sundays and Mondays.*) Born a minister's son, Handy absorbed various forms of African American music, including church gospel and chant rhythms from the workers on the Muscle Shoals canal, that would later turn up in his blues compositions. His most famous piece, "St. Louis Blues," begins with a line he overheard on a Mississippi levee: "I hate to see that evening sun go down." Handy, who left Florence at eighteen, found fame in Memphis and New York, but the museum here in a restored log cabin preserves his trumpet, piano, sheet music, and library.

Alabama Music Hall of Fame (*617 U.S. Highway 72, Tuscumbia; 800-239-AMHF*) The "Muscle Shoals sound" has been famous since 1959 when a group of white musicians created a studio, wrote songs, and played backup for black soul singers. Among the stars who recorded here include Wilson Pickett, Aretha Franklin, Clarence Carter, Percy Sledge, and Jimmy Hughes. The Muscle Shoals Rhythm Section played on dozens of hit records recorded at Rick Hall's Fame studio, including: "When a Man Loves a Woman," "Respect," and "Slip Away." Today, musicians ranging from Paul Simon to the Rolling Stones come to town to record in half a dozen studios. Hit songs in country and Christian genres are also produced here. The studios are not generally open to tourists, but the museum devotes a substantial section to the Muscle Shoals sound, with video interviews of Fame founder Rick Hall, Muscle Shoals Rhythm Section member Jimmy Johnson, and others.

Greensboro

Safe House Museum (*2401 Davis Street; 334-624-4228*) This restored "gin house," once used by workers at a nearby cotton gin, secretly sheltered Dr. Martin Luther King during a night of Klan violence. Its tidy display honors local residents—mostly women—who were the backbone of the civil rights movement. Acting largely outside the glare and protection of newspapers and TV, blacks in Hale and neighboring Perry and Greene Counties faced the most entrenched white supremacists. But they pressed for local rights, and joined larger demonstrations in Selma and Montgomery. Local rights weren't granted until after federal laws were prosecuted in 1965. Within a short time, three thousand blacks were registered. One of the most poignant displays features several photos of local civil rights pioneers from the 1960s juxtaposed against photos of eleven present-day officeholders— mayor, sheriff, councilmen, judges, and others—who are black. "If it had not been for this," said foot soldier Theresa Burroughs, pointing to herself and others being arrested, "this wouldn't have happened."

Hayneville

LOWNDES COUNTY COURTHOUSE SQUARE *(1 Washington Street)*
This poverty pocket in Alabama's black belt was discovered by civil rights workers when the Selma-to-Montgomery voting rights march passed through Lowndes County in March 1965. The night the march ended, March 25, Viola Liuzzo was shot to death in the county by Ku Klux Klansmen as she drove volunteers back to Selma. Several SNCC workers, including Stokely Carmichael and Bob Mants, returned to break white supremacy in a county where blacks outnumbered whites four to one but not one black was registered to vote.

The first mass demonstration in August 1965 led to the jailing of thirty demonstrators, including Jonathan Daniels, a white twenty-six-year-old Episcopal divinity student who had taken part in the Montgomery march. Released August 20, Daniels and three others walked to Varner's Cash Store for drinks and a ride. There, they were confronted by Tom Coleman, a part-time deputy sheriff, who waved his shotgun and told them to leave "or I'll blow your damned brains out." When Daniels pushed teenager Ruby Sales out of harm's way, Coleman fired. Daniels died instantly and another white man, Father Richard Morrisroe, was struck in the back. Coleman was acquitted by an all-white jury.

The courthouse and its square, where the jury members stretched their legs, are unchanged except for a monument on the southwest corner to Daniels. Erected by his classmates at the Virginia Military Institute, it reads: "He gave his life in the fight for integration of the churches and universal voter registration."

The county's resistance to the 1965 Voting Rights Act was so strong that the Department of Justice sent federal registrars. By November 1966 blacks held the majority. Unwilling to join Governor George Wallace's Democratic party, local blacks created an independent party, the Lowndes County Freedom Organization. To conform with state election law on behalf of illiterate voters, the party needed a symbol next to its candidates' names. An SNCC designer drew a black panther that stood out dramatically next to the Democrats' white rooster with its words "White Supremacy for the Right." The new party's jingle went, "Vote for the Panther and Go Home." Before the summer was out, Stokely Carmichael borrowed the black panther and the added slogan, "Black Power," to stir crowds in Mississippi. Before the year was out, militant blacks in California had created the Black Panthers. Meanwhile, Lowndes County "panthers" elected John Hulett as the first black sheriff in 1970. Soon after, African Americans controlled the county commission.

Marion

This town set off the deadly spark that launched the famous Selma-to-Montgomery voting rights march in the spring of 1965. Paralleling Selma's campaign to register voters, Marion blacks had been rallying at nightly meetings in the Zion United Methodist Church, just off the Perry County courthouse square. In February several hundred students were arrested for marching through the small business district. They were jammed into a stockade and forced to drink water from cattle tubs. Two hundred parents then were jailed for protesting those conditions. When campaign organizer James Orange was jailed, supporters decided to sing freedom songs outside the jail.

Fired up by a C. T. Vivian speech on the night of February 18, 1965, the crowd spilled out of the church to find streetlights out and agitated police and state troopers swinging nightsticks. Eighty-two-year-old Cager Lee, who had gone to the rally with his grandson, limped bleeding into Mack's Café behind the church, followed by swinging cops. Coming to his grandfather's aid, twenty-six-year-old Jimmie Lee Jackson was shot in the stomach. His death eight days later in a Selma hospital so outraged voting rights workers that they vowed to carry his body to Montgomery to lay before Governor George Wallace. Instead, Lee was buried in an emotional, rainy funeral in Marion, and the Selma-to-Montgomery voting march began with another confrontation with state troopers, "Bloody Sunday." The Marion melee had been more violent, but police that night had also attacked newsmen, destroying film of the event.

Historic markers have been erected by SCLC Women Inc. at the church, the jail, and the site of Mack's Café, all within sight of the courthouse. Lee's gravestone—"He was killed for man's freedom"—is in a slave cemetery a short drive on Highway 14. Visitors gather there every February.

Marion was also the birthplace of Alabama State University, which later moved to Montgomery; the Confederate "Stars and Bars" flag, which was designed here by teacher Nicola Marschall; and Coretta Scott, the future wife of Martin Luther King Jr. The Kings were married in 1953 at Mount Tabor Baptist Church on Highway 29.

Mobile

As a seaport, Mobile has been more diverse than the rest of Alabama since its founding by the French in 1702. This diversity convinced the city that it had the best race relations in Alabama, a belief longtime NAACP leader John LeFlore called a myth. By the 1920s 40 percent of the city was black and mostly blue collar, but there were also more than six hundred black professionals that included doctors, lawyers, and business owners, who held their own Mardi Gras. This elite, behind LeFlore's reconstituted NAACP, petitioned the city for a library "to place Mobile before the world as the most liberal and fair-minded Southern City in America." When union pressure forced the city to turn down a free Carnegie Library, voters passed a bond, built a main library for whites, and, in 1932, constructed a miniature, "separate but equal" version for blacks on Davis Avenue. It remained the city's only black library until 1961 when local black students began "read-ins" at the main library. When students arrived in large numbers, library director Guenter Jansen, Mayor George McNally, and city commissioner Joe Langan quietly opened the doors. By 1962 blacks and whites were reading books "in complete harmony," according to *A Right to*

Read, by Patterson Graham. Integration at other public accommodations proceeded in similar peaceable fashion under LeFlore and a coalition that included black dentist Robert Gilliard. Under Langan, the city desegregated buses, parks, and playgrounds, the police department, and other civil service jobs.

Mobile's go-easy attitude was shattered in March 1981 when members of the United Klans of America ambushed Michael Donald—simply because he was black. Donald, out walking to buy cigarettes, was abducted and taken to Baldwin County east of Mobile. Not only was he beaten unconscious, his throat was cut and his body brought back to Mobile to hang from a tree. Henry Hays was convicted and executed, and two others were sentenced to life in prison. The Klan group would later be bankrupted by civil rights lawyer Morris Dees.

THE MUSEUM OF MOBILE *(111 South Royal Street; 251-208-7569)* Mobile's three-hundred-year history is integrated in this city museum, as it traces the relationship and conflicts among Native Americans, Africans, and Europeans that created the port. Rare among public museums with competing stories to tell, race relations is a continuing story line through the displays. The civil rights era emphasizes the role of John LeFlore and the Nonpartisan Voters League (when the NAACP was outlawed in Alabama), and the "challenge" of school segregation.

The museum is also pursuing an underwater archaeological dig for the *Clotilde,* the last-known slave ship to the United States, sunk in Mobile Bay north of the city.

THE DAVIS LIBRARY *(564 Martin Luther King Jr. Avenue; 251-433-8511)* This former black library now holds an attic full of African American artifacts. Included are panels on the last African slave ship *Clotilde,* and the last survivor, Cudjoe Lewis. One corner portrays the Colored Carnival, a separate but equal version of Mardi Gras begun in 1938 that continues today with black royalty, parades, and balls. The first black "king" in 1940 was Alex Herman, father of Alexis Herman, who would become President Clinton's HEW secretary.

CUDJOE LEWIS MEMORIAL STATUE (*Old Pleateau Cemetery, Union Baptist Church, 506 Bay Bridge Road, Pleateau*) The U.S. Constitution outlawed the slave trade from Africa in 1808, but the market for slaves to work Alabama's cotton fields was so strong that illegal traders continued the practice when they could get away with it. In 1859 William Foster sailed the *Clotilde* into Mobile Bay carrying 130 slaves from a village in Togo, West Africa. Just before the slaves' sale at Mobile's downtown slave auction, authorities were alerted. The slaves were split up. The owner took twenty or thirty to his property in present-day Pleateau. Their village became known as "Africa Town." The last surviving member, Cudjoe Lewis, lived next door to the Union Baptist Church until his death in 1935. A tall white marker at the graveyard honors him, and the community is erecting a visitors center and grounds for an annual February heritage festival. The Museum of Mobile has begun an underwater archaeology project in search of the *Clotilde*.

HANK AARON STADIUM (*755 Bolling Brothers Boulevard; 251-479-BEAR*) Henry "Hank" Aaron, baseball's all-time home-run leader, was born in Mobile in 1934 and was such an outstanding high school baseball player that he soon joined the Indianapolis Clowns of the Negro American League. "I got the idea I could play professional baseball when I heard that Jackie Robinson had broken the color barrier," he said later. Before the 1954 season was over he had been signed by the Milwaukee Braves and became one of the first blacks in major league baseball. In 1974 Aaron broke Babe Ruth's lifetime home-run record of 714. Before and after the feat he was deluged with three thousand letters a day—most of them hate-filled and most from the north, according to ESPN.

"Dear Nigger Henry," read one letter. "You are [not] going to break this record established by the great Babe Ruth if I can help it. . . . My gun is watching your every black move."

Aaron finished his career with 755 home runs, a record still unsurpassed. The number was chosen as the street address for Hank Aaron Stadium, home to the Mobile Bay Bears. In front of the stadium, Aaron and four other Mobile players—all black—are honored for their membership in baseball's Hall of Fame. They include Satchel Paige, Willie McCovey, Billie Williams, and Ozzie Smith. Only New York City surpasses Mobile for the number of homegrown Hall of Famers.

Paige, a gangling youth from a large poor family, earned his nickname from carrying bags, or satchels, for train passengers. Confined to the black leagues until he was forty-five years old, he made his "rookie" debut in the newly integrated major leagues in 1948 with Cleveland. Paige is considered one of the best pitchers of all time, but he played in obscurity, winning an estimated two thousand out of twenty-five hundred games played.

Montgomery

No city encapsulates the human rights story better than Montgomery, which brags of being both the cradle of the Confederacy and the birthplace of the civil rights movement. In the space of a few blocks and a few hours a visitor can journey from slavery to freedom. The city is rich with ironic layers and intersections, such as the corner of Jefferson Davis Drive and Rosa Parks Avenue, which reflects both different histories and lingering tensions. At Courthouse Square, one can stand where slaves were sold, walk a few steps to where the telegraph clicked to fire on Fort Sumter, and look across the street to where Rosa Parks got on a bus that would carry her into history.

The loss of the Civil War was a shock to a city that had preened an antebellum facade atop the dirty work of slaves. Forced at military gunpoint to swallow black equality during Reconstruction, the old power structure reconstituted during Jim Crow did all it could to stop the nascent civil rights movement in the 1950s.

The famous bus boycott ended not with local assent but with a Supreme Court edict, and for two decades after, Montgomery remained the spiritual capital of segregation. A year after the boycott, for example, a city ordinance named "Segregation" divided city parks and pools. When ordered by a court to integrate, the city sold the parks. Black policemen, hired a year before the bus boycott, were fired. In 1968 a court order finally ended school segregation, although by then, a private "white" academy system was luring affluent families from public schools.

Over the years, despite Montgomery's loss of industries and reputation, various governors and mayors baited whites with racist campaigns and drove a wedge along the color line. Not until the 1990s did city government take a moderate turn. Today, race remains a divide, even as people from all over the world come to Montgomery to see a mecca of freedom. Their arrival has forced the city to appreciate its history and to erect the largest collection of civil rights museums and centers in the United States.

For orientation, maps, and brochures—and a free trolley ride to many sites—visit the **Chamber of Commerce in Union Station** (*Commerce Street near Embassy Suites*).

❚ **COURTHOUSE SQUARE AND FOUNTAIN** (*Dexter Avenue at Commerce and Montgomery Streets*) Beneath the iron cherubs, an artesian well once watered mules that carried bales of cotton down Commerce Street to riverboats on the Alabama River. Slaves by the thousands were sold at a market here and the nearby locations. Across Montgomery Street, on a corner occupied by a purplish bank building, was the Exchange, the city's premier hotel that hosted Jefferson Davis during his inauguration as president of the Confederacy. Davis strolled down Dexter from the capitol, held court in his suite, and gave the order to fire on Fort Sumter, an act that started the Civil War. The text of his order is engraved outside the former telegraph office a few steps up Dexter.

Across Dexter, behind a rectangular plaza, was the site of Montgomery Fair, a department store that employed Rosa Parks as a seamstress. She worked in a basement room next to a steam presser. Shortly after 5 P.M. on Thursday, December 1, 1955, she caught a Cleveland Avenue bus here. She paid her dime and took a seat halfway back that was already occupied by three black riders. The bus proceeded up Montgomery Street for two blocks where Mrs. Parks was arrested for refusing to give up her seat to a white man.

2 | **ROSA PARKS MUSEUM** *(252 Montgomery Street; 334-241-8615)*
A historic street marker pinpoints the bus stop that ignited the modern civil rights movement. It was here that white passengers filled the front of the segregated bus. Noticing one man standing, driver James Blake turned and said to four blacks seated in a center section: "Move y'all. I want those seats." When nobody moved he added, "Y'all better make it light on yourselves and let me have those seats." A black man and two black women got up, but Rosa Parks slid to the window and looked out at the Empire Theater, where the movie, *A Man Alone,* was advertised on the marquee. Blake approached her.

"Are you going to stand up?"

"No."

"Well, I'm going to have you arrested."

"You may do so."

At that moment, Mrs. Parks said years later, "I had the strength of my ancestors with me." She was also primed, if not radicalized, by years of activism with the NAACP, a summer desegregation workshop in Tennessee, and the recent arrests of three other women riders. Mrs. Parks said she did not plan her arrest, but she gave civil rights lawyers the test case they'd long been seeking.

The Rosa Parks Museum packs a big story and key artifacts into a small space. A multiscreen anteroom sets the scene for a spellbinding arrest re-creation in a restored city bus. The museum displays a copy of the mimeographed flyer, run off and distributed by Jo Ann Robinson and the Women's Political Council, calling for a boycott on Monday, December 5. At a mass meeting that night, after an inspiring speech by Martin Luther King Jr., black riders voted to continue the boycott indefinitely. The boycott brought King to fame, and established a model for forty-two other civil rights protests across the South. The boycott ended on December 20, 1956, with a Supreme Court ruling.

Rosa Parks's simple act of defiance made her world famous, but she lost her job, and after numerous death threats and growing jealousy among her boycott colleagues, she moved to Detroit, where she worked as a congressional aide until 1988.

3 | **DEXTER AVENUE KING MEMORIAL BAPTIST CHURCH** (*Dexter Avenue and Decatur Street*) Built by ex-slaves one block from the state capitol, "Dexter," as it is known, stands almost unchanged from the days when Martin Luther King Jr. was pastor between 1954 and 1960. King arrived at a propitious time—two weeks after the Supreme Court outlawed segregated schools. But with a Ph.D. thesis to write, a new family to raise, and his first congregation to reorganize, King did not envision a role as leader of the civil rights movement. That changed on Friday, December 2, 1955, when E. D. Nixon, the local NAACP leader, called King to inform him of Rosa Parks's arrest and to ask for his endorsement of a bus boycott. "Let me think about it," Dr. King said. Within a few hours, though, he helped persuade fifty ministers meeting at Dexter to endorse a Monday boycott from their pulpits during Sunday services.

By Monday afternoon, after the boycott proved a success, the ministers got cold feet and Nixon blew up. "You ministers have lived off these wash-women for the last hundred years and ain't never done nothing for them." Little boys with aprons, he called them, according to historian Taylor Branch. "It's time to take the aprons off . . . if we're gonna be mens, now the time to be mens." King, stung, said he was

Dexter Avenue King Memorial Baptist Church in Montgomery

not a coward. With that he was named president of a new boycott committee, the Montgomery Improvement Association. Any doubts the ministers may have had were blown away that night at the first mass meeting at Holt Street Baptist Church.

With eloquence and shrewdness belying his twenty-nine years, King became the face of the movement. Shortly after the boycott ended in December 1956, *Time* magazine put him on its cover. Now that he was a citizen of the world, King's dream of campaigns all over the South coincided with mounting pressure from his congregation— many of them teachers whose jobs were threatened by city and state officials—to leave. King became the first president of the Southern Christian Leadership Conference and moved to Atlanta in 1960.

Today, Dexter is both a church and museum, its small congregation aware of its historical importance and worldwide appeal. The church has preserved King's desk, many records, including his payroll checks, and, according to church documents, "the actual spaces where Dr. King regularly preached, counseled parishioners, performed the administrative duties of the pastorate and lived with his young family."

Money is being raised for a visitors center, a museum devoted to the role of the church in the movement, and a sanctuary that can be converted into a virtual theater to re-create the King years.

4 | **STATE CAPITOL** *(600 Dexter Avenue; 334-242-3935)* Atop Andrew Dexter's "goat hill" pasture, this Greek revival structure served as the founding capitol of the Confederate states before the Civil War and as the defiant anti-integrationist bastion of George Wallace. Jefferson Davis was sworn in on February 18, 1861, as the first president of the Confederate states. A star under the portico marks the spot. In late May, Davis and the Confederate capital moved to Richmond, Virginia, to be closer to battle.

During Reconstruction an integrated legislature met here, but by 1889, when the mighty Civil War soldier memorial was erected on the capitol's flank, elected blacks had disappeared, not to return until 1979.

After college students from Alabama State University staged a sit-in at the capitol's segregated snack bar on February 25, 1960, the governor ordered the students expelled and members of the Ku Klux Klan roamed downtown streets with baseball bats. On March 6, 1960, the streets in front of the capitol filled with thousands of angry whites trying to stop several hundred blacks from marching to protest the students' arrest. As one side sang, the other jeered. More than four hundred law enforcement personnel barely kept the surging crowds from coming to blows.

In January 1963, the capitol became the symbolic home for southern segregation when George Wallace was inaugurated governor with his famous vow: "segregation now, segregation tomorrow, segregation forever."

Two years later, in March 1965, at the end of the Selma-to-Montgomery voting rights march, a crowd of at least twenty-five thousand marked the pinnacle of the civil rights movement. From a platform on the street in front of the capitol, Dr. Martin Luther King Jr. recited four verses of the "Battle Hymn of the Republic," the Civil War anthem, to remind Wallace, who was in his office at the time, that freedom was destined. "Segregation," he said, "is on its deathbed."

The capitol grounds, still dominated by Confederate nostalgia, is slated to undergo a remodeling to include the civil rights story.

5 | **DEXTER AVENUE PARSONAGE** (*309 South Jackson Street*) This simple wood parsonage on Centennial Hill was home to Martin Luther King, his wife, Coretta, and their first two children during his time in Montgomery. Up at 5:30 each morning, King worked here on his Ph.D. dissertation, sermons, and strategy for the bus boycott. As the pressures of the boycott came to rest on his shoulders, King woke one night to a jarring and threatening phone call. Making coffee in the kitchen, he put his head in his hands and spoke aloud of his fear and need. At that moment, he later wrote, an inner voice told him to do what he thought was right.

A month later, on January 31, 1956, a bomb went off near the porch, which challenged King's nonviolent philosophy. Coretta and baby Yolanda were inside but uninjured. Summoned from a mass meeting, King stood amid shattered glass on the porch, arms raised, and told the angry crowd to take their guns home: "He who lives by the sword will perish by the sword . . . I did not start this boycott . . . if I am stopped, this movement will not stop . . . We must meet hate with love." The crowd dispersed. More than a year later, after the boycott succeeded, King responded to another "inner voice" and abandoned the house just before a second bomb exploded at a nearby taxi stand, crushing the front of the house. Unignited dynamite was found on the porch. Seven white men were charged with that and other boycott bombings, but were freed.

The parsonage has been remodeled with original King furniture. An adjacent visitors center offers additional background.

6 **CIVIL RIGHTS MEMORIAL AND SOUTHERN POVERTY LAW CENTER** (*400 Washington Avenue; 334-956-8200*) Civil rights attorney Morris Dees used the courts to defeat segregation and discrimination in a number of Alabama institutions, including the YMCA and state troopers, and to clear obstacles to black officehold-

Civil Rights Memorial designed by Maya Lin

ers, but he is best known for his nonstop pursuit of the Ku Klux Klan and other white supremacists nationwide.

After members of the Ku Klux Klan lynched Michael Donald in Mobile in 1981, Dees sued the Klan on behalf of the young man's mother, Beulah Mae. Dees won $7 million, forcing the Klan to sell off its headquarters to pay her. It would be the first of ten cases across the country that would bankrupt supremacists for their mayhem. In 2000 he ran the Aryan Nations out of Idaho and seized their rural seedbed of hate.

Dees and college friend Joe Levin founded the nonprofit Southern Poverty Law Center (SPLC) in 1971 to fund civil rights lawsuits, investigate the radical right, and produce the school-based Teaching Tolerance program, the Web site Tolerance.org, and a string of publications and films devoted to fighting hate and promoting tolerance.

In 1987, at a speech celebrating the Michael Donald court victory against the Klan, Dees mentioned the names of several "martyrs" of the civil rights movement. Students later asked him who they were. He came home, contacted Maya Lin, the sculptor of the Vietnam Memorial, and compiled a history of forty people who died between 1954 and 1968. Lin carved their names in a black granite fountain flowing with water and set it before a black wall engraved with the words from the Bible's book of Amos, used by Dr. Martin Luther King Jr. on the first night of the Montgomery bus boycott: "Until justice rolls down like water and righteousness like a mighty stream." With a few exceptions, the Civil Rights Memorial is the only monument to these deaths in the South.

A visitors center behind the memorial, to be opened in 2005, will recount SPLC's history and the destructive legacy of hate and violence. Visitors are urged to commit to promoting tolerance in their homes, communities, and workplaces.

7 | **GREYHOUND BUS TERMINAL/U.S. COURTHOUSE** (*210 South Court Street; 334-242-3184*) When the Freedom Riders arrived from Birmingham on May 20, 1961, Montgomery's promised police protection disappeared. When John Lewis stepped off the bus to meet reporters, a mob of men with pipes, bats, and bottles charged past newsmen and began knocking heads. Lewis fell unconscious. Jim Zwerg, a white Wisconsin student, was smashed repeatedly in the head. Some riders tried to flee in taxis, only to be blocked by a bigger crowd. John Seigenthaler, a Justice Department official, was clubbed senseless. While the mob burned suitcases, some riders jumped over a retaining wall and ran into the federal courthouse and post office behind the bus station. The next night, the shaken Freedom Riders appeared before a rally with Martin Luther King Jr. at First Baptist Church, only to be surrounded by a mob again. With U.S. marshals and National Guardsmen between them and the mob, riders escaped and moved on to Mississippi. After the bus beatings, Montgomery business leaders issued their first condemnation of the violence.

A historical sign stands before the bus station, in which Alabama's historical commission plans an $8 million Freedom Riders museum.

The U.S. courthouse directly behind the Greyhound station was the source of many civil rights victories during the movement years. In 1955, the year the bus boycott began, President Eisenhower appointed U.S. District Judge Frank Johnson, a native of Winston County. His first big case ended Montgomery's bus segregation, but he was best known for forcing Governor George Wallace and other public officials to desegregate and otherwise protect civil rights. Wallace called him an "integrating, scalawagging, carpetbagging liar." Among Johnson's decisions: integrating Alabama schools, adding blacks to voting rolls, and allowing the Selma-to-Montgomery voting rights march with state protection. For his efforts, his mother's home was bombed and he was threatened. In 1995 President Clinton awarded Johnson the presidential Medal of Freedom. The new federal courthouse carries Johnson's name.

Freedom Riders

One of the boldest moves of the civil rights movement—integrated bus rides into the segregated South—was launched in the spring of 1961 by the Congress of Racial Equality (CORE). It resulted in some of the most brutal confrontations of the movement, but, in short order, forced compliance of a 1960 Supreme Court decision (*Boynton v. Virginia*) that required interstate bus terminals to integrate.

The ride was the brainchild of James Farmer, a Ph.D. in religion who had embraced Gandhi's nonviolence philosophy and took over CORE in 1961. Acting against the wishes of established civil rights leaders, including Martin Luther King Jr. and the Kennedy administration, Farmer trained thirteen riders, black and white, in pacifism in Washington, D.C. John Lewis of SNCC recalled their "last supper" at a Chinese restaurant before six departed May 4 on a Greyhound and seven on a Trailways bus.

On their first stop, in Fredericksburg, Virginia, the COLORED and WHITE signs had been removed and the riders used different bathrooms without incident. Though signs were in place elsewhere in Virginia and they were often refused service, there was little trouble. In Rock Hill, South Carolina, John Lewis drew the first blood when he tried to enter the "whites" waiting room. He and Al Bigelow were beaten by thugs.

But it was in Anniston, Alabama, that the Freedom Riders met infamy. On May 14 a mob of white men attacked the station, slashing tires and breaking windows. The bus driver fled with fifty cars in pursuit. When tires went flat five miles west of town the driver ran away and the mob began smashing again, kept at bay from inside by two undercover investigators from Alabama. A firebomb, tossed through the rear window, set fire to seats, and filled the bus with black smoke. The mob held the door shut until one of the investigators, Eli Cowling, pulled his gun, fired into the air, and shouted, "Let these people off, or some of you are going to die." Several riders were beaten outside. The picture of the burning bus became worldwide news. Meanwhile the Trailways bus met a mob in Anniston, too. Men with clubs entered the bus, beating passengers to the floor. James Farmer had missed the melee because of his father's sudden death and funeral.

A few hours later in Birmingham, another group of white men with clubs met the Trailways bus and beat Jim Peck and other riders in the hallways of the station. Police, who knew about it, disappeared for fifteen minutes of mob rule. When asked later about their absence, Bull Connor blamed Mother's Day, when, he said, cops spend time with their mothers. Peck, an heir to the Peck & Peck clothing chain, had his skull exposed with five gashes and was bleeding profusely, his front teeth broken. Another rider, a sixty-year-old Michigan professor, Walter Bergman, kicked repeatedly in the head, suffered permanent brain damage that paralyzed him for the rest of his life.

Farmer wanted to call off the ride, but students from the Nashville movement volunteered to ride to Montgomery. They arrived in Birmingham, only to have Bull Connor drive them to the Tennessee line and dump them in the middle of the night. In his book *Walking with the Wind,* Lewis recalled the cold fear of being left in Klan country. They knocked on the door of a black family. "We're the Freedom Riders. We are in trouble. We need your help. Would you help us?" The frightened man shook his head no, but then a woman appeared in the door. "Honey, let them in."

The group returned to Birmingham and boarded the bus on May 17. Alabama's governor, John Patterson, meanwhile, told the White House that white citizens were so enraged at "this bunch of rabble rousers" that he couldn't guarantee the riders' safety. Bobby Kennedy sent assistant John Seigenthaler who arrived just as a white mob with bats, bricks, hoes, and chains began swinging. Jim Zwerg, John Lewis, Seigenthaler, and newsmen fell beaten to the pavement. Some fled into the federal courthouse and through the post office. Montgomery police stood by until the state public safety director, Floyd Mann, fired his gun and stopped the violence.

That night, fifteen hundred protesters gathered at First Baptist Church to hear Dr. Martin Luther King praise the riders. They were kept hostage inside by a mob that surrounded a thin line of U.S. marshals. Bricks were thrown, a car was bombed, and tear gas was launched. People inside prayed until Governor Patterson declared martial law and called out the National Guard. At midnight the congregation went home.

One thousand guardsmen escorted the last riders to the Mississippi line. They arrived without incident in Jackson, where they were arrested and jailed at the Parchman prison farm for three weeks.

That summer, 1961, brought an end to segregated bus stations in the South. Before the riders even arrived in Jackson, the Interstate Commerce Commission adopted regulations to end segregation in terminals.

8 | **HOLT STREET BAPTIST CHURCH** (*903 South Holt Street at Jefferson Davis Avenue;* 334-277-2088) In a movement full of inspiring scenes, the night of December 5, 1955, in this church ranks among the best. Thousands had packed the church and spilled out on the streets at the end of a successful one-day boycott of Montgomery's city bus line. Inside, Martin Luther King Jr. made his debut on the civil rights stage. He began with a preacher cadence of call-and-response, describing the arrest of Rosa Parks—"one of the finest citizens in Montgomery." He paused at each point as people answered, "Amen. That's right. Yes Lord." Then King raised his voice: "You know, my friends, there comes a time when people get tired of being trampled over by the iron feet of oppression." The crowd erupted as if gasoline had been poured on a fire. Feet stomped. Hands clapped. It sounded like thunder, long and rolling and full of anger and release, an emotional wave that took over King and Montgomery. From that moment on there was no stopping, not with buses or Montgomery or anywhere oppression existed.

King's speech and the crowd's response, caught on a tape recorder, remains chilling to hear. Rosa Parks, writing many years later, remembered her favorite line from his speech: "When the history books are written in the future somebody will have to say, there lived a race of people, a black people, fleecy locks and black complexion, a people who had the moral courage to stand up for their rights, and thereby they injected a new meaning in the veins of history."

Near the end of the boycott in December 1956, King spoke to another huge crowd here, in which he listed the lessons learned from the boycott. Unity in a common cause works, he said. The secret was "nonviolent resistance."

A historic sign stands outside the church. The congregation, which moved to new and larger quarters, plans to preserve Holt Street as a monument to that evening and subsequent mass meetings and strategy sessions through the Montgomery bus boycott.

9 | **FIRST BAPTIST CHURCH** *(347 North Ripley Street;* 334-264-*6921)*   The Reverend Ralph Abernathy was pastor here when Rosa Parks was arrested and many mass meetings were held during the boycott. Abernathy became Martin Luther King's trusted aide and friend, and both eventually moved to Atlanta to establish the Southern Christian Leadership Conference.

First Baptist's civil rights story began a century earlier in 1867 when newly freed slaves left the white First Baptist Church basement to form the first free Negro institution in Montgomery on this spot. For a time it was the largest black church in the United States. The present church was built literally brick by brick, as even the poorest parishioner was asked to bring one brick each day.

When the bus boycott ended, the church (and three others) were bombed so badly that it had to be rebuilt. Abernathy's house was also bombed. In 1961, during a mass meeting with King and injured Freedom Riders, First Baptist was surrounded by a violent white crowd that filled a park across the street (now the police department). The police, whose headquarters was a couple of blocks away at the time, did nothing. As the crowd sang "Leaning on the Everlasting Arms," federal marshals and National Guardsmen surrounded the church and allowed meeting goers to escape.

10 ALABAMA STATE UNIVERSITY *(809 South Jackson Street; 334-229-4291)* The oldest surviving black college in the state, ASU was founded in Marion as the Lincoln School and moved to Montgomery over the objection of Booker T. Washington, who feared competition with his Tuskegee Institute.

Fully accredited by 1943, Alabama State was the leading state-supported school for black teachers. Many of its staff members belonged to the "black elite" of Dexter Avenue Church. The 1955 bus boycott "awakened a new consciousness" among students, faculty, and staff, according to a school history, but it cost them and the school dearly.

ASU English professor Jo Ann Robinson, for example, who is credited with starting the bus boycott, lost her job. She and other colleagues had worked through the night to mimeograph thirty thousand boycott handbills and distribute them to black schools, churches, and businesses. After Robinson was fired, other ASU professors and administrators were threatened with being fired unless they abandoned Dr. Martin Luther King's campaigns. The pressure exerted on them was a major reason King left Montgomery in January 1960, according to historian J. Mills Thornton.

But in February, within days of the Woolworth's sit-in at Greensboro, North Carolina, students from ASU marched to the capitol and symbolically desegregated the basement lunch counter. Nine students were expelled on orders from Governor John Patterson. Led by Bernard Lee, the student body rallied, held a prayer service on the capitol steps, and later confronted police and Klansmen in a tense standoff that saw thirty-five students arrested. The state then cut so much funding for ASU that it lost its accreditation in 1961 for five years.

ASU plans a number of memorials to civil rights pioneers, including a mural at its National Center for the Study of Civil Rights and African-American Culture, and campus signposts commemorating Jo Ann Robinson and others.

11 | **CITY OF ST. JUDE/SELMA-TO-MONTGOMERY VOTING RIGHTS MARCH VISITORS CENTER** *(334-265-6849 or 265-6791)* This Catholic school, church, and hospital complex had long been a sanctuary from Montgomery's segregation. Established to help poor blacks on the west side of town, it became the final campground for the Selma-to-Montgomery march. On March 24, in what amounted to a civil rights musical rally, entertainers ranging from Sammy Davis Jr. to Joan Baez entertained the marchers.

The original campground has been designated part of a national trail and will be marked with signs. The National Park Service plans to build a visitors center in an adjacent shopping mall.

Scottsboro

As the site of one of the infamous miscarriages of racial justice, this city's name is wedded to that of the Scottsboro Boys, nine young black men accused of raping two white women on a train passing through the city on March 25, 1931. With inexperienced defense attorneys, they were convicted and eight sentenced to die. Thanks to the black press and the Communist party, their case received national publicity, and was overturned by the U.S. Supreme Court. A new trial was moved to Decatur where state Judge James Horton set aside the first conviction, a move that cost him his seat on the bench. In cases that dragged on for years, the men were eventually sentenced to long prison terms and paroled. The last, Clarence Norris, was pardoned by Governor George Wallace.

A marker briefly tells the story at the site of the old courthouse. Bricks and cells from the courthouse have been saved by the local historical society. There are plans to create a display about the trial at the city's Heritage Center.

Selma

Long mummified in faded antebellum glory, Selma was one of the last southern cities to open its door to modern human rights. Today, thanks to annual reenactments of the 1965 voting rights march and "Bloody Sunday," the city has made a mini-industry of the civil rights struggle.

Built on an Alabama River precipice in the heart of a cotton empire, Selma was home to a thriving slave and cotton market before the Civil War. Hundreds of slaves were sold on its banks and toiled at the top and bottom of the "cotton slide" used to rocket five-hundred-pound bales from shore to steamships. During the war, slaves worked in Selma's iron works making cannons and balls for the Confederate army. Afterward, as if the war hadn't happened, Selma and surrounding Clark County resettled into a white-dominated society for more than a century.

Efforts by blacks to vote in the 1950s and early 1960s were beat back, literally, by a Clark County sheriff and citizen "deputies." In 1965, ten years after the Montgomery bus boycott and two years after the Birmingham bombs and fire hoses, the civil rights movement came to Selma with a classic clash between marching blacks and a county sheriff with a club. When a sister protest in nearby Marion led to the death of Jimmy Lee Jackson, protesters in Selma vowed to take their demands to the state capital of Montgomery and confront Governor George Wallace. That attempt, a march over the Edmund Pettus Bridge into a phalanx of state troopers and a goon squad, turned out to be Wallace's waterloo. Protected by a federal court, the marchers succeeded in what has become known as the Selma-to-Montgomery voting rights march, the last major peaceful protest of the civil rights era. Four months later President Johnson signed the Voting Rights Act, the last major civil rights legislation that opened voter registration to virtually any adult.

In 1996 Congress authorized the Selma-to-Montgomery National Historic Trail, with plans to build visitors centers in Selma, Montgomery, and midroute Lowndes County. In 2000 Selma elected its first black mayor.

EDMUND PETTUS BRIDGE (*U.S. 80 across Alabama River off Water Avenue*) Named for a Confederate hero who, after the Civil War, lost a seat in the legislature to a black man, this steel arch has become the symbol for voting rights in the United States. Every March, a "ju-

Selma's Edmund Pettus Bridge

bilee" reenacts Bloody Sunday, the brutal and aborted protest march from Selma to Montgomery on March 7, 1965. Using tear gas, clubs, and horses, fifty state troopers and a posse of deputized citizens pushed marchers back across the bridge and into history. The bridge was covered with blood, according to witnesses, and the sound of screams, body blows, and heads hitting the pavement was sickening. Sixty-five people were injured in a melee shown on national television. Two days later, Martin Luther King Jr. led a symbolic protest march to the same spot, knelt and prayed but turned around. Protected by court order, King led a third march on March 21 that began a five-day trek to Montgomery and a huge rally on the steps of the capitol. A state historical marker stands on the Selma side of the river. A small memorial park has been built on the south side of the bridge, near the spot where the line of troopers waited, with memorials to the foot soldiers and two of the leaders, Hosea Williams and John Lewis.

NATIONAL VOTING RIGHTS MUSEUM (*1012 Water Avenue; 334-418-0800*)   This small, homemade museum reminds us of our most important civil right—the right to vote. Occupying a storefront once used by the white segregationist Citizens Council, the museum has a view of the Edmund Pettus Bridge. Its original intention was to honor those who walked across the bridge in 1965. But the museum has

247

become a catchall suffrage exhibit, surprising the average visitor with some unknown or forgotten bits of voting history. One room is devoted to blacks elected to Congress during Reconstruction—so many that they formed a highly visible voting block. One notable story belongs to Jeremiah Haralson, a Selma black who, in 1872, beat local Confederate hero Edmund Pettus for a seat in the state legislature. Haralson later was elected to Congress. The museum honors many local civil rights heroes, including J. L. Chesnut, a jazz musician–turned-attorney who, in 1958, reignited voting activism that had been going on since the 1940s. The exhibits are best explained by local guides who participated in the tumultuous marches and arrests of 1965.

Memorials outside Selma's Brown Chapel AME Church

BROWN CHAPEL AME CHURCH AND CIVIL RIGHTS WALKING TOUR *(410 Martin Luther King Street;* *334-874-7897)* Brown Chapel, in the heart of a tidy housing project, was an embattled sanctuary during the three-month voting rights campaign of 1965. White lawmen stationed themselves inside, bugged the pulpit with a microphone, and, during the Bloody Sunday march, chased citizens on horseback up the stairs and into the door. Martin Luther King Jr., Ralph Abernathy, Malcolm X, and other leaders spoke inside, and led daily mass marches from here across town to the Dallas County building in an attempt to register to vote. Monuments outside have been erected for James Reeb, Viola Liuzzo, and Jimmie Lee Jackson, all of whom died in the campaign. A large King bust notes that ten years after the Voting Rights Act, black voter enrollment jumped to 3,800,000 from 1,400,000. Black elected officials soared from 72 to more than 2,500; in 2000 the number had risen to over 9,000. Brown was designated by Congress as the beginning of a national historic trail. A short civil rights walking tour with informative kiosks runs along Martin Luther King Street beginning at First Baptist Church, just down the block.

DALLAS COUNTY COURTHOUSE *(105 Lauderdale Street; 334-876-4830)* Cream colored and serene today, this building was a monolith of exclusion as late as 1965. When blacks tried to register to vote, they were routinely rejected for "reasons" ranging from poor penmanship to failing arcane legal questions. They also lost their jobs. In 1964 SNCC activists began marching citizens to the door, only to be arrested by Sheriff Jim Clark. When Dr. Martin Luther King Jr. began a 1965 campaign of daily marches involving hundreds of demonstrators, Clark personally knocked heads and shocked bodies with cattle prods. He also turned loose a "posse" of deputized thugs who chased marchers on horseback. Following the Voting Rights Act of 1965, thousands of blacks signed up without incident.

The Right to Vote

Th Selma-to-Montgomery National Historic Trail is a unique monument to the heroic effort of blacks in central Alabama to secure America's most cherished right—to vote. Their victory, the Voting Rights Act of 1965, is considered the most successful civil rights law ever passed. It wiped out two hundred years of voting barriers to race and color, including those for disenfranchised American Indians, and was later amended to protect naturalized citizens who speak a foreign language.

The trail covers events in March of 1965 in four counties of Alabama, but the story goes back to the Depression with the arrival in Selma of

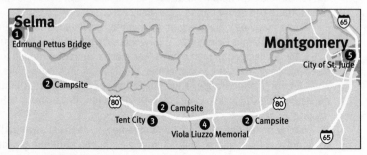

Route of Selma-to-Montgomery march

Memorial to James Orange in Marion

Amelia and Sam Boynton. While helping tenant farmers survive, the couple reestablished the Dallas County Voters League, which encouraged blacks to register. Between 1952 and 1962, seventy-five blacks tried and were rejected. Many lost their jobs. Their names formed an honor roll on the wall of the Boynton insurance firm.

Even after the Civil Rights Act of 1964 and Mississippi's Freedom Summer, voting was an uphill struggle for blacks in the South. Selma, the last segregationist stronghold, became an obvious target. At Boynton's invitation, Martin Luther King Jr. and the Southern Christian Leadership Conference converged on Selma in January 1965, and began mass marches to the Dallas County Courthouse. Beaten and jailed by the hundreds, protesters marched back and forth between black churches and the county building in repeated efforts to register. Sheriff Jim Clark led the resistance with help from deputized citizens. Clark himself struck activists Annie Lee Cooper and C. T. Vivian.

Similar marches were going on thirty miles away in Marion where police had jailed James Orange, an SCLC worker. On the night of February 18, 1965, locals decided to march one block from a church to the jail to sing freedom songs for Orange. As they did, the lights in the town square were shot out and a state trooper squad began beating protesters. During the melee, Jimmie Lee Jackson was shot. He died eight days later in a Selma hospital.

Protesters decided to march to Montgomery to confront segregationist Governor George Wallace. King announced a march and then decided to preach in Atlanta instead. On March 7, John Lewis and SCLC activist Hosea Williams led hundreds of people across the Edmund Pettus Bridge where they were beaten, teargassed, and trampled by horses of the state police and Jim Clark's posse. Two days later, King led a symbolic march to the same line of troopers but knelt, prayed, and turned around. That night, a white minister and protester, James Reeb, was hit with a club and died.

U.S. District Judge Frank Johnson ordered Governor Wallace to protect marchers with troopers and National Guardsmen. President Johnson also sent in two thousand army troops, FBI agents, and U.S. marshals.

On March 21 King and three thousand people began a five-day walk to Montgomery. King walked three days, left for a speech, and returned for the climax, but many hundreds walked the entire way. At the last campsite, at the Catholic City of St. Jude, on the edge of Montgomery, thousands of people were entertained by Harry Belafonte, Joan Baez, Peter, Paul and Mary, and others.

On March 25 twenty-five thousand people marched up Dexter Avenue to the Alabama capitol where, not far from where Governor Wallace had shouted "segregation forever," Dr. King asked, "How long will it take? Not long, because the arm of the moral universe is long, but it bends toward justice."

On June 4 President Johnson said in a speech, "At times history and fate meet at a single time in a single place to shape a turning point in man's unending search for freedom. So it was at Lexington . . . So it was last week in Selma." On August 6 he signed the Voting Rights Act, which allowed the Justice Department to take over voter registration in recalcitrant districts. The results were staggering. Today, more than 9,000 black politicians hold office.

The national historic trail, approved by Congress and President Clinton in 1996, stretches fifty-four miles from Brown Chapel in Selma to the Montgomery state capitol. When complete in 2008, the trail will include visitors centers in Selma, Lowndes County, and Montgomery, fifty-four roadside kiosks, and a nine-mile re-creation of the original U.S. 80 trekked by voting rights activists in March 1965.

The first center to be built, near White Hall in Lowndes County, focuses on the aftermath of the march. Two key stories are told there: the Klan shooting death of volunteer Viola Liuzzo from Detroit, and the eviction of poor tenant farmers for trying to vote. Liuzzo was gunned down on the night of King's speech while driving volunteers back to Selma through a lonely stretch of U.S. 80. A monument marks the spot. Up the road is "Tent City," the site where the evicted farmers were forced to live in tents for more than two years.

Tuscaloosa

UNIVERSITY OF ALABAMA CAMPUS First integrated by Autherine Lucy under a February 1956 federal court order, the school expelled Lucy for "her protection" after white rioters drove her away. The state legislature then outlawed her legal counsel, the NAACP. The university didn't accept integration until 1963 when another federal judge cleared the way for Vivian Malone and James Hood. On June 11, in a prearranged confrontation, Governor George Wallace made a "stand in the school house door"—long enough for news photos. Attorney General Nicholas Katzenbach escorted the students to their dorm where they were protected by National Guardsmen. That night, President Kennedy went on television to announce a civil rights bill to end segregation in American public life. A plaque on Foster Auditorium marks the spot where Wallace made his "stand."

The Crimson Tide football team under Bear Bryant was not integrated until 1971. In a storied account, Bryant arranged for a game with Southern Cal that starred Sam "Bam" Cunningham, a black player who scored two touchdowns in the first half of a USC rout. Bryant's unspoken lesson was that Alabama needed good black players to compete. The following year, Bryant integrated the team, which today is dominated by black players.

Tuskegee

A history with both noble and notorious turns, the Tuskegee Institute arose in the American conscience a century ago when Booker T. Washington built an influential black college from a chicken coop. Known for its agriculture, veterinary, and engineering schools, Tuskegee also gained fame with faculty member George Washington Carver, an agriculture genius who revolutionized the South's farming practices by rotating cotton with peanuts, soybeans, and other soil-enriching crops. He also invented products using peanuts and soybeans ranging from dyes to instant coffee.

In 1932 in Tuskegee the U.S. Public Health Service and Tuskegee Institute asked four hundred black sharecroppers to join in a study of "bad blood." In fact, they had syphilis, and they were watched—without treatment—for forty years, to study what happened to their bodies. They infected their wives and children and died. The story was finally leaked to the media in 1972 and the experiment was stopped. A $9 million lawsuit brought by attorney Fred Gray was divided among the survivors, and in 1997 President Clinton apologized on behalf of the nation.

During World War II, the first black fighter pilots were trained at Tuskegee's Moton Field. They had been denied training at the "white" Maxwell Air Base in Montgomery, but overcame their disadvantages and segregation to win fame in Europe. Today, their training field is a national park.

Despite a majority black population, Tuskegee and surrounding Macon County remained under white control until the civil rights movement. In 1951 the Alabama legislature gerrymandered the election districts to keep blacks off the city council. A 1957 lawsuit brought by Charles Gomillion and the Tuskegee Civic Association led to the Supreme Court's "one-man, one-vote" decision that ended gerrymandering to dilute black votes. Gomillion also led a downtown boycott to pressure businesses to hire blacks and treat black customers equally.

Following the Selma voting rights battles in 1965, SNCC organized Tuskegee students and began picketing stores and banks, swimming in segregated pools, and sitting in a "white" Methodist church. Led by student body president Gwen Patton, students gathered around the town square with its statue of a Confederate soldier and sang freedom songs. On January 3, 1966, student protester Samuel Younge Jr. was shot and killed by a gas station attendant. His death led to huge marches and threats of violence, though the shooter was acquitted.

In 1966 Lucius Amerson became the first black sheriff since Reconstruction. Today 80 percent of local officials are black, one of the highest proportions in the United States. Many whites left Tuskegee after the civil rights era. In 1990 317 whites were counted in a town of 12,000 citizens.

TUSKEGEE INSTITUTE NATIONAL HISTORIC SITE (*U.S. 80 to 1212 Old Montgomery Road; 334-727-3200*) During Reconstruction, when ex-slaves voted for the first time, Lewis Adams of Tuskegee traded local black votes for a "normal school for colored teachers." Adams then asked Hampton University in Virginia for a teacher recommendation. Booker T. Washington arrived in 1881 to find nothing but "hundreds of hungry, earnest souls who wanted to secure knowledge." One of them, a man of sixty, told Washington how he had been sold into Alabama in 1845: "There were five of us; myself and brother and three mules." Starting with a classroom in a church, Washington built an education system that taught practical trades, basic writing, arithmetic, and grooming skills, and an obeisant philosophy to show the ruling class that blacks could shape their destiny. Founded at the height of Ku Klux Klan violence in Alabama, Tuskegee was a safe place for a black to get an education.

Washington was criticized later for accommodation that smacked of Uncle Tom, yet he was funded by the Rockefellers, Carnegies, and Sears, Roebuck's Julius Rosenwald, and was even visited by Teddy Roosevelt. A famous sculpture on the campus, showing Washington lifting the "veil of ignorance" from the slave, captures his mind-set but it has been criticized as being paternalistic by today's standards.

Today the school is both a monument to black achievement and a prestigious college with strong schools of aerospace, veterinary medicine, engineering, and architecture. Many of the buildings were designed by the first black graduate of MIT, Robert Taylor. A museum devoted to George Washington Carver and Washington's home are open to the public.

TUSKEGEE AIRMEN NATIONAL HISTORIC SITE (*U.S. 81 and 1616 Chappy James Drive;* 334-724-0922) The Tuskegee Airmen are one of the great up-from-ignominy civil rights stories. So heroic were their war exploits that their second-class, segregated origins are often forgotten. When the United States entered World War II, the Army Air Force wanted nothing to do with blacks. Under pressure by civil rights groups, the Roosevelt administration forced the air force to train black pilots. But rather than use its existing training center at Maxwell Field in Montgomery, Alabama, the corps segregated the pilots at a small airfield in Tuskegee, forty miles away. It also trained them in the most difficult flying maneuvers—pursuit fighting—which washed many candidates out because of physical and technical requirements. Not until 1943, two years after its launch, was the Ninety-ninth Fighter Squadron sent to fight. Its success at escorting bombers into Italy and Germany, without the loss of a single bomber, and the downing of 251 enemy planes, won them wide respect and paved the way for integrated air units after the war. Nonetheless, until it closed in 1946, Tuskegee remained, as an official military history put it, "a powerful symbol of armed forces segregation."

In 2002 the National Park Service opened a temporary visitors center at Moton Field with plans for a full-scale park unit devoted to the story of military integration.

TUSKEGEE HUMAN AND CIVIL RIGHTS MULTICULTURAL CENTER (*104 South Elm Street; 334-724-0801*)   Launched by civil rights attorney Fred Gray and his daughter, Deborah, this museum's founding story was the Tuskegee syphilis study. Gray represented the untreated patients in a lawsuit against the federal government. Video clips include President Clinton's moving apology in 1997. The center plans an ambitious expansion that will eventually include the civil rights history of Macon County.

The center publishes a driving tour of the city and county. The county tour includes Shiloh Missionary Baptist Church, where syphilis patients were recruited, and its adjoining Rosenwald school, one of the first to be built by Booker T. Washington.

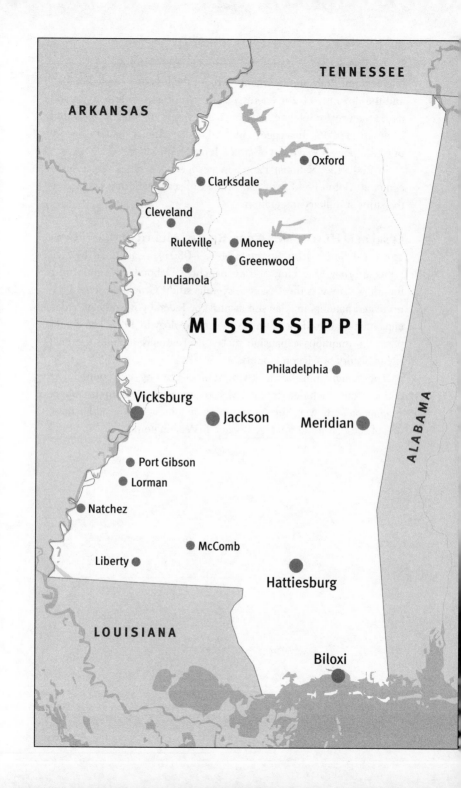

Mississippi

DESTINED BY ITS RIVERS, soil, and climate to a history of cotton, slavery, and rural poverty, Mississippi could be generations shaking its reputation as a backward, racist state. Host to more black lynchings (at least five hundred) and civil rights murders (twenty-five) than any state in the Union, old Mississippi, dead last in so many indexes of American life, seemed an appropriate birthplace of the blues.

Yet Mississippi today has more black officeholders than any state in the Union. It has faced its ghosts and prosecuted many for racial crimes. And reconciliation, once an unfamiliar, unfathomable concept, is heard in conversations whenever talk turns to ending three hundred years of racial division.

Mississippi's civil rights history is a local story about local people. The "stars" of the movement, such as Martin Luther King Jr., were not significant factors in Mississippi although several local people became nationally known because of their leadership or martyrdom. By and large, the grunt work of gaining civil rights in this most truculent of southern states was done by ordinary people. Among them, the young and the very old were the heroes.

Perhaps because of this, memorials to civil rights events, leaders, and venues are modest and often hard to find. As of this edition, there is one small, central museum in Jackson, one small community display in Port Gibson, and, sadly, many scattered headstones. Except in Jackson and Philadelphia, road signs to civil rights history are nonexistent. In towns with some of the most heroic events—McComb, Greenwood, Hattiesburg—a Confederate soldier on a pedestal still rules the public space. A stranger wandering Mississippi would have almost no idea that a revolution envied by the world took place there.

Still, Mississippi belongs on every civil rights itinerary. A tour through the state, even in search of sites, can be a telling experience. The state remains largely rural. Poverty is widespread. Ongoing prejudice makes each success story a small wonder.

To think that ordinary people with no visible support and everything to lose summoned the courage to challenge the Ku Klux Klan, tradition, and government is to understand the true heroism of the civil rights movement.

Mississippi and Civil Rights

Mississippi's civil rights history is entwined with cotton. By the time Mississippi became a state in 1817 a great migration of planters and their slaves was under way from the Carolinas and Virginia to plant cotton seeds in rich, wet, semitropical cropland along the Mississippi River and its tributaries.

Between 1810 and 1860, two hundred thousand slaves were imported, outnumbering whites, and Mississippi became the largest producer of cotton. From their antebellum mansions overlooking Ol' Man River, planters became hardened advocates of a separate slave nation. Seceding from the Union twenty days after South Carolina, Mississippi lent its U.S. senator, Jefferson Davis, to head the Confederacy in Civil War.

After the war, Mississippi passed through a hopeful period of power sharing. Hiram Revels, a northern-educated minister, was elected to fill Davis's senate seat, becoming the first black ever to serve in Congress. Planter Blanche Bruce, a former slave, served a full term, the last black senator to do so until the 1960s. The state legislature elected African American John Roy Lynch speaker of the house. Later he served three terms in Congress. Reconstruction legislatures built the state's first black colleges, including the first African American land-grant college, and established the state's public school system.

The promise of a shared future disappeared when white supremacists regained power. Although outnumbered 650,000 to 479,000, they instituted a reign of terror and grabbed control of government and sharecropped cotton production. A new state constitution of 1890 disenfranchised 123,000 blacks by imposing a two dollar poll tax and requiring all voters to read and understand the state Constitution, barriers that remained in effect (despite the Fifteenth Amendment) until the 1960s. Jim Crow laws quickly followed: segregated transportation, no intermarriage, and separate schools.

An independent black culture, built around churches and small businesses, developed. Its most famous product was Delta blues, sung and played by farmhands. Thousands of blacks left Mississippi for Memphis, Chicago, and other northern cities.

A descendant of one of those families, on a 1955 summer vacation to visit relatives in Money, Mississippi, was murdered for allegedly speaking "fresh" to a white woman. Emmett Till's murder, the open-casket display of his crushed face, and the all-white jury's acquittal of two white kidnappers ignited the fuse of black activism.

Black GIs who had fought in World War II and Korea formed the nucleus of the nascent movement. They were opposed by the Citizens Councils, first created in Indianola in 1954 to resist the Supreme Court's school integration decision. Their uneasy face-off exploded when hundreds of college students, white and black, came into the state to register black voters. With a couple of notable exceptions, traditional black leadership chafed at the intrusion, especially when Freedom Riders arrived on buses. But no one resisted like white supremacists.

In 1962 federal troops had to quell armed rioters fighting the court-ordered enrollment of James Meredith at the University of Mississippi. Two people died. In 1963 Medgar Evers, the NAACP state field secretary, was assassinated in his Jackson driveway. In June 1964 three civil rights workers—James Chaney, Michael Schwerner, and Andrew Goodman—were shot near Philadelphia. In the FBI's search for them, three more blacks were found dead in state rivers.

In that wake, the Freedom Summer campaign of 1964, a voter registration drive led by the Student Nonviolent Coordinating Committee, could be considered one of the most courageous human rights campaigns in history. Working virtually unaided, unprotected, and largely uncovered by the news media, young people walked door-to-door persuading black Mississippians to try, at least, to register and vote. Harassment was insidious and frightening, from economic strangulation to firebombings. Backed eventually by slow-moving federal enforcement of new civil rights legislation, nearly 100,000 African Americans registered over the next two years and began electing blacks to local, state, and federal offices.

Long after national media stopped covering the story, Mississippians pressed on. In 1967 the first black in the twentieth century was elected to the state legislature. Public school integration, averted for years by a "freedom of choice" plan, was finally struck down by the U.S. Supreme Court in 1970. In 1994, thirty years after he escaped prosecution, Byron De La Beckwith was convicted of murdering Medgar Evers. The following year, the state legislature ratified the Thirteenth Amendment (of 1865) abolishing slavery. But in 2001, by a two-to-one margin along race lines, voters decided to keep a state flag with Confederate colors.

"We've had to come further than any other state, and I think we have. There is still a lot of work that needs to be done," said former Governor William Winter.

The civil rights message in Mississippi, more powerfully told than anywhere else in the South, is the unfinished dream.

A Mississippi Civil Rights Tour

This guide recommends three tours:

The Mississippi Delta, with Oxford as side trip

A flat, green, fertile plain with heat and humidity, the Delta has a population that is 80 percent black and is dominated, economically, by cotton and catfish. Cotton bolls are never far away, and large ponds with nearby factories turn fingerlings into fillets in a matter of months. After the Civil War, many freed slaves moved into the Delta and carved out small farms. By the 1960s landholding blacks were not uncommon, and their homes served as refugee camps for voting-rights workers.

Starting at Memphis, the Delta can be crossed in a couple of hours, but a tour would take two days. Though very rural, even the smallest Delta towns have motels, and all small cities sport chains such as Hampton Inns.

The sites include quiet stories of triumph and sad reminders of the violence that accompanied the civil rights struggle. Visitors today are quite safe while traveling the well-kept roads of Mississippi's Delta. Towns to visit include Oxford, Clarksdale, Cleveland, Ruleville, Money, and Greenwood.

Central Mississippi

Mississippi's most notorious civil rights assassinations by members of the Ku Klux Klan occurred within seventy-five miles of each other: Medgar Evers in Jackson and three Freedom Summer workers in Philadelphia. Both events are commemorated by roadside markers and monuments (and Hollywood movies). The state capital has a driving tour of many "ordinary citizen" venues plus the first civil rights museum in the country.

Southern Mississippi

The fiercest resistance to voting and citizen rights occurred in a broad band across mid-southern Mississippi. Eight murders and vicious beatings were the price paid by civil rights workers. The state's only museum to the work of local people—in Port Gibson—is worth seeing. But in most communities, there is nary a whisper of the heroism that forced equal rights on Mississippi. This tour encompasses the towns of Port Gibson, Alcorn, Natchez, McComb and surroundings, and Hattiesburg.

City by City

Biloxi

One of Mississippi's first civil rights protests occurred on the spring morning of 1960 when a group of blacks entered the forbidden waters and beaches of the Gulf of Mexico. Sparked by the Greensboro lunch counter sit-in, they were ordered off the beach, and later, beaten and shot at. The "wade-in" forced a more militant stand by the state NAACP and led directly to public protests of libraries, theaters, and swimming pools elsewhere in the state. The U.S. Justice Department under Robert Kennedy sued Biloxi to integrate beaches and won seven years later.

Clarksdale

Revived by blues music tourism in recent years, downtown Clarksdale was the scene of Mississippi's longest and ugliest desegregation boycotts. It began in December 1961 when black marching bands were denied their normal place in the Christmas parade. "If we can't parade downtown should we trade downtown?" became the call. For two years, the boycott was led by Aaron Henry, a World War II veteran and pharmacist who headed the Mississippi NAACP. For his role, his home and business were firebombed—once while Detroit Congressman Charles Diggs was a house guest. Two years after the boycott began, the white mayor refused to even establish a biracial committee, and boycotters were arrested by the score. It was in Clarksdale that a coalition of national and local civil rights groups formed the Council of Federated Organizations to "take on" Mississippi. Henry was its first president.

During the Jim Crow era, Clarksdale's Fourth Street was hot with blues music. Bessie Smith, Muddy Waters, Sonny Boy Williamson, Robert Nighthawk, Kansas City Red, and Ike Turner, among others, performed, often staying at the Riverside Hotel. Sam Cooke was born in Clarksdale.

Today, blues and rock 'n' roll fans visit Clarksdale, often on a popular Delta-wide tour of blues sites. The city claims "the crossroads," the mythical spot where blues pioneer Robert Johnson sold his soul to the devil in return for guitar artistry. It is a fact that W. C. Handy first heard the blues from a street musician in nearby Tutwiler, and reinterpreted the music to wider audiences as the "father" of the blues.

CLARKSDALE'S DELTA BLUES MUSEUM *(Old Freight Depot, 1 Blues Alley; 662-627-6820; www.deltabluesmuseum.org)* This airy shed displays photos and interpretation of the Delta cotton culture and environment that produced the music. One section contains the simple log cabin once occupied by Muddy Waters, who was born in 1915 and grew up on the Stovall Plantation. Waters drove a tractor and did manual labor, but from age three was demonstrating musical talent. By age seven he played the harmonica. When Waters was twenty-six, Alan Lomax from the Library of Congress entered the cabin and recorded him playing guitar and singing. Within a year Waters left for Chicago and fame.

The museum's displays of Delta and Mississippi musical greats tempts the visitor to believe its assertion that "deprivation breeds inventiveness" and that in blues suffering becomes a lament. The discovery of, and dissemination of, this original American music, created in the Mississippi Delta by ex-slaves and their descendants, became an early bridge between races. In northern cities like Chicago, masterful blues musicians earned the respect of white patrons. Their performances to integrated crowds were harbingers of civil rights, and their music the soundtrack. Its upbeat child, rock 'n' roll, finished the job.

Cleveland

HOME OF AMZIE MOORE *(614 South Chrisman Avenue)*   Inside this unassuming beige and brick house, a civil rights revolution—Mississippi's black voter registration drive—was launched. At a time when "direct action" sit-ins and boycotts were the rage elsewhere in the South, Amzie Moore, a bear-like, ex-Army vet, postman, and gas station owner, persuaded Bob Moses, a New Yorker, to begin a door-to-door voter registration campaign. So poor were his Delta neighbors,

Amzie Moore's Cleveland home

Moore reasoned, that access to a lunch counter or department store would not materially affect their lives. He became "Godfather" to squads of young activists who eventually broke the back of Mississippi's Jim Crow.

Luminaries including Martin Luther King, Andy Young, and John Lewis ate and slept here, but it was young people that Moore believed in. Moses and Moore dispatched kids to Greenwood, Indianola, Belzoni, and down countless dirt roads to accompany locals, largely older residents, to county courthouses to attempt voter registration. They were usually turned away, often beaten, shot at, and firebombed for trying. For years, this tiny house served as strategy central, revolving dormitory, and safe house for fleeing, scared, and exhausted activists. Moore's house survived intact, perhaps because he slept with a gun by his head and had guests sleep in shifts with armed sentries. Moore died in 1982 and is buried in Cleveland's Westlawn Memorial Gardens. The house is in private hands, although it deserves to be a monument to one man's courage and impact.

AMZIE MOORE'S GAS STATION *(U.S. 61)* During Jim Crow, this station was said to offer the only restrooms for black drivers between Memphis and Vicksburg. Now boarded up, it has been eyed as a site for a local civil rights museum.

Ordinary Icons

For all the renown and consequence of the civil rights movement, its landmarks are remarkably ordinary: a Woolworth's lunch counter, a bus stop, a bridge, modest homes and schools.

By and large, these icons remain as they were fifty years after they helped revolutionize the American social fabric. Many are unmarked. Too many are falling down. None has been glorified with pillars and statues. Their significance in human rights seems all the more powerful because of their ordinariness.

Nowhere is this more evident than in Mississippi. There the movement was powered almost entirely by working people, many living in poverty. Amzie Moore's house in Cleveland was action central for the Delta's voting rights campaign. In this tiny house, civil rights notables and student activists ate, slept, and strategized around the clock.

In Jackson, the state capital, a unique civil rights driving tour takes you past a schoolteacher's house, a barbershop, and a library, just three of more than one hundred stops that in their heyday pulsed with ideas and energy that moved a city to integrate.

Schools that were battlefields on the integration front look the same, except for the color of the student body. In a few places, bullet holes remain. Most schools do not even have a plaque to mark the spot where so much pain was endured and years and opportunities were lost.

The notable exception is black churches, long established and quite magnificent monuments to black history. Many hosted mass meetings, provided refuge for the beaten, and fed sandwiches and faith to the discouraged. Indeed, it would be difficult to imagine a movement without the physical power and spiritual support of black churches.

But the struggle took place outside these black enclaves in the mundane venues of American life. It was in these places that blacks demanded admission to buy a cup of coffee, to check out a library book, to see a state fair, to ride a bus undisturbed. What they demanded, in the name of freedom, was a normal American life.

The resistance to this change was so broad that the movement had to repeat itself in scores of restaurants and public sites. Despite class-action Supreme Court decisions and new federal laws, implementation remained largely local. Someone, somewhere, had to be the first to sit down at the local café and order food. In hundreds of no-name crossroads, the civil rights movement came down to a handful of activists who stood face-to-face with people who, for generations, had considered them less than equal.

One unfortunate consequence of integration was the demise of healthy all-black neighborhoods. Once able to shop and eat and live (almost) anywhere, people did. Unable to compete against mass marketers, black businesses closed. Black neighborhoods, lacking political and economic clout, were sliced up and isolated by interstate highway construction and "urban renewal."

Today, a civil rights tourist will find many important sites in poor, scarred neighborhoods filled with potential. In some cities, a reverse migration of young professional blacks, artists, and bohemians are revitalizing historically black cityscapes. The state of these neighborhoods, and their civil rights icons, is a story in itself. There is work yet to be done.

Greenwood

Ground zero for the 1960s civil rights struggle in Mississippi's Delta, this county seat was home base for two powerful and competing organizations—SNCC and the Citizens Council. Fighting with nerves, largely nonviolent students took on the white power structure that encouraged vigilantes, including the Ku Klux Klan. The murder of Emmett Till six years earlier in the village of Money, eight miles north, hung over them, at once inspirational and terrifying. At the time, only 250 blacks were registered to vote.

In 1962 Sam Block, a twenty-three-year-old student, volunteered to move from his Cleveland hometown to Greenwood and begin recruiting for voter registration. "I had no car, no money, no clothes, no food, just me," Block later told historian Howard Zinn. Evicted once, Block slept in a car in a junkyard. Hanging out in the poor South Greenwood neighborhood, Block attracted

people to mass meetings where he led them in "freedom songs" while showing them how to register. After taking his first three volunteers to the imposing LeFlore County Courthouse, dominated by its huge Confederate memorial, he received a phone call from the Citizens Council: "If you take anybody else up to register you'll never leave Greenwood alive," according to historian John Dittmer. Later he was beaten, shot at, driven from SNCC's headquarters by goons with chains and shotguns, and firebombed. Local blacks were cowed and for six months Block walked the streets calming nerves.

During the winter of 1962–63, after James Meredith's integration of Ole Miss in Oxford, county officials cut off surplus food to the poor, an act of revenge that backfired. Comedian Dick Gregory flew in tons of food, Harry Belafonte sang at Carnegie Hall to raise funds, and SNCC became a moral force with the backing of hundreds of local people who marched, sang, and lined up for hours at the registrar's office.

Today, the public space at the LeFlore County Courthouse remains dominated by a Confederate soldier, and an economic divide between rich whites and poor blacks, across the Yazoo River, appears entrenched. But in a county with 26,000 registered voters, black voters outnumber whites, and every elected board is majority black.

GREENWOOD DRIVING TOUR

1 | LeFlore County Courthouse *(Market and Fulton Streets)* Guarded by three Confederate figures, including a woman nursing a wounded rebel, this building was the target of a brave effort to register black voters in the 1960s. On its steps and sidewalks, police and their dogs terrified and sometimes injured citizens seeking their constitutional rights.

2 | Greenwood City Hall *(Church and Main Streets)* In 1962 the mayor of Greenwood was a member of the Citizens Council, a white power group opposed to desegregation and equal rights. Peaceful black marchers were attacked on the sidewalk by police dogs as they passed by City Hall.

3 | Turner Chapel *(717 Walthall Street)* Mass meetings were held here. After the Reverend David Tucker was bitten by a police dog during a downtown march, the black community and other black protesters joined the movement.

4 | **CENTURY FUNERAL HOME** *(Walthall and Gibbs Streets)* The bodies of murdered Emmett Till and the revered Fannie Lou Hamer were handled by this longtime black funeral home founded by Henry Espy. Grandson Mike Espy became the first black congressman from Mississippi since Reconstruction.

5 | **BARBERSHOP** *(Broad Street and Avenue I)* Aaron Johnson, a barber and minister, was the bravest man in Greenwood in 1962 when he opened his church for mass meetings and SNCC voter registration schools. As an independent businessman, Johnson held strategy sessions in this shop.

6 | **SNCC HEADQUARTERS** *(616 Avenue I)* This now decrepit building was a vibrant beehive in the 1960s as young activists organized voter registrations, mass meetings, and food distribution. Across the street, a row of ramshackle shotgun houses bear witness to problems of equal opportunity that remain today.

7 | **BROAD STREET PARK** *(Broad Street and Avenue N)* Where swings now entertain children, a famous civil rights rally occurred in June 1966. Stokely Carmichael, who had worked for SNCC's nonviolent voter registration drive in the early 1960s, returned a militant. "Black power," he shouted. "We want . . . black power." The slogan signaled a split in civil rights organizations with Carmichael leading a militant wing largely based in urban areas of the United States.

Hattiesburg

The bustling college town of today bears little resemblance to the "gracious" Piney Woods capital of 1960 where Jim Crow reigned. Hattiesburg produced some of the saddest civil rights stories in Mississippi.

FORREST COUNTY COURTHOUSE *(Downtown at the corner of Main and Eaton Streets)* Up the front steps of this grand building with four imposing pillars and an adjacent Confederate soldier memorial, a welcoming arrow now points to voter registration. But in 1960, the door was blocked by a three-hundred-pound white supremacist named Theron Lynd. After his election as circuit clerk in 1959, Lynd refused to let blacks even apply, and fewer than fifty blacks were registered out of thousands of possible voters. Under Mississippi Jim Crow law, the local clerk could find almost any excuse for refusing registration.

After defying federal court injunctions, Lynd took on SNCC's campaign to bring black applicants in by the score. Many people learned to read and write in preparation for registration, and many lost their jobs after trying. When Lynd refused a Supreme Court order and defied contempt charges, a huge, emotional demonstration in the rain filled the courthouse and sidewalk outside. Freedom Day, January 22, 1964, gave local blacks the courage to register by the dozen. Demonstrations continued all summer in what became the largest Freedom Summer site in the state.

UNIVERSITY OF SOUTHERN MISSISSIPPI *(2701 Hardy Street; 601-266-7011; www.usm.edu)* In 1959 distinguished army paratrooper Clyde Kennard was forced to leave the University of Chicago in his senior year to nurse an ailing father and run the family farm in Eatonville, Mississippi. After applying to Mississippi Southern, the thirty-year-old Kennard was arrested on trumped up charges of stealing chicken feed, a felony that ended his dream of admission in a state school. Secret records from the Mississippi Sovereignty Commission later proved that the college president conspired with a black minister and others to keep Kennard from becoming the first black to integrate a state university. Kennard was sentenced to seven years in the state's notorious Parchman Penitentiary where he developed cancer. Just before his death, Governor Ross Barnett released Kennard. On his deathbed, Kennard told author John Griffin that his death would be worthwhile "if only it would show this country where racism finally leads. But the people aren't going to know it, are they?"

VERNON DAHMER GRAVESITE *(North of Hattiesburg, Interstate 59, exit 73 at Monroe Road. Turn east and head north to Shady Grove Church. Dahmer's gravestone is near the edge of the parking* *lot.*) Farmer-businessman Vernon Dahmer supported voter registration when it was unknown in the 1950s, during the 1963–1964 SNCC campaign, and again after passage of the 1965 Voting Rights Act. The Ku Klux Klan, in one of its death rattles, firebombed Dahmer's rural house during a January night in 1966. Helping his wife and children escape out the back, Dahmer grabbed his shotgun to fire back, opened the door to the living room, and was engulfed in flames. He returned shots, but was horribly burned on his skin and respiratory tract. He died the next day. Klan leader Sam Bowers escaped four jury trials and bragged that a white jury wouldn't convict. In 1998 an integrated jury sent him to prison for the rest of his life. Dahmer's gravestone reads: "Husband, father, community leader, voting rights activist. If you don't vote you don't count."

Indianola

To a poor, working African American in Sunflower County, the big courthouse in Indianola was a fearful seat of white power. The average sharecropper earned five hundred dollars a year, whites owned 90 percent of the

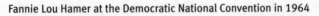
Fannie Lou Hamer at the Democratic National Convention in 1964

land, and though blacks outnumbered whites two to one, fewer than two hundred were voters, according to *Local People* by John Dittmer. Imagine the guts it took in 1962 for three black women to climb the steps, enter the clerk's office, and ask for voter registration forms. Charles McLaurin, the twenty-one-year-old SNCC recruiter who brought them, was struck with a sudden case of cold feet. But the women "went up the walk to the courthouse as if this was the long walk that led to the Golden Gate of Heaven, their heads held high," he told Dittmer. A week later, eighteen people tried to register, one of them Fannie Lou Hamer, a forty-four-year-old sharecropper's wife and plantation timekeeper. She took the test, a loosely defined requirement to interpret the state constitution, and was thrown off the plantation. Several days later, night riders fired into several homes, injuring two black girls. The campaign was halted temporarily, but Hamer found her calling. She became Mississippi's best loved local activist and her gravestone in Ruleville remains a pilgrimage site.

There are no signposts to the civil rights era in Indianola, and two of the most significant sites, the courthouse and city hall, have been rebuilt. While in town, visitors may contemplate the following civil rights stories.

- **Citizens Council:** Two months after the U.S. Supreme Court integrated public schools, angry white business leaders met in Indianola to form the Citizens Council to oppose it. No monument marks the spot but Citizens Councils spread throughout the South and became a potent political force that long delayed compliance with civil rights laws. Known to some civil rights workers as the "Klan in suits," the council's members blackmailed local activists, fired them, and foreclosed businesses, and distributed booklets in white public schools that claimed blacks were lazy, liars, and thieves. Leaders Bill Simmons and Tut Patterson set up an office in nearby Greenwood, and at one time claimed 250,000 members. Patterson told author William Doyle, "Everybody in the South felt like we did . . . we had the very finest people; ministers, lawyers, judges. It was a very fine, high-class patriotic organization."

- **The Sunflower County Courthouse:** Fannie Lou Hamer and other brave sharecroppers attempted voter registration at the courthouse, a raised, imposing structure, with stepped entrances on four sides. The old courthouse has been replaced. City Hall next door has been remodeled.

- **Minnie Cox:** Cox was the first black woman postmaster in the United States. She ran Indianola's post office in an unsung civil rights role. As the educated wife of a prominent black businessman, Cox was appointed by Republican presidents and ran the post office between 1891 and 1903. As Jim Crow took control in Mississippi, white supremacists tried to squeeze her out before her second term ended in 1904. Rather than submit to their demands, Teddy Roosevelt closed the post office, but continued to pay Cox until her term ended. A city park has been named in her honor, and efforts are under way to erect a plaque.

Jackson

Scarred by the assassination of civil rights hero Medgar Evers, the capital of Mississippi has done more than any other midsized city in the South to face its racist past and make it a lesson for citizens and visitors. Several landmarks are named for Evers, including the post office and a proposed new

civil rights museum. The first black mayor, Harvey Johnson Jr., also created a civil rights driving tour with a brochure and numbered steps that, in one day, dishes up a thoughtful, and by turns a troubling and optimistic message. The tour takes a visitor through black neighborhoods and past the occasional home that belonged to a pioneer, and not so different from other modest, run-down, homes or businesses in working-class neighborhoods, except for the numbered sign out front.

What impresses after viewing dozens of these modest venues is the widespread effort that racial equality required and generated, from schoolteachers suing for equal pay to students marching to the serving of countless church suppers.

(The driving tour brochure is available free at the city visitors center, 921 North President Street; 800-354-7695.)

▌ OLD CAPITOL MUSEUM *(100 State Street; 601-359-6920; www.mdah.state.ms.us/museum/)* The first permanent civil rights exhibit in the United States (1985) occupies a modest space of the museum on the first floor. Among the Jim Crow artifacts is a red tie and suspenders worn by white supremacist and U.S. Senator Theodore Bilbo, whose constituents were known as "red necks." In the 1946 primary, candidate Bilbo urged whites to "visit" blacks the night before the primary. He won the primary but left the Senate under a cloud, replaced by another racist, John Stennis. As the museum notes, Mississippi remained almost totally segregated until 1964: "Its established social order reinforced by rigid orthodoxy and fear of nonconformity."

This building, the state capitol until 1903, was the scene of dramatic racial reversals after the Civil War. Immediately following the war, Mississippi refused to pass the Thirteenth Amendment ending slavery. Instead, plantation owners persuaded the legislature to pass "Black Codes" that required blacks to have work contracts and set up severe punishment for violations ranging from vagrancy to insulting gestures to preaching without a license. These codes led Congress to pass both the first federal civil rights law—the Civil Rights Act of 1866—and the Fourteenth Amendment guaranteeing equal protection under law. In 1868 Mississippi's "black and tan convention" (with nineteen blacks among ninety-seven delegates) gave blacks equal rights for the first time. But in 1890, a mere twenty-five years after the end of the war, Mississippi became the first state to formally disenfranchise African Americans by setting up legal discrimination that was not abolished until the Voting Rights Act of 1965.

2 | **STATE FAIRGROUNDS** (*directly east behind the Old Capitol*)   This Mississippi landmark once hosted the Jim Crow phenomenon of "colored" and "white" fairs. For decades, the annual fair, for whites only, was followed by a "colored" fair. In 1961, according to Jackson's driving tour, the NAACP and its youth councils demonstrated against the "colored" fair. Their signs read, NO JIM CROW FAIR FOR US. Seven protesters were arrested. In the 1960s hundreds of sit-in protesters were hauled to livestock pens here. Surrounded by police dogs and spotlights, they resembled Nazi concentration camps.

3 | **GREYHOUND BUS STATION** (*219 North Lamar Street*)   Beautifully restored into a private architect's office, the former bus station was the end point of the famous Freedom Riders integration drive across the Deep South in 1961. Unlike the beatings and firebombings of Alabama, arriving riders were hustled away to prison by police.

4 | **FARISH STREET** (*on the edge of downtown*)   This was the thriving black business district before and during the civil rights era. Along this street, churches, funeral homes, and offices provided food, shelter, advice, and moral support for Jackson's long-suffering desegregation effort. The down-and-out street is slated for urban renewal.

5 | **JACKSON STATE UNIVERSITY** (*1400 J. R. Lynch Street; 601-979-2121; www.jsums.edu*)   In defiance of their administration, students at Jackson State repeatedly demonstrated and marched downtown to desegregate Jackson businesses and public facilities. After nine college students were arrested for trying to check out books at the Jackson Public Library, Medgar Evers led a "We want freedom" rally on campus. The school president ordered them to leave. Students boycotted classes the next day and marched again, but were met by clubs and tear gas. In May 1970 two students,

Phillip Gibbs and James Green, were killed by police gunfire during antiwar protests. The killings occurred eleven days after the murders of four Kent State students in a similar protest. A plaque at Alexander Hall honors the students, and bullet pockmarks remain in a stairwell.

6 | **HOME OF MEDGAR EVERS AND MURDER SITE** (*2332 Margaret Walker Alexander Drive; 601-977-7710; tours by appointment only*) Evers was among a small squadron of World War II GIs who returned to Mississippi to lay the groundwork for the civil rights revolution of the 1960s. As field secretary of the NAACP beginning in 1954, Evers toiled in relative isolation and barely contained rage, gathering files on lynchings, beatings, and endless discrimination cases common to the Jim Crow era. At least ten black murders by white Mississippians between 1956 and 1959 went unpunished. In 1961, spurred by the national sit-in movement, local college students led the charge into Jackson facilities. A month later the first "outside" activists, the Freedom Riders, arrived. Evers welcomed their energy and courage. Unfortunately the Jackson movement was blunted by

The Evers's home in Jackson

Sculpture of Medgar
Evers in Jackson

rivalries among civil rights groups and equivocal support by the Kennedy administration. Although the movement was reenergized in 1963 with a May 28 Woolworth's lunch counter sit-in, attention again focused on Evers, whose carport was firebombed the next night. Late on June 11, after a national civil rights address by President Kennedy, Evers was shot in the back as he arrived home and died in the arms of his wife and children. The slayer was Byron De La Beckwith, a member of the Citizens Council who was acquitted in his first trials but eventually was jailed in his old age. Evers's funeral with five thousand mourners nearly turned into a downtown riot. Tougaloo College, which owns the house, runs tours and plans an expanded daily operation.

7 | **MEDGAR EVERS STATUE** *(4215 Medgar Evers Boulevard)* Outside the Medgar Evers Library, this life-size bronze of Evers contains the following inscription: "Dedicated to everyone who believes in peace, love and nonviolence. Let's keep the torch burning." Inside the library a display provides significant detail about Evers's life and contribution to Mississippi civil rights.

8 | **TOUGALOO COLLEGE CAMPUS** *(500 West County Road; 601-977-7771; www.tougaloo.edu)* On the outskirts of Jackson, Tougaloo was Mississippi's first accredited black college. Founded by the American Missionary Association four years after the Civil War, the campus occupies a former cotton-and-slave plantation. Because of its independence from state funding, the school became a hotbed of civil rights activism. In 1961, spurred by the sit-in movement elsewhere in the South, nine Tougaloo students who were members of an NAACP youth group staged a book checkout at the segregated Jackson Public Library. The arrest of the "Tougaloo Nine" led to mass student sit-ins at the library, zoo, downtown stores, and swimming pools and the beginning of the modern movement statewide.

Liberty

In 1961 bitter irony abounded in this town named for America's original battle cry and home to Borden's condensed milk (made from contented cows). Amite County was majority black, but only one black resident was registered to vote. In what has been described as the "most heroic single act" of the civil rights movement, Bob Moses arrived and accompanied three blacks to the registrar's office in the imposing white courthouse. All were arrested. A week later, the sheriff's cousin, a brute named Billy Jack Caston, struck Moses to his knees with a knife butt. Moses filed charges, to no avail. One of Moses's hosts, cotton farmer Herbert Lee, drove Moses from house to house as he recruited volunteers. On September 25 Lee was gunned down at a Liberty cotton gin by state representative E. H. Hurst. A whitewash trial freed Hurst. The murder inspired the freedom song "We'll Never Turn Back," by Bertha Gober, which became the anthem of Mississippi's civil rights movement. Among its stanzas is this line: "We've been 'buked and we've been scorned. . . ."

Lorman

Alcorn State University, on the National Register of Historic Places, was the first land-grant college for blacks in the United States. Flush with the promise of Reconstruction, the integrated Mississippi legislature purchased Oakland College, a Presbyterian school abandoned during the Civil War, and turned it into Alcorn Agricultural and Mechanical College. The Oakland chapel, originally built by black craftsmen under white rule, is largely preserved. The school's first black president, Hiram Revels, led a dramatic and visible public life as an AME minister, black Civil War recruiter, founder of a freedman school, and U.S. senator. According to the school, most of Mississippi's black doctors and dentists are Alcorn graduates. Medgar and Charles Evers, brothers and civil rights activists, were graduates.

McComb

When President Kennedy was assassinated in 1963, many whites in this southern Mississippi town cheered. The Ku Klux Klan operated with unveiled support from city fathers. This was the atmosphere that greeted Bob Moses of SNCC when he arrived to push McComb and southwestern Mississippi toward civil rights.

Moses, a young black schoolteacher from Harlem, New York, held voter registration classes at the Masonic Hall in McComb in August 1961. Within days, pent-up frustration in the black community exploded. People filled out voter forms, sat in the Woolworth's lunch counter, and tried to integrate the Greyhound terminal. When the principal suspended two of the sit-in students, one hundred students marched out, singing, "We Shall Overcome."

Whites lashed back, killing Herbert Lee and beating Moses and assaulting a SNCC worker in Tylertown. Many black "leaders" objected, too, and the McComb campaign, with only six new registered voters, went inactive until 1964. As students moved back into town during Freedom Summer, the Klan threw bombs, burned churches, and beat activists. Yet slowly, blacks rallied, and after the September 20 dynamite bombing of Aylene Quin's home, in McComb, took to the streets with guns and Molotov cocktails. After Mrs. Quin met with President Johnson, and national media began covering the Klan's terrorism, the federal government threatened martial law. Police rounded up Klan suspects who then went free with a judge's lecture. In November 1964 the white business community, urged by a local newspaper editor, Hazel Brannon Smith, called for an end to violence and acceptance of federal civil rights laws.

Meridian

JAMES CHANEY GRAVESITE (*Valley Road exit off Interstate 20, south 3.4 miles through an industrial plant. Left on Fish Lodge Road at sign for Okatibbee Baptist Church. Road winds up to gravestone.*)   James Chaney was one of three activists murdered by the Klan in Philadelphia, Mississippi, during Freedom Summer 1964. The twenty-one-year-old Chaney, who was raised in Meridian, was one of the few local blacks on the staff of CORE, working with the husband-wife team of Mickey and Rita Schwerner. He and Schwerner had convinced the Mount Zion Methodist Church in rural Neshoba County to host a freedom school for voter education. On June 16, 1964, members of the White Knights of the Ku Klux Klan beat churchgoers and burned the church down. Feeling responsible, Schwerner, Chaney, and new volunteer Andy Goodman went to the church site to investigate. They were murdered and hidden in an earthen dam. Even in death, Chaney could find no peace. Black funeral directors declined his body, and segregated cemeteries refused to honor their parents' wish to bury Chaney and Schwerner side by side. Chaney's brother finally found this isolated spot four miles south of Meridian but continued to deal with vandalism. His stone has been defaced, and had to be secured in place by steel beams.

Money

Although it collapses more each year, the brick skeleton of a country store in this dried-up Delta town might be Mississippi's most eloquent civil rights icon. Enough remains to imagine fourteen-year-old Emmett Till, a streetwise Chicago kid, playing checkers on the store's porch on a hot August afternoon with other boys and bragging about his sexual exploits in the big city. On a dare, according to later conflicting testimony, Till walked inside, said something "fresh" to the twenty-one-year-old white woman at the counter, and exited with, "Bye, baby."

Three days later, when the woman's husband, truck driver Roy Bryant, returned, he and "Big" Milam showed up at midnight at Till's granduncle's house and took him away. His granduncle, Moses Wright, begged for a mere whipping.

Three days later, the boy's body was found in the Tallahatchie River, which flows in back of the store. He was held underwater by a cotton gin fan (an abandoned gin sits near the store). But Till had been so badly

What remains of the country store in Money

mauled that his face resembled nothing human. Till's mother, with courage and rage, displayed her son's face in an open casket and allowed a photograph to be published in *Jet* magazine. For many African Americans, the photo ignited personal civil rights activism.

The killers were tried. In an act of bravery before a white jury, Moses Wright stood before the suspects and identified one with, "Thar he." But the men were acquitted in the usual manner. Writing later, William Faulkner said of the country, "When we must murder children, no matter for what reason or what color, we don't deserve to survive, and probably won't."

Natchez

Carved from snake-infested swamp wilderness by slave labor, Natchez became a classic southern antebellum society with mansions on the bluff overlooking the Mississippi River, supported by legions of slaves picking cotton on huge plantations. Today what remains of this bifurcated culture are the mansions, many of which are open to a thriving tourist trade, and one road sign marking the slave trade post at the now-gone Forks of the Road, which operated until 1863. Except for a modest downtown African American museum and one brochure, the memory of lives of blacks who once outnumbered whites three to one is largely forgotten amid the magnolia-scented Spring Pilgrimage tours of historic homes that began in 1932. Tourists who ask about slaves are told, "We don't talk about that."

In 1954 a black group, the Natchez Business and Civic League, led a pioneering voter registration drive. Their gains, and the prospect of more a decade later during Freedom Summer, spawned the birth of a virulent Klan klavern, the Mississippi White Knights. During one night in April 1964, they burned sixty-four crosses across Mississippi. In May, after White Knights leader Sam Bowers urged "counterattacks against activists," klansmen stripped and whipped Archie Curtis, the head of the Natchez black league. Within days, two other black men were whipped and their houses firebombed, and Clinton Walker was shot to death. In nearby Meadville, the Klan killed Charles Moore and Henry Dee. Their broken bodies were found in the Mississippi River in July during the search for the three Philadelphia civil rights workers. Although a Klan member confessed, a judge dismissed the case.

When a modest Freedom Summer contingent came to town, local NAACP president George Metcalf put SNCC workers up until they could find lodging. On August 27, 1965, his car exploded as he left the Armstrong Rubber plant. He survived, but the bombing jolted local blacks into a nasty but successful rights boycott that closed many white businesses. Charles Evers, who had taken over the state NAACP from his slain brother Medgar, negotiated a modest victory—a desegregated city, six new black police jobs, a black on the school board, and a promise of jobs in stores. Natchez would be the last major Mississippi campaign.

The following year, in an effort to assassinate Martin Luther King Jr., the Klan tried to lure King to Natchez by murdering an innocent, elderly black man, Ben Chester White. Both killers confessed, but were acquitted. The next year, the Klan exploded a car bomb that killed NAACP treasurer Wharlest Jackson, after he was promoted to a white man's job at Armstrong Rubber. Though the mayor and police chief linked hands with black mourners and sang, "We Shall Overcome," Jackson's killers were never identified.

The Natchez school segregation case was not settled until the merger of two high schools in 1989, the same year that the National Park Service created a new park in Natchez, the first NPS unit required by Congress to include the African American story.

NATCHEZ MUSEUM OF AFRICAN AMERICAN HISTORY AND CULTURE *(301 Main Street; 601-442-0728; www.ncvb.natchez.ms.us/ natchez_museum_of_afro.htm)* After countless mansion tours of historic "white" Natchez, visitors to this modest space often say, "Thank you for presenting the other side." Even so, the story of black Natchez is severely censored. The museum, housed in an old post office, covers only the period from the Civil War to World War II. Still missing is the central role slaves played in creating Natchez wealth, and the city's brutal civil rights movement. As one docent put it: "Civil rights was very much alive in Natchez but nobody talks about it."

WILLIAM JOHNSON HOUSE *(210 State Street; 601-442-7047)* Now a National Park site, Johnson's house illustrates the promise and limits of a freed black man before the Civil War. Born a slave in 1809, Johnson parlayed an apprentice's job at a barber shop into a thriving real estate, farming, and barbering business that included thirty-one slaves of his own and white employees. Granted an exceptional position in Natchez, he could not vote or testify, but he could bring suit. In 1851 Johnson was shot and killed by a white man over a boundary dispute, a case that had to be moved because of heated reaction. But two years later, courts ruled that the white man could not be tried for murdering a black man. Johnson's 2,000-page diary was published on the one-hundredth anniversary of his death in 1951. According to local historians, at least three other mansions in Natchez were owned by free black entrepreneurs. China Grove Plantation and Glen Aubin Plantation were owned by ex-slaves after the Civil War.

DUNLEITH MANSION (*84 Homochitto Street; 601-446-8500; www.natchez-dunleith.com*) This is one of a number of grand plantations along the Mississippi that convey the sense of white wealth during the King Cotton era. But this mansion tells another story. John Lynch, a slave boy who once fanned guests in the mansion, was freed after the Civil War and worked as waiter, messenger boy, and photographic printer. He took night school classes from the Freedmen's Bureau and, sneaking a look from the second-floor photography studio across an alley, learned arithmetic by watching white children work on their chalkboards at the Natchez Institute. He became Speaker of the Mississippi House of Representatives, and, in 1873, Mississippi's first black congressman. His legislative record focused on civil rights. He later headed Capital Savings Bank in Washington, the first black bank in the United States. Thanks to the efforts of Historic Natchez Foundation, which is housed in the Institute's building, a photograph of Lynch now resides in the lobby of Dunleith and his story is told by interpreters.

RICHARD N. WRIGHT MARKER (*on Broadway at Bluff Park*) A marker honors Richard Wright, born to sharecroppers, author of *Native Son* and *Black Boy,* international best-sellers that told in stark detail what it was like to grow up black in America. He became an ex-patriot living in France, and died in 1960.

Oxford

Oxford's reputation as the Deep South's literary capital and home of gracious "Ole Miss" is marred by one notorious civil rights incident—the attempt by James Meredith to integrate the University of Mississippi and the U.S. military's intervention to quell a white supremacist insurrection. To its credit, forty years later, the university acknowledged this history with a memorial and the creation of a campus walking tour mapping the events of 1962. Reunions and seminars are held annually on the October 1 anniversary. In 2003 Ole Miss erected a public sculpture commemorating the integration of higher education. The school's effort put Ole Miss ahead of most southern colleges, including many historically black colleges.

James Meredith was an air force staff sergeant in Japan in 1957 when President Eisenhower sent military troops to Little Rock, Arkansas, to enforce integration of public schools. Five years later, Meredith precipitated an even uglier constitutional crisis when he chose to enroll at Ole Miss. In a sixteen-month legal battle engineered by NAACP lawyer Constance Baker Motley, federal courts ordered Ole Miss to admit Meredith in the fall semester of 1962.

"Never!" shouted Mississippi Governor Ross Barnett in a televised diatribe that brought students, Klansmen, and white supremacists to Oxford with guns and hate. When U.S. marshals surrounded the Lyceum and escorted Meredith inside to register, a crowd of several thousand greeted them with jeers, eggs, Molotov cocktails, and bullets. As snipers fired, two people, a newsman and a bystander, died from stray bullets. After a night of rioting, eleven thousand federalized National Guard and twenty thousand U.S. troops massed into the "Circle," a picturesque grove of trees at the center of campus—a story told in detail in *An American Insurrection* by William Doyle.

On the morning of October 1, 1962, Meredith calmly filled out registration forms. As he walked to his first class, escorted by soldiers who would be with him all year, he was showered with racial epithets, but one black cleaning man "gently touched him with his broom handle," Doyle reported. Meredith's first class was titled, "The Beginnings of English Colonization."

In 1966, three years after graduation, Meredith began a "march against fear" across Mississippi to show blacks it was safe to register to vote. On his second day, near Hernando, a white man in the bushes fired a shotgun at him, striking Meredith with buckshot. While he recuperated, Martin

Luther King Jr., Floyd McKissick, Stokely Carmichael, and others took up the walk to Jackson. By this time, the eleven-year-old civil rights movement was in turmoil, its leaders fighting over tactics and direction, a dispute played out on what became the last big march of the modern civil rights era.

Philadelphia

MOUNT ZION CHURCH (*from the center of Philadelphia, drive east on 16E for eight miles. Turn left, or north, on County Road 747 for 2.2 miles.*) A standard state historical road sign ten miles east of Philadelphia marks the most infamous lynching in Mississippi history—the murders of three civil rights workers during Freedom Summer 1964. They weren't killed here, but the young men had visited on June 21, the day they disappeared, to investigate the fire-bombing of the Methodist church.

Less than a month earlier, CORE organizers Michael Schwerner and James Chaney had persuaded the church congregation to host a "freedom school" to teach blacks how to pass voter registration tests. After the Ku Klux Klan burned the church, Schwerner and Chaney, feeling responsible, drove from Meridian to investigate. They brought along a new volunteer, Andrew Goodman. Heading home, their car was stopped by Deputy Sheriff Cecil Price who jailed them in Philadelphia until 10:30 P.M. Released, they were pulled over again by Price, who turned them over to the Klan. Not until a paid informant tipped the FBI on August 4 were their bodies found in a new earthen dam twenty miles southwest of the church. Schwerner and Goodman, who were white, were shot once. Chaney, who was black, had been shot three times, twice in the head. His skeleton was also crushed, as if, a pathologist said, he had been in an airplane crash. Investigators concluded that the bulldozer used to bury them had caused the additional travesty. Schwerner and Goodman were buried out of state. Chaney's grave is outside Meridian.

Not until the second anniversary of the murders did the federal government announce the trial of eighteen men, including Sheriff Lawrence Rainey and Deputy Sheriff Price. In a disquieting scene before the trial, Martin Luther King Jr. spoke in Philadelphia with Rainey and Price standing behind. "I believe in my heart that the murderers are somewhere around me at this moment," King said. A

Memorial marker in Philadelphia

white man hollered, "They're right behind you," and the crowd roared. Price and six others were convicted of violating the civil rights of the three men. Sheriff Rainey walked free.

The case, captured much later in a factually false but emotional film, *Mississippi Burning,* outraged the nation while sobering and steeling hundreds of other young volunteers. During the summer of 1964, the Mount Zion fire was just one of sixty-six bombings and burnings, thirty-five shootings, and one thousand arrests of activists that included eighty beatings. The FBI search for the three turned up the bodies of three other black victims in other parts of Mississippi: Charles Moore, a twenty-year-old college student; Henry Dee, twenty-one, and Herbert Oarsby, fourteen, who was found wearing a CORE T-shirt. Their killers escaped.

In his book *Local People,* historian John Dittmer concludes that the Philadelphia murders, involving two white middle-class men, finally persuaded the federal government to pressure Mississippi. FBI Director J. Edgar Hoover, until then no friend to activists, sent in 150 agents and privately told the governor and law enforcement officials that the Klan must be stopped and civil rights laws enforced. According to Dittmer, Hoover gave the governor a list of highway patrolmen who were Klan members and they were fired.

Mount Zion erected a granite memorial in front of the church, and the church holds an annual ceremony to honor the men. In the village of Philadelphia, Mt. Nebo Missionary Baptist Church, whose congregation first invited the three activists to Philadelphia, has erected a memorial with photos of the three men. It is on the corner of Adams and Carver Streets.

Port Gibson

A small but smart display in the Claiborne County administration building chronicles the local civil rights movement. Rarely described in civil rights histories, local dramas mirrored better known events and often demanded more fortitude. They occurred outside the watchful eye of the national media, which normally attracted federal intervention, and they involved neighbor against coworker, some of whom were the entrenched racists.

Port Gibson's events didn't begin until 1966, when a group of citizens asked the county to desegregate facilities, hire blacks, and denounce extremist groups. Turned away, blacks began a nine-month boycott of stores. Stores sued the NAACP for losses and the thirteen-year legal battle ended in a 1982 Supreme Court decision upholding the right of peaceful protest through economic boycott. Local residents also began registering voters. The number of black voters rose from 150 in 1964 to 2,600 two years later. In 1967 the first black county supervisor, clerk, judge, and coroner were elected, more governmental representation here than in any other Mississippi county. In 1970 black voters in the county held a majority.

The Port Gibson display, "No Easy Journey," was the work of a nonprofit community group and the white Crosby family. Daughter Emily Crosby studied the local movement for a Ph.D. thesis, gathered photos, and mounted the exhibit.

The display is in the William "Matt" Ross building, named for the first black supervisor in the twentieth century. In a community where race equality is a daily exercise, the display stands as a historic benchmark.

Ruleville

(*U.S. 49W, turn east on Bryon Street. Gravestone is near the end.*)   The gravestone of Fannie Lou Hamer may be the most visited—certainly the most cited—civil rights memorial in Mississippi. On a modest granite stone is inscribed Hamer's most famous line: "I am sick and tired of being sick and tired." As a result, Ruleville is now best known as Fannie Lou Hamer's hometown.

In 1961 Mrs. Hamer was a forty-four-year-old sharecropper's wife who held the job of timekeeper on the Marlowe plantation. She learned of SNCC's voter drive and agreed to try to register at the Indianola courthouse with seventeen other Sunflower County residents. When plantation owner B. D. Marlow learned of her activity, he demanded she withdraw her application. She refused and he threw her out of her home.

Mrs. Hamer became a pugnacious SNCC organizer, dodging bullets, enduring a severe beating by police, and speaking on national TV to the 1964 Democratic Convention in Atlantic City. As part of an alternate Mis-

Fannie Lou Hamer's grave in Ruleville

sissippi delegation, Mrs. Hamer told her life story and demanded to be seated to represent her state. Unbeknownst to her, she and other members of the Freedom Democratic Party, along with Martin Luther King Jr., were wiretapped by the FBI, under President Johnson's orders. But she did learn that Senator Hubert Humphrey's nomination as vice president depended on his keeping the alternative party out. She told Humphrey: "Do you mean to tell me that your position is more important to you than 400,000 black people's lives?" It was. Amid picketing by black alternates, only two members of her party were seated. Said Mrs. Hamer in her Delta accent: "We didn't come all this way for no two seats."

When SNCC voted in 1966 to expel white members, Mrs. Hamer resigned. She spent her last years organizing a Freedom Farm cooperative for sharecroppers, building housing and a day-care center in Ruleville. She died penniless on April 14, 1977. Her grave is on co-op land that was used to grow food for the poor.

Vicksburg

VICKSBURG NATIONAL BATTLEFIELD (*3201 Clay Street; 601-636-0583; www.nps.gov/vick*) Not until the Civil War was half over did President Lincoln allow blacks to fight for their own freedom. Nowhere was their effort as total as Milliken's Bend, an early battle in the fall of Vicksburg. Milliken's Bend was a loop (now gone) in the Mississippi River where Union soldiers were massing to prepare for the Vicksburg campaign. Six months after President Lincoln's Emancipation Proclamation allowed blacks to serve as soldiers, hundreds of ill-prepared troops (they were called the "colored" units) were ordered to guard the terrain.

Some fifteen hundred Confederate soldiers attacked in a day of bayonet bloodletting. Failing, the Confederates withdrew and the siege of Vicksburg began. A few hours after the battle, Rear Admiral David Porter arrived to find "dead Negroes lined the ditch . . . most were shot on the top of the head." Nearly 45 percent of the Ninth Louisiana Infantry (Fifth U.S. Colored Heavy Artillery) died, the highest proportion in a single Civil War battle—17 percent higher than the famed losses of the First Minnesota Infantry at Gettysburg. Their valor changed the military's attitude about the contribution African Americans could make to the war effort.

Milliken's Bend disappeared in a Mississippi flood. The National Park Service plans to tell the story of the black soldiers in a new downtown visitors center, and the state has appropriated money to build a display honoring them.

The Vote

In American democracy, ultimate equality is the right to vote. For African Americans it was a long time coming.

When the United States was founded, voting was a right granted only to white men who owned property. This changed with the Fifteenth Amendment after the Civil War when black men joined the privileged ranks. This flush of democracy elected scores of blacks to offices ranging from sheriff to U.S. senator. During Reconstruction, twenty-two congressmen were elected in the South. They were Republicans—the party of Lincoln.

Backlash from white supremacists and Democrats led to America's worst terrorism: lynching by the Ku Klux Klan, voter intimidation, fraud, and slander. Having their way in state legislatures, Democrats enacted a blizzard of restrictions to disenfranchise blacks. In 1890 Mississippi wrote a new constitution with a two-dollar poll tax and a quiz on the Constitution. Overnight, according to Richard Kluger in *Simple Justice,* 123,000 black voters disappeared from the state's polls. Louisiana followed with a "grandfather clause" guaranteeing white votes but forcing the withdrawal of 125,000 black votes.

The Supreme Court, fresh from its "separate but equal" approval of railcars and other public accommodations, approved the vote stealing in 1898. Their decision read: "It has not been shown that their actual administration was evil but only that evil was possible under them."

Between 1900 and World War II, only 3 percent of eligible blacks were registered in the South, according to *Quiet Revolution in the South.*

Although women finally won the right to vote in 1920, the NAACP's effort to regain the votes for blacks did not begin to pay off until 1944, when the Supreme Court overturned Texas's "whites-only" primary. Lawsuits begun in the 1950s struck down gerrymandering and established the ruling of one person, one vote. But it took the murderous resistance of Deep South officialdom in places like Philadelphia, Mississippi, and Selma, Alabama, to persuade the country and President Johnson that a sweeping, federal law was needed.

The Voting Rights Act of 1965 has been called the most successful civil rights legislation in American history. It eliminated all barriers to registration and voting. It put seven southern states on special notice for violations, and it gave the U.S. attorney general the power to "preclear" any change in voter rules.

But it couldn't anticipate the crafty, ongoing efforts of politicians in power to deny certain groups the full equity of their vote. All kinds of ways to dilute votes have been practiced, including at-large elections, majority-vote runoffs, and redrawing district lines so that a group of voters loses its majority or is confined to a single district safely "corralling" all its votes. The 1965 act has been amended several times to close loopholes.

In 1993, in a reversal of historic trends, a sharply divided Supreme Court (in *Shaw v. Reno*) ruled that legislative districts drawn in a "bizarre" way to create black representation can violate the constitutional rights of white voters. The ruling invalidated North Carolina's majority African American twelfth congressional district and opened the door to other "reverse" discrimination cases.

Still, the Voting Rights Act of 1965 changed the political landscape of the South. Between 1970 and 2000, the number of black elected officials rose from 1,469 to 9,040. Mississippi added more than 800 black officeholders and led the nation with 19 percent of its public officials African Americans. Alabama was second with 731.

In a growing number of cities, blacks were being elected to represent majority-white districts. The most common statewide position for an elected black was as a judge.

In 2000 blacks in the District of Columbia held 58 percent of the posts in a city with a 56 percent black population. Nationwide, the number of black U.S. representatives rose from nine in 1970 to thirty-nine in 2001.

Black elected statistics are kept up to date by the Joint Center for Political and Economic Studies. The center's Web site is www.jointcenter.org.

Louisiana,
Arkansas, Tennessee

LOUISIANA
Louisiana and Civil Rights

For centuries, the French, Spanish, British, and Americans lusted after Louisiana as the gateway to a rich continent. Under every jurisdiction, Africans did the laboring.

The French were the first to formulate rules. Their Code Noire, or black code, of 1724 allowed slaves to marry and take Sundays off, but it outlawed gatherings, drinking, and carrying guns without permission. Violators were branded, tortured, whipped, mutilated, and executed. Runaways were common, and they sometimes joined with Indians in maroon swamp communities. In 1729, Ira Berlin writes, Natchez Indians teamed up with blacks and slaughtered two hundred French settlers, about 10 percent of Louisiana's population at the time. In retaliation, authorities lynched many rebels and dismembered their leader, Samba.

Louisiana became a state wedded to cotton, and the number of slaves rose quickly from forty-two thousand in 1812, the year of statehood, to four hundred thousand by the Civil War. One thousand planters each owned at least seventy slaves.

Under French Catholic influence, a group known as "free men of color" thrived in the racial soup that developed in New Orleans. Many black French Creoles, both men and women, lived as aristocrats. At the time of statehood, 18 percent of Louisiana's blacks were free, the highest percentage in the South, and by 1860, free blacks owned $15 million worth of property. During the Civil War, they formed units to fight for the United States. A whole society of quadroon (having one-quarter black ancestry) women who were envied for their light-brown skins and European features worked for the pleasure of white men. They met at quadroon balls—one of their dance halls is now occupied by the Bourbon Orleans Hotel.

New Orleans bankers and traders weren't keen on civil war—their customers included Yankees—but planters persuaded them to secede. Within a year, the Confederacy lost New Orleans to the Union navy and with it the ability to finance the war with cotton from the Mississippi Delta. In 1862, three years before Appomattox, Louisiana became a laboratory for Lincoln's reformation of the South. All the issues that would soon strangle Reconstruction, especially sharing power between ex-slaves and ex-Confederates, erupted in Louisiana. The result was chaos.

In the summer of 1866 ex-Confederate police waded into delegates attending a New Orleans constitutional convention, which was about to award the vote to blacks. Thirty-four blacks and three supporters were murdered in the convention hall. General Philip Sheridan called the scene "an absolute massacre." When an outraged Congress insisted on black suffrage in the 1868 presidential election, white supremacists led by the new Ku Klux Klan staged "Negro hunts" that killed two thousand in Louisiana, including at least two hundred in St. Landry Parish, according to Stetson Kennedy in *After Appomattox*. A New Orleans gang called the Innocents "entered the houses to drive out the blacks, shooting them like rabbits as they ran."

Even in this political climate, black legislators were elected, including state senator P. B. S. Pinchback, who later was chosen president pro tem. Upon the death of the lieutenant governor, also black, Pinchback succeeded him, and then became governor when the incumbent was impeached. Pinchback's forty-three-day reign made him the first black governor in the United States at a time when antiblack massacres were occurring statewide. For a short while, Louisiana outlawed segregated schools, an idea that collapsed when white gangs terrorized educators. Louisiana's Reconstruction ended after massacres at the Colfax courthouse on Easter Sunday, 1873, and Coushatta and New Orleans in 1874. The

1866 New Orleans melee, memorialized by the victors as the Battle of Liberty Square, overthrew a biracial government.

Jim Crow arrived in Louisiana with a law to separate railcars by race. During a staged test in June 1892, Homer Plessy, a shoemaker who was seven-eighths white, sat down in a "white" East Louisiana Railroad car and was arrested. The judge, John Ferguson, ruled that Louisiana could segregate public accommodations within its borders. *Plessy v. Ferguson,* upheld by the U.S. Supreme Court in 1896, affirmed legal segregation under the so-called separate but equal doctrine until 1954.

Louisiana's 1898 constitution set up so many roadblocks to black voters—property ownership, literacy, a grandfather clause, and an "interpretation" test—that by 1900 blacks, who were half the population, accounted for only 4 percent of voters. During this same period, lynchings killed 391. Police violence against blacks was "so routine that it caused little comment outside the pages of the Negro press," Adam Fairclough wrote in *Race and Democracy: The Civil Rights Struggle in Louisiana, 1915–1972.*

During the darkest days of Jim Crow, jazz developed in New Orleans. It arose from the music of brass bands, blues, and minstrels. "Segregation probably accelerated the development of jazz," historian Gerald Early wrote on PBS.org, "because such a large number of talented young men (and some women) went into it who might have, if the society had been less racially restrictive, either played some other form of music or not played music at all."

As jazz spread worldwide, the civil rights movement made early gains in Louisiana: Louisiana State University admitted black students in 1950, a four-day Baton Rouge bus boycott reduced seat shifting in 1953, and New Orleans quietly integrated its library in 1954. The NAACP, meanwhile, increased black voter registration from 7,000 to 161,000 and elected the first black city councilmen in Crowley in 1954.

But the Supreme Court's order to integrate public schools brought out rabid racists. Led by Leander Perez, the district attorney of St. Bernard Parish near New Orleans, and state senator William Rainach, groups such as the Citizens Council, the Southern Gentlemen, and the state legislature did all in their power to preserve segregation.

Mass demonstrations were squelched. The legislature took control of schools and formally segregated virtually every public facility and activity.

Under an old anti-KKK law that targeted "conspiracies," police raided and closed down the NAACP. In a coordinated purge unlike anything in the South, members of the Citizens Council removed nine thousand black voters from the rolls through a little-used law that allowed two people—in this case, white people—to prove by affidavits that someone was illegally registered. In Monroe, wrote Fairclough, three thousand black votes were purged.

New Orleans's school integration case, originally filed in 1951 by attorney Alexander Pierre Tureaud, came to a head in 1960 in an unprecedented legal standoff between federal judge J. Skelly Wright and the legislature over four black girls who were the first to attend two white schools. As white women screamed obscenities at the girls each morning, and the Klan burned a cross in the judge's yard, the legislature cut off teacher pay to the two schools and, for good measure, welfare benefits to twenty-eight thousand poor families. As Louisiana's reputation approached that of South Africa, the Urban League sent in food under "Operation Feed the Babies." The crisis passed in a year.

In 1963 CORE set up shop in Plaquemine to register voters in fear-ridden parishes along the Mississippi River. It took months of calm persuasion to get blacks to meetings, let alone into courthouses. In August CORE's James Farmer led a thousand people to the Plaquemine city hall where they were met with cattle prods, tear gas, and billy clubs. As a mob hunted for him, Farmer hid in a funeral home and fled town in a hearse. The following year, Tensas became the last Louisiana parish to add blacks to its pure-white voter list. But it took several Justice Department lawsuits to dismantle Louisiana's arcane voting rights barriers. And not until 1969 did New Orleans, the "big easy," finally, legally, integrate its bars.

Eight years later, New Orleans elected its first black mayor, Ernest Morial, who with son Marc, dominated local politics for the next twenty years. But a decade later, white supremacist David Duke shocked Louisiana by garnering a seat in the state legislature and then winning a Republican runoff to become the party's candidate for governor. The 1991 "race from hell" pitted Duke against Edwin Edwards, a Cajun pro–civil rights ex-governor who had been charged with bribery while in office. With bumper stickers that said VOTE FOR THE CROOK, NOT THE KOOK, Edwards won. Both he and Duke later wound up in prison.

Today, half of Louisiana's children, the majority of them black, live below the poverty level. But black voter registration approaches that of whites (66 percent versus 72 percent), and blacks, who make up 30 percent of the state population, constitute an important voting block. In 2000 there were 701 black elected officials, about 14 percent of all elected officials, including thirty-one members of the state legislature.

The State of Louisiana and the cities of Baton Rouge and New Orleans publish detailed black history brochures. They are available at the state capitol or visitors centers (800-395-1939).

Baton Rouge

STATE CAPITOL *(100 North Boulevard; 800-488-2968)* Louisiana's art-deco capitol is a tourist attraction because of its audacious size and its pint-sized builder, Huey Long, whose assassination inside and burial on the grounds made the building his tombstone. But Louisiana's capital, old and new, witnessed far worse crimes in the state's long history of suppressing and terrorizing its black citizens.

The old capitol, a white medieval-looking museum downtown, was the setting for Louisiana's 1861 secession from the Union. Abandoned during the Civil War, the building was not restored as the seat of government until 1882. By then, Louisiana had tried and rejected Reconstruction, and with it, the promise of a shared democracy with freed slaves. The new capitol, opened in 1932, preserved the contribution of slave labor in bas-relief figures around the portal.

In May 1956 the government here joined in a massive, coordinated attempt to stop integration. With the support of Citizens Councils statewide and Baton Rouge's upper-crust racists, the Southern Gentlemen, laws were passed to segregate everything in Louisiana, including personal relationships. Legislators seized control of schools and tried to expel blacks already enrolled in white colleges.

In 1960, in an attempt to stop the integration of the New Orleans school system, legislators displayed a petulance unmatched in the South. In what can only be described as legal kung fu with federal judge J. Skelly Wright, the legislature met in five special sessions and passed one hundred bills, each one annulled by Wright, sometimes within minutes of its passage. It was, according to historians, "a legislative carnival." Years later, Wright recalled how the legislature refused to accept his orders. "We told the marshals to throw the orders on the floor in front of them. Then legislative officers ordered plastic put over them and sealed so they couldn't be touched . . . the whole thing was ludicrous," he told the *Times-Picayune*.

On December 15, 1961, a crowd of two thousand blacks massed before the capitol building to protest segregation. After a two-block march to the Baton Rouge courthouse, a melee erupted with tear gas and dogs, and police made 290 arrests. Leader Elton Cox was sent to prison for nearly two years.

Three years later, a new Louisiana Ku Klux Klan was organized in a lodge hall in Baton Route and in 1965 massed five thousand supporters before the capitol. Louisiana held out for years before finally bowing to federal legislation safeguarding voting rights and equal access.

KRESS STORE *(Third Street and Main Street)*   Closed but still marked by its marquee, this historic building witnessed Baton Rouge's first sit-in protest on March 28, 1960, when seven black Southern University students sat down at the lunch counter. They were arrested. The next day, sixteen students were arrested. School president Felton Clark crushed the protest in four days and outgoing Governor Earl Long said the students should return to their "native Africa." Nonetheless, they became heroes of the black community and plaintiffs in a suit that went to the Supreme Court. Nearly a year later, their cases, consolidated under *Garner v. Louisiana,* and argued before the Supreme Court by Thurgood Marshall, established the right for peaceful demonstrations everywhere.

MT. ZION FIRST BAPTIST CHURCH *(356 East Boulevard)*   In 2003 this church was still led by the Reverend Theodore Jemison whose civil rights credits predate the commonly accepted "movement years." In June 1953, after the Baton Rouge bus company backed away from a first-come, first-served seating rule, Jemison led a bus boycott, complete with mass meetings and carpools. This was two years before Montgomery's famous boycott. Jemison ended the strike in four days after a compromise reduced the amount of seat shifting blacks had to endure. The promise was later abandoned, and the bus system didn't fully integrate until 1962 when a lawsuit filed by Jemison was settled.

SOUTHERN UNIVERSITY *(U.S. 61 and Louisiana Route 408; 225-294-2129; www.subr.edu)*   On a beautiful bluff of the Mississippi River, one of the largest black colleges in the country played a small historic role in civil rights activism. Students staged a four-day sit-in in 1960 at the Kress store downtown, a case that established the right to peaceful protest for civil rights activists everywhere. After a march to the state capitol and two hundred arrests, school president Felton Clark pressured students to end the protest for the sake of the school's reputation. Students held several angry mass meetings in front of the president's home in a vain attempt to get his support for further action.

On November 16, 1972, during another student protest aimed at inadequate state support for the school, law enforcement officers from outside the campus were called to disperse it. In the midst of tear gas, a deputy sheriff apparently shot two students to death in front of the administration building. No one was arrested and the families of the students, Leonard Brown and Denver Smith, were never able to prosecute for their loss. The university named the student union for Smith and Brown and a fraternity erected a *Lift Every Voice and Sing* sculpture in the courtyard. A marker where the young men were shot is near the entrance to the arts museum.

Southern was cofounded by the first black governor in the United States, Pinckney Pinchback. A historic marker honoring Pinchback and the tombs of President Felton Clark and his parents sit on the river bluff.

PORT HUDSON *(U.S. 61, twenty miles north of Baton Rouge)* The first use of black U.S. troops in a major battle occurred here in May 1863 when the Louisiana Native Guards made a stalwart if suicidal attack on Confederate forces guarding the Mississippi River. A fifth of the men died, but their skill and spirit on behalf of freedom "marked a turning point in attitudes toward the use of black soldiers," according to *The Civil War's Black Soldiers*. The First Native Guards was a unique New Orleans group made up entirely of free men of color with black officers. When the Confederates spurned their offer to fight for the South, and abandoned New Orleans, Union General Benjamin Butler, who had earlier made history by enlisting ex-slaves as "contraband," welcomed them. In a month the Native Guard were fighting in Port Hudson.

At the time, Port Hudson and Vicksburg were the last Confederate forts controlling the Mississippi River. The First Native Guards and the Third, made up of ex-slaves with white officers, were ordered to make a frontal assault on a dug-in enemy. Free black Andre Cailloux led the charge on May 23, and was killed. After repeated attempts, the men fell back and joined a siege of the fort that lasted until the fall of Vicksburg in July. Many are buried in a nearby national cemetery. The sight of freed slaves fighting their former masters was exhilarating for Yankees. The *Detroit Free Press* reported they fought with the "desperation of tigers"—one enraged soldier tore flesh from the face of rebel soldiers with his teeth. One white officer wrote: "You have no idea how my prejudices with regard to Negro troops have been dispelled." More Louisiana blacks fought as Union soldiers—nearly twenty-five thousand—than from any other state.

Bogalusa

Louisiana's most virulent Ku Klux Klan group called Bogalusa home and carried out the worst terrorism in the state. According to Adam Fairclough's *Race and Democracy,* a 1965 clash between the Klan and the Deacons for Defense, an armed black group, was a turning point in Louisiana's movement. It forced the government and businesses to comply with the Civil Rights Act of 1964.

A unionized sawmill and paper mill attracted a large black population to Bogalusa. But the mill and city were segregated "from cradle to coffin," according to one judge, and the Crown-Zellerbach plant made lame integration efforts—like cutting a hole in the wall between "white" and "black" bathrooms. The advent of legal integration prompted many whites to join the Ku Klux Klan, including one hundred mill employees. Eight hundred

Klansmen rallied here in May 1964 and terrorism began soon after. Crosses were burned, a white worker with black friends was whipped, bricks were thrown at blacks on the street from passing cars. At the time, according to the Southern Poverty Law Center, there were more Klan members per capita in Bogalusa than anywhere in the South.

In response, a black union leader and World War II veteran, A. Z. Young, took over the Bogalusa Voters League. In one of the most stirring speeches of the civil rights movement, Fairclough wrote, "Young stood before a mass meeting at a labor hall and said: 'Will you let your sons and daughters be hit by billy clubs, have live snakes thrown at them, have cigarettes put out on their bodies and be chased by police dogs on picket lines and marches, while you stay at home?'"

He and other activists came under the protection of Deacons for Defense, who arrived with guns and walkie-talkies to patrol black neighborhoods and stand watch atop CORE's headquarters in Bryon Burris's barbershop. As every racist nutcase in the South was drawn to Bogalusa— one particular Klan motorcade stretched three miles—a federal judge ordered police to protect demonstrators. In the midst of this, in the neighboring village of Vernando, a black deputy sheriff was shot to death in a drive-by attack while he was on duty. A Crown-Zellerbach employee was charged with murder, but no one was ever convicted.

Assistant Attorney General John Doar, sent by President Lyndon Johnson, couldn't believe how the Klan roamed the street, intimidating demonstrators. He made Bogalusa a test case of the 1964 Civil Rights Act. Doar filed charges against police, initiated a flurry of lawsuits to integrate facilities, and enjoined the Klan. One hundred and twenty FBI agents were sent to Bogalusa to gather evidence. Federal Judge John Minor Wisdom called the Klan "ignorant bullies" and ordered them to report their every move each month for three years. Sporadic violence continued as schools integrated in the fall of 1965.

The following year, black picketer Clarence Triggs was found shot to death in his car. Police arrested two white men, but after the first was acquitted, the other was released. In 1967 the Bogalusa Voters League staged a march to the capital, which led to the hiring of the first black state troopers.

There is nothing in Bogalusa to mark the tumultuous human rights struggle.

New Orleans

In a city where race has always been an artificial construct, a 1952 Mardi Gras fund-raiser exposed the artifice of segregation. Staged at the Municipal Auditorium adjacent to Congo Square on behalf of the United Negro College Fund, the event invited upper-crust whites and blacks. At the time, however, the city auditorium was officially off-limits to blacks. When police arrived to search for them, they found everyone in masks. In the city's most famous tradition black and white meant nothing. From that point on, Municipal Auditorium was integrated. But the rest of the city put up a long fight. New Orleans's school integration case was one of the ugliest in America. And advances came incrementally, largely case by case filed by black attorney Alexander Pierre Tureaud.

On February 14, 1957, the Southern Christian Leadership Conference, with Martin Luther King Jr. in charge, was formally organized at New Zion Baptist in New Orleans. Almost immediately, local SCLC member Abraham Lincoln Davis, a black minister, launched a campaign to integrate buses. In March 1956, he challenged a crowd of twenty-five hundred people: "The time is out for segregation and for all that this evil monster stands for." Under a federal court order from federal judge J. Skelly Wright, buses integrated on May 31, 1958. That night, a cross was burned on Wright's lawn.

Two years later, Wright ordered four black girls to integrate two elementary schools in working-class white neighborhoods. A supportive group called Save Our Schools was overwhelmed by screaming women, rioting white kids, and a reactionary legislature.

Sit-ins and pickets at stores on Dryades and Canal Streets started and stopped in 1960 and 1961, dampened by arrests. Under court order, city parks were integrated in 1963. Federal judge John Minor Wisdom wrote: "There is no excuse left . . . New Orleans, here and now, must adjust to the reality of having to operate desegregated public facilities." To press the point, ten thousand blacks marched from Shakespeare Park to city hall to protest delays in integration. The Reverend Avery Alexander staged a sit-in at the city hall cafeteria. Police dragged him away by his ankles. That same year, Tulane was integrated against the wishes of benefactor Paul Tulane who had specified in his will "white males" as students, and Canal Street stores began hiring blacks. Meanwhile, the archbishop integrated Catholic schools and summarily excommunicated two archsegregationists: Una Gail-

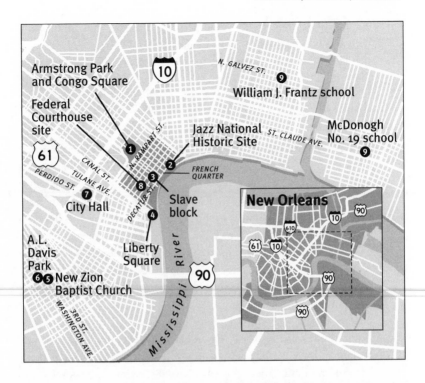

lot, the housewife in charge of the "Cheerleaders" who screamed at the black girls, and Leander Perez, the parish's chief white supremacist. Perez died in 1969, the year New Orleans integrated its bars.

New Orleans's civil rights history is not well marked, but it has a wealth of sites. A black heritage guide, available at city tourist centers, leans toward the arts.

I | **ARMSTRONG PARK AND CONGO SQUARE** (*North Rampart at Dumaine, adjacent to French Quarter*)   A gathering spot for Indians, slavers, traders, and, eventually, Africans and their descendants, Congo Square was famous for its Sunday dancing and fervent music at the time of the Louisiana Purchase in 1803. A visitor, Benjamin Latrobe, found it by the noise, "like horses trampling on a wooden floor." A century later, during Jim Crow segregation, the music had evolved into blues, rhythm and blues, and jazz. In the adjacent black tenderloin district of Storyville, the music became the sound track to the

301

work of prostitutes. In 1980 the park was renamed Armstrong Park, with a statue dedicated to the jazz great.

Plans have been announced to move the Jazz National Historic Site within the park, adjacent to WWOZ, the public radio station that broadcasts jazz music. A visitors center will anchor a "history of jazz neighborhood."

2 | **JAZZ NATIONAL HISTORIC SITE** *(916 North Peters Street, French Quarter;* 877-520-0677; *www.nps.gov/neor)*   This temporary headquarters houses the National Park Service's effort to memorialize black New Orleans's most famous product. Jazz grew out of the multiple roots of African and Caribbean music and slavery and freedom that lived side by side in New Orleans. Jazz played an unstated role in civil rights as black musicians performed worldwide, often with more acclaim and respect in Europe than in the United States. Many jazz greats, like Sidney Bechet, settled in France because of hometown discrimination.

New Orleans gets mixed grades for preserving the history of jazz. While venues such as Preservation Hall thrive, a number of sites important in the lives of jazz greats have been torn down for parking lots. Several Louis Armstrong sites have disappeared. Armstrong was baptized at the Sacred Heart of Jesus Church at 139 South Lopez Street on August 25, 1901. At age five, he attended the Fisk School at 507 South Franklin. Armstrong worked at the Funky Butt Hall and heard jazz for the first time at Kinney's Hall where Joe "King" Oliver was playing.

3 | **SLAVE BLOCK** *(Old Mint, Decatur Street)*   A splintered wood block in this museum is a rare artifact from New Orleans's history as a thriving slave mart. The block once sat in the rotunda of the St. Louis Motel (now the Royal Orleans) at St. Louis and Royal Streets. According to the *Times-Picayune,* "men, women and children once stood on the block and waited with horror as other men and women bid to purchase them." There were also blocks at the St. Charles Exchange, the St. Charles Hotel, and various corners in the French Quarter.

Reporter Stephen Camier wrote that one trader, Theophilus Freeman, held slaves in a St. Charles Avenue pen located in what today is the business district at Place St. Charles between Gravier and Common Streets. Solomon Northup, a freed slave, later wrote how Freeman "would make us hold up our heads, walk briskly back and forth, while customers would feel of our hands and arms and bodies, turn us about, ask us what we could do, make us open our mouths and show our teeth, precisely as a jockey examines a horse which he is about to purchase."

4 | **BATTLE OF LIBERTY SQUARE** (*Canal Street near aquarium and ferry entrance*) This obelisk is a rare monument to white supremacy and the failure of Reconstruction. In 1874, in a pitched gun battle in front of the Customs House, the White League defeated an integrated militia. The White League, according to Eric Foner's *Reconstruction,* was "openly dedicated to the violent restoration of white supremacy. It targeted local Republican officeholders for assassination, disrupted court sessions and drove black laborers from their homes."

On September 14 thirty-five hundred White League supporters, ex-Confederate soldiers largely, fought and defeated an equal number of black militiamen and police. They then occupied city hall, the statehouse (at the time in New Orleans), and the arsenal. Foner writes that the insurrection shocked President Grant into sending troops, but it also signaled an inevitable end to the dream of a democratic South. In short order, a white government was in power and remained until the 1970s.

Until then, the obelisk stood in the middle of Canal Street with a plaque reading, DEDICATED TO THE RESTORATION OF WHITE SUPREMACY. Those words were covered after the election of black leadership in New Orleans. The obelisk was moved from its once prominent spot on Canal, and the city added a plaque honoring the city militiamen who died in the fight.

5 | **NEW ZION BAPTIST CHURCH** (*2319 Third Street*) On February 14, 1957, the Southern Christian Leadership Conference met here and formally established itself as a permanent organization. Launched in January 1957 in Atlanta, SCLC helped replace the NAACP, which had been banned in Alabama and gutted in Louisiana. About one hundred people convened here, among them, the Reverend Martin Luther King Jr., the Reverend T. J. Jemison of Baton Rouge, Dr. C. O. Simpkins of Shreveport, Clarence "Chink" Henry of the longshoremen's union, and the host, the Reverend Abraham Lincoln Davis. Hoping to capitalize on the Montgomery success, a bus boycott was soon launched in New Orleans by Davis. A historic sign sits outside the church.

6 | **A. L. DAVIS PARK** (*LaSalle Street and Washington Avenue*) Called Shakespeare Park during the 1960s, it was the site of many protest rallies. Now chockablock with tennis and basketball courts, swimming pools, and other attractions, the park has been renamed for the Reverend A. L. Davis. On September 10, 1963, he led a huge march from the park to city hall to demand an end to segregation. Davis later became New Orleans's first black councilman.

7 | **CITY HALL AND THE REVEREND AVERY ALEXANDER MEMORIAL PLAZA** (*1300 Perdido Street*) The park across the street from city hall contains several slices of civil rights history. One of the older memorial busts honors Edward White, a member of a wealthy sugar-beet plantation family, who had fought for the South in the Civil War at age sixteen, and had worked hard to "redeem" white supremacy after Reconstruction. Named to the U.S. Supreme Court in 1894, he voted with the majority on *Plessy v. Ferguson,* the 1896 ruling that legalized segregation. As chief justice, however, he struck down Oklahoma's grandfather clause that required voters to descend from previous voters, a restriction aimed at stopping new black registrations. The ruling upheld the Fifteenth Amendment, which gave the vote to blacks.

A second bust honors John McDonogh, a former wealthy slave owner whose philanthropy carried with it a strong sense of paternalism. McDonogh donated City Park to New Orleans, although it was segregated for many years. He also built many schools, each named McDonogh No. 1, 2, 3, etc. Every May for years, New Orleans's schoolchildren gathered before a statue of McDonogh in Lafayette

Square, laid flowers, sang songs, and then picked up keys to the city from the mayor. The white children performed the ceremony first while black children waited in the hot sun. In 1954, in a preview of coming events, blacks boycotted the event. Only thirty-four black children showed up, according to the Southern Institute. The boycott continued for two subsequent years, and presaged the civil rights movement against segregated schools, parks, and life in general.

The third monument, of the Reverend Avery Alexander in full stride, memorializes the day in October 1963 when he marched into city hall, declaring "today is the day." He sat down at the segregated lunch counter in the basement and refused to move. Police dragged him up two flights of stairs by his heels. His action followed the city's single massive protest march in September to city hall to demand an end to Jim Crow. Alexander served as a state legislator from 1976 to 1999.

Though long-gone, Jane Alley, across from city hall, was the birthplace of Louis Armstrong.

8 | **FEDERAL COURTHOUSE SITE** *(400 Royal)*   In this beautifully ornate building in the heart of the French Quarter, U.S. District Court Judge J. Skelly Wright fought a duel with the entire Louisiana legislature and thousands of segregationists. His February 15, 1956, order to integrate New Orleans schools was the first such action in the Deep South. In May 1957 Wright desegregated New Orleans's buses, an order upheld a year later by the Supreme Court. He also integrated City Park.

On May 16, 1960, six years to the day after the Supreme Court's *Brown* decision integrating schools, Wright ruled that black students could choose a school to integrate, an order that set off one of the most extraordinary standoffs between state and federal power since Little Rock. Wright struck down a blizzard of laws and tricks to stop school integration in New Orleans. Finally, he ordered four girls into two schools on Monday, November 14, 1960.

On the weekend before, the state school superintendent declared a school holiday on the fourteenth. Wright canceled it. When the governor fired the New Orleans school board and assumed control, the judge ordered the board to ignore the governor. Wright "left ultra-segregationists seething with anger and gasping in disbelief," wrote historian Adam Fairclough.

In 1962 President Kennedy named Wright to a seat on the Washington, D.C., appellate court. The building has gone through several tenants, and is scheduled to house the state Supreme Court.

9 **WILLIAM J. FRANTZ SCHOOL** (*3811 North Galvez Street at Alvar*) and **McDONOGH No. 19 SCHOOL** (*St. Claude Street and Alabo Street*)   School integration in New Orleans began in secret on November 14, 1960, when federal marshals in unmarked cars outfoxed state troopers sent to stop them en route to these two schools with four little girls—three to McDonogh and one to Frantz. After a hate rally led by Leander Perez that night, white parents withdrew their children from the schools, and a group of women known as the "Cheerleaders" met the girls every day with what writer John Steinbeck described as "bestial and filthy and degenerate" epithets. One woman's daily threat to poison student Ruby Bridges at Frantz prompted Bridges to hide her mother's homemade sandwiches in a cupboard.

Ruby Bridges's story is the most famous, thanks to psychiatrist Robert Coles who wrote a book, Norman Rockwell who painted a famous scene of her surrounded by four marshals, and the Walt Disney Company, which made a fairly accurate movie about her ordeal called *Ruby Bridges*. As crowds jeered, Ruby walked into the school each day surrounded by four U.S. marshals. Mrs. Barbara Henry, a new teacher from Boston, was assigned to Bridges—and no one else. Coles, then a military psychiatrist in New Orleans, counseled Ruby and her parents. When white parents Jimmy and Daisy Gabrielle refused to withdraw their daughter from Frantz, Jimmy's fellow city workers taunted him out of town. Three other white parents lost their jobs for cooperating. The second year, her school integrated without incident, and Bridges went on to a career as a travel agent and head of her own civil rights foundation and became a mother of four.

The three girls at McDonogh—Leona Tate, Tessie Prevost, and Gail Etienne—had the school to themselves for the entire year. The next year, twelve blacks attended six white schools.

Ruby Bridges in 1960

There is little recognition of this momentous case at the two schools today, although physically, neither has changed much. Both are now all black. At Frantz, a copy of the Norman Rockwell painting, *The Problem We All Face*, hangs in the principal's office, but nothing marks Bridges's old Room 202, which looks remarkably the same as it did in 1960. The McDonogh school, renamed for Louis Armstrong, has a single plaque to the three girls on the library door, and portraits of the three as adults hang in the library.

Shreveport

As much a part of Texas as Louisiana, the cotton and oil Red River port was a tough place for civil rights activists. The Klan was active here, and the Citizens Council held sway for years. For a time, between 1900 and 1930, the rate of lynchings was said to be the highest in the South, and blacks tried to mind their own business down on the "Avenue," the black district. But the city also had a small, moderate group of citizens who wanted better race relations.

In 1957 the United Christian Movement quietly integrated city buses. Police stopped them, and a desegregation lawsuit dragged on for years despite attempts by Dr. C. O. Simpkins, a local minister, who brought in Dr.

Martin Luther King in August 1958. Attempts by CORE, the NAACP, and SCLC to organize were squelched or lost on a quiescent population. For his effort, the Klan firebombed Simpkins's home. At Centenary College, a quiet Methodist school, crosses were burned on the lawns of liberal professors. The Klan also firebombed a church and a Masonic lodge.

In late September 1963 a group staged a commemoration to mourn the bombing deaths of four girls in a Birmingham church. They marched from the Thirteenth District Baptist Auditorium to the Little Union Baptist Church for a memorial. When they exited, cops beat the NAACP president, Harry Blake, and mounted police rode into the crowd on the steps. The next day, according to historian Adam Fairclough, protesting high school students and police clashed.

In the midst of this, the NAACP's second-in-charge, beautician Ann Brewster, committed suicide. She reportedly was deeply depressed over apathy among African Americans, and burdened both by personal debts and overwhelming opposition, led by the city's two newspapers that preached a hard line against integration.

ARKANSAS

Arkansas and Civil Rights

Born a slave state in 1836, Arkansas developed a split personality among its Mississippi Delta planters, mountain farmers, and western cowboys. The state also picked up an early reputation for "persistent poverty and relative cultural backwardness," as historian Morris Arnold gently put it. Mark Twain was more blunt: He called Arkansans "lunkheads." Kicking the state became a sport, as visiting writers portrayed hanging judges, Ozark hillbillies, and the ubiquitous "Arkansas traveler." As late as 1874, the *New York Times* called Arkansans a "bilious hog and corn-eating people."

Because of differences in geography, the state was divided for months about whether to secede from the Union. When it came to consensus, however, every county voted yes. At the time, Arkansas counted 111,000 black slaves, most of them in the east and south. Liberated, they followed in the wake of Union troops and more than 5,000 joined up as soldiers.

They exulted in the end of the war, and under a liberal new constitution voted by the thousands to put sheriffs, clerks, forty-five state legislators, and black congressman James Hinds in office.

But Reconstruction was a lawless failure. The Ku Klux Klan assassinated Congressman Hinds. In Pine Bluff, whites burned out a black neighborhood and left twenty-four black men, women, and children hanging from trees. In one rare case, freedmen lynched three whites accused of killing a black lawyer, according to Eric Foner. Reconstruction ended with the Brooks-Baxter war, a civil commotion between two gubernatorial candidates, both of whom claimed to be governor. When federal troops withdrew, white supremacists took control.

In the summer of 1919 black farmers in Phillips County met to demand better cotton prices, but railroad officials opened fire on them. Two hundred blacks were "hunted down in the fields and swamps to which they had fled and shot down like animals," according to an NAACP field report. Those who survived were given a forty-five-minute trial, and twelve were sentenced to death and sixty-seven to life in prison. All were later freed by the Supreme Court. It was the last of the twenty-six "Red Summer" race riots.

Under Jim Crow, blacks, who made up 25 percent of the population, directed their energies into creating an independent culture of small farms, businesses, and schools. Little Rock's Dunbar school, built in 1929, was their pride and joy. With a close-knit family of faculty, parents, and motivated students, Dunbar produced graduates that were welcomed by major universities.

In the Delta, meanwhile, Arkansas cotton pickers were doing as much as their colleagues across the Mississippi River to give birth to the blues. Helena, Arkansas, eighty miles southwest of Memphis, was considered the blues capital in the 1930s, primarily because of radio station KFFA and its daily radio show, "King Biscuit Time." From 12:15 to 12:30 it hawked Sonny Boy Cornmeal and began with the line, "Pass the biscuits, 'cause it's King Biscuit Time." The star was Robert Lockwood Jr. from Turkey Scratch who had learned his licks from Robert Johnson, the mysterious guitar genius. Among the field hands who huddled around radios at dinnertime was Riley King from Mississippi who later took the nickname "B.B." and perfected his chops in the black clubs of West Memphis, Arkansas. While performing in nearby Twist one night a fight between men touched off a fire that consumed the juke joint. King ran in and rescued his guitar. The fight, it turned out, was over Lucille, a woman whose name thereafter graced his guitars.

The blues muffled tragedy and second-class citizenship that was black Arkansas' social order. One lynching in Little Rock brought out the National Guard. Near Elaine in the Delta, wrote LeRoy Williams, tenant farmers and their landlords shot it out and killed five whites and twenty-three blacks. In tiny Stamps, Maya Angelou entered back doors and endured the daily emasculation of black spirit, later chronicled in her book *I Know Why the Caged Bird Sings.*

During World War II, seventeen thousand Japanese Americans from California suddenly showed up at two Delta internment camps, at Jerome and Rohwer. They spent the war guarded like prisoners, their children fighting in the war and their sick and elderly dying in this strange land with so much heat and humidity. Their cemetery at Rohwer is a registered national historic site.

Beginning in the 1940s black Arkansas began agitating for equal rights and the state led the South in early integration. Daisy Bates and her husband L. C. bought the *Arkansas State Press* and crusaded against injustices. The first black students were admitted to state law and medical schools in 1948. Black police were hired, neighborhoods, parks, and libraries were integrated, one community integrated its Baptist churches, and, according to Juan Williams in *Eyes on the Prize,* 33 percent of blacks registered to vote. When the Supreme Court issued its 1954 *Brown* decision integrating public schools, two school districts integrated and the Little Rock school board "was the first in the South to issue a statement of compliance," Williams wrote. Bates, by then head of the state NAACP, called Little Rock a "liberal southern city."

Little Rock adopted a tentative schedule to integrate Central High in the fall of 1957, a three-year delay that allowed opposition to grow. Governor Orville Faubus announced a poll in 1956 that found 85 percent of the state opposed integrated schools. When seventy-five blacks registered at Central, the legislature passed four anti-integration bills, one requiring prointegrationists, namely members of the NAACP, to register with the state.

Winthrop Rockefeller, grandson of John D. Rockefeller, who had moved to Arkansas in 1941 to farm and who headed the Arkansas Industrial

Development Commission, tried to talk Faubus out of his segregationist stand saying it was bad for business. But Faubus went on the air to warn that unless he called out the National Guard to stop the court order, "Blood will run in the streets."

President Eisenhower, who had been conspicuously silent on the *Brown* decision, did not want to get involved. But once federal courts issued a direct order, and Faubus called out his armed forces, the old World War II supreme commander had no choice. It was, according to Taylor Branch, "the most severe test of the Constitution since the Civil War." When Faubus pulled his guardsmen from Little Rock High and a white mob rioted, Eisenhower telephoned General Maxwell Taylor and, according to Branch, told him to "show how fast he could deploy . . . Taylor put a thousand soldiers into Little Rock before nightfall."

Integration went slowly, however, interrupted by violence after Martin Luther King Jr. was assassinated. Later, governors Winthrop Rockefeller and Bill Clinton created integrated, inclusive administrations, and by 2002 Arkansas had elected 502 black officeholders, a dramatic rise from the twenty-five in 1970.

Arkansas publishes an integrated History and Heritage Trail Guide, available at visitors centers and on its Web site: www.arkansasheritage.com. Little Rock publishes an African American heritage brochure (*800-844-4781*).

Little Rock

CENTRAL HIGH SCHOOL NATIONAL HISTORIC SITE (*2125 West Fourteenth Street; 501-374-1957; www.nps.gov/chsc*) This magnificent public school—the most expensive high school in the country when it was built in 1927—was the stage for the first major constitutional test between the Supreme Court and southern governors over integration. The story began with a good-faith, if reluctant, effort by the Little Rock school board to integrate Central High in 1957 with a few students. But by then, three years after the Supreme Court ruling on public schools, opponents were raising shrill objections and the board got cold feet. An NAACP lawsuit forced the board to proceed in September, even though the seventy-five enrolled black kids had dwindled to nine. Two weeks before school, a rock with a note crashed through a window at the home of Daisy Bates, head of the state NAACP: "Stone this time. Dynamite next." Nonetheless, Bates took charge of the nine students. They were to meet each morning at her house and walk or ride as a group to school.

Governor Orville Faubus created the crisis when he called out the Arkansas National Guard on September 2 to keep the nine students out of school. He acknowledged that it was a "test of authority" as the children were turned away. A prosegregationist group organized by Faubus, called the Mothers' League, gathered at Central High at sunrise on the second day and sang "Dixie." Again the nine children went home. The following morning, they tried again, creating the most painful scene of the standoff—Elizabeth Eckford trying to flee from screaming women. "I tried to see a friendly face somewhere in the mob—someone maybe would help," she said later. "I looked into the face of an old woman and it seemed a kind face, but when I looked at her again, she spit on me." On the fourth day, Eisenhower told Faubus that the federal court order would be upheld.

On September 20 Faubus removed the National Guard, the children entered, and people rioted. "Oh God," one of them cried, "the niggers are in the school." Calling the scene "disgraceful," Eisenhower sent in twelve hundred members of the 101st Airborne and nationalized the state guard. Faubus complained, "We are now an occupied territory."

Inside the school, some white kids harassed and brutalized the nine pioneers. When Minniejean Brown spilled chili on two boys in retribution and was suspended, a note went around: "One down and eight to go." The Klan burned crosses on the lawn of newspaper editor Harry Ashmore, who later won a Pulitzer for editorials supporting integration. The school year ended with the graduation of Ernest Green, one of the Little Rock Nine. Martin Luther King Jr. quietly attended the ceremony, but when Green's name was called, no one applauded.

Faubus then closed Little Rock high schools for a year—although his ruling did not affect the white football team, which was allowed to play its schedule. Federal courts reopened them in August 1959. Little Rock's elementary schools integrated under separate court order in 1968.

When the crisis passed, Central High became a living integration laboratory. In 1970 Deborah Mathis because the first African American editor of the *Tiger,* the school newspaper, and in 1971 Sandra Hill was crowned the first black homecoming queen. In 1975 Lloyd Myers became the first black student body president. According to a memorial garden near the school, Little Rock became Arkansas's premier high school, "not by returning to old form but by modeling the diversity and pluralism that caused the original storm of protest."

Under President Clinton, the school became part of a National Park Service historic site in 1998. A temporary visitors center was built across the street in a restored Mobil gas station. Plans call for a new visitors center and development of Ponder's Drug Store, which closed its doors to Elizabeth Eckford, and the late Daisy Bates's home on Twenty-eighth Street.

DUNBAR JUNIOR AND SENIOR HIGH SCHOOL (*Wright Avenue and Ringo Street*)   Opened in 1929, Dunbar was the premier black school in Arkansas, accredited as a junior college, and visited by many black luminaries. In 1943 black teacher Susie Morris filed suit for pay equal to white teachers. She lost her job, but the case established a federal precedent for "equal pay based on professional qualifications and services rendered." Dunbar was a vibrant black school at the time the NAACP petitioned for integration of Little Rock. Many older blacks in Little Rock remain nostalgic for the Dunbar atmosphere where teachers and parents embraced the students in a supportive community. It closed as a high school in 1955 and reopened as a magnet school for gifted children.

TENNESSEE

Tennessee and Civil Rights

"Davy Crockett, King of the Wild Frontier" and other odes to Tennessee have created the enduring vision of a wilderness tamed by white men in coonskin hats. Teddy Roosevelt, for example, called the migration of five hundred North Carolinians in 1779 "the great leap westward." Fact is, they brought their slaves and took Tennessee from Cherokee, Creek, and Chickasaw Indians. Tennessee became a state by 1796, its history dominated by Andrew Jackson, whose life work seemed to be Indian "removal."

Geography dictated multiple personalities in its new owners. The eastern mountains bred independent farmers, the gentler terrain of the middle attracted a brew of entrepreneurs and intellectuals, and the west encouraged slaveholding planters tied to the Mississippi cotton culture. By 1810 20 percent of the population consisted of slaves, concentrated in the West, while in the eastern mountain village of Jonesboro, in 1819, Elihu Embree started the nation's first abolitionist newspaper, the *Manumission Intelligencer*, later the *Emancipator*. The state had "little enthusiasm" for civil war, according to a state history, and didn't send a delegation to the Alabama secession convention. After Fort Sumter was fired upon, and Lincoln called up troops, the state's middle counties changed their minds and Tennessee became a Confederate state.

The Civil War, according to the state's official *Blue Book,* was a "grim, brutish time when death and ruin ruled the land." The Shiloh battle on April 6–7, 1862, killed more men, 23,746, than all of America's previous wars. Memphis fell to the Union in June 1862. Surrender freed 275,000 slaves who poured into cities. North Nashville and south Memphis became black "towns." One group of ex-slaves established a village called Promise Land.

The first southern state to officially abolish slavery, and the only one not occupied by military Reconstruction, Tennessee made a reasoned attempt at the new order. The legislature approved black voting, and thirteen blacks were sent to the state legislature, led by Sampson Keeble of Nashville. Missionary groups established black colleges, including Fisk, LeMoyne, Tennessee Central, Lane, and Knoxville. Meharry Medical College of Nashville was the first, and is now the largest, medical school for blacks in the United States. Such schools gave Nashville the nickname of the black Athens of the South.

Yet, the Ku Klux Klan was launched in Pulaski and began terrorizing Republicans away from polls. In 1881 Tennessee pioneered Jim Crow segregation with a law mandating the separation of blacks from whites on trains, depots, and wharves. Many blacks protested. After a 1905 law segregated streetcars, boycotts erupted in Chattanooga, Memphis, and Nashville, and blacks started their own livery companies to compete. In Nashville in 1916, blacks won their own Carnegie library.

In 1946 an unusual clash in Columbia portended the civil rights movement. Arguing over a broken radio, a white man picked a fight with a black navy veteran fresh from World War II who knocked him through a window. When rumors of a lynching surged through the city, blacks armed themselves and took up positions in the "Bottom," or "mink slide," as their part of town was known. Police were wounded in a shootout, two black prisoners were killed, and white mobs sacked buildings before hundreds of state guardsmen and state police broke it up. In a remarkable trial, Thurgood Marshall and Nashville attorney Z. Alexander Looby won the acquittal of twenty-five black defendants. Marshall was nearly lynched afterward. Looby went on to become one of Nashville's first black councilmen in 1951.

Tennessee's white political leaders, meanwhile, refused to join their Deep South colleagues in harsh segregationist stands. Neither of the U.S. senators, Estes Kefauver nor Albert Gore, would sign the Southern Manifesto that promised that "every lawful means" would be used to oppose the Supreme Court's school integration decision.

In an even lonelier stand, Governor Frank Clement used the National Guard to protect integrating black children in Clinton, near Knoxville, in 1956. The Clinton case had been filed by black parents in 1950. When a dozen black students registered in Clinton schools, out-of-town white supremacists fomented a riot. Clement sent six hundred National Guardsmen. One year later, in May 1957, Bobby Cain became the first black student to graduate from an integrated high school in the South. Later that year, three bombs destroyed the Clinton high school.

In September 1957, under a separate lawsuit, Nashville's first grades were integrated, which led to the bombing of that city's Hattie Cotton Elementary School. Despite their early start, only 169 out of Tennessee's 146,000 black students were in integrated schools by 1960.

Tennessee was also home to the Highlander School in Monteagle, a liberal training camp for human rights. Among those who studied there was Rosa Parks and several of the college students who led the movement in the 1960s. They networked, strategized, and learned old labor songs like "Keep Your Eyes on the Prize." The school's impact so incensed Tennessee that the attorney general closed it in 1959 on integration and liquor violations. But by then, Highlander's lessons had spread like pollen across the South.

That same year in rural Fayette County, just east of Memphis, tenant farmers opened a grassroots program to vote and serve on juries after a local

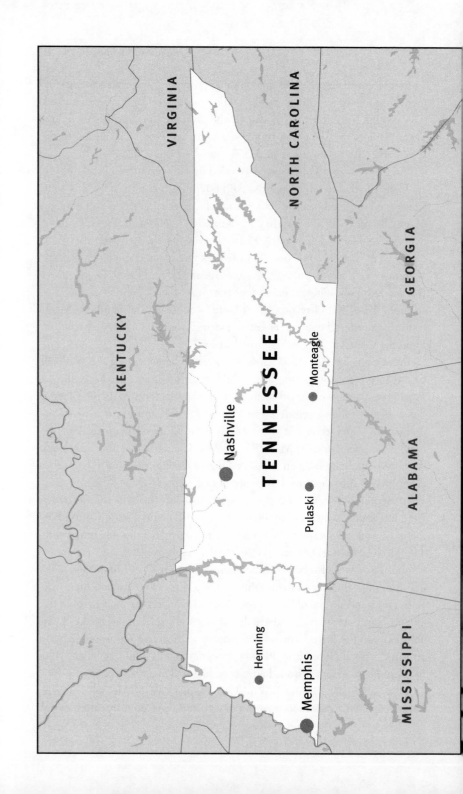

black man had been wrongfully convicted of killing a white sheriff's deputy. As they tried to vote in the August Democratic primary, however, they were rejected by the hundreds. They appealed to John Doar of the Justice Department, who sued the county under the new 1957 Civil Rights Act. In retribution, hundreds of tenants were thrown out of their houses. Quakers helped set up army tents that served as homes for the winter. The following June, President Kennedy sent surplus food to Fayette's "tent city." A federal consent decree in this case, prohibiting interference with voting, set a precedent that was later used by Doar in dozens of Mississippi cases.

In Nashville, meanwhile, a yeasty combination of bright students, black colleges, strong church leadership, and a visionary mentor developed what became the 1960 sit-in movement. Though it started spontaneously in Greensboro, North Carolina, the movement's core of pacifists had been training in Nashville for more than a year under the Reverend Jim Lawson. Their first sit-in took place on February 13, 1960, and by mid-May, stores were integrating. Their discipline and intellectual and spiritual grasp of the issues soon made them the leaders of the student crusade across the South. Later that year, in Jackson, Tennessee, students at all-black Lane College staged the swiftest, most successful bus boycott in the South—two days, in October 1960.

When Lawson moved to a new church in Memphis in 1962, he was discouraged to find most civil rights battles there yet to be waged. Buses were integrated but restaurants, schools, and parks remained under Jim Crow. Local black leadership, wrote David Halberstam, "was exhausted by years and years of trying to coexist with the intense institutional racism all around them." In 1968 Lawson invited Martin Luther King Jr. to help break a stalemated strike by black sanitation workers. While there on April 4, 1968, King was assassinated at the Lorraine Motel.

His death left Tennessee with blood on its hands and holding the shards of the civil rights movement. Its redemption was serious progress in race relations, and leadership in memorializing civil rights history. Much work remains, but Tennessee seems more open about its history. The boldness of turning the Lorraine Motel into the country's premier civil rights museum is one example. The state also does a singular job of integrating African American and civil rights stops into tourism marketing. Civil rights is mixed with attractions as varied as the Grand Ole Opry and Oak Ridge, as they should be. It is, after all, American history.

Henning

ALEX HALEY'S BOYHOOD HOME AND GRAVESITE *(200 S. Church Street; 901-738-2240)* This quiet corner in an impoverished town is a worthy stop for anyone who appreciates the power of stories. When he was a boy, Alex Haley listened to the women in his family retell the oral history of their kidnapped African ancestor who was made a slave in Virginia. Kunta Kinte, his son Chicken George, and five other generations led to Haley on the front porch of his grandmother's home. There and inside, around the modest tables and parlor, Grandma, Cousin Georgia, Aunt Plus, Aunt Liz, and Aunt Till spun the stories that Haley later wove into *Roots*, the book that won a Pulitzer Prize and was turned into the TV miniseries that won nine Emmys. *Roots* resurrected interest in genealogy in people of all colors, but especially blacks whose slave pasts are difficult to find. Haley's account—barely disguised fiction—of returning to Africa and finding an old tribal oral historian who recited the village's history back to Haley's ancestor is one of the most thrilling scenes of any American life.

Haley, whose father was a professor, spent his early years and many summers living here with his grandparents, Cynthia and Will Palmer. In 1960 Haley retired from a twenty-year hitch in the Coast Guard and began freelance writing. He also wrote the acclaimed biography *Malcolm X*. Haley died in 1992 and is buried in the front lawn. Chicken George is buried in nearby Bethlehem Cemetery.

The home, filled with era pieces, was Tennessee's first historic site to a black citizen.

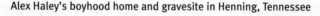

Alex Haley's boyhood home and gravesite in Henning, Tennessee

Memphis

With the possible exception of Atlanta, no Deep South city has done more to transform itself than Memphis. This one-time slave mart stained by the assassination of Dr. King has become a showcase for civil rights. Turning the Lorraine Motel into a museum was a daring but brilliant move. Today, the city seems to exude diversity in music, and public and business affairs.

As the unofficial capital of the Mississippi Delta, Memphis was the center of the slave and cotton empires of northern Mississippi and western Tennessee. After the Civil War, the city swelled with ex-slaves, creating South Memphis as an enduring black ghetto. On May 1, 1866, after two hacks collided, one with a white driver and the other with a black driver who was arrested, freshly discharged black Union soldiers took issue and Irish cops began beating them. Forty-six blacks and two whites were killed and hundreds of homes, shops, and schools in South Memphis were destroyed or ransacked. The riot, along with one in New Orleans a month later, influenced the rise of radical Reconstruction, which, for a while, gave freed slaves full citizenship, including the vote.

With the rise of Jim Crow segregation many blacks left Tennessee for Chicago, among them Ida B. Wells, a teacher-turned-journalist who fled for her life after publishing in her *Memphis Free Speech* the details of a lynching that killed three friends. Her *Red Record,* published in Chicago, was the first statistical compilation of lynchings, later picked up the NAACP, which she cofounded.

Blacks began a concerted attack on Memphis segregation as early as 1957 when two students applied to Memphis State University. Buses were integrated and sit-ins at lunch counters began in 1960. Police bodily removed protesters during a library "read-in." The Mid-South Fair wasn't integrated until 1962 but by 1965, Memphis had sent a black representative to the state legislature.

Black garbage workers struck on February 12, 1968, for better wages—including pay when weather rained them out, a benefit white workers got—plus the right to join a union. During the strike, they wore simple protest signs reading, "I am a man." Opposed by Mayor Henry Loeb, the union asked the Reverend Jim Lawson to help, and he, in turn, asked Martin Luther King Jr. to join a protest march. At the time, economic injustices were King's focus. He was planning the Poor People's Campaign to Washington to demand an economic bill of rights.

319

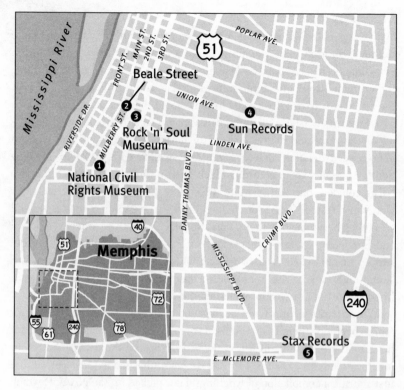

Dr. King spoke on March 18, 1968, and proposed a general strike to close Memphis down. The march was postponed for nearly a week because of a snowstorm. That march, from Clayborn Temple (*280 Hernando Street*) to City Hall on March 28, turned violent when vandals broke two hundred windows, and one suspected black looter, sixteen-year-old Larry Payne, was shot and killed by police. Police used mace and tear gas and arrested 280. The following day, without King, 300 striking workers walked the same route as National Guardsmen kept the peace. On April 3, King returned and at the Mason Temple (*930 Mason Street*) gave a prophetic speech: "I've been to the mountaintop . . . I've looked over and I've seen the Promised Land. I may not get there with you . . ."

He was shot the next day.

On Monday, April 8, Mrs. Coretta Scott King led a peaceful march downtown. The next day, King was buried in Atlanta. On April 16 striking sanitation workers accepted a contract giving them a fifteen-cent per hour pay raise and the right to withdraw union dues from their pay.

Ten years later, Memphis hired the first black superintendent of schools, Willie Herenton, who became mayor in 1991. In 1974 Harold Ford of Memphis was elected the state's first black congressman.

Memphis Heritage publishes a civil rights walking tour called "I Am a Man," marked with the route of the March 28 march and other black history sites (*901-529-9828*).

▌ **NATIONAL CIVIL RIGHTS MUSEUM** (*450 Mulberry Street; 901-521-9699; www.civilrightsmuseum.org*) As if frozen in time at 6:01 P.M., Thursday, April 4, 1968, with two Cadillacs still parked in front of Room 306, the Lorraine Motel is an eerie denouement of the civil rights movement. As you look up at the balcony marked with a wreath, you can turn around and see the window where the killer fired at Dr. Martin Luther King Jr. The boarding house room rented to James Earl Ray is now part of the museum. Between the two, the civil rights movement and King's life and death are exhaustively presented. A day or two spent here in quiet contemplation is a course in civil rights history.

Opened as a museum in 1991, the motel was gutted to allow a walk through every major civil rights story, including the Montgomery bus boycott, lunch counter sit-ins, the Ole Miss standoff between President Kennedy and Governor Barnett (complete with taped telephone calls), Birmingham, Selma, and the "I Have a Dream" march on Washington. Replicas of buses and garbage trucks have been squeezed into and under ramps. At some point in the tour, the din from competing loudspeakers grows—as the movement did—into a cacophonous cry. The "tour" ends in Memphis, where the elevated walkway looks physically and metaphorically back over the movement. Here, at the end of the line, is the room the way King left it, with crumpled beige bedspreads and room service coffee and the soft sound of "Precious Lord Take My Hand," the song King was asking for on the balcony moments before he was shot.

The museum's expansion, across the street, would satisfy any conspiracy theorist, for the investigation of King's death is treated in

The Lorraine Motel in Memphis, now the National Civil Rights Museum

excruciating detail. The museum also has re-created Room 5B rented by Bessie Brewer to one "John Willard" and the shabby bathroom where he had a clear shot of King's balcony. It almost requires another visit to appreciate the museum's "legacy" section that examines what changed in the United States and Memphis after 1968.

Saving the Lorraine was a heroic tale unto itself. When King was shot, the Lorraine's owner ran into the courtyard, suffered a heart attack, and died. Soon after, the motel went bankrupt. In 1982 Chuck Scruggs of the radio station WDIA began a "Save the Lorraine" campaign. It took many years to raise funds, but the museum has transformed the neighborhood into an art district and important tourist attraction.

2 | **BEALE STREET** A little too gussied up for its roots, Beale Street remains a place where people of all colors and backgrounds come together for music and a good time. The modern Beale, embedded with brass notes of fame, gives little hint of the racy "black" section that during the Jim Crow era was open to whites only one night a week—

Thursday's "midnight ramble." Still, there is a palpable sense of the whirlpool of rhythms that created in Memphis blues and soul and rock 'n' roll—styles of music that both mirrored human needs and urged them as rights.

W. C. Handy transcribed music on the bar at Pee Wee's Saloon. Elvis Presley hung out at Lansky Brothers. In the 1960s urban renewal gutted much of Beale Street, leaving just three blocks as a nationally recognized historic place. During the 1968 march led by King, rowdy protesters broke windows and looted shops along the street.

3 | **ROCK 'N' SOUL MUSEUM** *(Gibson Guitar Building, 145 Lt. George W. Lee Avenue; 901-543-0800; www.memphisrocknsoul. org)* It would take more than five hours to listen to all the tracks available at this fine museum devoted to the various strains of American music that came together in Memphis. This Smithsonian exhibit was given a permanent home by Gibson in an airy wing of its guitar factory. It tells the story of Memphis, Beale Street, Sun Records and Stax Records, and much more. The museum's message is that music was a unifying force. As one curator put it: "Races were reaching toward each other in the 1950s. In Memphis, it was happening right in front of us."

When Sam Phillips opened Sun Records in Memphis, black and white kids couldn't dance in the same room. Soon, however, kids of both colors were listening to his records on Dewey Phillips's "Red, Hot and Blue" show in WHBQ or WDIA's "Tan Town Jamboree" with Nat Williams, the first black DJ.

Among musicians, the issue of race disappeared early. "I can't remember that color was ever thought about," said Jim Stewart, co-founder of Stax. But as the civil rights movement changed the nation, the music evolved with it. Soul titles became pointed: "I Am Somebody," "Wooly Bully," and, "Say It Loud, I'm Black and I'm Proud." The death of Dr. King in Memphis split the music world into black and white camps. With the rise of "black power," race in the music business, including ownership and money, became divisive issues.

The Music of Civil Rights

The civil rights movement had a sound track that calmed the frightened, inspired the weary, and awakened America to a pulse that was unstoppable. Music and protest became inseparable, although the linkage evolved over two decades, spurred by and influencing parallel trends—the secularization of church music, the popularity of folk, and the creation of soul and rock 'n' roll.

Although no one saw the connection at the time, it was no coincidence that in the same month that the Supreme Court issued the *Brown v. Board of Education* ruling integrating schools, a young hillbilly named Elvis Presley walked into Sun Studios in Memphis, Tennessee, and with "That's All Right, Mama," integrated music.

That was 1954. The following year, the Montgomery bus boycott infused new meaning into hymns and spirituals that had been a staple at church services. Lyrics about freedom were as old as slavery, so it was natural that on Sunday morning, December 4, as preachers all over Montgomery spread the word of a Monday boycott, their choirs sang, "Walk Together Children" and "Joshua Fit de Battle of Jericho."

On Monday night, December 5, the first mass meeting is remembered for Martin Luther King's inspiring speech. But before he arrived, according to author Roberta Wright, the huge crowd had vibrated Holt Street Baptist Church with "Onward, Christian Soldiers" and "Leaning on the Everlasting Arms."

By 1960 Ray Charles and other artists had transformed gospel to rhythm and blues and soul music by altering lyrics of "This Little Light of Mine" to "This Little Girl of Mine," and recording songs with sly titles like "Hallelujah, I Love Her So." Soul music, as Peter Guralnick has written, was a racial collision that introduced white teens to black musicians and nurtured a mix of sex and equality that defined a liberal counterculture soon to define a generation.

When one hundred college students arrived at the Highlander School in Monteagle, Tennessee, in April 1960 to hone and spread their first sit-in protests, a quartet of them sang a doo-wop version of "You Better Leave Segregation Alone," according to historian Taylor Branch. Over the next three days, resident musician Guy Carawan taught them a number of old labor organizing songs from the 1930s: "We Shall Not Be Moved," "Keep Your Eyes on the Prize," "I'm Gonna Sit at the Welcome Table," and "We Shall Overcome."

They became the movement's anthems, shared at mass meetings, sung in jails, shouted at cops. No single campaign did more to fuse song and protest than Albany, Georgia, in November 1961. At the first mass meeting, SNCC activist Cordell Reagon and two local students, Bernice Johnson and Rutha Harris, led the group in songs. They were so good that they became the core of the SNCC Freedom Singers who sang for protests across the South.

Ms. Johnson, who later married Reagon, became a leading musicologist of the movement and founder of the group Sweet Honey in the Rock, has written at length about the process by which gospel songs were localized and new songs written on the spot to target authority. When mass meetings were invaded by menacing lawmen or when police waded in to street protests to fill paddy wagons, songs erupted, serving both as balm and nonviolent defiance. The music and protests quickly influenced the folk music craze then sweeping college campuses. Protest or "message" songs became hits, led by Bob Dylan's "Blowin' in the Wind." Dylan and Phil Ochs churned out "news" songs, based on real civil rights events—both published songs on Oxford, Mississippi, for example—and Joan Baez reworked singalong standards like "Kumbaya" and "We Shall Overcome," sung at the 1963 march on Washington, into huge swaying mass protests.

These artists, in turn, influenced black soul writers, among them balladeer Sam Cooke, who recorded "A Change Is Gonna Come," and Otis Redding, who wrote "Respect" for Aretha Franklin. As the movement peaked between 1963 and 1965, John Lewis, who headed the SNCC, remembered the sound track in his autobiography, *Walking With the Wind:*

> Some of the deepest, most delicious moments of my life were getting out of jail in a place like . . . Selma and finding my way to the nearest Freedom House, taking a good long shower, putting on a pair of jeans and a fresh shirt and going to some little Dew Drop Inn . . . where I'd order a hamburger . . . and walk over to the jukebox and stand there with a quarter in my hand, and look over every song on that box because this choice had to be *just* right . . . and then I would finally drop that quarter in and punch up Marvin Gaye or Curtis Mayfield or Aretha, and I would sit down with my sandwich, and I would let that music wash over me, just wash right *through* me. I don't know if I've ever felt anything so sweet.

4 | SUN RECORDS *(706 Union Avenue; 800-441-6249; www.sunstudio. com)* A small recording studio next to a radiator shop—things haven't changed much since Sam Phillips opened the Memphis Recording Service and began recording anybody who walked in the door. Now a full-time tourist stop and part-time studio, Sun Records offers an engaging tour among crammed artifacts that gives a sense of the music created here. This was where teenaged Elvis Presley recorded black music that became rock 'n' roll. When Elvis signed a forty-five hundred dollar record contract on November 15, 1955, Phillips's early work of capturing black blues and gospel was forgotten in the stampede to rock.

In 1951 Phillips recorded what is now considered the first rock song, "Rocket 88," by a Clarksdale, Mississippi, group featuring Ike Turner and singer Jackie Brenston. The first Sun "hit" was Rufus Thomas's "Bear Cat" in 1953. Phillips also recorded five inmates from the Tennessee State Penitentiary who were brought to the studio in chains. The Prisonaires were an Elvis favorite, and through them he learned of the studio, and began dropping in. Many blacks resented Elvis's "theft" of their music and style, but his success opened doors to others. Little Richard later said he probably wouldn't be known but for Elvis. The roll call of musicians at Sun included Carl Perkins (with the first million-seller, "Blue Suede Shoes"), B.B. King, Johnny Cash, Roy Orbison, and Jerry Lee Lewis.

5 | **Stax Records** *(926 East McLemore; 901-946-2535; www. soulsvilleusa.com)* This re-created music studio and academy is a unique gamble to reverse the flow of fortune that occurred in the 1950s and 1960s at Soulsville. At the time, musicians literally walked out of the black neighborhood and into fame and fortune. David Porter, who cowrote "Soul Man" with Isaac Hayes, for example, bagged groceries across the street.

Stax was established in an abandoned movie theater on this spot by a white brother-sister team, Jim Stewart and Estelle Axton—"Stax" derived from their names. With a house band that later became known as Booker T. and the MGs, and a revolving group of white and black musicians, the homemade studio recorded and made stars of Otis Redding, the Staple Singers, Wilson Pickett, Sam and Dave, and dance innovators ("Funky Chicken") Carla and Rufus Thomas. Isaac Hayes, who wrote or contributed to two hundred Stax songs, including "Hold On, I'm Coming" and "Soul Man," later won an Oscar for

Sun Records studio in Memphis

the music from *Shaft*. The original Stax studio was torn down. The re-created studio is an attempt to redevelop the neighborhood.

Monteagle

HIGHLANDER SCHOOL SITE AND CEMETERY (*U.S. 41, 1.5 miles east of Monteagle; 865-933-3443; www.highlandercenter.org*) This bucolic think tank on the Cumberland plateau was a training camp for revolutionaries in the South. Myles Horton started Highlander Folk School in 1932 to organize labor unions and Appalachian communities but he turned to civil rights activism in the 1950s. His workshops, led by Septima Clark, were rare integrated gatherings in the South. Old labor songs were refashioned into movement anthems by musician Guy Carawan. Among the famous students was Rosa Parks, who was so quiet and shy during two weeks in August 1955 that organizers were surprised to hear of her arrest in Montgomery four months later. Martin Luther King Jr. spent a week there in September 1957, sleeping in a log cabin. A photo of King, Horton, and Parks became a billboard purporting to show a "Communist school."

In September 1959 Tennessee's attorney general raided Highlander, found alcohol and integrated classes, and revoked the school's charter. The school reopened in Knoxville, but was run out of town by right-wing businessman Cas Walker. In 1970 Highlander moved to a one-hundred-acre farm near New Market and remains an activist organization. Myles Horton died in 1990. Though subdivided for new homes, the original site contains many of the original buildings including the library (now a house), the log cabin where King stayed, and a graveyard where Horton and his family are buried.

Nashville

Nashville could have gone down in civil rights history as the birthplace of the student sit-in movement—were it not for four young men in Greensboro, North Carolina, who walked into a Woolworth's lunch counter on February 1, 1960. For more than a year, a group of Nashville students had been training for similar action, and their names soon became familiar as leaders of the movement—Diane Nash, James Bevel, John Lewis, Marion Berry, and Bernard Lafayette.

Twelve days after Greensboro, they and more than 100 other students sat down at several Nashville lunch counters. A week later, 340 students protested, and 81 were arrested. The protests spread with a "Don't Buy Downtown" boycott enforced by black ministers.

Two months later, a predawn dynamite blast heavily damaged the home of black lawyer Alexander Looby. That afternoon, April 19, several thousand protesters converged on city hall in what is considered the first mass civil rights march. In a dramatic verbal confrontation between Mayor Ben West, Diane Nash, and the Reverend C. T. Vivian, the mayor blurted out that he supported integrating lunch counters. On May 10 six Nashville stores were integrated, the first in a major southern city. The Nashville leaders soon headed the Student Nonviolent Coordinating Committee, a national organization that led protests and voter registration drives in Mississippi, Georgia, Alabama, and North Carolina.

In Nashville, protests resumed a year later against movie theaters and continued four years, aimed at the Krystals hamburger chain, hotels, churches, and libraries. As Taylor Branch put it: leader John Lewis "was marching through Nashville's yellow pages."

Nashville has done a better-than-average job in marking civil rights hot spots, and publishes a free African American Historic Sites booklet. It is available from the **Visitors Bureau** (*161 Fourth Avenue, Nashville, TN 37219; 615-259-4700*).

CLARK MEMORIAL METHODIST CHURCH (*1014 Fourteenth Avenue North*) This modest red-brick church could rightly be called the nursery of the student sit-in movement. Here, in September 1958, the Reverend Jim Lawson began workshops in nonviolent protest. Students from Fisk University, Tennessee A&I, Meharry Medical, and the American Baptist Theological Seminary gathered on Tuesday evenings and learned Gandhian philosophy and practical strategy.

Lawson, who had gone to prison as a conscientious objector rather than serve in the Korean War, had spent three years as a missionary in India. After reading of the Montgomery bus boycott, he vowed to get involved in the movement. At Clark, he assigned students the works of Reinhold Neibuhr, Thoreau, and Lao-tzu. They role-played being attacked verbally and physically. They were counseled to dress well, act courteously, and endure the worst that a segregated society could dish up, possibly including death. In the winter of 1959, they made practice runs to segregated lunch counters.

Congressman John Lewis, then a student at American Baptist, later wrote: "That little building played a major role in educating, preparing and shaping a group of young men and women who would lead the way for years to come in the nonviolent struggle for civil rights in America."

FIRST BAPTIST CHURCH SITE *(Eighth Avenue North and Charlotte Pike)* A historic marker denotes the headquarters and staging site for Nashville's sit-in movement. First Baptist Church was led by the Reverend Kelly Miller Smith, a dynamic speaker who opened his church to workshops, strategy sessions, and meetings. The first mass meeting of the student movement occurred here on February 12, 1960, eleven days after the famous Woolworth's sit-in in Greensboro, North Carolina.

By then, half a dozen cities were under sit-in siege, and Jim Lawson's seventy-five disciples were joined by five hundred new volunteers, according to movement historian Taylor Branch. "We were young, free and burning with belief," said John Lewis. Lawson led a crash course on etiquette, dress, threats, and physical protection, and they met at the church the next morning. Walking in fresh snow at 11 A.M., 124 students marched from here to Fifth Avenue to sit in at Woolworth's, Kress's, and McClellands.

THE ARCADE AND FIFTH AVENUE HISTORIC DISTRICT *(Fifth Avenue)* "Oh my god, here's the niggers," cried a waitress at Woolworth's on February 13, 1960, as more than one hundred college students began Nashville's sit-in movement to integrate lunch counters. To reach Fifth, they walked through the Arcade mall. The area is now a historic district marked by a sign that includes the protester rules of conduct as summarized in a Nashville newspaper at the time: "Do show yourself friendly at the counter at all times. Do sit straight and always face the counter. Don't strike back or curse if attacked. Remember love and nonviolence."

METRO COURTHOUSE *(1 Public Square)*   One of the most satis-
fying victories in civil rights history occurred on the steps of city hall
on April 19, 1960, when Mayor Ben West met thousands of protesters upset over the bombing of a black attorney's home. Two months of
sit-ins and a shopping boycott had left the city on edge. Hundreds of
students had been arrested, and some had been beaten. As they gathered at the steps, folksinger Guy Carawan led them in verses of "We
Shall Overcome." Then, in what amounted to a "good cop, bad cop"
exchange with the mayor, the Reverend C. T. Vivian berated the city
for the violence while student leader Diane Nash asked a series of
measured questions. When the mayor appealed to citizens to end discrimination, Nash pressed: "Do you mean to include lunch
counters?"

"Little lady," West answered, "I stopped segregation seven years
ago at the airport . . ."

"Then, mayor, do you recommend that the lunch counters be
desegregated?"

"Yes," West said.

The crowd, John Lewis wrote, "exploded, cheering and applauding."

On the thirty-fifth anniversary of the event, Mayor Phil Bredesen
invited the original protesters to unveil a plaque on which he had inscribed words from the Book of Joshua: "And the people shouted with
a great shout; so that the wall fell down."

FISK UNIVERSITY AND JUBILEE HALL *(1000 Seventeenth Avenue;
615-329-8500; www.fisk.edu)*   Regarded as a brain trust for the
civil rights movement, Fisk University was long famous as the home
of the Jubilee Singers. Founded in 1867 by the American Missionary
Association, it was named for Clinton Fisk, the Freedmen's Bureau
chief in Tennessee who supported black education. At the time, tu-
ition was twelve dollars a year. Within five years Fisk University was
nearly bankrupt.

Treasurer George White assembled a group of student singers—all
but two had been slaves—and dubbed them the Jubilee Singers. With
the help of teacher Ella Sheppard, White took them on a fund-raising
tour. Traveling hand-to-mouth, they finally won fame in their second

year. Carrying home twenty thousand dollars, White was able to start a campus. The first building was a dormitory, Jubilee Hall, which has become a landmark. Fisk developed into a prestigious black university and counts among its alums W. E. B. Du Bois, John Hope Franklin, Constance Baker Motley, and James Weldon Johnson.

In 1958 Fisk students joined Jim Lawson's nonviolent protest workshops at nearby Clark Memorial Methodist Church. On February 3, 1960, Lawson stood before five hundred students in the Fisk chemistry building auditorium and announced that sit-ins would begin in Nashville. Among Fisk students who participated were Diane Nash and Marion Barry.

The campus area is a historic district and worth seeing for the architecture alone. A number of **historical markers** are on or near the campus including one (*D. B. Todd Boulevard and Jefferson Street*) marking the route of the mass protest to city hall in April 1960. A campus brochure is available from public affairs in the **Du Bois building** (*Eighteenth Street and Jackson Street*).

EAST HIGH SCHOOL (*110 Gallatin Avenue*)   Nashville's schools were first desegregated in 1957 after barber Alfred Kelley filed a lawsuit to enroll his son Robert into this "white" school near their home. Represented by Alexander Looby and Avon Williams, their lawsuit won early backing under the Supreme Court's *Brown* decision, and Nashville was ordered to integrate one grade at a time. The school board evaded with redrawn zones and a voluntary transfer program, but nineteen black children pioneered integration at six elementary schools on September 9. They endured jeers and epithets, and later that night a bomb destroyed Hattie Cotton Elementary in East Nashville. Police blamed an outside white supremacist, John Kaspar. By 1963 more than seven hundred blacks were integrated into Nashville schools.

Pulaski

KU KLUX KLAN BIRTHPLACE (*209 Madison Street*)   The historic plaque has been turned face-in to stop white supremacists from posing for pictures, but the "Klan building" is still ruefully present in this quiet town. The plaque's hidden side reads: "Ku Klux Klan organized in this, the law office of Judge Thomas M. Jones December 24th, 1865."

The six founders, whose names are on the plaque, had been Confederate soldiers, and, supposedly, sought nothing more than each other's company in a social club. Their club's name was derived from the Greek word, *kuklos,* or circle. According to early histories, the men met later at a private house where founder James Crowe recommended costumes made of sheets. When they rode through town in silence, the effect on blacks was chilling. What allegedly started as a gag, however, soon turned deliberate intimidation. Communities from as far away as North Carolina began copying costumes and tactics, and in 1867, a central organization was formed in Nashville. By then, "radical" Yankees in Congress were forcing southern states to give blacks their citizenship, including the vote. The Klan's reaction was "maintenance of the supremacy of the white race." The Klan became the "invisible empire" and Nathan Bedford Forrest, a former slave trader and Confederate general, its "grand wizard."

People in Pulaski cling to the original notion of the Klan as a social club. But by 1868 the Klan's mission was clear—terrorizing and preventing blacks from gaining equal rights. Klan members or their imitators killed hundreds of blacks and white supporters before 1890, and participated in many of the five thousand lynchings during Jim Crow segregation. There would be many manifestations of the Klan over the next 140 years, including a period in the 1920s when it was politically expedient to belong. The use of a burning cross as an intimidating symbol began in 1915. As late as 1985, Klansmen were murdering blacks in the South.

For many years, Klansmen, skinheads, and other white supremacists gathered in Pulaski on Martin Luther King's birthday, stopped for pictures, kissed the plaque, and generally caused an embarrassment. In 1989 Pulaski closed down the town in a silent protest. A few years later, the owner of the building turned the plaque around. "We turned our back to the Klan and our plaque to the wall," she said. Despite an annual unity parade, and the election of black officials, Pulaski has had trouble recruiting black professionals like doctors.

Philadelphia's Liberty Bell, one of the first American symbols of freedom

Other States, Other Sites

Kansas • Kentucky • Maryland •
Massachusetts • Michigan • Ohio •
Oklahoma • Pennsylvania

KANSAS

"BLEEDING KANSAS," wrote historian John Hope Franklin, was the "preliminary battleground of the Civil War." Violence between abolitionists and proslavery forces began after Congress left it up to the territory to decide for itself whether to be slave or free. The most infamous abolitionist was John Brown, a white fanatic who with his sons murdered several proslavery citizens. He later reached martyrdom when he was hanged in Harpers Ferry, West Virginia, after a failed attempt to start a revolt.

After the Civil War and Reconstruction, forty thousand blacks left the terrorism of the South to begin again in Kansas, but many returned home after facing Midwestern winters and its own brand of racism. For a century, Kansas remained divided over race. More whites than blacks were lynched—thirty-five versus nineteen—but segregation was allowed by law and was widespread.

Topeka

BROWN V. BOARD OF EDUCATION NATIONAL HISTORIC SITE (*Fifteenth and Monroe Streets; 785-354-4273; www.cr.nps.gov/nr/travel/civilrights/ka1.htm*) On land once owned by an abolitionist, former slaves established a community in southeast Topeka after the Civil War. In 1877 the Topeka school board built a school for them and named it Monroe Elementary. The school, three buildings later, remained all black and parents began agitating for a school more on a par with Topeka's white schools. The school board offered new light-bulbs and hand-me-down desks. Linda Brown walked to Monroe across a busy railroad yard from her home. Her father, railroad welder and assistant pastor Oliver Brown, wanted to enroll her in the all-white Sumner Elementary, a school not only closer but better than Monroe. When she was denied, he joined with a dozen other parents to sue. Because his name came first in the alphabet, and because the Supreme Court decided to make the Kansas case the lead in a con-solidated review of school segregation, the landmark case became known as *Brown v. Board of Education of Topeka.*

Brown v. Board of Education

On May 17, 1954, the U.S. Supreme Court ruled that public schools must integrate to give black and white children equal rights. The decision, nine-teen months before the Montgomery bus boycott began, launched the modern civil rights era.

The ruling reversed—the rarest of Supreme Court acts—a fifty-eight-year-old policy known as "separate but equal" that had established legal segregation in the South and extralegal segregation in much of the coun-try. The court found that separate schools for blacks denied them equal opportunity and that separation by race generated feelings of inferiority among blacks that could last a lifetime. In short, it said segregated edu-cation violated the Fourteenth Amendment, which guaranteed equal pro-tection of the law. The ruling was the most sweeping civil rights mandate from the federal government since the Emancipation Proclamation. With dozens of other related cases before and after, *Brown* ended legal segre-gation in the United States.

Brown was named for Oliver Brown, a welder from Topeka, Kansas, who tried to enroll his daughter, Linda, in a "white" elementary school that was closer to home, safer to walk to, and better equipped. Kansas law permitted, but did not require, segregated schools. Denied his request, Brown and other parents sued the Topeka Board of Education. The case was handled by the NAACP's Thurgood Marshall. *Brown* was chosen by the court as the lead case of five school cases to demonstrate that school segregation was a national and not strictly a southern problem.

"Separate but equal" came from an 1896 Supreme Court case called *Plessy v. Ferguson,* which upheld separate-race railroad cars in Louisiana. At the time, the court argued, segregation did not imply second-class citizenship for blacks. In practice, however, "black" facilities, whether cars, schools, or toilets, were never equal.

Until the *Brown* case, the NAACP had pressed for equal schools but never challenged the underlying segregation. This strategy worked at state law and graduate schools, beginning in Texas, where the cost of creating a truly equal law school for blacks made integration the only solution.

But suing individual cases became a nightmare when it came to independent public school districts. In Virginia alone, 124 school systems were sued. Even when courts went along with equalization, victories were hollow. School districts dragged their feet in building new schools for black kids. Each case required endless follow-up trips to court, according to Richard Kluger's *Simple Justice,* the leading history of school desegregation.

Brown attacked the unspoken concept behind "separate but equal"—that blacks were inferior. When the argument was drawn so starkly, Chief Justice Earl Warren saw immediately that segregation had to end. To soften the blow to the South, he delayed a compliance order for a year, and even then made the yardstick "all deliberate speed."

The reaction in the South, nonetheless, was swift and ugly. Virginia vowed "massive resistance" and closed some schools for up to five years. Mississippi business leaders created the Citizens Council to oppose integration, and the state legislature ordered state officials not to comply. In 1957 Arkansas's governor defied a federal court order under the *Brown* precedent, forcing President Eisenhower to send the army to Little Rock High School. Ten years after the decision, according to John Hope Franklin, less than 2 percent of African American students in the eleven states of the former Confederacy were in desegregated schools.

By then, a slew of civil rights cases had extended the reasoning of *Brown* to buses, lunch counters, libraries, parks, and bedrooms. NAACP attorney Constance Baker Motley told PBS: "I think the greatest impact of the *Brown* decision was on the black community itself. It was a statement . . . that they had friends, so to speak, in the Supreme Court. It emboldened communities of blacks around the country to move forward to secure their rights."

The other cases consolidated under *Brown* came from:

Clarendon County, South Carolina, where black residents had been denied a bus to carry their children to their school. Filed in November 1949, *Briggs v. Elliott* claimed that the children of gas station attendant Harry Briggs (and twenty other plaintiffs) suffered "irreparable damage" because they were not treated equally by a school district chaired at the time by Roderick Elliott. During the 1952 *Briggs* trial, psychologist Kenneth Clark used a now-famous doll test to show that black children preferred white dolls and felt "bad" about their black identity.

Wilmington, Delaware, where black kids were bused away from a beautiful "white" high school in suburban Claymont to an overcrowded "black" school downtown. Ethel Belton and other parents who tried unsuccessfully to get their kids enrolled in the neighborhood school sued the state board of education in 1951. Delaware's highest court sided with the parents but *Gebhart v. Belton*—Francis Gebhart was on the board—was filed by Delaware and consolidated with the other cases.

Farmville, Virginia, where sixteen-year-old student Barbara Johns led a student walkout to protest "temporary" tar-paper shack classrooms at the overcrowded Moton High School. The students persuaded the NAACP to take their case, which was filed in May 1951 and called *Davis v. County School Board of Prince Edward County. Davis* was Dorothy Davis, daughter of a farmer.

Washington, D.C., where, on September 11, 1950, longtime activist Gardner Bishop had led a group of black children to a new white school to enroll. Turned away, they became plaintiffs in a case brought by James Nabrit, a law professor at Howard University. *Bolling v. Sharpe* is named for twelve-year-old student Spottswood Bolling Jr. and Melvin Sharpe, the president of the D.C. school board. The case, decided separately but concurrently by the Supreme Court, turned on the Fifth Amendment's guarantee of "liberty," which the court extended to cover in the federal district the same equal protection that the Fourteenth Amendment required in states.

Key to *Brown*'s victory, according to Richard Kluger's *Simple Justice*, was the testimony of Dr. Louisa Holt, a counselor at Topeka's Menninger Clinic, a psychiatric hospital. She said that "the mere fact of segregation" denoted a belief, held by whites and blacks, in the inferiority of blacks, and that segregation at an early age affected attitudes and development of blacks for the rest of their lives. Much of her language ended up in the Supreme Court ruling, which eventually forced desegregation in twenty-one states. A series of subsequent lawsuits and decisions were required to overcome southern resistance, which lasted, in some cases, into the 1980s.

Monroe was closed in 1975, but the building was saved by a nonprofit foundation headed by Linda's sister, Cheryl Brown Henderson. After "people laughed in my face," she convinced Congress to approve a national park in 1992. The National Park Service planned to open its site in the old Monroe school on the fiftieth anniversary of the *Brown* decision, in May 2004.

The Sumner school *(330 Southwest Western Avenue)* is a registered historic place.

Osawatomie

JOHN BROWN CABIN *(Tenth and Main Streets; 913-755-4384; www.kshs.org/places/johbrown/index.htm)* In this cabin, abolitionist John Brown ran an antislavery guerrilla camp and a stop on the Underground Railroad. On May 24 and 25, 1856, Brown and his sons murdered six proslavery citizens at Pottawatomie Creek. In 1858 Brown harbored at the cabin slaves en route to Canada. Operated as a state park, the cabin was moved and restored in near-original condition.

A life-sized statue of John Brown, with the inscription "Erected . . . by a Grateful People," was donated to Western University in Kansas City *(2804 Sewell)* by black citizens who raised the two-thousand-dollar sculpting fee. The state capitol building in Topeka also features a large and dynamic mural of John Brown.

KENTUCKY

Berea

One of the "border" states, with loyalties to both North and South, Kentucky elected not to secede. During the Civil War, Camp Nelson recruited black soldiers, who later settled in and around Berea at the urging of camp minister John Fee. He named the settlement Berea after a biblical town known for tolerance. Fee was run out of town by white supremacists but later returned to establish an integrated church in 1855 and an integrated school in 1866, which grew into Berea College, the only integrated college in the South at the time. One of its graduates in 1903 was Carter Woodson, a black historian and founder of Black History Month. The following year, when Jim Crow segregation rolled over Kentucky, the state legislature ordered the school to segregate. The school appealed to the Supreme Court, which upheld Kentucky. The law remained on the books until 1950. As a result, Berea's black population dropped from 25 percent to less than 8.

Berea has published a driving tour guide about this African American heritage, with stops at Center Street—a planned integrated neighborhood—and Berea College.

MARYLAND

Maryland was established by George Calvert, Lord Baltimore, who sailed into Chesapeake Bay in 1634. With him was Mathias de Sousa, a man of African and Portuguese descent and one of nine indentured servants aboard who worked for Jesuit missionaries. In four years, de Sousa worked himself to freedom and became a sailor, Maryland's first black voter and its first black legislator, a member of the 1642 assembly of freedmen. Later, however, Maryland became a slave state, and although it did not secede, endured a long history of segregation and discrimination. Two of the most famous black abolitionists, Frederick Douglass and Harriet Tubman, escaped slavery in Maryland. A century later, the state produced two famous civil rights activists, Thurgood Marshall and H. Rap Brown, who attacked racism with polar-opposite methods. George Wallace, the former Alabama governor and segregationist, was shot and paralyzed at a Laurel shopping center on May 15, 1972, while running for president. Assailant Arthur Bremer was white.

Annapolis

KUNTA KINTE—ALEX HALEY MEMORIAL (*city harbor; www. kintehaley.org*) *Roots* writer Alex Haley determined that his slave ancestor, Kunta Kinte, stepped foot in America at the port of Annapolis. Near the waterfront, sculptor Ed Dwight created a statue of Haley reading a book to three children.

BANNEKER-DOUGLASS MUSEUM *(84 Franklin Street; 410-216-6180; www.marylandhistorialtrust.net/bdm.htm)* Named for two of Maryland's famous African Americans, this state museum describes the history of blacks since slavery. Benjamin Banneker was a surveyor hired by George Washington to help Pierre L'Enfant lay out Washington, D.C. When L'Enfant quit in a huff and took the plans with him, Banneker recalled the design and the construction went foward. The other honoree, Frederick Douglass, escaped slavery to become the leading black abolitionist.

Baltimore

No city has erected more statues to its black heroes than Baltimore. An African American museum is in the works, and black history walks and tours are readily available on the waterfront. Black Baltimore Tours leads walks focusing on Harriet Tubman, Alex Haley, and Frederick Douglass.

THURGOOD MARSHALL STATUE *(Pratt Street and Hopkins Place, outside federal building)* Born Thoroughgood Marshall in 1908, raised in West Baltimore, and graduated from Howard University, Marshall was a struggling private attorney in the early 1930s when he agreed to serve as counsel to the Baltimore branch of the NAACP. The branch had been nursed back to life in 1934 by Lillie Jackson, an outspoken housewife, and Carl Murphy, publisher of the *Afro-American* newspaper. For his work, Marshall was paid an annual retainer of twenty-five dollars, plus five dollars a day when specifically working on NAACP cases. One of his first big cases, researched by Marshall and argued by his mentor, Howard law school dean Charles Houston, forced the University of Maryland to admit its first black law student in 1936. They argued that "separate but equal" segregation, the law in the South since the late 1890s, did not, in fact, provide equal education. Marshall later expanded this argument to desegregate all public schools in the United States. Marshall became the first black justice of the U.S. Supreme Court in 1967, appointed by President Johnson. He died in 1993.

LILLIE JACKSON'S HOME *(1320 Eutaw Place)* Like many black urban neighborhoods that developed during Jim Crow, West Baltimore nurtured its own and more or less accepted segregation. Not until Thurgood Marshall, Lillie Jackson, and Carl Murphy stirred things up did long-hidden feelings of resentment spill onto the streets. They and other black leaders, including Jackson's daughter Juanita, met here in strategy sessions to end segregation in Baltimore. One of their first efforts, "Don't Buy Where You Can't Work," took aim at white-owned retail stores on Pennsylvania Avenue that catered to black customers but refused to hire black clerks. Patterned after a successful picketing campaign in Washington, D.C., the boycott prompted the stores to sue the NAACP. Defended by Marshall, the activists won and blacks were hired. In the 1970s Jackson's home became Baltimore's only civil rights museum, but it closed for lack of funds.

AFRO-AMERICAN (*2519 North Charles Street*) A weekly black newspaper, founded in the 1890s by white-washer John H. Murphy in his basement, had an initial circulation of 250. At its height in the 1970s, it sold 150,000 copies. It is still in business. Murphy's son, Carl, who took over the paper after his father's death in 1922, had been denied admission to Johns Hopkins University because of his race. His outrage became the paper's, and it campaigned tirelessly for an end to Jim Crow. Murphy's office on Eutaw Street served as the NAACP headquarters when Thurgood Marshall was beginning his legal battles.

FREDERICK DOUGLASS MARKER (*Fells Point Square*) Douglass's spirit still lingers around the Baltimore waterfront where, as a child slave, he learned to read, and he became a ship's laborer. Donning a sailor's suit and hopping a train, he later wrote, he took advantage of the "kind feeling that prevailed in Baltimore . . . towards those who go down to the sea in ships . . . my knowledge of ships and sailors' talk came much to my assistance, for I knew a ship from stem to stern, and from keelson to crosstrees, and could talk sailor like an 'old salt.'" Challenged on the northbound train by a conductor, he flashed some official looking papers and escaped to Philadelphia. He became an eloquent spokesman for abolition, published a newspaper in Rochester,

New York, and consulted President Lincoln. His home in Washington is a national park.

According to Louis Fields, who leads a Douglass tour, Douglass bought books at a store near Caroline and Thames Streets, and lived at what is now a garage at Durham and Aliceanna Streets.

Cambridge

In the 1960s Cambridge made headlines for violent standoffs between civil rights activists and police. In 1963, in the first grassroots campaign outside the Deep South, Gloria Richardson and the Cambridge Nonviolent Action Group demanded integration of stores and improvements in slum housing. After activists clashed with police and the National Guard were called out, Attorney General Bobby Kennedy negotiated the Cambridge Accord, which ended demonstrations in exchange for school integration and new public housing and jobs. But progress was slow. The fire department hired its first black firefighter in 1986 after additional federal pressure.

In 1967 H. Rap Brown, the newly elected head of SNCC, went to Cambridge to stir things up. That summer race riots broke out in Detroit, Harlem, Minneapolis, and other cities. "If America don't come around, we're going to burn it down," Brown shouted from a car top. "Don't be trying to love that honky to death. Shoot him to death, brother." Brown then went to Cambridge's Race Street, the main shopping district, where he was struck in the face with a shotgun pellet. Within hours, an elementary school was set on fire, snipers were reported, and the fire department refused to fight the flames that spread through a black neighborhood.

Governor Spiro Agnew responded with an order to arrest people for violent speech. Brown was charged with arson and other violations, and he and black militancy became an issue nationwide. In 1970, while driving to a Brown trial on firearms violations near Baltimore, SNCC worker Ralph Featherstone and a companion, Che Payne, were blown up in their car. The FBI said it suspected Featherstone carried a bomb, but activists suspected it was planted. A year later Brown was wounded in a holdup-shootout in Manhattan. After serving prison time, Brown became a Muslim cleric and moved to Atlanta, where, in 2002, he killed a sheriff's deputy. That same year, Brown, now known as Jamil Abdullah Al-Amin, was captured in Lowndes County, Alabama, and sentenced to life in prison.

Nothing in Cambridge memorializes this chapter in civil rights history.

HARRIET TUBMAN MUSEUM *(424 Race Street; 401-228-0401; www.harriettubmanmuseum.org)* A simple historical marker on Maryland Route 397 in Bucktown, ten miles outside Cambridge, designates the spot where, around 1820, Harriet Tubman was born as the slave Araminta. After escaping, she became a fearless "conductor" of the Underground Railroad. She journeyed nineteen times into Maryland, often disguised as a man, to lead some three hundred slaves north to freedom. Never caught, despite a forty-thousand dollars' bounty on her head, she later said of her own Underground Railroad: "I never lost a passenger." She also served as nurse and spy for the Union army during the Civil War. She died in Auburn, New York, in 1913.

MASSACHUSETTS

Boston

Liberty is Boston's mantra, and it remains a great irony that the first man to die here to help make America free was an African American. The year was 1770. England had just sent a contingent of soldiers to enforce import taxes. Among the outraged citizens was Crispus Attucks, a forty-seven-year-old black-Indian dockworker. On the evening of March 5, Attucks joined a "motley rabble" to harass the British soldiers. When shooting broke out, Attucks was the first of five to fall in what became known as the "Boston Massacre," the first skirmish that preceded the Revolution.

In the early 1800s Boston was a nest of abolitionists who defied the South and the federal government's support of slavery. After slaves Ellen and William Craft escaped from Georgia, fugitive hunters went to Boston to pick them up. The new Fugitive Slave Act gave bounty hunters the right to retrieve runaways, but they were harassed and banished by citizenry who hid the Crafts. When President Fillmore vowed to enforce the law, abolitionists sent the couple to England and openly challenged Fillmore to jail them.

Brochures for the Freedom Trail and the Black Heritage Trail are available from a kiosk on the Common.

CRISPUS ATTUCKS MEMORIAL AND GRAVE *(Boston Common)*
The first to fall in preliminary skirmishes with British soldiers, Attucks was buried in the Granary Burial Ground and honored with a monument on the Boston Common, one of the stops on the famous "freedom trail." The burial ground is directly north on Tremont Street. His memorial, an obelisk with a bronze figure holding a broken chain, was erected in 1888.

AFRICAN MEETING HOUSE *(46 Joy Street; 617-725-0022; www.afroammuseum.org)* The first black church in America, built in 1806, became the center of black activism in New England. Inside, William Lloyd Garrison founded the New England Anti-Slavery Society in 1832. Known thereafter as the "abolition" church, it was later used by the military to enlist members of the famed Massachusetts Fifty-fourth Regiment, the first northern unit of black soldiers in the Civil War. The church is now a black museum.

ROBERT GOULD SHAW AND FIFTY-FOURTH MASSACHUSETTS COLORED INFANTRY REGIMENT MONUMENT *(Boston Common)*
When President Lincoln's Emancipation Proclamation opened the Civil War to black soldiers, the first one thousand recruits were organized into the Fifty-fourth Regiment, commanded by a white officer, Robert Gould Shaw. Among his soldiers were two sons of Frederick Douglass who watched as the twenty-six-year-old Shaw led the regiment through Boston's streets en route south. Chosen to assault Fort Wagner, at the edge of Charleston, South Carolina's harbor, the men were cut down by Confederate fire. Shaw and 272 of his men were killed. They were eventually buried together in the sandy spit that later washed away.

Using real male models, sculptor Augustus Saint-Gaudens worked for twelve years on the bronze of a mounted Shaw leading his men. Fifteen feet high and eighteen feet long and renowned for its accurate depiction of black features, the sculpture was dedicated in 1897 with Booker T. Washington as lead speaker. The story of the Fifty-fourth is depicted in the movie *Glory.*

Boston monument to the 54th Massachusetts Regiment

MICHIGAN

Detroit

THE FIST (*Woodward Avenue at Jefferson Avenue*) Joe Louis of Detroit became an American hero when he fought Max Schmeling of Germany in 1938 in what was considered a propaganda match pitting white supremacy against American diversity. Louis beat him in one round and the country went wild. When a young fan, Coleman Young, grew up to be mayor of Detroit, he arranged for *Sports Illustrated* to pay for a sculpture to Louis. Robert Graham created a gargantuan fist rising from a long arm. Though it reverberated at the time as "black power," the Fist today is seen as a spectacular symbol of black pride.

MOTOWN MUSEUM (*2648 West Grand Boulevard; 313-875-2264; www.motownmuseum.com*)   In the basement of this house, Barry Gordy created Motown (short for Motor Town) Records and recorded the Supremes, Michael Jackson, Smokey Robinson, Gladys

Knight, and many more. After the company moved to California, Gordy's home was turned into a museum with original control room and studios.

Dearborn

HENRY FORD MUSEUM *(20900 Oakwood Boulevard; 313-982-6100; www.thehenryford.org)* This sprawling collection of Americana pulled a civil rights coup in 2002 with the discovery and purchase of the bus on which Rosa Parks was arrested in 1955. Her act touched off the civil rights movement. But the bus's story is one of neglect and intrigue. It sat unwanted and rusting in a farmer's pasture outside Montgomery for thirty years. When the owner tried unsuccessfully to sell it on eBay, another online auction company discovered scrapbooks that supposedly proved that this was the actual bus Mrs. Parks boarded on December 1, 1955. Although the bus had been completed gutted, Ford bid $427,000 for the hulk, then spent another $300,000 replacing it with parts from other buses of the era. Before it was even ready for display, visitors were asking to see it.

Rosa Parks's bus at the Henry Ford Museum in Dearborn, Michigan

OHIO

Cincinnati

NATIONAL UNDERGROUND RAILROAD FREEDOM CENTER *(312 Elm Street; 513-412-9100; www.undergroundrailroad.org)* Scheduled to open in summer 2004, the Freedom Center is the first major museum about the Underground Railroad, the ingenious network of abolitionists and ex-slaves who helped thousands of slaves escape their bondage. But the museum's displays cover also the entire spectrum of the African American experience.

The Underground Railroad was not a railroad in the literal sense but an informal system of moving slaves to freedom, often by foot, sometimes by wagons with hidden compartments. Boats were used, and in at least one celebrated Virginia case, a shipping crate. Most slaves escaped to the north, where slavery had been outlawed and sympathizers helped them find homes and jobs. Because of the 1850 Fugitive Slave Act, which allowed bounty hunters to chase slaves into any state, many escaped slaves went on to Canada. The Railroad also ran southward, along the Atlantic coast where black watermen helped slaves through swamps and barrier islands into Florida, when it was a Spanish territory. Many fled to the Bahamas, Haiti, and the Caribbean islands. Mexico was also a refuge.

Escapes shattered the southern planters' myth that their slaves were "happy" toiling in cotton and rice fields. Slaves attempted escape in numerous ways and disguises. With help from a white sympathizer, "Box" Brown shipped himself from Richmond to Philadelphia. Dockworker Frederick Douglass disguised himself as a "free" sailor and simply rode a train north from Baltimore. Fair-skinned mulatto Ellen Craft was able to pose as a male slave owner traveling north with "his" slave, who was actually her darker-skinned husband.

The most famous Underground Railroad "conductor" was Harriet Tubman who escaped from a Maryland plantation while in her twenties and later returned to Maryland to usher perhaps three hundred other slaves north. White "conductors" included many Quakers, a denomination that had spoken out against slavery as early as 1688.

Levi Coffin sheltered so many slaves in his homes in Indiana and Ohio that he became known as the "president" of "Grand Central Station."

The $65 million museum sits, appropriately, on the northern bank of the Ohio River, the last barrier between slave states and the north. In one of the most famous scenes in American literature, *Uncle Tom's Cabin,* based on a true story, a slave woman and child escaped across the frozen Ohio River.

OKLAHOMA

Tulsa

GREENWOOD CULTURAL CENTER (*322 North Greenwood Avenue; 918-596-1029*) As if it happened yesterday, Tulsa today is coming to grips with a race riot—in 1921. Lawsuits, reparations, and reconciliation have all risen from a state commission report issued in 2000 that reexamined the once forgotten uprising.

On June 1, 1921, after a shoeblack named Dick Rowland touched the arm of Sarah Page, a white woman, in an elevator, thousands of whites charged across the railroad track into Greenwood, a large and affluent black neighborhood. They shot, hanged, and burned up to three hundred black residents, and set fire to forty square blocks, including an entire business district and twelve hundred homes. By the time the National Guard was called, the uprising was over.

Walter White of the NAACP saw the devastation a week later and wrote, "The Tulsa riot, in sheer brutality and willful destruction of life and property, stands without parallel in America." Historians Scott Ellsworth and John Hope Franklin later concluded that the term "riot" was inadequate, that "massacre, a pogrom, or, to use a more modern term, an ethnic cleansing" took place. "One thing is certain," they wrote in the legislative commission's report, "when it was all over, Tulsa's African American district had been turned into a scorched wasteland of vacant lots, crumbling storefronts, burned churches, and blackened, leafless trees."

The story was largely forgotten until the fiftieth anniversary in 1971 when a memorial service was held for victims and survivors. Subsequent news stories prompted a reexamination by the legislature.

The Greenwood Cultural Center has a permanent exhibit with photographs of the riot.

PENNSYLVANIA

Pennsylvania, the birthplace of the U.S. government, was also the heart of the movement to abolish slavery. The first-known antislave sentiments arose among Mennonites in Germantown at the time of the Revolution, who asked, "Have these Negroes not as much right to fight for their freedom as you have to keep them slaves?" Later, Pennsylvania-based Quakers established Underground Railroad depots.

One of the first skirmishes of the coming Civil War took place in the Quaker village of Christiana near the Maryland border when a slave owner came hunting for his runaways. When he and his sons found their slaves in a home on September 11, 1851, he was killed in a shootout. "The Battle of Christiana" was, according to a Pennsylvania newspaper, "the first blow struck."

Philadelphia

INDEPENDENCE NATIONAL HISTORICAL PARK *(Market and Sixth Streets; 215-597-8947; www.nps.gov/inde)*   The theories of an experimental democracy were written into two documents—the Declaration of Independence and the Constitution—in this area preserved as a national park. Thomas Jefferson's first draft of the Declaration was written in June 1776 in an upstairs room of a house at Seventh and Market Streets. That house, now called the Declaration House, and forty other buildings tell the story of the founding of the United States. The full promise of those documents was finally delivered by the civil rights movement.

Philadelphia is home to a number of icons and stories important in the human rights struggle: Benjamin Franklin, who tried to get Congress to outlaw slavery; Quakers and other abolitionists who founded integrated schools and stirred the pot before the Civil War; Mother Bethel AME Church, the American Missionary Association, and other denominations that founded educational institutions and schools specifically for freed slaves and served as moral compasses; and the Liberty Bell, the most famous symbol of America's founding, which began life as the Old State House bell and was renamed "Liberty Bell" by abolitionists before the American Revolution.

During the Jim Crow segregation era, Philadelphia became a restricted city for blacks, and earned the nickname "The northern-most southern city." A long period of activism over police brutality, integration, and equal opportunity began in the 1960s.

Innumerable brochures, programs, and guided tours can be chosen at the visitors center. A Philadelphia Civil Rights Struggle tour of north Philadelphia runs periodically from the visitors center.

MOTHER BETHEL AME CHURCH *(419 Sixth Street; 215-925-0616; tours by appointment only)* A grand and stately church near Independence Hall, this was the first church of the first black religious denomination in the United States. Founder Richard Allen had been born a slave, but found religion and convinced his owner to free him. He bought this lot in 1793 and built the church on it. Allen and Absalom Jones, another freed slave, also formed the Free African Society, a charity and activist group that fought plans to send blacks back to Africa. In 1830 the AME denomination's first national convention was held here at the "mother" church to tackle segregation, disenfranchisement, and slavery. Allen is buried in the basement, near a museum.

GIRARD COLLEGE *(2101 South College; 215-787-2600; www.girardcollege.edu)* In 1968 this school for orphaned white boys became a cause célèbre when the NAACP organized a nine-month protest to integrate it. The school had been established by wealthy banker Stephen Girard whose will only allowed white orphan boys in grades one through twelve. The school was surrounded by a massive stone wall, in what had become an all-black neighborhood, and the administration resisted efforts to integrate. The NAACP's "March to the Wall" campaign was led by Cecil B. Moore. A court suit in 1968 forced the school to admit black boys. Later, girls were admitted.

PROGRESS PLAZA (*1501 Broad Street*) In 1968 the Reverend Leon Sullivan of the Zion Baptist Church opened Progress Plaza, the city's first black-owned shopping center. Called the "Lion of Zion," Sullivan is best known for his Sullivan's Principles, written in 1977 to encourage corporations to support "universal human rights" and stop trading with South Africa. The principles were a cornerstone of the international campaign that forced an end to apartheid. Twenty years later, Sullivan created a similar set of global principles of social responsibility.

As this book went to press, a number of new memorials were planned. To update information, to suggest sites, or to comment, please write: *jimcarrier@msn.com*.

Bibliography

Anderson, James. *The Education of Blacks in the South*. University of North Carolina Press, 1988.

Angelou, Maya. *I Know Why the Caged Bird Sings*. Bantam Books, 1983.

Aptheker, Herbert. *American Negro Slave Revolts*. International Publishers, 1993.

Ashe, Arthur. *A Hard Road to Glory: A History of the African American Athlete*. Penguin Books, 1993.

Bailey, Richard. *Neither Carpetbaggers nor Skalawags: Black Officeholders During the Reconstruction of Alabama*. R. Bailey Publishers, 1991.

Bass, Jack and Jack Nelson. *The Orangeburg Massacre*. Mercer University Press, 1996.

Berlin, Ira. *Many Thousands Gone: The First Two Centuries of Slavery in North America*. Harvard University Press, 1998.

Bennett, Jr., Lerone. *Before the Mayflower: A History of Black America*. Penguin Books, 1988.

Blight, David W. *Race and Reunion: The Civil War in American Memory*. Harvard University Press, 2001.

Bond, Julian and Andrew Lewis (eds). *Gonna Sit at the Welcome Table*. American Heritage/Custom Publishing, 1995.

Branch, Taylor. *Parting the Waters: America in the King Years 1954–63.* Touchstone/Simon & Schuster, 1988.

——. *Pillar of Fire: America in the King Years 1963–65.* Touchstone/Simon & Schuster, 1999.

Bryant, Isa. *We Florida.* Palm Beach Post, 1996.

Brinkley, David. *Rosa Parks.* Viking, 2000.

Bullard, Sara. *Free At Last: A History of the Civil Rights Movement and Those Who Died in the Struggle.* Oxford University Press, 1993.

Cecelski, David. *Along Freedom Road: Hyde County, North Carolina, and the Fate of Black Schools in the South.* University of North Carolina Press, 1994.

——. *The Waterman's Song: Slavery and Freedom in Maritime North Carolina.* University of North Carolina Press, 2001.

Chafe, William. *Civilities and Civil Rights.* Oxford University Press, 1981.

Chafe, William, Raymond Gavings, and Robert Korstad (eds). *Remembering Jim Crow: African Americans Tell about Life in the Segregated South.* New Press, 2001.

Cheseborough, Steve. *Blues Traveling: The Holy Sites of Delta Blues.* University Press of Mississippi, 2001.

Colburn, David. *Racial Change and Community Crisis.* University of Florida Press, 1991.

Colburn, David, and Jane Landers (eds). *The African American Heritage of Florida.* University Press of Florida, 1997.

Crow, Jeffrey, Paul Escott, and Flora Hatley. *A History of African Americans in North Carolina.* North Carolina Division of Archives and History, 1992.

Curry, Constance. *Silver Rights.* Harvest Books, 1995.

Curtis, Nancy. *Black Heritage Sites: The North.* The New Press, 1996.

——. *Black Heritage Sites: The South.* The New Press, 1996.

Davison, Chandler, and Bernard Grofman (eds.). *Quiet Revolution in the South: The Impact of the Voting Rights Act 1965–1990.* Princeton University Press, 1994.

Davies, David. *The Press and Race: Mississippi Journalists Confront the Movement.* University Press of Mississippi, 2001.

Davis, Townsend. *Weary Feet, Rested Souls: A Guided History of the Civil Rights Movement.* W.W. Norton, 1998.

Derr, Mark. *Some Kind of Paradise: A Chronicle of Man and the Land in Florida*. University Press of Florida, 1998.

Dees, Morris. *A Lawyer's Journey: The Morris Dees Story*. American Bar Association, 2001.

Dittmer, John. *Local People: The Struggle for Civil Rights in Mississippi*. University of Illinois Press, 1994.

Douglas, Marjory Stoneman. *Everglades: River of Grass*. Pineapple Press, 1988.

―――. *Florida: The Long Frontier*. Harper & Row, 1967.

D'Orso, Michael. *Like Judgment Day*. Boulevard Books, 1996.

Doyle, William. *An American Insurrection: The Battle of Oxford, Mississippi, 1962*. Random House, 2001.

Du Bois, W. E. B. *The Souls of Black Folk*. Dover Publications, 1994.

Dunn, Marvin. *Black Miami in the Twentieth Century*. University Press of Florida, 1997.

Egerton, Douglas. *Gabriel's Rebellion: The Virginia Slave Conspiracies of 1800 and 1802*. University of North Carolina Press, 1993.

Ellis, Joseph J. *Founding Brothers: The Revolutionary Generation*. Vintage, 2002.

Erenrich, Susie (ed.). *Freedom Is a Constant Struggle: An Anthology of the Mississippi Civil Rights Movement*. Black Belt Press, 1999.

Escott, Colin, with Martin Hawkins. *Good Rockin' Tonight: Sun Records and the Birth of Rock 'n' Roll*. St. Martin's Press, 1991.

Fairclough, Adam. *Race and Democracy: The Civil Rights Struggle in Louisiana 1915–1972*. University of Georgia Press, 1999.

Fitzpatrick, Sandra, and Maria Goodwin. *The Guide to Black Washington*. Hippocrene Books, 2001.

Flynt, Wayne, William Rogers, Robert Ward, and Leah Atkins. *Alabama: The History of a Deep South State*. University of Alabama Press, 1994.

Foner, Eric. *Reconstruction: America's Unfinished Revolution 1863–1877*. Harper & Row, 1988.

Frank, Andrew. *The Routledge Historical Atlas of the American South*. Routledge, 1999.

Franklin, John Hope, and Alfred Moss Jr. *From Slavery to Freedom: A History of African Americans*. Alfred Knopf, 1994.

Fullerton, Christopher. *Every Other Sunday*. Boozer Press, 1999.

Glatthaar, Joseph. *The Civil War's Black Soldiers.* Eastern National Park and Monument Association, 1996.

Graham, Patterson. *A Right to Read: Segregation and Civil Rights in Alabama's Public Libraries.* University of Alabama Press, 2002.

Grant, Donald. *The Way It Was in the South: The Black Experience in Georgia.* University of Georgia Press, 2001.

Grant, Joanne. *Ella Baker: Freedom Bound.* John Wiley & Sons, 1998.

Guralnick, Peter. *Sweet Soul Music: Rhythm and Blues and the Southern Dream of Freedom.* Little, Brown & Company, 1999.

———. *Last Train to Memphis: The Rise of Elvis Presley.* Little, Brown & Company, 1994.

Halberstam, David. *The Children.* Random House, 1998.

Haley, Alex. *Roots.* Dell, 1976.

Ham, Debra Newman (ed.). *The African American Odyssey.* Library of Congress, 1998.

Haskins, James, and Joanne Biondi. *The Historic Black South.* Hippocrene Books, 1993.

Horton, James, and Lois Horton. *Hard Road to Freedom: The Story of African America.* Rutgers University Press, 2001.

Hurston, Zora Neale. *Their Eyes Were Watching God.* University of Illinois Press, 1995.

———. *Dust Tracks on a Road.* Harper Perennial, 1995.

Jackson, Harvey H., III. *Rivers of History: Life on the Coosa, Tallapoose, Cahaba and Alabama.* University of Alabama Press, 1995.

Jacoway, Elizabeth, Dan Carter, Lester Lamon, Robert McMath (eds.). *The Adaptable South.* Louisiana State University Press, 1991.

Jones, Maxine, and Kevin McCarthy. *African Americans in Florida.* Pineapple Press, 1993.

Kasher, Steven. *The Civil Rights Movement: A Photographic History, 1954–68.* Abbeville Press, 1996.

Kennedy, Frances (ed.). *The Civil War Battlefield Guide.* Houghton Mifflin, 1998.

Kennedy, Stetson. *After Appomattox: How the South Won the War.* University Press of Florida, 1995.

———. *Jim Crow Guide.* Florida Atlantic University Press, 1990.

King, Martin Luther, Jr. *A Call to Conscience: The Landmark Speeches of Dr. Martin Luther King Jr.* Time Warner Audio Books, 2001.

Kluger, Richard. *Simple Justice.* Vintage Books, 1977.

Lewis, Anthony. *Gideon's Trumpet.* Vintage Books, 1989.

Lewis, Jan Ellen, and Peter S. Onuf (eds.). *Sally Hemings & Thomas Jefferson: History, Memory and Civic Culture.* University Press of Virginia, 1999.

Lewis, John. *Walking with the Wind: A Memoir of the Movement.* Harcourt, 1998.

Madigan, Tim. *The Burning: Massacre, Destruction, and the Tulsa Race Riot in 1921.* St. Martin's Press, 2001.

MacGregor, Morris Jr. *Integration of the Armed Forces 1940–1965.* U.S. Government Printing Office, 1981.

McPherson, James. M. *Battle Cry of Freedom: The Civil War Era.* Oxford University Press, 1988.

McWhorter, Diane. *Carry Me Home.* Simon & Schuster, 2001.

Morgan, Edmund S. *American Slavery, American Freedom: The Ordeal of Colonial Virginia.* W.W. Norton & Company, 1975.

Mykle, Robert. *Killer 'Cane: The Deadline Hurricane of 1928.* Cooper Square Press, 2002.

Nash, Gary B. *Red, White & Black: The Peoples of Early North America.* University of California, 2000.

Newby, I. A. *Black Carolinians: A History of Blacks in South Carolina from 1895 to 1968.* University of South Carolina Press, 1973.

Norrell, Robert. *Reaping the Whirlwind: The Civil Rights Movement in Tuskegee.* University of North Carolina Press, 1998.

Opala, Joseph. *The Gullah.* Eastern National/National Park Service, 2000.

O'Reilly, Kenneth. *Nixon's Piano: Presidents and Racial Politics from Washington to Clinton.* Free Press, 1995.

Porter, Kenneth. *The Black Seminoles.* University of Florida Press, 1996.

Prather, Leon. *We Have Taken a City.* Farleigh Dickenson University Press, 1983.

Rabby, Glenda. *The Pain and the Promise: The Struggle for Civil Rights in Tallahassee, Florida.* University of Georgia Press, 1999.

Rampersad, Arnold. *Jackie Robinson.* Alfred A. Knopf, 1997.

Randel, William Peirce. *The Ku Klux Klan: A Century of Infamy.* Chilton, 1965.

Remini, Robert. *Andrew Jackson and His Indian Wars.* Penguin Books, 2002.

Rose, Willie Lee. *Rehearsal for Reconstruction: The Port Royal Experiment.* University of Georgia Press, 1999.

Rubin, Louis. *Virginia: A Bicentennial History.* Norton, 1977.

Rymer, Russ. *American Beach.* Harper Perennial, 2000.

Savage, Beth, (ed.). *African American Historic Places.* The Preservation Press, 1994.

Savage, Curt. *Standing Soldiers, Kneeling Slaves.* Princeton University Press, 1999.

Sears, Stephen. *Landscape Turned Red: The Battle of Antietam.* Ticknor & Fields, 1983.

Thornton, J. Mills. *Dividing Lines.* University of Alabama Press, 2002.

Torres, Sasha. *Black, White and in Color: Television and Black Civil Rights.* Princeton University Press, 2003.

Tyson, Timothy. *Radio Free Dixie.* University of North Carolina Press, 1999.

Wadelington, Charles, and Richard Knapp. *Charlotte Hawkins Brown.* University of North Carolina Press, 1999.

Washington, Booker T. *Up From Slavery.* Signet, 2000.

Williams, Eric. *From Columbus to Castro.* Vintage, 1984.

Williams, Juan. *Eyes on the Prize: America's Civil Rights Years 1954–1965.* Penguin Books, 1988.

Williams, Lou Falknew. *The Great South Carolina Ku Klux Klan Trials, 1871–1872.* University of Georgia Press, 1996.

Wills, Gary. *Lincoln at Gettysburg: The Words That Remade America.* Simon & Schuster, 1993.

WPA. *The WPA Guide to 1930s Alabama.* University of Alabama Press, 2000.

———. *The Negro in Virginia.* John F. Blair, 1994.

Wright, Roberta. *The Birth of the Montgomery Bus Boycott.* Charro Books, 1991.

Zinn, Howard. *A People's History of the United States, 1492–Present.* Perennial Classic, 2001.

Acknowledgments

In 1996, Bonnie Gilbert, a senior editorial assistant at the *Denver Post,* told me of an unusual vacation she had taken through the South to visit civil rights sites. She had read several histories of the movement, plotted the scenes on maps, and charted an itinerary. She was in the vanguard of what is known as heritage tourism.

Three years later, I found myself in Montgomery, Alabama, doing civil rights work, and witnessing scores of people on similar pilgrimages. They often wandered around, because signposts were few and far between. I borrowed Gilbert's idea for this guidebook, and I thank her.

For initial guidance, site nominations, and the recommendation that I take a broad view of civil rights history, I thank James Horton, Debra Newman Ham, Dwight Pitcaithley, John Sprinkle, Jr., Heather Huyck, Skip Thomas, Roger Kennedy, Frances Kennedy, Jerry Eisterhold, and Spencer Crew. My editor, Kati Hesford, remained patient and enthusiastic as the book grew.

I traveled to virtually every site, accompanied by a seat full of books. To the civil rights pioneers, especially U.S. Representative John Lewis, and writers and historians who witnessed events or did the hard work of preserving these compelling stories, I am indebted. Many are quoted in the text, and listed in the bibliography. I found that many state and local travel bureaus are attempting to commemorate this history, but their drum major is Frances Smiley of the Alabama Bureau of Tourism and Travel.

Thanks to the Southern Poverty Law Center for supporting initial research. To my former colleagues—Penny Weaver, Kelvin Datcher, Jim Carnes, Sara Bullard, Richard Cohen and Morris Dees, especially—I am grateful for support, feedback, and friendship. Librarians Vincent Thacker and Jeanne Holladay went out of their way to help, as did Jerry Mitchell of the Jackson, Mississippi, *Clarion-Ledger*. Through two years of research and writing, my partner Trish O'Kane was a daily supporter, editor, and conscience.

Index

Aaron, Edward, 220
Aaron, Hank, 150, 184, 224, 230–31
  Hank Aaron Stadium (Mobile, AL),
    230–31
Abbott, Robert, 69, 141–42
Abernathy, Ralph, 118, 152, 166, 221,
  243–44, 248
  First Baptist Church (Montgomery, AL),
    240, 242, 243–44
Accomack County, VA, 41–42
Adams, Clinton, 156
Adams, Lewis, 253
African American Civil War Monument
  (Washington, D.C.), 26–27
African American monument (Savannah,
  GA), 159
African Meeting House (Boston, MA), 345
Afro-American (newspaper), 69, 341, 342
Afro-American Life Insurance Company
  (Jacksonville, FL), 190, 191–93, 194
Agee, James, 216
Agnew, Spiro, 343
Alabama, 210, 211–55
  Anniston, 219–20
  Birmingham, 220–24
  Florence-Muscle Shoals, 224–25
  Greensboro, 225–27
  Hayneville, 226–27
  Marion, 227–28
  Mobile, 228–31

  Montgomery, 231–45
  Scottsboro, 245
  secession of, 214
  Selma, 160, 246–51
  Tuscaloosa, 252
  Tuskegee, 28, 252–55
Alabama Music Hall of Fame (Tuscumbia,
  AL), 225
Alabama State University (Montgomery, AL),
  228, 236–37, 244–45
Albany, GA, 145–48
Albany Civil Rights Movement Museum at
  old Mt. Zion Church (Albany, GA),
  146–47
Albany Movement, 145–48
Alcorn State University (Lorman, MS), 277
Alexander, Archer, 22
Alexander, Avery, 300, 305
  Memorial (New Orleans, LA), 304–5
Alexander, Fred, 81–82
Alexander, Kelly, 81–82
Alexandria, VA, 41–43
Alexandria/Black History Resources Center
  (Alexandria, VA), 42
Algonquin Indians, 56
Allen, Louis, 89
Allen, Richard, 351
All Star Bowling Lanes (Orangeburg, SC),
  129
Allwright, S. E., 20

Index

Alpha Phi Alpha fraternity, 9
American Beach (Amelia Island, FL), 189, 193–94
American Civil Liberties Union (ACLU), 68
American Colonization Society, 51
American Missionary Association, 53, 98, 103–4, 276, 331, 351
American Tennis Association (ATA), 58–59, 104
Amerson, Lucius, 253
Amnesty International, 104
Amoros, Sandy, 183
Amsterdam News (New York), 69
Amzie Moore's gas station (Cleveland, MS), 264
Anacostia Museum and Center for African American culture (Washington, D.C.), 13
Anderson, James, 95–96
Anderson, Marian, 11–12
Anderson, Robert, 119
Angelou, Maya, 159, 310
Annapolis, MD, 340–41
Anniston, AL, 219–20
Antietam Battlefield (MD), 7, 31
Appomattox Court House (Appomattox, VA), 42–44
Aptheker, Herbert, 47, 89
Arcade and Fifth Avenue Historic District (Nashville, TN), 330
Arkansas, 290, 308–13
Arkansas Industrial Development Commission, 310–11
Arkansas State Press, 310
Armfield, John, 42
Armstrong, James, 222
Armstrong, Louis, 302, 305, 307
Armstrong, Samuel, 54
Armstrong Park (New Orleans, LA), 301–2
Arnold, Morris, 308
Arrington, Richard, 222, 223–24
Aryan Nations, 239
Ashe, Arthur, 58–59, 182–84
  Memorial (Richmond, VA), 65–66
Ashe, Samuel, 65
Ashmore, Harry, 312
Association for the Study of Negro Life and History, 3, 26
Atlanta, GA, 148–55
Atlanta Braves, 150
Atlanta-Clark University Center (Atlanta, GA), 154
Atlanta Daily World, 153
Atlanta University, 154
Atlanta World, 69
Atlantic Life Insurance Company, 148–49
Attucks, Crispus, 14, 344

Memorial and Grave (Boston, MA), 345
Auburn Avenue (Atlanta, GA), 153
Ax Handle Saturday Memorial (Jacksonville, FL), 190–91
Axton, Estelle, 326

Baez, Joan, 133, 245, 251, 325
Bailey, Cornelia, 157
Bailey, Richard, 120
Baker, Ella, 79, 93, 166
Baker, Frank, 53
Baker, John, Jr., 92
Ball, Thomas, 22
Baltimore, MD, 341–43
Banneker, Benjamin, 341
Banneker-Douglass Museum (Annapolis, MD), 341
Barbershop (Greenwood, MS), 268
Barnes, Roy, 144
Barnett, Ross, 269, 283
Barry, Marion, 3, 21, 93–94, 332
Barton, Clara, 51
Bass, Jack, 129
Bates, Daisy, 310, 312–13
Bates, L. C., 310
Baton Rouge, LA, 295–98
"Battle Hymn of the Republic" (song), 237
Battle of Liberty Square (New Orleans, LA; 1866), 292–93, 303
Baxley, William, 223
Beale Street (Memphis, TN), 322–23
Beaufort, SC, 114
Beauregard, Pierre, 110
Bechet, Sidney, 302
Belafonte, Harry, 150, 251, 267
Belle Glade, FL, 177–80
Belton, Ethel, 338
Bennett College (Greensboro, NC), 83, 85
Bennett, Edward, 41
Bennett, Lerone, Jr., 162
Berea, KY, 339–40
Berea College (Berea, KY), 339–40
Berendt, John, 157
Bergman, Walter, 241
Berks, Robert, 23
Berlin, Ira, 109, 204, 291
Beschloss, Michael, 16
Bethune, Mary McLeod
  Home (Daytona Beach, FL), 185
  Home (Washington, D.C.), 23, 25–26
  sculpture in Lincoln Park (Washington, D.C.), 23, 185
Betsch, MaVynee, 193, 194
Bevel, James, 221, 328
Bickett, Thomas, 76
Bigelow, Albert, 132, 241
Bilbo, Theodore, 273

364

Bill of Rights (National Archives, Washington, D.C.), 4–6
Biloxi, MS, 261
Birmingham, AL, 220–24
Birmingham Barons, 224
Birmingham Civil Rights Institute (Birmingham, AL), 221–22
Birth of a Nation (film), 15
Bishop, Gardner, 26, 338
Bishop, Judine, 26
Black Archives, History and Research Foundation of South Florida (Miami, FL), 197–98, 208
Black Awareness Coordinating Committee, 128
Black Barons, 224
Black Heritage Trail, 345
Black History Month, 26, 150, 340
Black History Museum & Cultural Center (Richmond, VA), 64
Black Horse Cavalry, 141
Black Panthers, 227
Black Patriots Memorial (proposed; D.C.), 13–14
Blair, Ezell, Jr., 83, 85
Blake, Harry, 308
Blake, James, 216, 233
Blanton, Thomas, Jr., 223
Blind Phillip, 122
Block, Margaret, 89
Block, Sam, 266–67
Bloody Sunday (1965), 71, 160, 218, 227–28, 246–48
Blunt, Samuel, 48
Bogalusa, LA, 298–99
Bolling, Spottswood, Jr., 338
Bolling v. Sharpe, 338
Bond, Julian, 143, 150
Booker T. and the MGs, 326
Booker T. Washington High School (Miami, FL), 198
Booker T. Washington National Monument (Hardy, VA), 54
Booth, John Wilkes, 10
Boston, MA, 27, 344–46
Boston Massacre (1770), 344
Boston University, 186
Bowers, Sam, 270, 280
Boyle, Sarah, 44
Boynton, Amelia, 249–50
Boynton, Bruce, 20
Boynton, Sam, 249–50
Boynton v. Virginia, 20, 240–41
Branch, Taylor, 13, 67, 85, 93, 121, 148, 161, 162, 167, 234, 311, 324, 329, 330
Braxton, Sadie, 189–90
Bredesen, Phil, 331

Bremer, Arthur, 340
Brenston, Jackie, 326
Brewer, Bessie, 322
Brewster, Ann, 308
Bridges, Ruby, 306–7
Briggs, Harry, 112, 133–34, 337–38
Briggs-Delaine Foundation, 134
Briggs v. Elliott, 112, 124, 126, 133–34, 337–38
Brinkley, Douglas, 216
Broad Street Park (Greenwood, MS), 268
Brooke, Edward, 25
Brooklyn Dodgers, 181–84
Brooks, Preston, 110
Brookshire, Stanford, 82
Brotherhood of Sleeping Car Porters, 24
Brown, Charlotte Hawkins, 166
    Historic site (Sedalia, NC), 98
Brown, H. Rap, 128, 340, 343–44
Brown, Henry "Box," 61, 348
Brown, J. Arthur, 115
Brown, John, 335, 339
    Cabin (Osawatomie, KS), 339
    Harpers Ferry (WV), 30–31, 335
Brown, John (Dr.), 196
Brown, Leonard, 297
Brown, Linda, 336–39
Brown, Mike, 58
Brown, Millicent, 115
Brown, Minniejean, 312
Brown, Oliver, 336–37
Brown, Sage, 162–63
Brown Chapel AME Church and Civil Rights Walking Tour (Selma, AL), 248–49
Brown v. Board of Education National Historic Site (Topeka, KS), 335–36
Brown v. Board of Education of Topeka, 17–19, 20, 24, 49, 69–70, 77–78, 124, 133, 222, 305, 310, 311, 324, 332, 335–39
Bruce, Blanche, 258
Bryan, Andrew, 160
Bryant, Bear, 252
Bryant, Roy, 279
Buchanan, James, 119
Bunche, Ralph, 24
Burlington, NC, 81
Burns, Ken, 32
Burris, Bryon, 299
Burroughs, Theresa, 226
Bush, George W., 14, 175–76
Bushnell, FL, 180–81
Butler, Benjamin, 53, 298
Butler, Frank, 205
Byrd, Harry, 50

Cabbage Row (Charleston, SC), 123
Cailloux, Andre, 298

Cain, Bobby, 315
Calhoun, John C., 110, 116, 122–23
Callender, James, 45
Calvert, George (Lord Baltimore), 340
Cambridge, MD, 343–44
Cambridge Accord (1963), 343
Cambridge Nonviolent Action Group, 343
Camier, Stephen, 303
Campanella, Roy, 182, 183
Campbell, "Cull," 145
Campbell, Ralph, Jr., 94
Campbell, William, 92
Cape Fear Museum (Wilmington, NC), 105
Capital Savings Bank (Washington, D.C.), 282
Carawan, Guy, 324, 328, 331
Carmichael, Stokely, 128, 166, 226, 227, 268, 283–84
Carnegie, Andrew, 55, 254
Carney, William, 120
"Carry Me Back to Old Virginia" (song), 39
Carter, Clarence, 225
Carter, Jimmy, 121, 138, 143–44
Carver, George Washington, 252, 254
Cash, Johnny, 326
Casor, John, 41
Caston, Billy Jack, 277
Catfish Alley (Charleston, SC), 123
Cecelski, David, 98–99
Center for Political and Economic Studies, 289
Central High School National Historic site (Little Rock, AK), 15, 310, 311–13
Century Funeral Home (Greenwood, MS), 268
Chafe, William, 74, 85, 96
Chambers, Julius, 81–82
Chambliss, Robert "Dynamite Bob," 223
Chaney, James, 259, 284
  Gravesite (Meridian, MS), 278–79
Chappell, Johnnie Mae, 190
Charles, Ray, 189, 324
Charleston, SC, 114–27
Charlotte, NC, 81–82
Charlotte Hawkins Brown Historic site (Sedalia, NC), 98
Charlottesville, VA, 44–46
Charlotte Three, 82
Chase, Judith, 122
Chase, Salmon, 132
Chavis, Ben, 79, 101, 103
Chavis, John, 91–92
Cherokee, 139–40, 313–14
Cherry, Bobby Frank, 223
Chesapeake Indians, 53

Chesnut, J. L., 248
Chicago Cubs, 182
Chicago Defender, 69, 141–42
Chickasaw, 313–14
Chicken George, 318
Cincinnati, OH, 348–49
Citadel Parade Ground and Park (Charleston, SC), 122–23
Citizens Councils, 131
  in Alabama, 217, 247
  in Louisiana, 293–94, 295, 307
  in Mississippi, 259, 266, 267, 271, 276, 337
  in South Carolina, 131
City Hall (New Orleans, LA), 304–5
City of St. Jude/Selma-to-Montgomery voting rights march visitors center (Montgomery, AL), 245
Civil Rights Act (1866), 17, 273
Civil Rights Act (1957), 21, 317
Civil Rights Act (1964), 1, 10, 17, 21, 68, 71, 129, 143, 150, 194, 203, 217, 250, 298, 299
Civil Rights Memorial (Montgomery, AL), 238–39
Clarendon County, SC, 337–38
Clark, Felton, 296, 297
Clark, Jim, 249, 250, 251
Clark, Joe, 187
Clark, Kenneth, 108, 134, 338
Clark, Nerie, 120–21
Clark, Septima, 166
  citizenship schools and, 124–25, 133, 165
  Gullah culture and, 112, 121–22, 124–25
  at Highlander School, TN, 121, 125, 328
  Memorial (Charleston, SC), 120, 121–22
Clark Memorial Methodist Church (Nashville, TN), 329–30, 332
Clarksdale, MS, 262–63
Clarksdale's Delta Blues Museum (Clarksdale, MS), 262–63
Clement, Frank, 315
Cleveland, MS, 263–64
Clinton, Bill, 52, 229, 240, 251, 253, 255, 311, 313
Coachman, Alice, 184
Cobb, Ty, 224
Coca-Cola Company, 138
Code Noire (black code of 1724), 291
Coffin, Levi, 348–49
Cohen, Bernard, 68
Colburn, David, 174–75, 203–5
Cole, James "Catfish," 78, 88
Cole, Johnnetta, 193
Cole, Nat King, 220
Coleman, Tom, 226
Coles, Robert, 306

Collins, Addie Mae, 223
Collins, LeRoy, 175, 188, 207
Collins, Sarah, 223
Colored Farmers' Alliance, 142
Columbia, SC, 126–27
Colvin, Claudette, 216
Commission for Racial Justice, United
    Church of Christ, 103–4
Committee of 100, 158
Confederate States of America, 53, 110, 140,
    214, 231, 233, 258, 292, 314, 333
Conference on Negro Problems, 154
Congo, 125
Congo Square (New Orleans, LA), 301–2
Congressional Medal of Honor, 62, 67, 120,
    181
Congress of Racial Equality (CORE), 52, 96,
    196, 207, 240–41, 278, 284, 294, 299,
    308
Connor, Bull, 71, 211, 217, 220, 221, 241–42
Conroy, Pat, 135
Contanchobee Park (Tampa, FL), 209
Cooke, Sam, 262, 325
Cooper, Annie Lee, 250
Cornmeal, Sonny Boy, 309
Cornwell, Rudy, 116
Clotilde slave ship, 229, 230
Council of Federated Organizations, 262
Council of Laborers, 142
Courthouse Square and Fountain
    (Montgomery, AL), 232–33
Courtland, VA, 46–48
Cowling, Eli, 241
Cox, Elton, 296
Cox, Minnie, 272
Craft, Ellen, 140, 344, 348
Craft, William, 344
Creek, 171, 213, 313–14
Creswell, NC, 82–83
Crimson Tide, 252
Crosby, Emily, 286
Crowe, James, 333
Crown-Zellerbach plant, 298–99
Culmer, John, 196
Cunningham, Sam "Bam," 252
Curtis, Archie, 280
Cuthbert-Kerr, Simon, 166

Dade, Francis, 180, 209
Dade Battlefield (Bushnell, FL), 180–81
Dahmer, Vernon, gravesite (Hattiesburg,
    MS), 269–70
Daily Record (North Carolina), 100–101, 103
Dallas County Courthouse (Selma, AL), 249,
    250
Daniels, Jonathan, 226–27
Darden, Colgate, 44

Daughters of the American Revolution, 12
Davies, David, 70
Davies, Lawrence, 51
Davis, Abraham Lincoln, 300, 304
    Park (New Orleans, LA), 304
Davis, Dorothy, 338
Davis, Jefferson, 51, 53, 63, 214, 233, 236, 258
Davis, Sammy, Jr., 245
Davis Library, The (Mobile, AL), 229
*Davis v. County School Board of Prince
    Edward County,* 338
Day, Thomas, House (Milton, NC), 88–89
Daytona Beach, FL, 181–86
Daytona Cubs, 182
Deacons for Defense, 90, 298, 299
Dearborn, MI, 347
Declaration of Independence (National
    Archives, Washington, D.C.), 3–4, 107,
    350
    Jefferson and, 3–4, 8, 35–36, 38, 45, 350
Decoration Day, 115
Dee, Henry, 280, 285
Dees, Morris, 80, 229, 238–39
Defenders of State Sovereignty and
    Individual Liberty, 50
De La Beckwith, Byron, 260, 276
DeLaine, Joseph, 134
Delaney, Elizabeth "Bessie," 94
Delaney, Sarah, 94
Delaware, Wilmington, 338
DePasquale, Paul, 61, 62
Derr, Mark, 171, 173
de Sousa, Mathias, 340
Detroit, MI, 346–47
Dexter Avenue King Memorial Church
    (Montgomery, AL), 49, 234–36, 244
Dexter King Parsonage (Montgomery, AL),
    237–38
Diggs, Charles, 262
Dinkins, David, 25
Dittmer, John, 89, 267, 271, 285
"Dixie" (song), 44
Doar, John, 299, 317
Donald, Beulah Mae, 239
Donald, Michael, 229, 239
Dorchester Academy (Savannah, GA), 165
Dorsey, Dana, 197
Dorsey, George, 29
Dorsey, Hugh, 141
Dorsey, May, 155–56
D'Orso, Michael, 201
Douglas, Marjory Stoneman, 172, 173, 177
Douglas, Stephen, 110
Douglass, Frederick, 21–22, 27, 340, 341,
    342–43, 345, 348
    Home (Washington, DC), 21–22
    Marker (Annapolis, MD), 342–43

Doyle, William, 16, 30, 271, 283
Drayton, John, 125–26
Drayton Hall (Charleston, SC), 125–26
Du Bois, W. E. B., 55, 59, 89, 123, 131, 137, 141, 149, 154, 332
Duke, David, 294
Dunbar Junior and Senior High School (Little Rock, AK), 309, 313
Dunleith Mansion (Natchez, MS), 282
Dunn, Marvin, 195, 199
Dwight, Ed, 13, 127, 340
Dylan, Bob, 325

Early, Gerald, 293
Eaton, Hubert, 58, 101, 104
East High School (Nashville, TN), 332
Eaton, Hubert, 58, 101, 104
  Home (Wilmington, NC), 104–5
Eaton, Josiah, 186
Eatonville, FL, 186–87
Ebenezer Baptist Church (Atlanta, GA), 150, 153–54
Eckford, Elizabeth, 312, 313
Edgar, Walter, 108
Edmund Pettus Bridge (Selma, AL), 246–47, 251
Edwards, Edwin, 294
Egerton, Douglas, 60
1898 Memorial Park (Wilmington, NC), 102
Eisenhower, Dwight D., 15, 240, 283, 311, 312, 337
Eliot, William, 22
Ellington, Duke, Home (Washington, D.C.), 25
Elliott, Roderick W., 134, 337–38
Ellis, Joseph, 6, 35, 45
Ellsworth, Scott, 349
Elmore, George, 127
Emancipation Proclamation (National Archives, Washington, D.C.), 6–7, 10, 22, 27, 31, 55, 184, 287, 336, 345
Embree, Elihu, 314
Emmanuel AME Church (Charleston, SC), 123
English, William, 171
Espy, Henry, 268
Espy, Mike, 268
Etienne, Gail, 306
Evans, Lillian, 25
Evans, Walker, 216
Evers, Charles, 277, 281
Evers, Medgar, 29, 90, 259, 260, 261, 272–73, 274, 277, 281
  Home and murder site (Jackson, MS), 275–76

Medgar Evers Library (Jackson, MS), 276
Medgar Evers statue (Jackson, MS), 276
Executive Order 8802, 24
Executive Order 9981, 29

Fairclough, Adam, 293–94, 298, 299, 306, 308
Falwell, Jerry, 58
Farish Street (Jackson, MS), 274
Farmer, James, Jr., 241–42, 294
  Home (Fredericksburg, VA), 52
Farmville, VA, 48–50, 338
Faubus, Orville, 310–11, 312
Faulkner, William, 280
Featherstone, Ralph, 343
Federal Court (Charleston, SC), 123–24
Fee, John, 339
Ferguson, John, 293
Fields, Louis, 343
Fifty-fourth Massachusetts Regiment, 27, 28, 119–20, 345
Fillmore, Millard, 344
First African Baptist Church (Savannah, GA), 160
First Baptist Church (Montgomery, AL), 240, 242, 243–44
First Baptist Church (Petersburg, VA), 67
First Baptist Church site (Nashville, TN), 330
First Landing State Park (Hampton/Norfolk, VA), 53
Fisk, Clinton, 331
Fisk University (Nashville, TN), 96, 161, 331–32
Fist, The (Detroit, MI), 346
Fitzpatrick, Sandra, 25
Flagler, Henry, 173, 194
Fleming, Francis, 172
Florence-Muscle Shoals, AL, 224–25
Florida, 168, 169–209
  Belle Glade, 177–80
  Bushnell, 180–81
  Daytona Beach, 181–86
  Eatonville, 186–87
  Groveland, 187–88
  Jacksonville, 188–94
  Miami, 194–99
  Mims, 199–200
  Ocoee, 200
  Rosewood, 200–202
  St. Augustine, 202–5
  Tallahassee, 205–8
  Tampa, 208–9
Florida A&M University (Tallahassee, FL), 161, 208
Floyd, Harry, 129
Floyd, James, 160

Floyd, John, 47
Flynt, Wayne, 217
Foner, Eric, 89, 161, 172, 303, 309
Ford, Harold, 321
Ford, Henry, Museum (Detroit, MI), 347
Forrest, Nathan Bedford, 333
Forrest County Courthouse (Hattiesburg,
    MS), 268–69
Fort Mill (Columbia, SC), 127
Fort Monroe/Freedom's Fort (Hampton, VA),
    38, 53–54
Fort Mose (St. Augustine, FL), 204
Fort Sumter (Charleston, SC), 110, 114, 119,
    233, 314
Fort Wagner site (Charleston, SC), 27,
    119–20, 345
Foster, William, 230
Founding Fathers, 5–7, 8, 26, 35–38,
    44–45, 164, 350–51
Franklin, Aretha, 225, 325
Franklin, Benjamin, 350–51
Franklin, Isaac, 42
Franklin, John Hope, 3, 19, 20, 38, 139, 164,
    332, 335, 337, 349
Franklin and Armfield slave trading firm
    (Alexandria, VA), 42
Frantz, William J., William J. Frantz school
    (New Orleans, LA), 306–7
Frederick Douglass marker (Annapolis, MD),
    342–43
Fredericksburg, VA, 50–51
Free African Society, 351
Freedmen's Bureau, 24, 54, 89, 95, 162, 172,
    173, 282, 331
Freedom Day (January 22, 1964), 269
Freedom Democratic Party, 287
Freedom Riders, 20, 44, 52, 70, 132, 219,
    220, 222, 239–42, 244, 259, 274,
    275–76
Freedom Singers, 146–47, 148, 324–25
Freedom Summer (1964), 250, 259–60, 261,
    269, 278, 280, 284
Freedom Trail, 345
Freeman, Theophilus, 303
Fugitive Slave Acts, 344, 348
Fullerton, Christopher, 224
F. W. Woolworth Co. store (Greensboro,
    NC), 13, 70, 74, 78, 79, 83, 84–86, 96,
    207, 209, 244, 278, 328, 330

Gabrielle, Daisy, 306
Gabrielle, Jimmy, 306
Gabriel's Rebellion (Richmond, VA), 60–61
Gadsden, Walter, 221
Gaillot, Una, 300–1
Gaines, Lloyd, 20

Gaines v. Canada, 20
Gandhi, Mahatma, 52, 88, 151, 154–5, 183,
    186
Gantt, Harvey, 80, 113
Gardner, Michael, 15
Garner v. Louisiana, 296
Garrido, Juan, 170
Garrison, William Lloyd, 345
Gaston, Paul, 44
Gaston Motel (Birmingham, AL), 221, 222
Gates, William, 183
Gault, Prentiss, 184
Gebhart, Francis, 338
Gebhart v. Belton, 338
Georgetown University, 140
Georgia, 136, 137–67
    Albany, 145–48
    Atlanta, 148–55
    Monroe, 155–56
    Sapelo Island, 156–57
    Savannah, 157–65
    secession of, 140
Georgia Equal Rights Association, 142
Georgia Federation of Colored Women's
    Clubs, 142
Gettysburg Address, 5, 32–33
Gettysburg Battlefield (PA), 32–33
Gibbs, Jonathan, 172
Gibbs, Phillip, 275
Gibson, Althea, 58–59, 65, 101, 104, 105,
    184
Gibson, Theodore, 175, 196, 198
Gilbert, Ralph Mark, 160
    Ralph Mark Gilbert Civil Rights Museum
        (Savannah, GA), 159–60
Gilliam, Jim, 183
Gilliard, Robert, 229
Girard, Stephen, 351–52
Girard College (Philadelphia, PA), 351–52
Glory (film), 27, 120, 345
Gober, Bertha, 277
Godfrey, Donald, 190
Godfrey, Iona, 190
Gomillion, Charles, 253
Gone with the Wind (Mitchell), 148, 149–50,
    213
Goodman, Andrew, 259, 278, 284
Goodwin, Maria, 25
Gordy, Barry, 346–47
Gore, Albert, Jr., 175–76
Gore, Albert, Sr., 315
Gracia Real de Santa Teresa de Mose (FL),
    202
Graham, Edward, 196, 198
Graham, Patterson, 220, 228–29
Graham, Robert, 346

Index

Grant, Donald, 140, 142, 149
Grant, Jehu, 57
Grant, Ulysses S., 22, 43–44, 111, 130, 303
Gravely, Samuel, 29
Graves, G. E., 196
Graves, Louise, 122
Gray, Deborah, 255
Gray, Fred, 253, 255
Great Awakening, 75
Greater Bethel AME Church (Miami, FL), 198
Green, Ernest, 312
Green, James, 275
Greene, Nathanael, 163–64
Greenlee, Charles, 187–88
Green-Meldrim House (Savannah, GA), 162
Greensboro, AL, 225–27
Greensboro, NC, 13, 74, 83–86
  Woolworth store sit-in (1960), 13, 70, 74, 78, 79, 83–86, 96, 207, 244, 261, 328, 330
Greensboro Four, 84–85, 96
Greensboro Historical Museum (Greensboro, NC), 86
Greenwood, MS, 266–68
Greenwood City Hall (Greenwood, MS), 267
Greenwood Cultural Center (Tulsa, OK), 349–50
Gregory, Dick, 267
Gregory Congregational Church (Wilmington, NC), 103–4
Greyhound Bus Station (Jackson, MS), 274
Greyhound Bus terminal/U.S. Courthouse (Montgomery, AL), 239–40
Griffin, John, 269
Griffin, Marvin, 142
Grimes, Willie, 79
Groveland, FL, 187–88
Gullah (Geechee) culture, 112, 113, 120–21, 123, 124–25, 135, 156–57
Gullah Jack, 122
Guralnick, Peter, 324

Habitat for Humanity, 143
Hadley, Phillip, 207
Halberstam, David, 70–71, 317
Haley, Alex, 37, 50–51
  Boyhood Home and Gravesite (Henning, TN), 318
  Kunta Kinte-Alex Haley Memorial (Annapolis, MD), 340
Hall, Rick, 225
Hamburger Grill (Washington, D.C.), 26
Hamer, Fannie Lou, 268, 271, 286–87
Hammond, Samuel, Jr., 129

Hampton, Wade, 111, 126
Hampton Institute, 54
Hampton/Norfolk, VA, 52–54
Hampton University (Hampton/Norfolk, VA), 53, 54, 253
Handy, W. C., 262, 323
  W. C. Handy Birthplace Museum (Florence, AL), 225
Haralson, Jeremiah, 215, 248
Hardy, John, 213
Hardy, VA, 54–5
Harlem Globetrotters, 105
Harlem Renaissance, 187, 191
Harpers Ferry (WV), 30–31, 335
Harris, Rutha, 324–25
Hartley, Broadus, 206
Hartsfeld, William, 138
Harvest of Shame (CBS documentary), 177, 178
Hattiesburg, MS, 268–70
Hawkins, Reginald, 82
Hawkins, Virgil, 174
Hayes, Isaac, 326–28
Hayling, Robert, 203, 204
Hayneville, AL, 226–27
Hays, Henry, 229
Hazard, Robert, 177
Healy, Michael, 140
Hearth, Amy Hill, 94
Heart of Atlanta Motel v. United States, 21
Helms, Jesse, Jr., 80, 87
Helms, Jesse, Sr., 87
Hemings, Sally, 8, 45–46
Henderson, Cheryl Brown, 339
Henning, TN, 318
Henry, Aaron, 262
Henry, Barbara, 306
Henry, Clarence "Chink," 304
Henry Ford Museum (Detroit, MI), 347
Herenton, Willie, 321
Herman, Alex, 229
Herman, Alexis, 229
Herndon, Alonzo, 148–49
Higginson, Thomas Wentworth, 27–28
Highlander School Site and Cemetery (Monteagle, TN), 121, 125, 216, 315, 328
Hill, Oliver, 38–39, 42, 64
Hill, Sandra, 313
Hinds, James, 309
Hinton, James, 112
Historical Museum of Southern Florida (Miami, FL), 199
Holifield, Marilyn, 207
Hollings, Fritz, 124
Holmes, Hamilton, 143
Holt, Joseph, 94

370

Holt, Louisa, 338
Holt Street Baptist Church (Montgomery, AL), 236, 242–43
Home of Denmark Vesey (Charleston, SC), 122
Hood, James, 252
Hoover, J. Edgar, 129, 285
Hope, John, 154
Horton, James, 245
Horton, Myles, 328
Hose, Sam, 141
Houston, Charles, 24, 26, 341
Howard, Oliver, 24
Howard University (Washington, D.C.), 24–25, 161, 186, 341
Hughes, Jimmy, 225
Hulett, John, 227
Humphrey, Hubert, 287
Humphries, Solomon, 140
Hunter, Charlayne, 143
Hurricane monument and museum at Belle Glade library (Belle Glade, FL), 178–79
Hurst, E. H., 277
Hurst, Rodney, 190
Hurston, Zora Neale, 176, 178
    Zora Neale Hurston art museum (Eatonville, FL), 186–87

Ibo, 139
Ickes, Harold, 12
Independence National Historical Park (Philadelphia, PA), 350–51
Indianapolis Clowns, 230
Indianola, MS, 270–72
Innocents (Louisiana gang), 292
Inter-Civic Council (ICC), 206
Interstate Commerce Commission (ICC), 242
Irvin, Walter, 187–88
Ivory, C. A., 131

Jackson, Andrew, 169, 171, 180–81, 202, 314
Jackson, Harvey, 213
Jackson, Jesse, 79
Jackson, Jimmie Lee, 218, 227–28, 246, 248, 250
Jackson, Juanita, 342
Jackson, Lillie, 341–42
    Home (Baltimore, MD), 341–42
Jackson, Mahalia, 13
Jackson, Maynard, 138, 144, 150, 155
Jackson, Michael, 346–47
Jackson, MS, 272–76
Jackson, Rachel, 169
Jackson, Wharlest, 281
Jackson State University (Jackson, MS), 274–75

Jacksonville, FL, 188–94
Jackson Ward (Richmond, VA), 38, 59, 64–65
Jakes, Wilhelmina, 206
James Monroe Library (Fredericksburg, VA), 51
Jamestown, NC, 86
Jamestown, VA, 35, 36–37, 40, 53, 55–57
Jamestown Island (Jamestown/Yorktown, VA), 56
Jamestown Settlement (Jamestown/Yorktown, VA), 56
Jansen, Guenter, 228
Jazz National Historic Site (New Orleans, LA), 302
Jefferson, Thomas
    Declaration of Independence and, 3–4, 8, 35–36, 38, 45, 350
    Louisiana Purchase (1803) and, 16, 301
    Monticello, VA, 9, 44–46
    slavery and, 8, 26, 35–36, 38, 44–46, 61, 164
    Thomas Jefferson Memorial (Washington, D.C.), 8
Jeffries, Jim, 184
Jemison, Theodore J., 296–97, 304
Jenkins, Esau, 124–25
Jim Crow, 14
    African American culture and, 161
    in Alabama, 220, 231
    in Arkansas, 309
    black schools and, 95–96
    in Florida, 188–89, 204–5
    in Georgia, 147, 153, 157–58
    in Kentucky, 340
    in Louisiana, 293, 301–2, 305
    in Maryland, 341–42
    in Mississippi, 259, 262, 264, 268–70, 272, 273, 274, 275
    in North Carolina, 74, 76–77, 90–91, 97, 101, 103
    in Pennsylvania, 351
    rules of, 114–15
    in South Carolina, 111, 116–17, 127, 133
    in Tennessee, 314, 317, 319, 322–23, 333
    in Virginia, 38, 40, 55, 57, 59, 64, 66, 68
    in Washington, D.C., 15
John Birch Society, 128, 203
"John Brown's Body" (song), 31, 115
Johns, Barbara, 48–50, 338
Johns, Charley, 174
Johns, Ralph, 85
Johns, Vernon, 49
Johns Committee, 175
Johnson, Aaron, 268
Johnson, Andrew, 141, 157

Johnson, Anthony, 41, 56, 111
Johnson, Bernice, 324–25
Johnson, Earl, 189–90
Johnson, Frank, 240, 251
Johnson, Harvey, Jr., 273
Johnson, Jack, 183–84
Johnson, James Weldon, 3, 188, 191, 332
Johnson, Jimmy, 225
Johnson, John Rosamond, 191
Johnson, Leroy, 131
Johnson, Lyndon B., 16, 17, 143, 246, 251, 279, 287, 289, 299, 341
Johnson, Robert, 262, 309
Johnson, Walter, 58–59, 65, 104
  Home (Lynchburg, VA), 58–59
Johnson, Warren "Gator," 138, 145
Johnson, William, House (Natchez, MS), 281–82
Jones, Absalom, 351
Jones, Charles, 145
Jones, Thomas M., 333
Jordan, Abigail, 159
Jordan, Michael, 101, 105
Jordon, Vernon, 25
Journal of Negro History, The, 26
Jubilee Hall (Nashville, TN), 331–32
Jubilee Singers, 331–32
Juneteenth (holiday), 7

Kansas, 335–39
  Osawatomie, 339
  Topeka, 335–39
Kansas City Red, 262
Kaspar, John, 332
Katzenbach, Nicholas, 252
Keeble, Sampson, 314
Kefauver, Estes, 315
Kelley, Alfred, 332
Kelley, Robert, 332
Kelly Ingram Park (Birmingham, AL), 221, 223–24
Kennard, Clyde, 269
Kennedy, John F., 15, 23, 52, 70, 150, 162, 163, 221, 241, 252, 276, 278, 306, 317
Kennedy, Robert, 15, 52, 68, 242, 261, 343
Kennedy, Stetson, 130, 174, 292
Kentucky, Berea, 339–40
King, Alberta, 154
King, Boston, 57
King, C. B., 145, 146
King, Coretta Scott, 144, 150, 152, 167, 228, 237–38, 320–21
King, Lonnie, 150
King, Marion, 145
King, Martin Luther, Jr., 16, 67, 103, 133, 137, 138, 185–86, 211, 257, 281, 287

  in Alabama, 217, 220–22, 225–26, 228, 233–45, 247, 248, 249, 250–51
  Albany Movement and, 145–48
  in Arkansas, 312
  assassination (1968), 25, 51, 152–53, 207, 311, 317, 319, 321–22, 323
  birth and family background, 142, 150, 153–54
  boyhood home, 153
  bust in the U.S. Capitol, 17
  Dexter Avenue King Memorial Church (Montgomery, AL), 234–36, 244
  Dexter King Parsonage (Montgomery, AL), 237–38
  in Florida, 71, 196, 203, 205, 208
  "I Have a Dream Speech," 9–10, 13, 153, 154–55, 162
  "Letter from Birmingham Jail," 221, 222
  in Louisiana, 304, 307–8
  Martin Luther King Day, 39, 144, 152, 333
  Martin Luther King Jr. memorial site (Washington, D.C.), 9–10
  Martin Luther King Jr. National Historic Site (Atlanta, GA), 144, 150, 151–53
  in Mississippi, 264, 283–85
  MLK Memorial Park (Raleigh, NC), 94
  Montgomery bus boycott, 233–45
  Morehouse College, King Statue and "I Have a Dream" Speech in Bronze (Atlanta, GA), 154–55
  nonviolent protest and, 88, 90, 145–48, 154, 160, 166, 183, 242–43
  in North Carolina, 79, 83, 88, 93–94
  Southern Christian Leadership Conference (SCLC) and, 142–43, 150, 152, 165, 166, 203, 205, 206, 220–22, 236, 300
  statue in Kelly Ingram Park (Birmingham, AL), 223–24
  Student Nonviolent Coordinating Committee (SNCC) and, 145–46, 150
  in Tennessee, 317, 319–22, 323, 324, 328
  tomb, 151
King, Martin Luther, Sr., 142, 150, 153–54
King, Primus, 142
King, Riley "B. B," 309–10, 326
King, Slater, 145
King, William, 183
Kingsley, Zephaniah, 193
Kingsley Plantation (Fort George Island, FL), 193
Kluger, Richard, 3, 21, 95, 133, 288, 337, 338
Knight, Gladys, 346–47
Knowles, Christene, 207
Knowles, Harold, 207
Kraemer, Louis, 20
Kress Store (Baton Rouge, LA), 296

Ku Klux Klan
  in Alabama, 215, 220, 221, 223, 225–27, 229, 236–39, 244–45, 251, 254
  in Arkansas, 309, 312
  in Florida, 71, 172, 173–74, 190–91, 200, 203, 204–5
  formation of, 130, 215, 314, 332–33
  in Georgia, 141
  in Louisiana, 292, 293–94, 296, 298–99, 307–8
  in Mississippi, 258, 261, 266, 270, 271, 277–79, 280, 281, 283, 284, 285, 288
  in North Carolina, 73–74, 78, 79, 80, 89–90, 99, 103–4
  in South Carolina, 111, 126, 127
  in Tennessee, 314, 332–33
  in Virginia, 44
Ku Klux Klan Birthplace (Pulaski, TN), 332–33
Kunta Kinte, 37, 50, 318
  Kunta Kinte–Alex Haley Memorial (Annapolis, MD), 340

Lafayette, Bernard, 328
Lane, Mills, 158
Lane College (Jackson, TN), 317
Langan, Joe, 228
Latrobe, Benjamin, 301
La Union Marti-Maceo (Tampa, FL), 208–9
Law, W. W., 160
Lawson, James, 93–94, 317, 319, 329–30, 332
Lee, Bernard, 244
Lee, Cager, 227
Lee, Herbert, 277, 278
Lee, Robert E., 38, 40, 66
  Antietam Battlefield (MD), 7, 31
  end of Civil War and, 43–44, 64, 171–72
  Harpers Ferry (WV), 30–31
Lee, Spike, 155
LeFlore, John, 156, 228–29
LeFlore County Courthouse (Greenwood, MS), 267
Lemon, Meadowlark, 101, 105
L'Enfant, Pierre, 341
Levin, Joe, 239
Levine Museum of the New South (Charlotte, NC), 82
Levy's department store site (Savannah, GA), 162–63
Lewis, Abraham Lincoln, 188–89, 191–93, 194
Lewis, Anthony, 71
Lewis, Cudjoe, 229
  Memorial Statue (Mobile, AL), 230
Lewis, Jerry Lee, 326

Lewis, John, 71, 132, 150, 239–40, 241–42, 247, 251, 264, 325, 328, 329, 330, 331
Liberia, 51, 66
Liberty, MS, 277
Liberty Bell (Philadelphia, PA), 351
Liberty Hill AME Church (Summerton, SC), 132–33
Liberty Square (Charleston, SC), 118–19
Liberty Square (New Orleans, LA), 293–94, 303
Liele, George, 160
Lin, Maya, 239
Lincoln, Abraham, 13, 27, 293, 314, 342–43
  assassination, 10, 64
  election as president, 10, 110, 119, 126, 214
  Emancipation Proclamation, 6–7, 10, 22, 27, 31, 55, 184, 287, 336, 345
  Freedom's Memorial monument in Lincoln Park (Washington, D.C.), 22
  Gettysburg Address, 5, 32–33
  Lincoln Memorial (Washington, D.C.), 8–11, 153
  Lincoln statue and trail (Richmond, VA), 63
  in Virginia, 51, 59, 63
Lincoln Memorial (Washington, D.C.), 8–11, 153
Lincoln Park (Washington, D.C.), 22–23, 185
Lincolnville Historic District (St. Augustine, FL), 204–5
Little Rock, AK, 311–13, 337
Little Rock Nine, 90, 312
Liuzzo, Viola, 226, 248, 251
Lockwood, Robert, Jr., 309
Loeb, Henry, 319
Lomax, Alan, 262
Long, Earl, 296
Long, Huey, 295
Looby, Z. Alexander, 315, 329, 332
Lorman, MS, 277
Lorraine Motel (Memphis, TN), 321–22
Louis, "Brown Bomber," 184
Louis, Joe, 183–84, 346
Louisiana, 290, 291–309
  Baton Rouge, 291–93, 295–98
  Bogalusa, 298–299
  New Orleans, 291–95, 300–7
  secession of, 292, 295
  Shreveport, 307–8
Louisiana Native Guards, 297–98
Louisiana Purchase (1803), 16, 301
Louisiana State University, 293
Loving, Mildred and Richard, 68
Loving v. Virginia, 68
Lowndes County Courthouse Square (Hayneville, AL), 226–27

Lowndes County Freedom Organization, 227
Lowry, Leon, 209
Lucas, Bill, 150
Lucy, Autherine, 252
Lumbee Indians, 78
Lynch, John Roy, 258, 282
Lynchburg, VA, 58–59
Lynchburg Legacy Museum (Lynchburg, VA), 59
Lynd, Theron, 269
Lyric Theater (Miami, FL), 197–98

MacGregor, Morris, Jr., 29
Maddox, Lester, 138, 143
Maggie Walker National Historic Site (Richmond, VA), 64
Malcolm, Dorothy, 155–56
Malcolm, Roger, 155–56
Malcolm X, 248, 318
Mallory, Shepard, 53
Malone, Vivian, 252
Mandela, Nelson, 65, 148
Manly, Alex, 100–1
    historic marker and site of newspaper fire (Wilmington, NC), 102–3
Mann, Floyd, 242
Mants, Bob, 226
Manumission Society, 86
Marble, Alice, 104–5
Marion, AL, 227–28
Marlow, B. D., 286
Marschall, Nicola, 228
Marshall, Thurgood, 17, 24, 59, 340
    as NAACP attorney, 18, 20, 44, 88, 124, 134, 187, 188, 189–90, 296, 315, 336–37, 340–41
    statue (Baltimore, MD), 341
    as Supreme Court justice, 341
Martin Luther King Day, 39, 144, 152, 333
Martin Luther King Jr. memorial site (Washington, D.C.), 9
Martin Luther King Jr. National Historic Site (Atlanta, GA), 144, 150, 151–53
Maryland, 340–44
    Annapolis, 340–41
    Antietam Battlefield, 31
    Baltimore, 341–43
    Cambridge, 343–44
Mason, George, 35
Mason-Dixon line, 6
Massachusetts
    Boston, 27, 344–45
    Fifty-fourth Massachusetts Regiment, 27, 28, 119, 345
Mathews, Zeke, 146
Mathis, Deborah, 313
Mays, Benjamin, 154

Mays, Willie, 184, 224
McCain, Franklin, 85, 96
McCall, Willis, 187–88, 200
McClain, W. B., 220
McComb, MS, 277–78
McCovey, Willie, 231
McCoy, Irene, 131
McCray, John, 112
McCray School (Burlington, NC), 81
McCrory's lunch counter site (Rock Hill, SC), 131–32
McDaniel, Hattie, 149–50
McDonogh, John, 304–5
McDonogh No. 19 school (New Orleans, LA), 306–7
McDuffie, Arthur, 196, 198
McKinley, William, 101
McKissick, Floyd, 96, 283–84
McLaurin, Charles, 271
McLean, George, 70
McNair, Denise, 223
McNair, Robert, 128
McNally, George, 228
McNeil, Joseph, 85
McPherson, James, 27, 63, 110
McWhorter, Diane, 221
Medal of Freedom, 52, 240
Medal of Honor, Congressional, 62, 67, 120, 181
Memphis, TN, 319–28
Mendenhall, Richard, 86
Mendenhall Plantation (Jamestown, NC), 86
Menendez, Francisco, 204
Mennonites, 350
Meredith, James, 29, 30, 90, 259, 267, 283–84
Meridian, MS, 278–79
Merrick, George, 195
Merrill, Lewis, 111
Metcalf, George, 281
Metro Courthouse (Nashville, TN), 331
Miami, FL, 194–99
Michigan, 346–47
    Dearborn, 347
    Detroit, 346–47
Middleton, Delano, 129
Middletown, Dick, 221
Migrant parking lot (Belle Glade, FL), 178
Milam, "Big," 279
Miles, James, 62
Miller, Glenn, 80
Miller, John Chester, 45
Miller, Phineas, 164
Milton, NC, 86–88
Milwaukee Braves, 230
Mims, FL, 199–200
Mississippi, 256, 257–89

Biloxi, 261
Clarksdale, 262–63
Cleveland, 263–64
Greenwood, 266–68
Hattiesburg, 268–70
Indianola, 270–72
Jackson, 272–76
Liberty, 277
Lorman, 277
McComb, 277–78
Meridian, 278–79
Money, 279–80
Natchez, 280–82
Oxford, 283–84
Philadelphia, 284–85
Port Gibson, 285–86
Ruleville, 286–87
secession of, 258
Vicksburg, 287–88
Mississippi Burning (film), 285
Mississippi Sovereignty Commission, 269
Missouri Compromise (1820), 16
Mitchell, Margaret, 149–50
MLK Memorial Park (Raleigh, NC), 94
Mobile, AL, 228–31
Mobile Bay Bears, 230
Mohl, Raymond, 195–96
Money, MS, 279–80
Monroe, GA, 155–56
Monroe, James, 38, 60
   James Monroe Library (Fredericksburg,
      VA), 51
Monroe, NC, 87–88
Monteagle, TN, 328
Montgomery, AL, 231–45
   Montgomery bus boycott (1955), 8, 19, 29,
      70, 122, 142–43, 166, 206, 212–13,
      216–17, 222, 231, 233–45, 246, 324
   Selma-to-Montgomery voting rights march
      (1965), 13, 212–13, 218, 222, 226–28,
      237, 240, 245–51
Montgomery, Hugh, 14
Montgomery Advertiser, 70
Montgomery Improvement Association, 206,
   236
Monticello, VA, 9, 44–46
Montreal Royals, 181–84
Moore, Amzie, 263–65
   gas station (Cleveland, MS), 264
   home (Cleveland, MS), 263–65
Moore, Cecil B., 352
Moore, Charles, 280, 285
Moore, Evangeline, 175–76
Moore, Gary, 201
Moore, Harriette, 199–200
Moore, Harry T., 174, 175–76, 187, 188,
   199–200

Homesite (Mims, FL), 199–200
Moore's Ford (Monroe, GA), 155–56
Morehouse College (Atlanta, GA), 150, 152,
   154, 161, 186, 206
Morgan, Edmund, 38
Morgan, Irene, 20
Morgan v. Virginia, 20
Morial, Ernest, 294
Morial, Marc, 295
Mormino, Gary, 169
Morris, Susie, 313
Morrison, Toni, 25
Morrisroe, Richard, 226
Moses, Bob, 89, 263, 277–78
Mother Bethel AME Church (Philadelphia,
   PA), 351
Mothers' League, 312
Motley, Constance Baker, 189–90, 283, 332,
   337
Moton, Robert Russa, 10, 89–90
   Robert Russa Moton Museum (Farmville,
      VA), 48–50
Motown Museum (Detroit, MI), 346–47
Motown Records, 346–47
Mount Zion Baptist Church (Miami, FL),
   198
Mount Zion Church (Philadelphia, MS),
   278, 284–85
Mt. Zion First Baptist Church (Baton Rouge,
   LA), 296–97
Moving Star Hall (Charleston, SC), 124–25
"Mr. Bojangles" (song), 64
Mulberry Grove Plantation (Savannah, GA),
   163–64
Murphy, Carl, 341
Murphy, John H., 342
Murray, Ellen, 132
Murrow, Edward R., 177
Muscle Shoals, AL, 224–25
Muscle Shoals Rhythm Section, 225
Myer, Russ, 190
Myers, Lloyd, 313
Mykle, Robert, 178–79

NAACP, 15, 19–20, 28, 83–84, 104, 107–8,
   134, 166, 289
   in Alabama, 216–17, 228, 229, 233, 234,
      252, 303–4
   in Arkansas, 310, 311, 312–13
   in Florida, 175, 187, 188, 189–90, 191, 196,
      198, 199–200, 203, 209
   in Georgia, 142, 148–49, 153, 156, 160, 163
   in Kansas, 336–37
   in Louisiana, 293–94, 303–4, 307–8
   in Maryland, 341–42
   in Mississippi, 259, 261, 262, 274, 275,
      276, 281, 283, 286

NAACP (*continued*)
  in North Carolina, 73–74, 78, 79, 81–82,
    87, 88–90
  in Oklahoma, 349
  origins of, 25, 141, 142, 148–49, 153, 319
  in Pennsylvania, 351–52
  in South Carolina, 112, 116–17, 120–21,
    127, 131
  in Tennessee, 319
  in Virginia, 44, 49, 69–70, 338
Nabrit, James, 24, 26
Nash, Diane, 131–32, 328, 329, 331, 332
Nash, Gary, 37, 56–57
Nashville, TN, 315, 317, 328–32
Natchez, MS, 280–82
Natchez Business and Civic League, 280
Natchez Indians, 291
Natchez Museum of African American
    History and Culture (Natchez, MS), 281
National African American Museum
    (proposed; Washington, D.C.), 14
National Archives (Washington, D.C.), 3,
    4–6
  Bill of Rights, 6
  Declaration of Independence, 4–5, 8
  Emancipation Proclamation, 6–8
  U.S. Constitution, 5–6
National Association of Colored Women, 25
National Basketball Association, 183
National Center for the Study of Civil
    Rights, 245
National Civil Rights Museum (Memphis,
    TN), 321–22
National Council of Negro Women, 23, 185
National Football League, 177, 183
National Museum of American History,
    Smithsonian Institution (Washington,
    D.C.), 13
National Negro Congress, 3
National Park Service, 12, 21, 26, 30, 31, 32,
    55, 56, 62, 64, 113, 118, 144, 151, 193,
    245, 253, 255, 281, 288, 302, 313, 339
National Underground Railroad Freedom
    Center (Cincinnati, OH), 348–49
National Voting Rights Museum (Selma,
    AL), 247–48
Negro American League, 230
Negro National League, 224
Nelson, Jack, 129
New Bern, NC, 90–91
Newby, I. A., 107–8, 111, 129
Newcombe, Don, 182
New Deal, 23
New England Anti-Slavery Society, 345
New Orleans, LA, 291–95, 300–307
Newton, Huey P., 88
New York Giants, 224

New York Times, The, 71
New Zion Baptist Church (New Orleans,
    LA), 301, 303–4
Nigeria, 139
Nighthawk, Robert, 262
Nixon, E. D., 70, 216–17, 234
Nixon, Richard M., 3
Nobel Peace Prize, 151
Nonpartisan Voters League, 229
Norman, Jessye, 25
Norman, Mose, 173, 200
Norris, Clarence, 245
North Carolina, 72, 73–105
  Burlington, 81
  Charlotte, 81–82
  Creswell, 82–83
  Greensboro, 83–86
  Jamestown, 86
  Milton, 86–87
  Monroe, 87–88
  New Bern, 90–91
  Princeville, 91
  Raleigh, 91–94
  Salisbury, 97–98
  Sedalia, 98
  Swanquarter, 98–99
  Walnut Grove, 99
  Wilmington, 99–105
North Carolina A&T University, 78, 79, 85,
    86, 96, 161
North Carolina Museum of History (Raleigh,
    NC), 92
Northrup, Solomon, 303

O. A. Peay School (Swanquarter, NC),
    98–99
Oak Grove–Freedman's Cemetery Memorial
    (Salisbury, NC), 97–98
Oarsby, Herbert, 285
O'Brien, Marian, 173
Ochs, Phil, 325
Ocoee, FL, 200
Oglethorpe, James, 138–39, 159, 204
Ohio, Cincinnati, 348–49
Oklahoma, 349
  Second Seminole War, 180–81, 209
  Tulsa, 349–50
Old Capitol Museum (Jackson, MS),
    273–74
Old Slave Mart (Charleston, SC), 123
Old Williamsburg, VA, 68–69
Oliver, Joe "King," 302
Opala, Joseph, 135
Orange, James, 227, 250
Orangeburg, SC, 128–29
Orangeburg Massacre (SC), 128–29
Orbison, Roy, 326

O'Reilly, Kenneth, 13
Osawatomie, KS, 339
Outlaw, Wyatt, 75
Overtown (Miami, FL), 197
Owens, Jesse, 183–84
Oxford, MS, 283–84

Padgett, Norma, 187
Page, Sarah, 349
Paige, Satchel, 224, 231
Palmer, Alice, 98
Palmer, Cynthia, 318
Palmer, Will, 318
Palmer Institute (Sedalia, NC), 96, 98
Parker, Eli, 43
Parks, Raymond, 216–17
Parks, Rosa, 71, 88, 121, 151, 182, 211
  employment history of, 233, 234
  at Highlander School, TN, 121, 216, 315,
    328
  Montgomery bus protest (1955), 70, 122,
    166, 212, 216–17, 231, 233, 242–43, 347
  in the NAACP, 216–17, 233
  Rosa Parks Museum (Montgomery, AL),
    233–34
Patterson, Carrie, 206
Patterson, John, 242, 244
Patterson, Tut, 271
Patton, Gwen, 253
Payne, Che, 343
Payne, Larry, 320
Peabody, Mrs. Malcolm, 203
Peake, Mary, 95
Pearsall Committee, 77–78
Pearson, Rutledge, 190
Peay, O. A., 99
  O. A. Peay School (Swanquarter, NC),
    98–99
Peck, Jim, 241
Penn School Historic District and Museum
  (Saint Helena Island, SC), 133
Pennsylvania, 350–352
  Gettysburg Battlefield, 32–33
  Philadelphia, 350–52
Perdue, Sonny, 144
Perez, Leander, 293, 301, 306
Perkins, Carl, 326
Perry, Albert, 87–88
Perry, July, 173, 200
Person, Charles, 44
Peter, Paul and Mary, 251
Petersburg, VA, 66–67
Petersburg National Battlefield (Petersburg,
  VA), 66–67
Petersburg Public Library (Petersburg, VA),
  67
Pettus, Edmund, 248

Edmund Pettus Bridge (Selma, AL), 246–47
Philadelphia, MS, 284–85
Philadelphia, PA, 350–52
Phillips, Dewey, 323
Phillips, Sam, 323, 325–26
Pickett, Wilson, 225, 326
Pinchback, P. B. S., 292
Pinchback, Pinckney, 297
Pinckney, Charles, 107, 109–10
Pittsburgh Courier, The, 69
Plaza de la Constitución (St. Augustine, FL),
  205
Plessy, Homer, 20, 293
Plessy v. Ferguson, 19–20, 293, 304, 337
Pocahontas, 56
Poinsette, Peter, 120
Pollard, Mother, 166
Ponce de León, Juan, 170
Porgy and Bess (opera), 123
Porter, David, 288, 326
Port Gibson, MS, 285–86
Port Hudson (Baton Rouge, LA), 297–98
Port Mayaca Mass Grave (Belle Glade, FL),
  179
Port Royal Experiment, 132–33
Prather, H. Leon, 100
Preservation Hall (New Orleans, LA), 302
Presley, Elvis, 323, 324, 326
Preston, J. S., 110
Prevost, Tessie, 306
Price, Cecil, 284–85
Princeville, NC, 91
Pritchett, Laurie, 145
Progress Plaza (Philadelphia, PA), 352
Prosser, Gabriel, Gabriel's Rebellion
  (Richmond, VA), 38, 60–61, 89
Pulaski, TN, 332–33
Punch, John, 37

Quakers, 73, 75, 86, 317, 348, 350, 351
Quin, Aylene, 278

Rabby, Glenda, 206–7
Radio Free Dixie, 78, 88, 90
Radio Havana, 78, 88, 90
Rainach, William, 293
Raines, Dollie, 89
Rainey, Lawrence, 284–85
Raleigh, NC, 91–94
Raleigh City Museum (Raleigh, NC), 92–93
Ralph Mark Gilbert Civil Rights Museum
  (Savannah, GA), 159–60
Rampersad, Arnold, 181
Randolph, A. Philip, 12–3, 24
Randolph, Benjamin, 127
Randolph Cemetery (Columbia, SC), 127
Range, Athalie, 196

Rapier, James, 215
Ravenel, Arthur, 127
Rawick, George, 161
Ray, James Earl, 321
Reagan, Ronald, 16
Reagon, Bernice Johnson, 146
Reagon, Cordell, 145, 146, 324–25
Redding, Otis, 325, 326
Redford, Dorothy, 82
Red Shirts, 75, 101, 111, 113, 130
Red Summer (1919), 3, 28, 130–31, 309
Reeb, James, 248, 251
Reeves, Garth, 198
Regulators, 130, 141
Remini, Robert, 180–81
Reno, Janet, 196
Revels, Hiram, 258, 277
Reynolds, Quintus, 220
Reynolds, R. J., 157
Richard, Little, 326
Richardson, Gloria, 343
Richmond, David, 85, 96
Richmond, VA, 59–66
Richmond National Battlefield Park
    (Richmond, VA), 62
Rickey, Branch, 182, 183
Rickwood Field (Birmingham, AL), 220, 224
Ridgway, Matthew, 29
Riley, Joe, 113
Ritz Theatre and LaVilla Museum
    (Jacksonville, FL), 191
Riverfront Canal Walk (Richmond, VA),
    61–62
Roberts, Joseph Jenkins, 66
Robertson, Carole, 223
Robertson, W. G., 213–14
Robinson, Bernice, 125
Robinson, Bill "Bojangles," 64, 66
Robinson, Frank, 184
Robinson, Jackie, 141–42, 146, 176, 181–84,
    224, 230
  Jackie Robinson Ballpark and monument
    (Daytona Beach, FL), 181–82
Robinson, Jo Ann, 166, 234, 244, 245
Robinson, Millie, 141–42
Robinson, Rachel, 182
Robinson, Robert, 160
Robinson, Smokey, 346–47
Rockefeller, John D., 55, 254, 310–11
Rockefeller, Winthrop, 310–11
Rock Hill, SC, 131–32
Rock Hill Seventy, 131–32
Rock 'n' Soul Museum (Memphis, TN), 323
Rockwell, Norman, 306, 307
Rolfe, John, 57
Rolfe, Thomas, 57
Rolling Stones, The, 225

Roosevelt, Eleanor, 15, 23, 25–26, 185
Roosevelt, Franklin D., 15, 23, 24, 25–26,
    185
Roosevelt, Teddy, 15, 55, 254, 272, 313–14
Roots (Haley), 37, 50, 82, 193, 318, 340
Rose, Willie Lee, 132
Rosenwald, Julius, 55, 77, 95–96, 99, 254
Rosewood (film), 201
Rosewood, FL, 200–202
Ross, William "Matt," 286
Rough Riders, 75, 90–91, 130
Rowan, Carl, 90
Rowland, Dick, 349
Royal African Company, 138–39
Ruby Bridges (film), 306
Ruleville, MS, 286–87
Russell, Donald, 112
Russell, Richard, 142
Rustin, Bayard, 13
Ruth, Babe, 150, 224, 230
Rymer, Russ, 188

Safe House Museum (Greensboro, AL),
    225–26
St. Augustine, FL, 202–5
St. Augustine's College (Raleigh, NC), 94
Saint-Gaudens, Augustus, 27, 345
St. Helena Island, SC, 132–33
St. Mary's Missionary Baptist Church (St.
    Augustine, FL), 205
St. Paul AME church (St. Augustine, FL),
    205
St. Paul AME Church (Tampa, FL), 209
Sales, Ruby, 226
Salisbury, NC, Oak Grove–Freedman's
    Cemetery Memorial, 97
Sam and Dave, 326
Sanford, Terry, 74, 79, 92
Sapelo Island, GA, 156–57
Savage, Kirk, 22
Savannah, GA, 157–65
Save Our Schools, 300
Schell, Greg, 177–78
Schmeling, Max, 184, 346
Schwerner, Michael, 259, 278, 284
Schwerner, Rita, 278
SCLC Women Inc., 228
Scott, Charlotte, 22
Scott, Coretta. *See* King, Coretta Scott
Scott, Dred, 19
Scottsboro, AL, 245
Scottsboro Boys, 216, 245
Scott's Branch School site (Summerton, SC),
    133–34
Scruggs, Chuck, 322
Sears, Roebuck & Co., 55, 74, 77, 95–96,
    99, 254

Sears, Stephen, 31
Second African Baptist Church (Savannah, GA), 162
Second Seminole War (1835), 180–81, 209
Secret Nine, 100–101
Sedalia, NC, 98
Seigenthaler, John, 70, 240, 242
Sellers, Cleveland, 108, 128, 129
Selma, AL, 160, 246–51
    Bloody Sunday (1965), 71, 160, 218, 227–28, 246–48
    Selma-to-Montgomery voting rights march (1965), 13, 212–13, 218, 222, 226–28, 237, 240, 245–51
    Selma-to-Montgomery National Historic Trail, 218, 246, 249–51
Seminoles, 139, 171, 176, 180–81, 209
Sewell, John, 194
Seymour, Truman, 120
Sharpe, Melvin, 338
Shaw, Robert Gould, 119–20, 345
    Robert Gould Shaw and Fifty-fourth Massachusetts Colored Infantry Regiment Monument (Boston, MA), 27, 345
Shaw University (Raleigh, NC), 79, 91, 93–94
Shaw v. Reno, 289
Shelley, J. D., 20
Shelley the Playboy, 221
Shelley v. Kraemer, 20
Shepherd, Sam, 187–88
Sheppard, Ella, 331–32
Sheridan, Philip, 292
Sherman, William Tecumseh, 140–41, 148, 157, 162
Sherrod, Charles, 89, 145, 146, 148
    Charles Sherrod Civil Rights Park (Albany, GA), 148
Shiloh Baptist Church (Albany, GA), 145, 147–48
Shiloh Old Site Baptist Church, The (Fredericksburg, VA), 51–52
Shinhoster, George, 162–63
Shores, Arthur, 222
Shreveport, LA, 307–8
Shuttlesworth, Fred, 90, 220, 221–22
Sierra Leone, 109, 125, 156
Sifford, Charlie, 184
Simkins, Modjeska, 126, 166
Simmons, Bill, 271
Simon, Paul, 225
Simpkins, C. O., 304, 307–8
Sit In Inc., 85
Sitton, Claude, 146
Sixteenth Street Baptist Church (Birmingham, AL), 220, 221, 222–23

Sledge, Percy, 225
Smalls, Robert, 114, 115
    memorial and grave site (Beaufort, SC), 114
Smith, Bessie, 262
Smith, Denver, 297
Smith, Hazel Brannon, 278
Smith, Henry, 129
Smith, John, 56
Smith, Kelly Miller, 330
Smith, Lonnie, 20
Smith, Mary Louise, 216–17
Smith, Ozzie, 231
Smith, Samuel, 62
Smithsonian Institution, National Museum of American History (Washington, D.C.), 13
Smith v. Allwright, 20
Somerset Place State Historic Site (Creswell, NC), 82–83
Sons of Confederate Veterans, 80
South Africa, 65, 294, 352
Southampton County Historical Society (VA), 48
South Carolina, 74–75, 106, 107–35
    Beaufort, 114
    Charleston, 30, 114–26
    Clarendon County, 337–38
    Columbia, 126–27
    Orangeburg, 127–29
    Rock Hill, 131–32
    St. Helena Island, 132–33
    secession of, 110, 119, 126
    Summerton, 133–34
South Carolina Capitol (Columbia), 126–27
South Carolina Negro Citizens Committee, 112
South Carolina State University (Orangeburg, SC), 127–29
Southern Christian Leadership Conference (SCLC), 67, 89, 153
    in Alabama, 217, 220–22, 236, 243, 250–51
    in Florida, 203, 205, 206
    formation of, 142–43, 150, 152, 243
    in Georgia, 144, 165
    in Louisiana, 300, 303–4, 307–8
    in North Carolina, 93
Southern Christian Leadership Program, 134
Southern Gentlemen, 293, 295
Southern Institute, 305
Southern Manifesto, 315
Southern Poverty Law Center (SPLC; Montgomery, AL), 238–39, 299
Southern Regional Council, 44
Southern University (Baton Rouge, LA), 296, 297

Sparta, VA, 68
Spelman College (Atlanta, GA), 154–55
Spencer, Anne, 59
Spradley, Dorothy, 159
Stanley, Thomas, 50
Stanton, Edwin, 140–41, 162
Stanton, Lucia, 46
Staple Singers, 326
State Capitol (Baton Rouge, LA), 295–96
State Capitol (Montgomery, AL), 236–37
Stax Records (Memphis, TN), 323, 326–28
Steele, Charles Kenzie, 206–7
    Charles Kenzie Steele Memorial and bus
        station (Tallahassee, FL), 208
Steinbeck, John, 306
Stennis, John, 273
Stephens, John, 75
Stephens, Patricia, 207
Stephens, Priscilla, 207
Steptoe, E. W., 88
Stewart, Jim, 323, 326
Stowe, Harriet Beecher, 172
Stroman, John, 128–29
Student Nonviolent Coordinating Committee
    (SNCC), 23, 88–89
    in Alabama, 226, 227, 249, 253
    Freedom Singers, 146–47, 148, 324–25
    in Georgia, 143, 145–48, 150, 324–25
    headquarters (Greenwood, MS), 268
    in Maryland, 343–44
    in Mississippi, 259–60, 266, 267, 268,
        269, 270, 271, 277, 281, 286–87
    origins of, 79, 91, 93–94
    in South Carolina, 128, 131–32
    in Tennessee, 329
Styron, William, 48
Sullivan, Leon, 352
Sullivan's Island (Charleston, SC), 122
Sullivan's Principles, 352
Sullivan v. New York Times, 71
Summerton, SC, 133–34
Sumner, Charles, 110
Sunflower County Courthouse (Indianola,
    MS), 271
Sun Records (Memphis, TN), 323, 324,
    325–26
Supremes, The, 346–47
*Swann v. Charlotte-Mecklenburg Board of
    Education,* 81
Swanquarter, NC, 98–99
Swanson, Gregory, 44
Sweet Honey in the Rock, 146, 325
Swinton, David, 127

Tallahassee, FL, 205–8
Talmadge, Gene, 142
Tampa, FL, 208–9

Tampa Technique, 209
Taney, Roger, 19
Tanner, Henry, 54
Tate, Leona, 306
Taylor, Fannie, 201
Taylor, Maxwell, 311
Taylor, Robert, 254
Teaching Tolerance program, 239
Temple, Shirley, 64
Tennessee, 290, 313–33
    Henning, 318
    Memphis, 319–28
    Monteagle, 328
    Nashville, 328–32
    Pulaski, 332–33
    secession of, 314
Terrell, Mary Church, 3
    home (Washington, D.C.), 25
Texas, 337
Thomas, Carla, 326–28
Thomas, Ernest, 187–88
Thomas, Henry, 203
Thomas, Rufus, 326–28
Thornton, J. Mills, 244
Thurman, Howard, House/Cultural Park
    (Daytona Beach, FL), 185–86
Thurmond, Strom, 107, 112, 113, 124, 126
Till, Emmett, 69–70, 259, 266, 268,
    279–80
Tillman, "Pitchfork Ben," 17, 111, 113
Tonies Vineyard (VA), 41
Topeka, KS, 335–39
Torres, Sasha, 71
Tougaloo College (Jackson, MS), 161, 276
Tougaloo Nine, 276
Towne, Laura, 132
Townsend, James, 53
Townsend, Sarah, 162–63
Travis, Joseph, 48
Triggs, Clarence, 299
Truman, Harry S., 15, 29, 112, 126, 155–56
Truth, Sojourner, 165–66
Tubman, Harriet, 340, 348
    Harriet Tubman Museum (Cambridge,
        MD), 344
Tucker, David, 267–68
Tucker, Samuel, 42
Tucker, William, 37
Tulane, Paul, 300
Tulsa, OK, 349–50
Tureaud, Alexander Pierre, 294, 300
Turner, Benjamin, 215
Turner, Ike, 262, 326
Turner, John, 196
Turner, Nat, Nat Turner's rebellion
    (Courtland, VA), 38, 40, 46–48, 89
Turner, Ted, 150

Turner Chapel (Greenwood, MS), 267–68
Tuscaloosa, AL, 252
Tuskegee, AL, 28–29, 252–55
Tuskegee Airmen National Historic Site
  (Tuskegee, AL), 253, 254–55
Tuskegee Human and Civil Rights
  Multicultural Center (Tuskegee, AL), 255
Tuskegee Institute National Historic Site
  (Tuskegee, AL), 12, 55, 90, 131, 215–16,
  244, 252, 253–54, 255
Tyson, Timothy, 77–78, 88, 89

Uncle Tom's Cabin (Stowe), 172, 349
Underground Railroad, 66, 73, 86, 109, 160,
  339, 344, 348–49, 350
Union Station (Washington, D.C.), 24
United Christian Movement, 307–8
United Klans of America, 223, 229
United Negro College Fund, 300
U.S. Capitol (Washington, D.C.), 16–17
U.S. Civil Rights Commission, 17, 21,
  175–76
U.S. Constitution (National Archives,
  Washington, D.C.), 5–6, 35, 107, 350
  Bill of Rights, 6
  Fifteenth Amendment, 5–6, 20, 259, 288,
    304
  Fifth Amendment, 338
  Fourteenth Amendment, 6, 17, 18, 20, 273,
    336
  Nineteenth Amendment, 6
  Thirteenth Amendment, 6, 10, 17, 260, 273
United States Historical Society, 64
U.S. Justice Department, 17, 21, 129, 146,
  227, 240, 261, 294, 317
University of Alabama campus (Tuscaloosa,
  AL), 217, 252
University of Maryland, 341
University of Mississippi, 259, 283
University of Southern Mississippi
  (Hattiesburg, MS), 269
University of Virginia, 44, 45
Urban League, 294
Urban League of Greater Miami, 198, 199
USS *Mason*, 29
USS *Sea Cloud*, 29
U Street Neighborhood (Washington, D.C.),
  25–26

Vandiver, Ernest, 142
Vaughn, Rebecca, 48
Vesey, Denmark, 89, 122, 123
  home (Charleston, SC), 122
Vicksburg, MS, 287–88, 298
Vicksburg National Battlefield (MS), 287–88
Virginia, 34, 35–71
  Accomack County, 41–42

Alexandria, 42
Appomattox, 42–43, 63–64
Charlottesville, 44–46
Courtland, 46–48
Farmville, 48–50, 338
Fredericksburg, 50–52
Hampton/Norfolk, 52–54
Hardy, 54
Jamestown/Yorktown, 55–58
Lynchburg, 58–59
Monticello, 44–46
Petersburg, 66–67
Richmond, 40, 59–66
Sparta, 68
Williamsburg, 68–69
Virginia Historical Association (Richmond,
  VA), 64
Virginia Key Beach (Miami, FL), 198–99
Virginia Military Institute, 227
Vivian, C. T., 227, 250, 329, 331

W. C. Handy Birthplace Museum (Florence,
  AL), 225
Waddell, Alfred, 76
Walker, Alice, 155, 187
Walker, Cas, 328
Walker, Clinton, 280
Walker, Jerry Jeff, 64
Walker, Maggie I., 38, 64
  Maggie Walker National Historic Site
    (Richmond, VA), 64
Walker, William, 28
Walker, Wyatt T., 67, 165, 166, 222
Wallace, George, 211, 220, 227, 236, 240,
  252, 340
  segregation pledge, 212, 217, 237, 251
  Selma-to-Montgomery voting rights march
    (1965), 228, 237, 245–51
Walls, Josiah, 172
Walnut Cove, NC, 99
Walt Disney Company, 306
Ware, Charlie, 145
Waring, Julius Waties, 112, 123–24
Warren, Earl, 17–18, 337
Washington, Booker T., 15, 38, 54, 95, 255,
  345
  Booker T. Washington High School
    (Miami, FL), 198
  Booker T. Washington National Monument
    (Hardy, VA), 54
  Tuskegee Institute, 55, 90, 215–16, 244,
    252, 253–54, 255
Washington, D.C., 1–33, 338
  African American Civil War Monument,
    26–27
  Black Patriots Memorial (proposed), 13–14
  Carter Woodson House, 26

Washington, D.C., (*continued*)
  Home of Duke Ellington, 25
  Home of Frederick Douglass, 21–22
  Home of Mary Church Terrell, 25
  Home of Mary McLeod Bethune, 25–26
  Howard University, 24–25
  Thomas Jefferson Memorial, 8
  Martin Luther King Jr. memorial site, 9–10
  Lincoln Memorial, 10–13, 153
  Lincoln Park, 22–23
  march on Washington (1963), 12, 167, 321,
    325
  National African American Museum
    (proposed), 14
  National Archives, 4–8
  National Museum of American History,
    Smithsonian Institution, 13
  planning of, 341
  Supreme Court, 17–21
  Union Station, 24
  U.S. Capitol, 16–17
  U.S. Constitution, 5–6
  U Street Neighborhood, 25–26
  The White House, 15–16
Washington, George, 14, 341
Washington, Kenny, 183
Washington, Walter, 3
Waters, Muddy, 262
Watson, Robert, 48
"We'll Never Turn Back" (song), 277
Wells, Ida B., 55, 89, 131, 166, 319
"We Shall Overcome" (song), 146, 278, 281,
  324, 325, 331
Wesley, Cynthia, 223
Wesley United Methodist Church
  (Charleston, SC), 125
West, Ben, 329, 331
West Africa, 230
Western Sanitary Commission, 22
West Palm Beach mass grave (Belle Glade,
  FL), 179–80
West Virginia, Harpers Ferry, 30–31, 335
White, Ben Chester, 281
White, Edward, 304
White, George, 331
White, George Henry, 76
White, Walter, 349
White Citizens Councils, 79, 131, 217
White House, The (Washington, D.C.), 15–16
White Knights, 278, 280
White League, 303
Whitman, Walt, 51
Whitney, Eli, 139, 163–64
Wilder, Douglas, 25, 39, 50
Wilkins, Robert, 14
Wilkinson, Bud, 184

William J. Frantz school (New Orleans, LA),
  306–7
Williams, Adam Daniel, 142, 153
Williams, Avon, 332
Williams, Billie, 231
Williams, Hosea, 89, 144, 160, 163, 205, 247,
  251
Williams, Juan, 17, 310
Williams, LeRoy, 310
Williams, Lou Falkner, 130
Williams, Mrs. Hosea, 13
Williams, Nat, 323
Williams, R. B., 67
Williams, Robert, 78, 87
  Gravesite (Monroe, NC), 87–88
Williams, Serena, 105
Williams, Venus, 105
Williamsburg, VA, 68–69
Williamson, Sonny Boy, 262
Wilmington, DE, 338
Wilmington, NC, 100–105
Wilmington Ten, 79, 101, 104
Wilson, Woodrow, 15, 191
Wine, Rosa, 124
Winter, William, 260
Wisdom, John Minor, 299, 300
Women's Political Council, 166, 234
Woodruff, Robert, 138
Woodson, Carter, 3, 340
  House (Washington, D.C.), 26
Woodward, Isaac, 29
Woolworth Co. Store (Greensboro, NC), 13,
  70, 74, 78, 79, 83–86, 96, 207, 244, 261,
  328, 330
Work, Monroe, 131
WPA Writers' Program, 187
Wright, J. Skelly, 294, 295–96, 300, 305–6
Wright, John, 202
Wright, Moses, 279–80
Wright, Richard N., Richard N. Wright
  Marker (Natchez, MS), 282
Wright, Roberta, 324

Yale–New Haven Teachers Institute, 89, 129,
  130
Yancey, William, 214
Yorktown, VA, 57
Young, A. Z., 299
Young, Andrew, 25, 143–44, 150, 264
Young, Coleman, 346
Younge, Samuel, Jr., 253

Zinn, Howard, 37, 266
Zora Neale Hurston art museum (Eatonville,
  FL), 186–87
Zwerg, Jim, 240, 242

Photo Credits

Photos by Jim Carrier with the following exceptions:

Washington, D.C.—p. 9 © CORBIS; p. 11 © Hilton-Deutsch Collection/CORBIS; p. 17 © Bettman/CORBIS; p. 23 Courtesy Washington, D.C. Convention and Tourism Corporation; p. 27 Courtesy Washington, D.C. Convention and Tourism Corporation; p. 32 © CORBIS

Virginia—p. 62 (left and right): Courtesy Richmond Riverfront Corporation; p. 64 Courtesy Richmond Riverfront Corporation

North Carolina—p. 78 © Jack Moebes/CORBIS; p. 100 © CORBIS

South Carolina—p. 122 Courtesy Highlander Research and Education Center

Georgia—p. 151 Courtesy Kathleen Parker; p. 152 © 1995 Kevin C. Rose/Atlanta Photos.com; p. 159 Courtesy Penny Weaver

Florida—p. 208 Reprinted with permission of Florida Department of State, Division of Historical Resources. For further information, call 1-800-847-7278, or visit www.flheritage.com

Alabama—p. 212 © Bettman/CORBIS; p. 219 © Bettman/CORBIS; p. 223 Courtesy Alabama Bureau of Tourism & Travel and Dan Brothers;